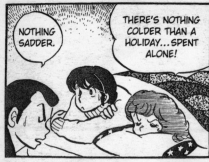

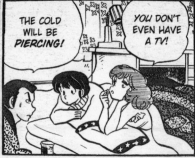

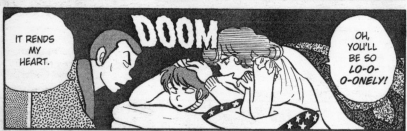

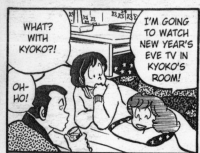

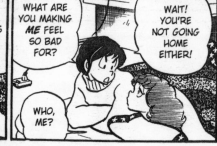

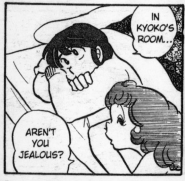

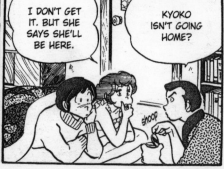

5

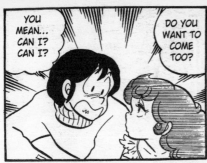

YOU MEAN... CAN I? CAN I?

DO YOU WANT TO COME TOO?

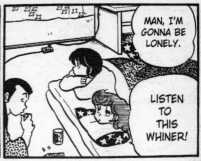

MAN, I'M GONNA BE LONELY.

LISTEN TO THIS WHINER!

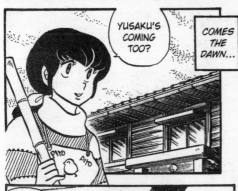

YUSAKU'S COMING TOO?

COMES THE DAWN...

piyo piyo

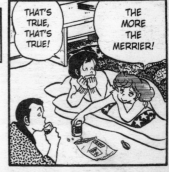

THAT'S TRUE, THAT'S TRUE!

THE MORE THE MERRIER!

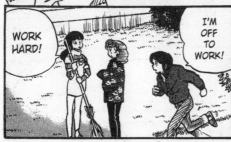

WORK HARD!

I'M OFF TO WORK!

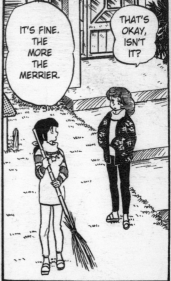

IT'S FINE. THE MORE THE MERRIER.

THAT'S OKAY, ISN'T IT?

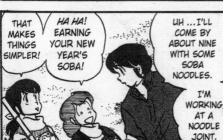

THAT MAKES THINGS SIMPLER!

HA HA! EARNING YOUR NEW YEAR'S SOBA!

UH ...I'LL COME BY ABOUT NINE WITH SOME SOBA NOODLES.

I'M WORKING AT A NOODLE JOINT.

6

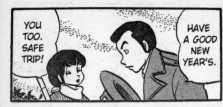

YOU TOO. SAFE TRIP!

HAVE A GOOD NEW YEAR'S.

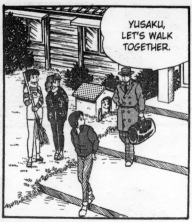

YUSAKU, LET'S WALK TOGETHER.

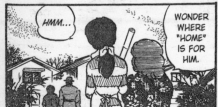

HMM...

WONDER WHERE "HOME" IS FOR HIM.

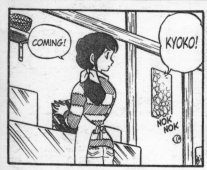

COMING!

KYOKO!

NOK NOK

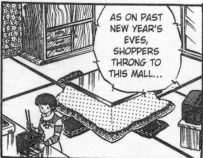

AS ON PAST NEW YEAR'S EVES, SHOPPERS THRONG TO THIS MALL...

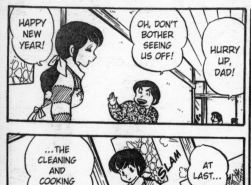

HAPPY NEW YEAR!

OH, DON'T BOTHER SEEING US OFF!

HURRY UP, DAD!

...THE CLEANING AND COOKING ARE DONE!

SLAM

AT LAST...

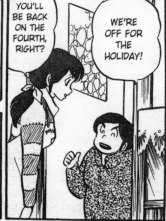

YOU'LL BE BACK ON THE FOURTH, RIGHT?

WE'RE OFF FOR THE HOLIDAY!

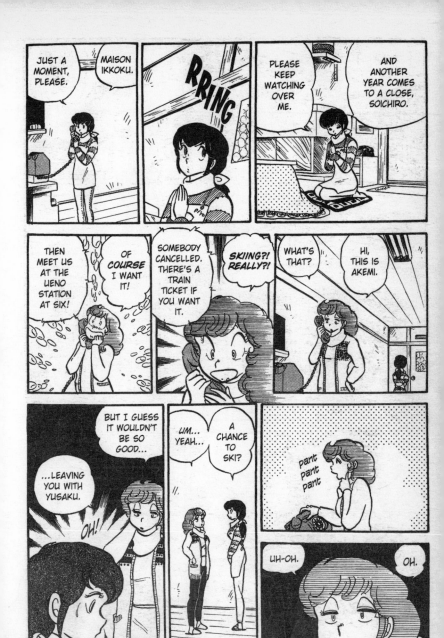

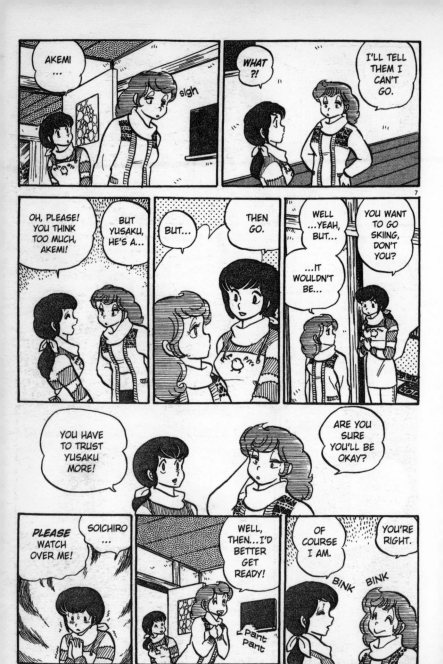

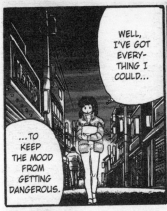

WELL, I'VE GOT EVERYTHING I COULD...

...TO KEEP THE MOOD FROM GETTING DANGEROUS.

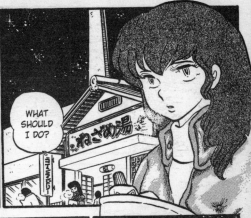

WHAT SHOULD I DO?

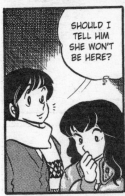

SHOULD I TELL HIM SHE WON'T BE HERE?

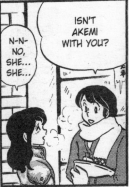

N-N-NO, SHE... SHE...

ISN'T AKEMI WITH YOU?

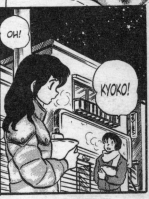

OH!

KYOKO!

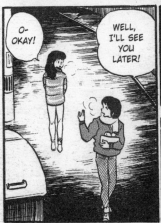

O-OKAY!

WELL, I'LL SEE YOU LATER!

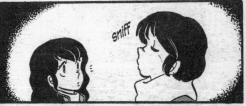

sniff

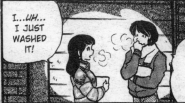

I...UH... I JUST WASHED IT!

MM

YOUR HAIR SMELLS GREAT.

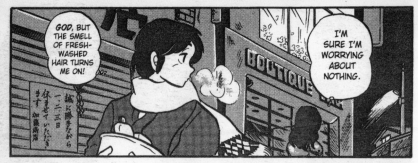

GOD, BUT THE SMELL OF FRESH-WASHED HAIR TURNS ME ON!

I'M SURE I'M WORRYING ABOUT NOTHING.

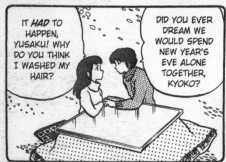

IT *HAD* TO HAPPEN, YUSAKU! WHY DO YOU THINK I WASHED MY HAIR?

DID YOU EVER DREAM WE WOULD SPEND NEW YEAR'S EVE ALONE TOGETHER, KYOKO?

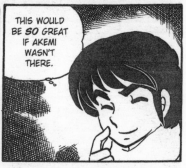

THIS WOULD BE *SO* GREAT IF AKEMI WASN'T THERE.

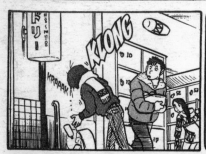

KLONG

KRAAAK

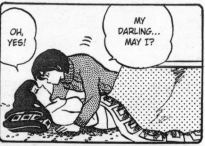

OH, YES!

MY DARLING... MAY I?

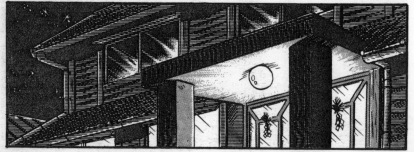

11

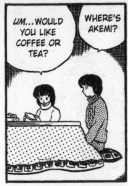

UM...WOULD YOU LIKE COFFEE OR TEA?

WHERE'S AKEMI?

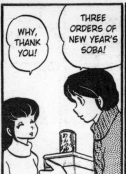

WHY, THANK YOU!

THREE ORDERS OF NEW YEAR'S SOBA!

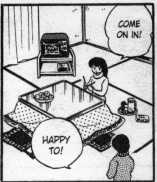

COME ON IN!

HAPPY TO!

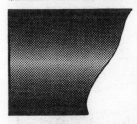

FINE.

UH-HUH.

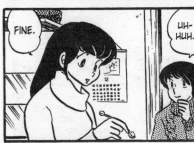

DO YOU TAKE SUGAR?

WHERE'S AKEMI?

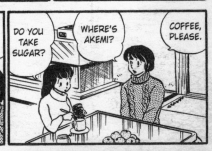

COFFEE, PLEASE.

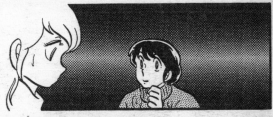

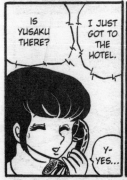

IS YUSAKU THERE?

I JUST GOT TO THE HOTEL.

Y-YES...

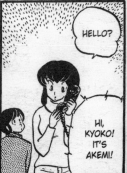

HELLO?

HI, KYOKO! IT'S AKEMI!

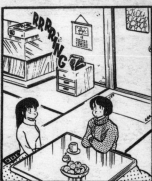

12

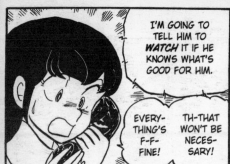

I'M GOING TO TELL HIM TO *WATCH* IT IF HE KNOWS WHAT'S GOOD FOR HIM.

EVERY-THING'S F-F-FINE!

TH-THAT WON'T BE NECES-SARY!

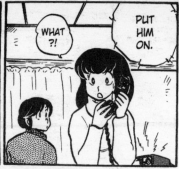

WHAT ?!

PUT HIM ON.

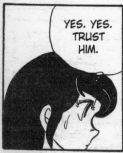

YES. YES. TRUST HIM.

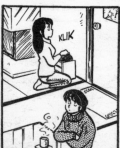

KLIK

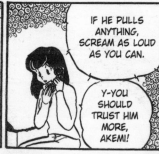

IF HE PULLS ANYTHING, SCREAM AS LOUD AS YOU CAN.

Y-YOU SHOULD TRUST HIM MORE, AKEMI!

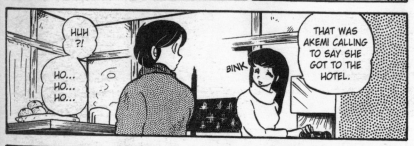

HUH ?!

HO... HO... HO...

BINK

THAT WAS AKEMI CALLING TO SAY SHE GOT TO THE HOTEL.

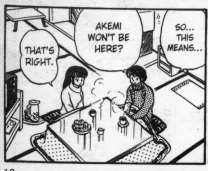

THAT'S RIGHT.

AKEMI WON'T BE HERE?

SO... THIS MEANS...

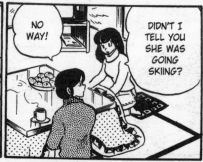

NO WAY!

DIDN'T I TELL YOU SHE WAS GOING SKIING?

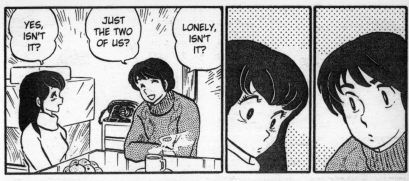

YES, ISN'T IT?

JUST THE TWO OF US?

LONELY, ISN'T IT?

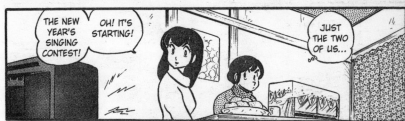

THE NEW YEAR'S SINGING CONTEST!

OH! IT'S STARTING!

JUST THE TWO OF US...

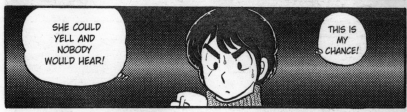

SHE COULD YELL AND NOBODY WOULD HEAR!

THIS IS MY CHANCE!

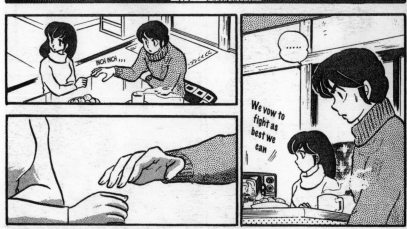

INCH INCH

.....

We vow to fight as best we can

14

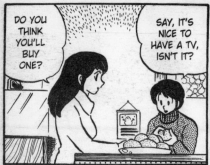

DO YOU THINK YOU'LL BUY ONE?

SAY, IT'S NICE TO HAVE A TV, ISN'T IT?

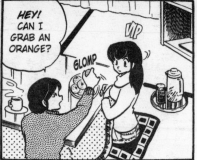

HEY! CAN I GRAB AN ORANGE?

GLOMP

UP

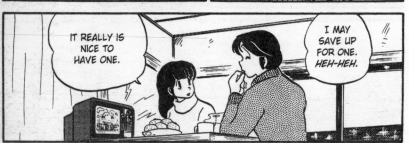

IT REALLY IS NICE TO HAVE ONE.

I MAY SAVE UP FOR ONE. HEH-HEH.

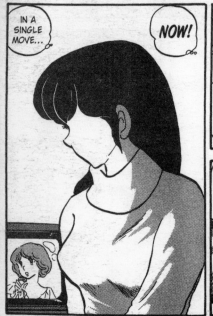

IN A SINGLE MOVE...

NOW!

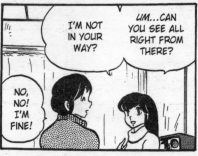

I'M NOT IN YOUR WAY?

UM...CAN YOU SEE ALL RIGHT FROM THERE?

NO, NO! I'M FINE!

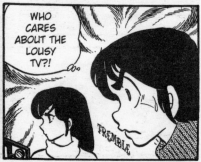

WHO CARES ABOUT THE LOUSY TV?!

TREMBLE

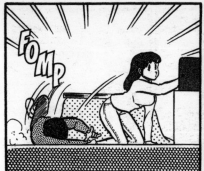
FOMP

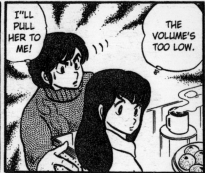
I'LL PULL HER TO ME!

THE VOLUME'S TOO LOW.

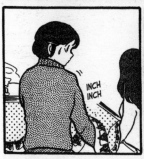
INCH INCH

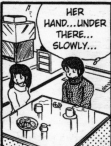
HER HAND...UNDER THERE... SLOWLY...

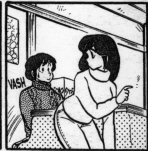
VASH

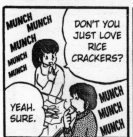
MUNCH MUNCH MUNCH MUNCH MUNCH

DON'T YOU JUST LOVE RICE CRACKERS?

YEAH. SURE.

MUNCH MUNCH MUNCH

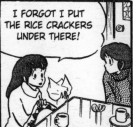
I FORGOT I PUT THE RICE CRACKERS UNDER THERE!

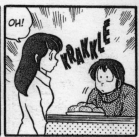
OH!

KRAKKLE

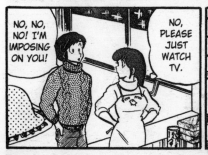
NO, NO, NO! I'M IMPOSING ON YOU!

NO, PLEASE JUST WATCH TV.

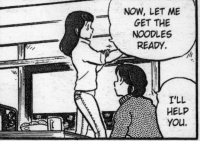
NOW, LET ME GET THE NOODLES READY.

I'LL HELP YOU.

16

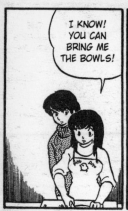

I KNOW! YOU CAN BRING ME THE BOWLS!

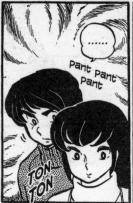

......

Pant pant pant

TON TON

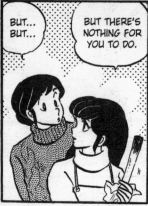

BUT... BUT...

BUT THERE'S NOTHING FOR YOU TO DO.

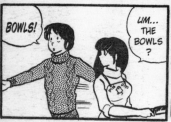

BOWLS!

UM... THE BOWLS?

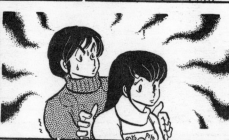

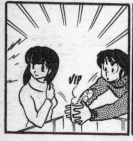

VIP

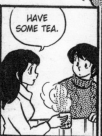

HAVE SOME TEA.

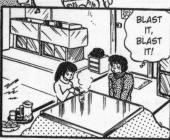

BLAST IT, BLAST IT!

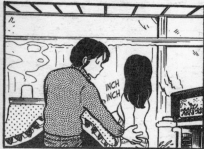

INCH INCH

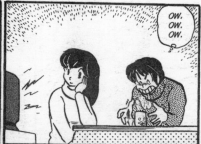

OW. OW. OW.

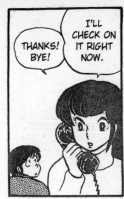

THANKS! BYE!

I'LL CHECK ON IT RIGHT NOW.

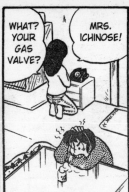

WHAT? YOUR GAS VALVE?

MRS. ICHINOSE!

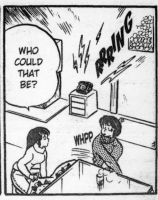

WHO COULD THAT BE?

RRRING

WHPP

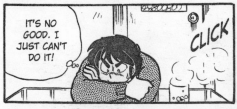

IT'S NO GOOD. I JUST CAN'T DO IT!

CLICK

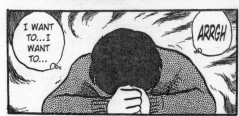

I WANT TO...I WANT TO...

ARRGH

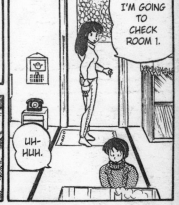

I'M GOING TO CHECK ROOM 1.

UH-HUH.

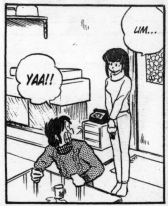

UM...

YAA!!

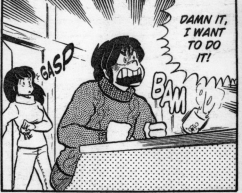

GASP

DAMN IT, I WANT TO DO IT!

BAM

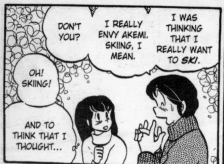

OH! SKIING!

AND TO THINK THAT I THOUGHT...

DON'T YOU?

I REALLY ENVY AKEMI. SKIING, I MEAN.

I WAS THINKING THAT I REALLY WANT TO *SKI*.

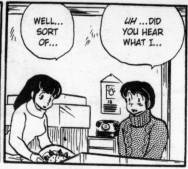

WELL... SORT OF...

UH ...DID YOU HEAR WHAT I...

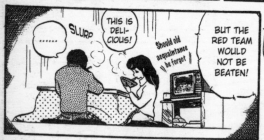

......

SLURP

THIS IS DELICIOUS!

Should old acquaintance be forgot

BUT THE RED TEAM WOULD NOT BE BEATEN!

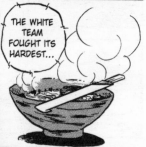

THE WHITE TEAM FOUGHT ITS HARDEST...

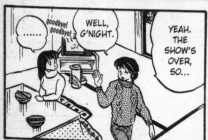

......

goodbye! goodbye!

WELL, G'NIGHT.

YEAH. THE SHOW'S OVER, SO...

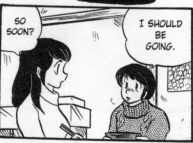

SO SOON?

I SHOULD BE GOING.

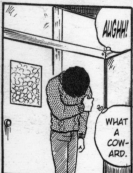

AUGHH!

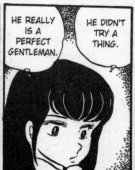

HE REALLY IS A PERFECT GENTLEMAN.

WHAT A COWARD.

HE DIDN'T TRY A THING.

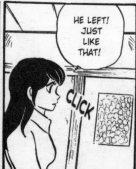

HE LEFT! JUST LIKE THAT!

CLICK

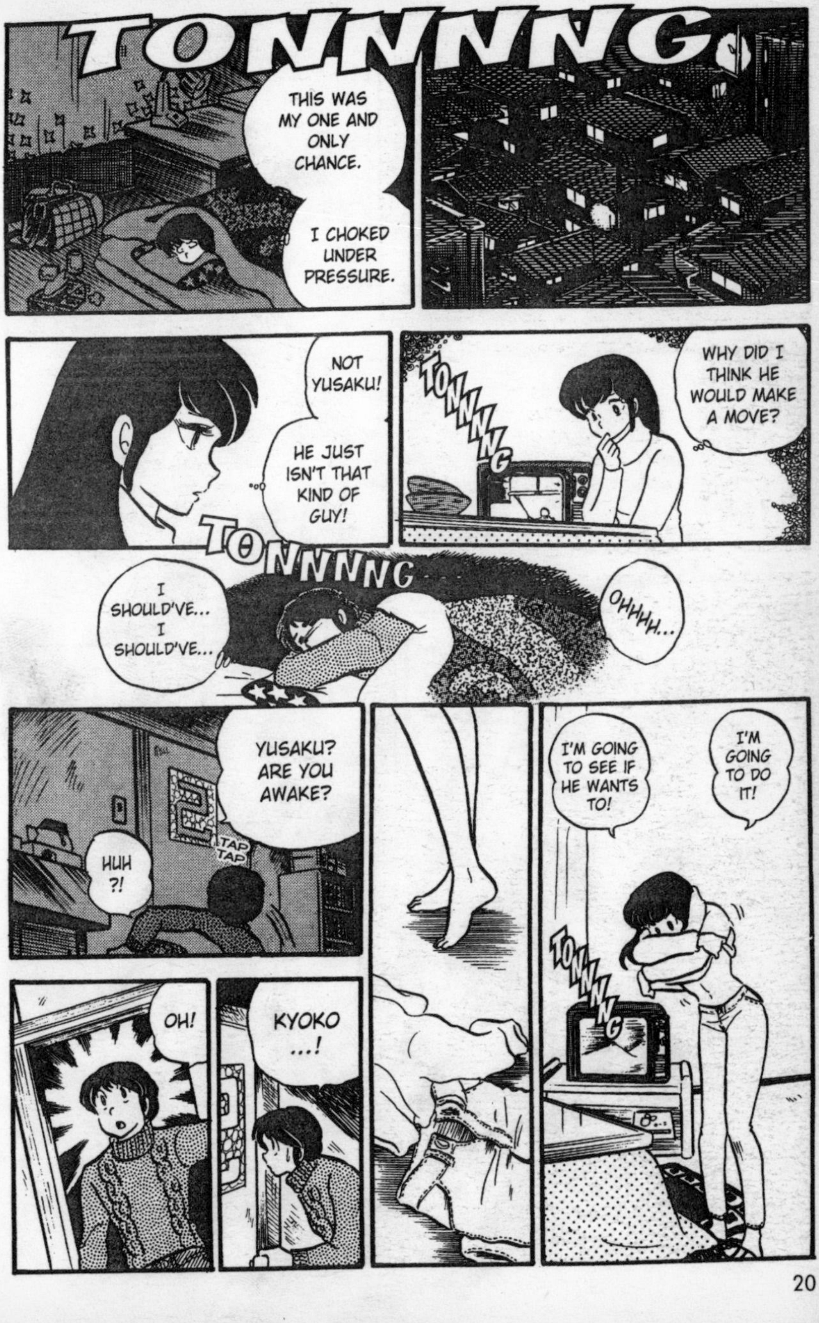
TONNNNG
THIS WAS MY ONE AND ONLY CHANCE.
I CHOKED UNDER PRESSURE.
TONNNNG
WHY DID I THINK HE WOULD MAKE A MOVE?
NOT YUSAKU!
HE JUST ISN'T THAT KIND OF GUY!
TONNNNG
OHHHH...
TONNNNG
I SHOULD'VE... I SHOULD'VE...
I'M GOING TO DO IT!
I'M GOING TO SEE IF HE WANTS TO!
TONNNNG
YUSAKU? ARE YOU AWAKE?
TAP TAP
HUH ?!
KYOKO ...!
OH!

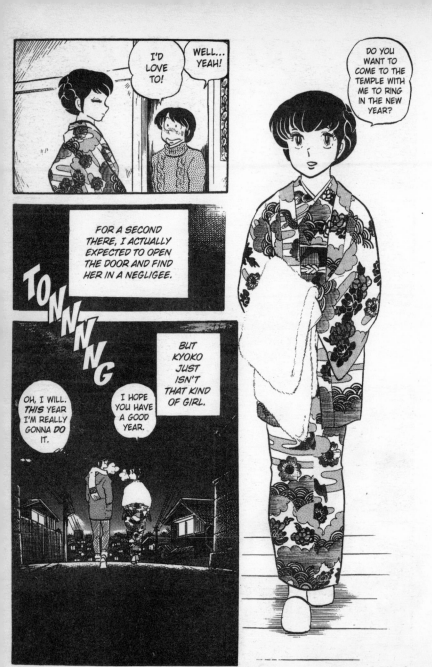

DO YOU WANT TO COME TO THE TEMPLE WITH ME TO RING IN THE NEW YEAR?

WELL... YEAH!

I'D LOVE TO!

FOR A SECOND THERE, I ACTUALLY EXPECTED TO OPEN THE DOOR AND FIND HER IN A NEGLIGEE.

TONNNNNG

BUT KYOKO JUST ISN'T THAT KIND OF GIRL.

OH, I WILL. *THIS* YEAR I'M REALLY GONNA *DO* IT.

I HOPE YOU HAVE A GOOD YEAR.

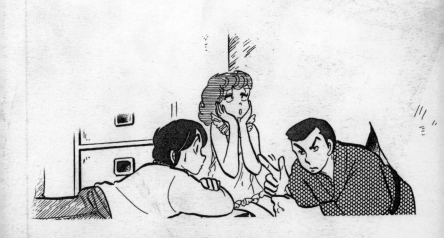

PART TWO
"I'LL BE BACK"

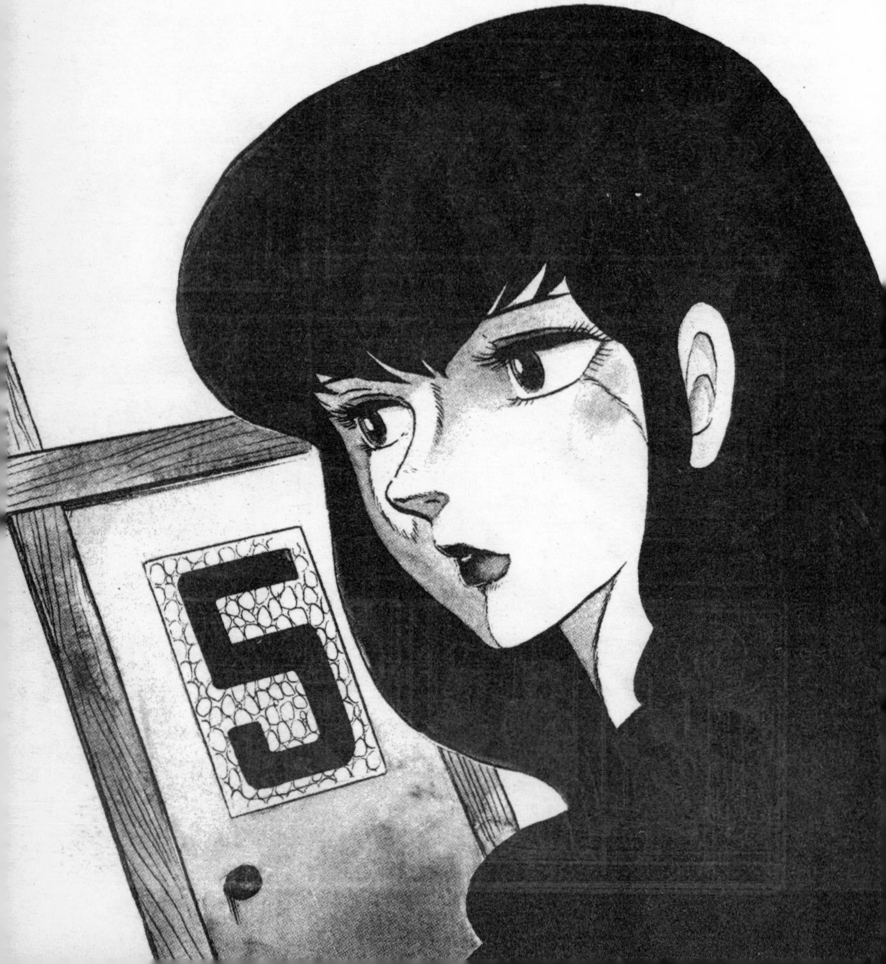

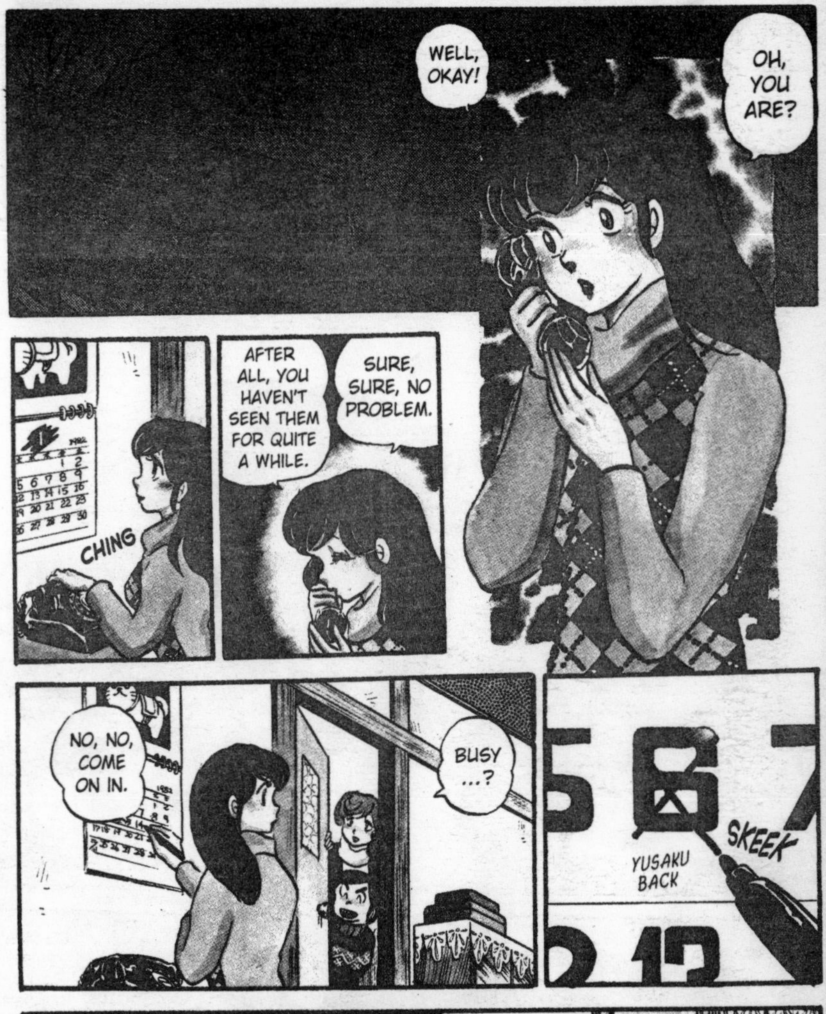
OH, YOU ARE?
WELL, OKAY!
SURE, SURE, NO PROBLEM.
AFTER ALL, YOU HAVEN'T SEEN THEM FOR QUITE A WHILE.
CHING
SKEEK
YUSAKU BACK
BUSY ...?
NO, NO, COME ON IN.

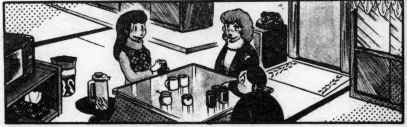

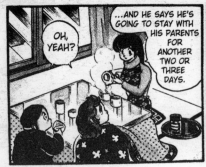

OH, YEAH?

...AND HE SAYS HE'S GOING TO STAY WITH HIS PARENTS FOR ANOTHER TWO OR THREE DAYS.

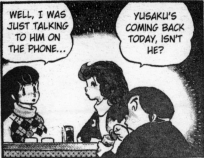

WELL, I WAS JUST TALKING TO HIM ON THE PHONE...

YUSAKU'S COMING BACK TODAY, ISN'T HE?

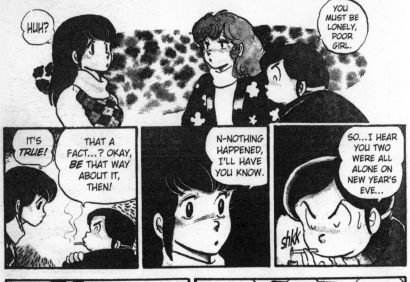

HUH?

YOU MUST BE LONELY, POOR GIRL.

IT'S *TRUE!*

THAT A FACT...? OKAY, *BE* THAT WAY ABOUT IT, THEN!

N-NOTHING HAPPENED, I'LL HAVE YOU KNOW.

SO...I HEAR YOU TWO WERE ALL ALONE ON NEW YEAR'S EVE...

shkk

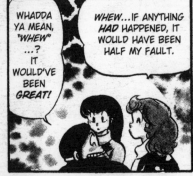

WHADDA YA MEAN, *"WHEW"* ...? IT WOULD'VE BEEN *GREAT!*

WHEW...IF ANYTHING *HAD* HAPPENED, IT WOULD HAVE BEEN HALF MY FAULT.

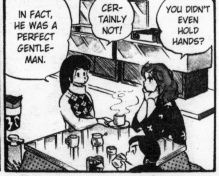

IN FACT, HE WAS A PERFECT GENTLE-MAN.

CER-TAINLY NOT!

YOU DIDN'T EVEN HOLD HANDS?

25

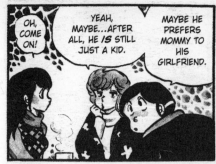

OH, COME ON!

YEAH, MAYBE...AFTER ALL, HE *IS* STILL JUST A KID.

MAYBE HE PREFERS MOMMY TO HIS GIRLFRIEND.

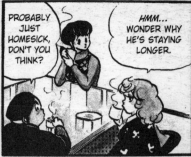

PROBABLY JUST HOMESICK, DON'T YOU THINK?

HMM... WONDER WHY HE'S STAYING LONGER.

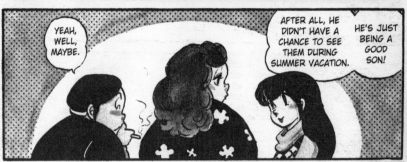

YEAH, WELL, MAYBE.

AFTER ALL, HE DIDN'T HAVE A CHANCE TO SEE THEM DURING SUMMER VACATION.

HE'S JUST BEING A GOOD SON!

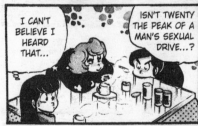

I CAN'T BELIEVE I HEARD THAT...

ISN'T TWENTY THE PEAK OF A MAN'S SEXUAL DRIVE...?

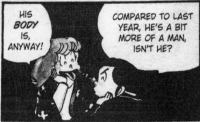

HIS *BODY* IS, ANYWAY!

COMPARED TO LAST YEAR, HE'S A BIT MORE OF A MAN, ISN'T HE?

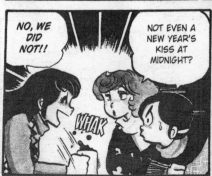

NO, WE DID NOT!!

NOT EVEN A NEW YEAR'S KISS AT MIDNIGHT?

WHAK

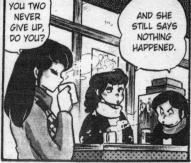

YOU TWO NEVER GIVE UP, DO YOU?

AND SHE STILL SAYS NOTHING HAPPENED.

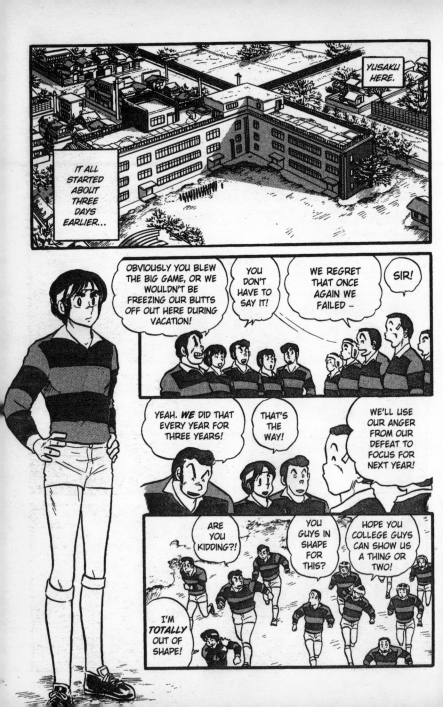

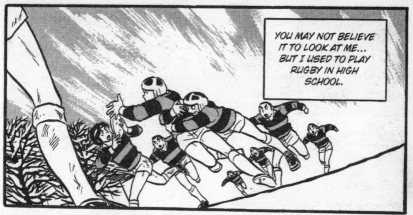

YOU MAY NOT BELIEVE IT TO LOOK AT ME... BUT I USED TO PLAY RUGBY IN HIGH SCHOOL.

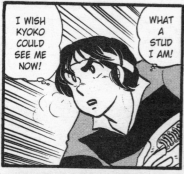

I WISH KYOKO COULD SEE ME NOW!

WHAT A STUD I AM!

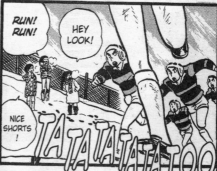

RUN! RUN!

HEY LOOK!

NICE SHORTS!

TATATATATATOOM

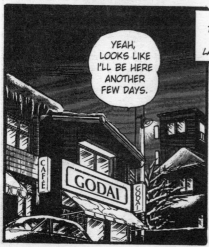

AND THREE DAYS LATER...

YEAH, LOOKS LIKE I'LL BE HERE ANOTHER FEW DAYS.

CAFE

GODAI

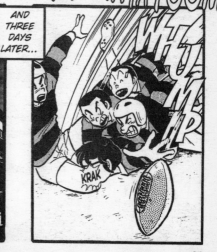

WHUMP

KRAK

28

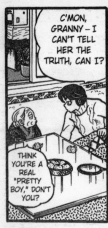

C'MON, GRANNY — I CAN'T TELL HER THE TRUTH, CAN I?

THINK YOU'RE A REAL "PRETTY BOY," DON'T YOU?

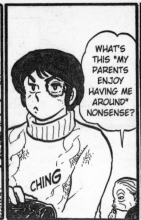

WHAT'S THIS "MY PARENTS ENJOY HAVING ME AROUND" NONSENSE?

CHING

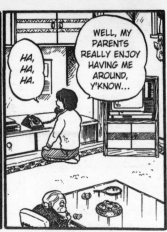

HA, HA, HA.

WELL, MY PARENTS REALLY ENJOY HAVING ME AROUND, Y'KNOW...

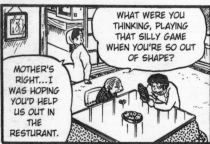

WHAT WERE YOU THINKING, PLAYING THAT SILLY GAME WHEN YOU'RE SO OUT OF SHAPE?

MOTHER'S RIGHT...I WAS HOPING YOU'D HELP US OUT IN THE RESTURANT.

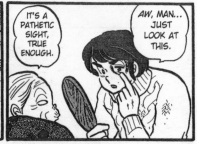

IT'S A PATHETIC SIGHT, TRUE ENOUGH.

AW, MAN... JUST LOOK AT THIS.

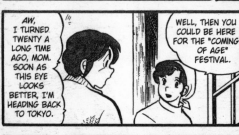

AW, I TURNED TWENTY A LONG TIME AGO, MOM. SOON AS THIS EYE LOOKS BETTER, I'M HEADING BACK TO TOKYO.

WELL, THEN YOU COULD BE HERE FOR THE "COMING OF AGE" FESTIVAL.

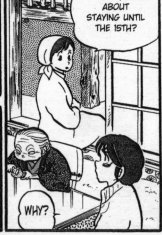

YUSAKU, HOW ABOUT STAYING UNTIL THE 15TH?

WHY?

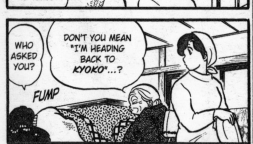

WHO ASKED YOU?

DON'T YOU MEAN "I'M HEADING BACK TO KYOKO"...?

FUMP

29

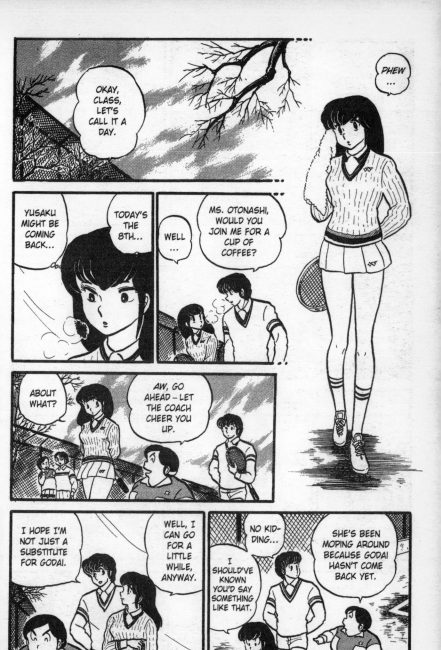

30

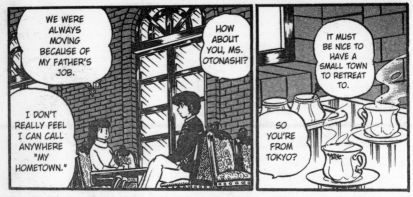

WE WERE ALWAYS MOVING BECAUSE OF MY FATHER'S JOB.

HOW ABOUT YOU, MS. OTONASHI?

IT MUST BE NICE TO HAVE A SMALL TOWN TO RETREAT TO.

I DON'T REALLY FEEL I CAN CALL ANYWHERE "MY HOMETOWN."

SO YOU'RE FROM TOKYO?

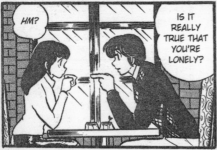

HM?

IS IT REALLY TRUE THAT YOU'RE LONELY?

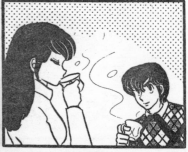

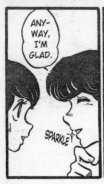

ANY-WAY, I'M GLAD.

SPARKLE

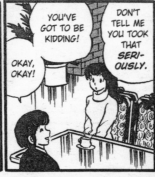

YOU'VE GOT TO BE KIDDING!

DON'T TELL ME YOU TOOK THAT *SERI-OUSLY.*

OKAY, OKAY!

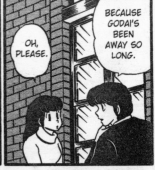

OH, PLEASE.

BECAUSE GODAI'S BEEN AWAY SO LONG.

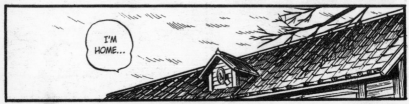

I'M HOME...

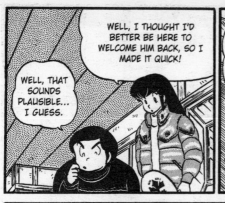

WELL, THAT SOUNDS PLAUSIBLE... I GUESS.

WELL, I THOUGHT I'D BETTER BE HERE TO WELCOME HIM BACK, SO I MADE IT QUICK!

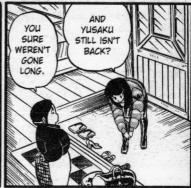

YOU SURE WEREN'T GONE LONG.

AND YUSAKU STILL ISN'T BACK?

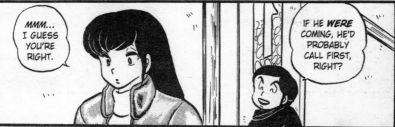

MMM... I GUESS YOU'RE RIGHT.

IF HE *WERE* COMING, HE'D PROBABLY CALL FIRST, RIGHT?

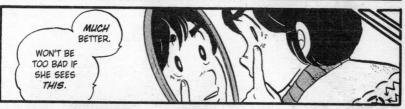

MUCH BETTER.

WON'T BE TOO BAD IF SHE SEES *THIS*.

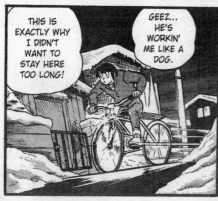

THIS IS EXACTLY WHY I DIDN'T WANT TO STAY HERE TOO LONG!

GEEZ... HE'S WORKIN' ME LIKE A DOG.

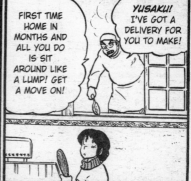

FIRST TIME HOME IN MONTHS AND ALL YOU DO IS SIT AROUND LIKE A LUMP! GET A MOVE ON!

YUSAKU! I'VE GOT A DELIVERY FOR YOU TO MAKE!

32

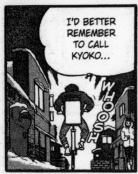

I'D BETTER REMEMBER TO CALL KYOKO...

WHOOSH

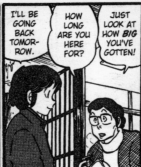

I'LL BE GOING BACK TOMORROW.

HOW LONG ARE YOU HERE FOR?

JUST LOOK AT HOW *BIG* YOU'VE GOTTEN!

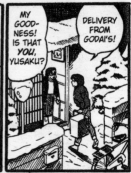

MY GOODNESS! IS THAT *YOU*, YUSAKU?

DELIVERY FROM GODAI'S!

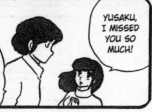

I'M BACK, NOW. I'M SORRY TO LEAVE YOU ALONE FOR SO LONG...

YUSAKU, I MISSED YOU SO MUCH!

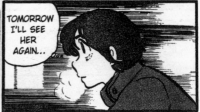

TOMORROW I'LL SEE HER AGAIN...

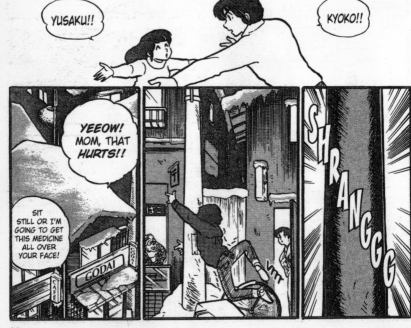

YUSAKU!!

KYOKO!!

YEEOW! MOM, THAT *HURTS!!*

SIT STILL OR I'M GOING TO GET THIS MEDICINE ALL OVER YOUR FACE!

GODAI

CAFÉ GODAI

VTT

SHRANGGG

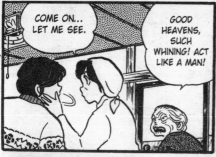

COME ON... LET ME SEE.

GOOD HEAVENS, SUCH WHINING! ACT LIKE A MAN!

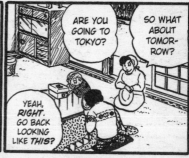

ARE YOU GOING TO TOKYO?

SO WHAT ABOUT TOMORROW?

YEAH, *RIGHT.* GO BACK LOOKING LIKE *THIS*?

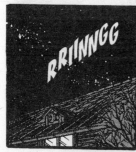

R-RIINNGG

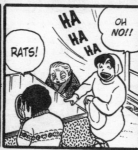

HA HA HA HA

RATS!

OH NO!!

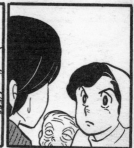

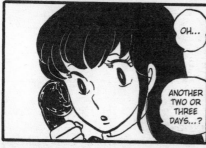

OH...

ANOTHER TWO OR THREE DAYS...?

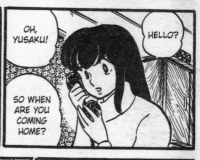

OH, YUSAKU!

SO WHEN ARE YOU COMING HOME?

HELLO?

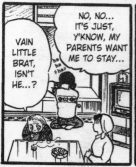

VAIN LITTLE BRAT, ISN'T HE...?

NO, NO... IT'S JUST, Y'KNOW, MY PARENTS WANT ME TO STAY...

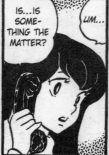

IS...IS SOMETHING THE MATTER?

UM...

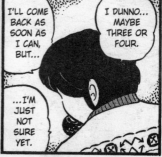

I'LL COME BACK AS SOON AS I CAN, BUT...

...I'M JUST NOT SURE YET.

I DUNNO... MAYBE THREE OR FOUR.

34

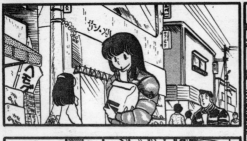

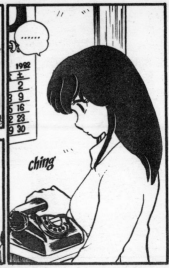

......

ching

OH, KOZUE.

HEY, MS. OTONASHI!

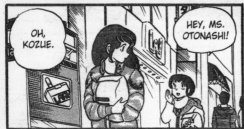

SO YOU DON'T KNOW WHY HE'S STAYING AWAY SO LONG, EITHER.

NOPE.

WE EVEN HAD A DATE TO SEE A MOVIE ON THE 10TH.

THAT DUMMY...

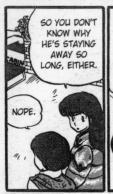

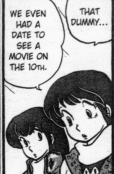

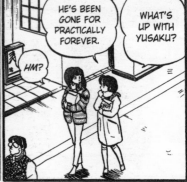

HE'S BEEN GONE FOR PRACTICALLY FOREVER.

WHAT'S UP WITH YUSAKU?

HM?

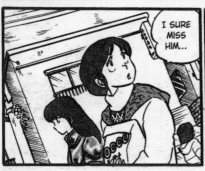

I SURE MISS HIM...

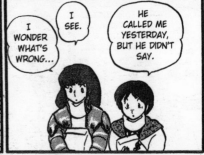

I WONDER WHAT'S WRONG...

I SEE.

HE CALLED ME YESTERDAY, BUT HE DIDN'T SAY.

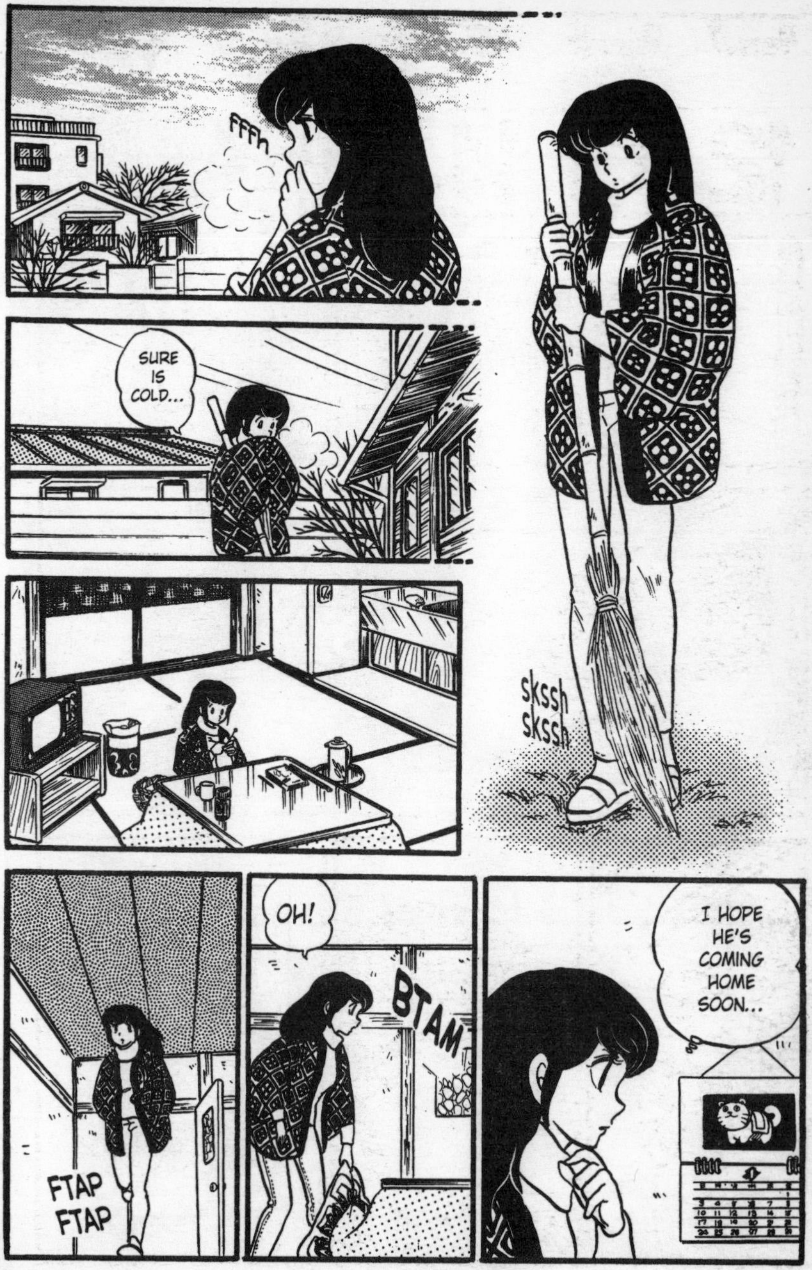
skssh
skssh
fffh
SURE IS COLD...
I HOPE HE'S COMING HOME SOON...
OH!
BTAM
FTAP FTAP

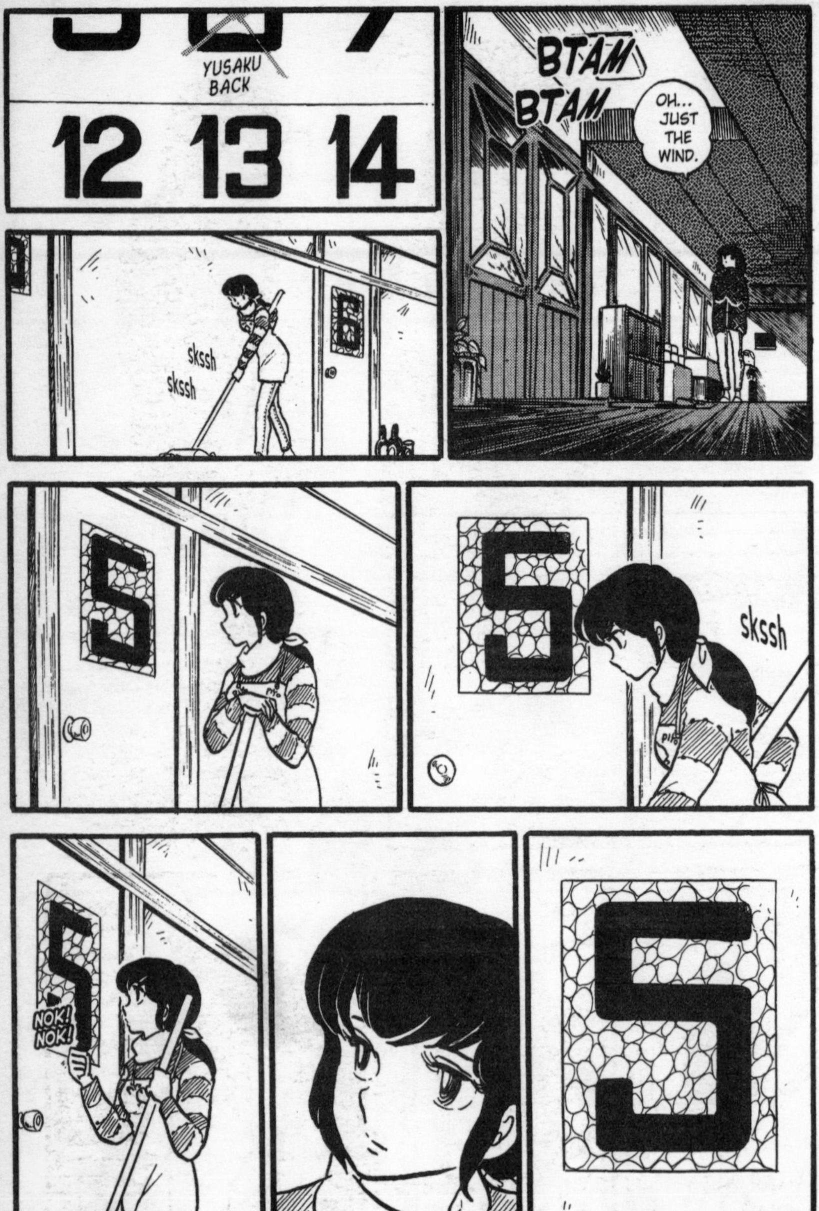
BTAM
BTAM
OH... JUST THE WIND.
YUSAKU BACK
12 13 14
skssh
skssh
skssh
NOK! NOK!

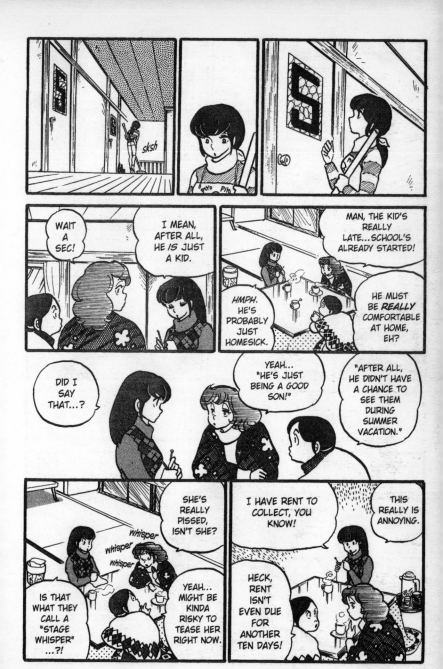

38

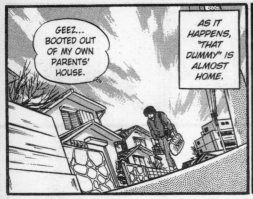

GEEZ... BOOTED OUT OF MY OWN PARENTS' HOUSE.

AS IT HAPPENS, "THAT DUMMY" IS ALMOST HOME.

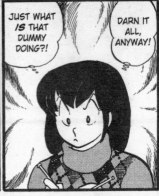

JUST WHAT *IS* THAT DUMMY DOING?!

DARN IT ALL, ANYWAY!

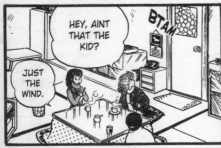

HEY, AINT THAT THE KID?

JUST THE WIND.

BTAM!

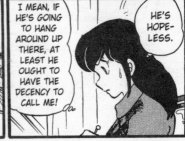

I MEAN, IF HE'S GOING TO HANG AROUND UP THERE, AT LEAST HE OUGHT TO HAVE THE DECENCY TO CALL ME!

HE'S HOPE-LESS.

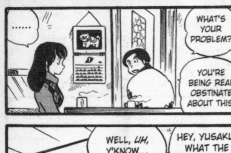

......

WHAT'S YOUR PROBLEM?

YOU'RE BEING REAL OBSTINATE ABOUT THIS.

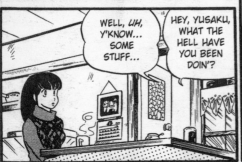

WELL, *UH*, Y'KNOW... SOME STUFF...

HEY, YUSAKU, WHAT THE HELL HAVE YOU BEEN DOIN'?

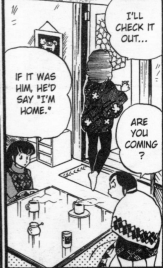

I'LL CHECK IT OUT...

IF IT WAS HIM, HE'D SAY "I'M HOME."

ARE YOU COMING?

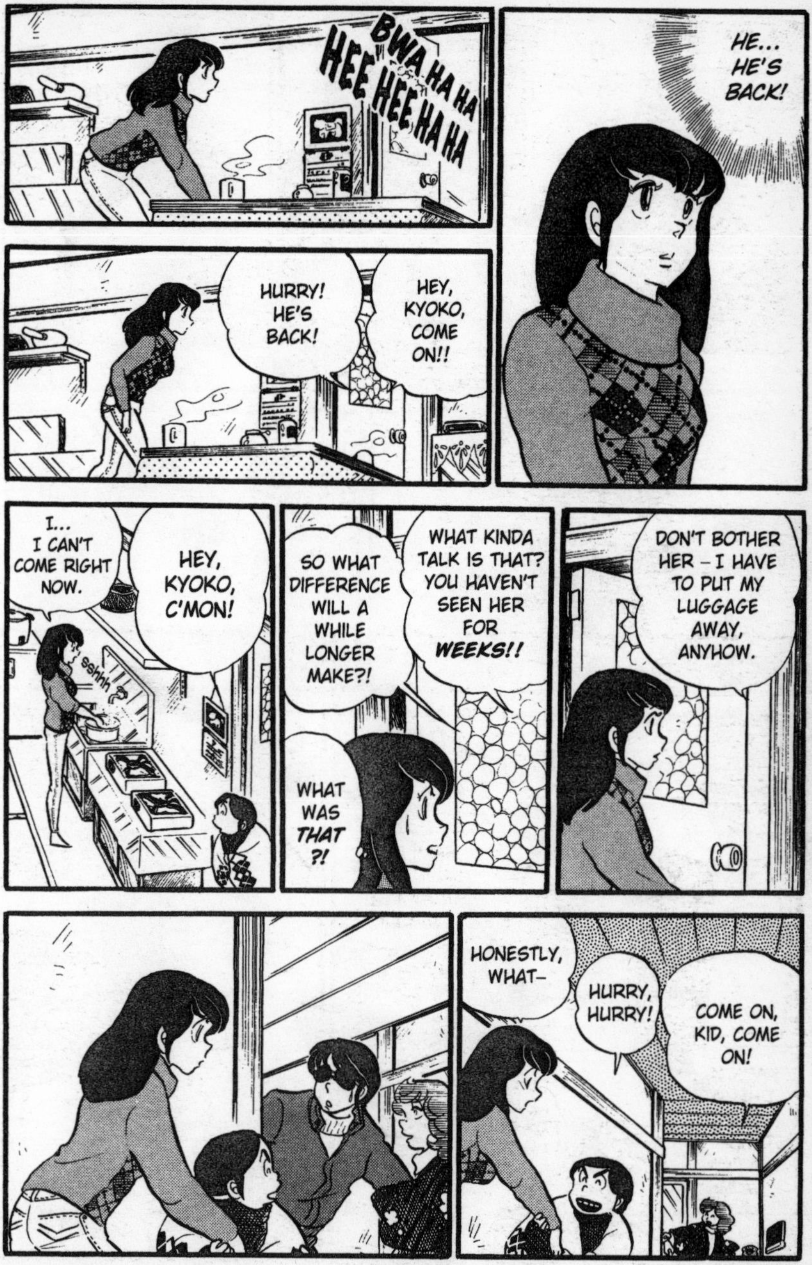
HE... HE'S BACK!
BWA HA HA HEE HEE HA HA HA
HEY, KYOKO, COME ON!!
HURRY! HE'S BACK!
DON'T BOTHER HER – I HAVE TO PUT MY LUGGAGE AWAY, ANYHOW.
WHAT KINDA TALK IS THAT? YOU HAVEN'T SEEN HER FOR WEEKS!!
SO WHAT DIFFERENCE WILL A WHILE LONGER MAKE?!
WHAT WAS THAT?!
HEY, KYOKO, C'MON!
I... I CAN'T COME RIGHT NOW.
sshhh
COME ON, KID, COME ON!
HURRY, HURRY!
HONESTLY, WHAT–

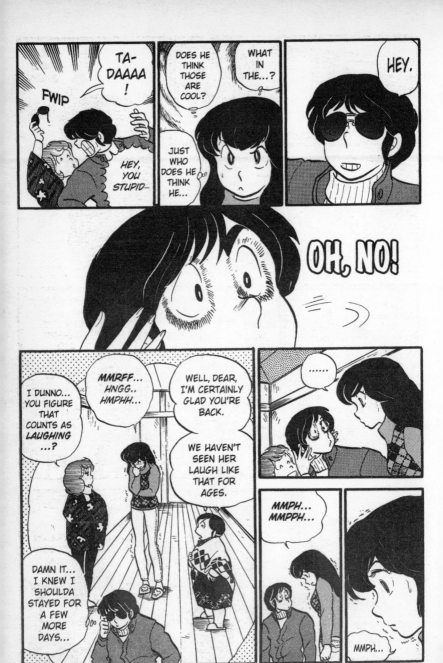

41

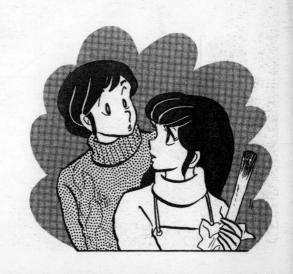

PART THREE

STAKE IT ON THE RINK!

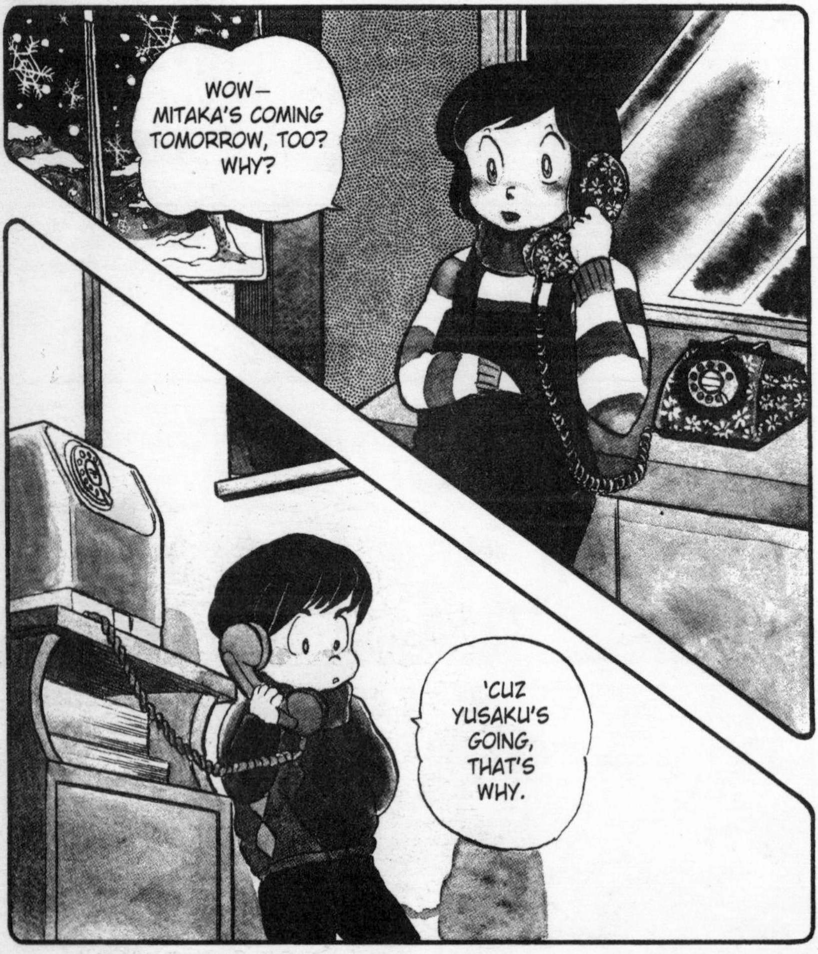
WOW— MITAKA'S COMING TOMORROW, TOO? WHY?
'CUZ YUSAKU'S GOING, THAT'S WHY.

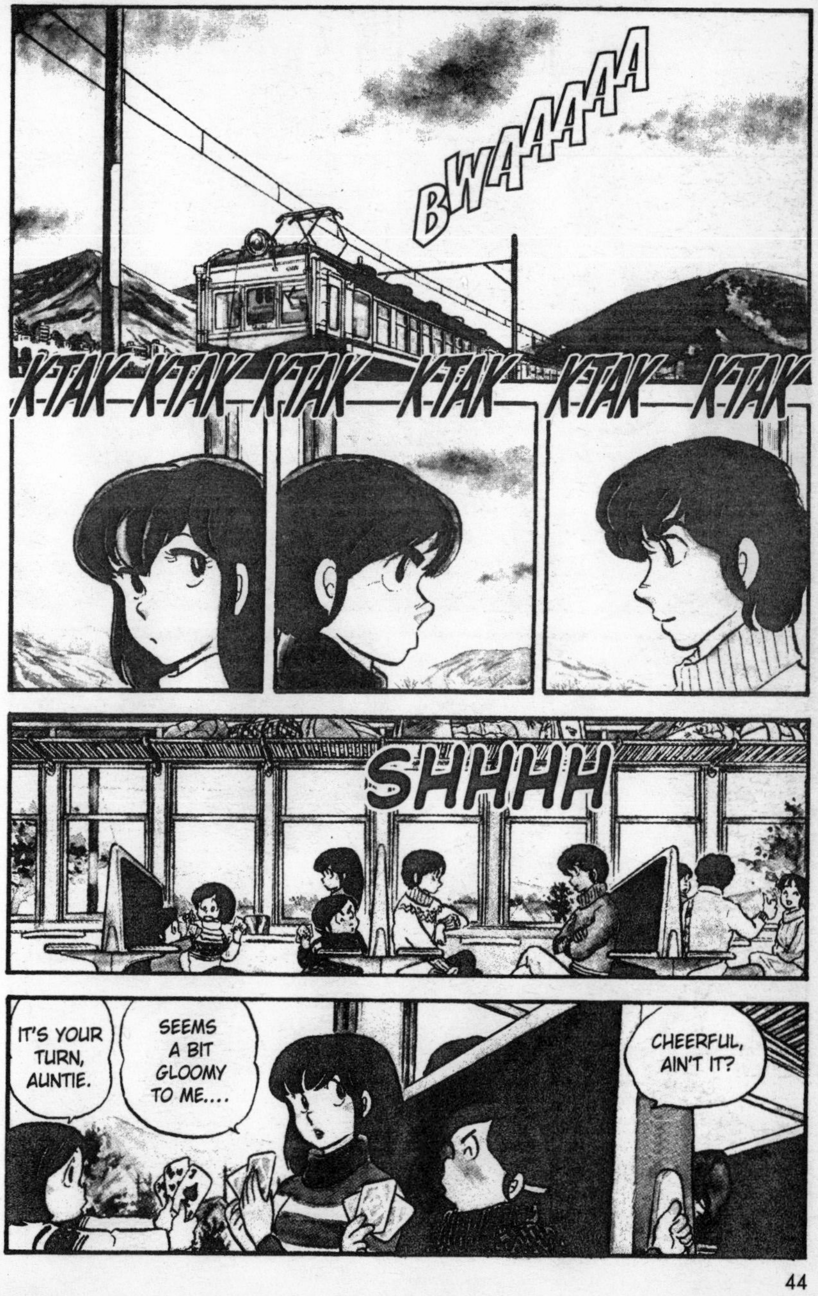
BWAAAAAA
KTAK KTAK KTAK KTAK KTAK KTAK
SHHHH
CHEERFUL, AIN'T IT?
SEEMS A BIT GLOOMY TO ME....
IT'S YOUR TURN, AUNTIE.

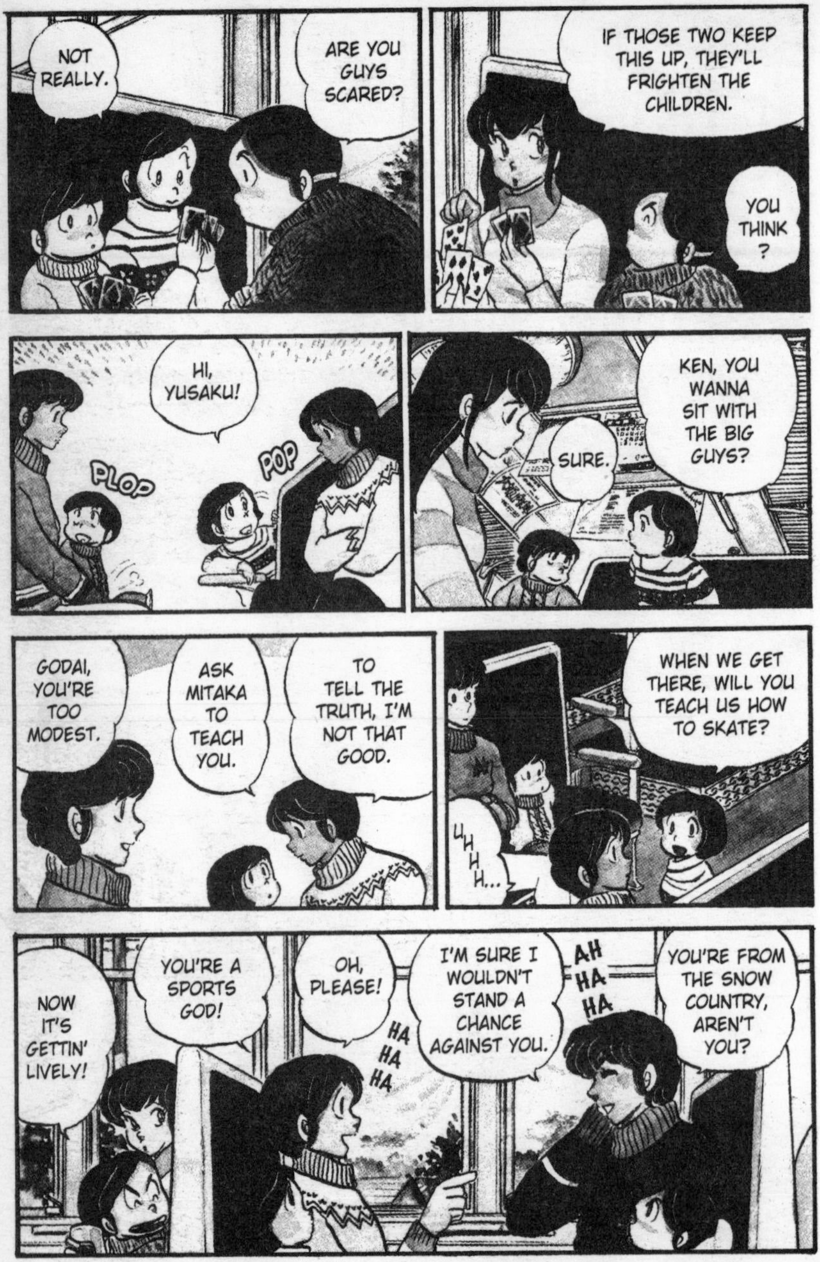
IF THOSE TWO KEEP THIS UP, THEY'LL FRIGHTEN THE CHILDREN.
YOU THINK ?
ARE YOU GUYS SCARED?
NOT REALLY.
KEN, YOU WANNA SIT WITH THE BIG GUYS?
SURE.
HI, YUSAKU!
POP
PLOP
WHEN WE GET THERE, WILL YOU TEACH US HOW TO SKATE?
UHHH...
TO TELL THE TRUTH, I'M NOT THAT GOOD.
ASK MITAKA TO TEACH YOU.
GODAI, YOU'RE TOO MODEST.
YOU'RE FROM THE SNOW COUNTRY, AREN'T YOU?
AH HA HA
I'M SURE I WOULDN'T STAND A CHANCE AGAINST YOU.
HA HA HA
OH, PLEASE!
YOU'RE A SPORTS GOD!
NOW IT'S GETTIN' LIVELY!

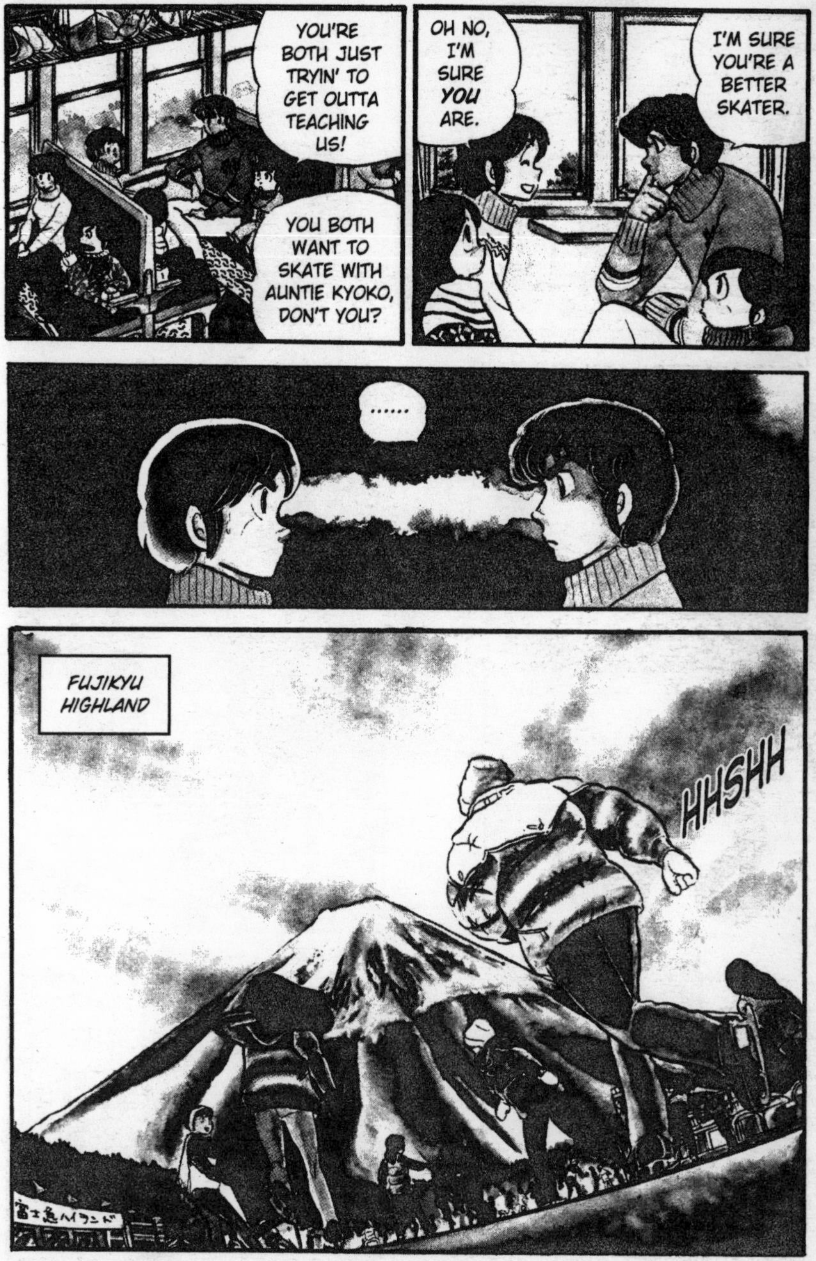
I'M SURE YOU'RE A BETTER SKATER.
OH NO, I'M SURE *YOU* ARE.
YOU'RE BOTH JUST TRYIN' TO GET OUTTA TEACHING US!
YOU BOTH WANT TO SKATE WITH AUNTIE KYOKO, DON'T YOU?
......
FUJIKYU HIGHLAND
HHSHH
富士急ハイランド

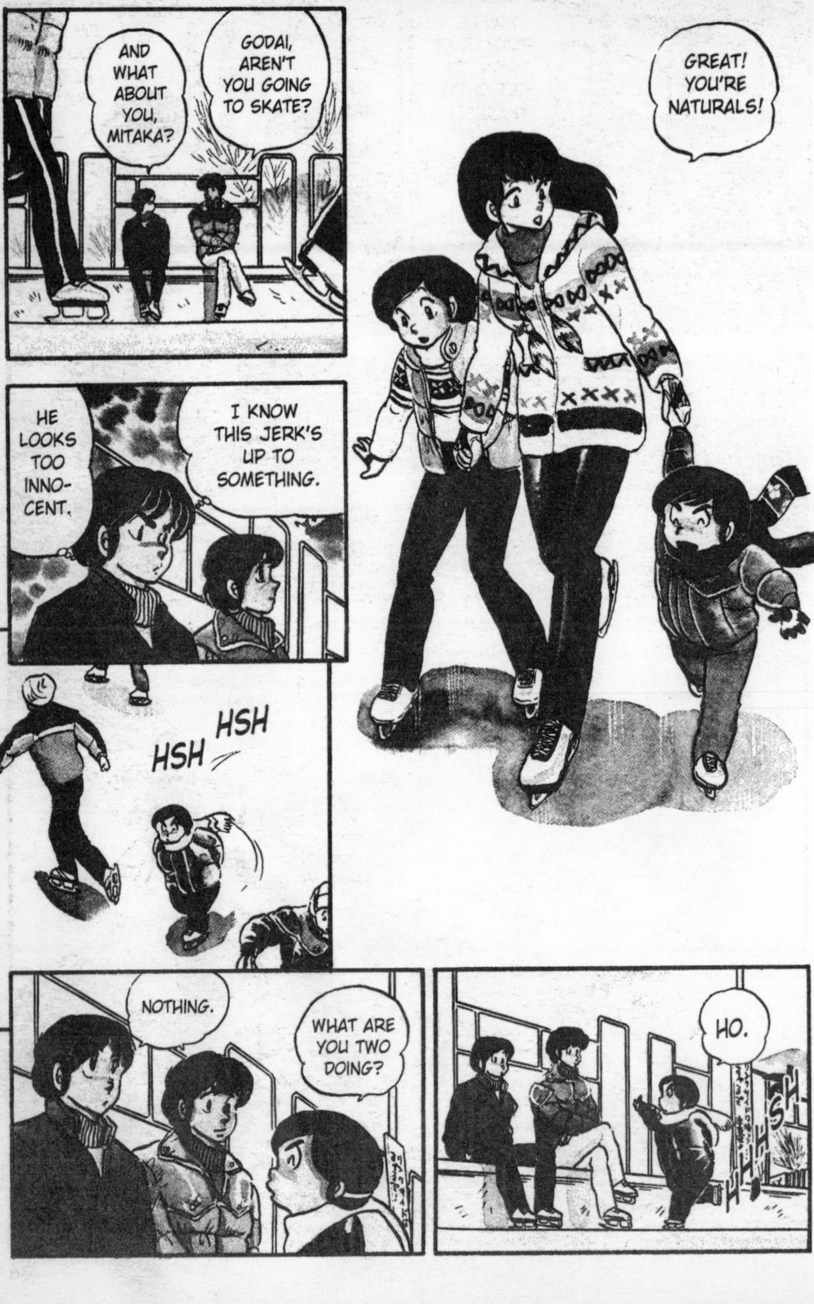
GREAT! YOU'RE NATURALS!
GODAI, AREN'T YOU GOING TO SKATE?
AND WHAT ABOUT YOU, MITAKA?
I KNOW THIS JERK'S UP TO SOMETHING.
HE LOOKS TOO INNO-CENT.
HSH
HSH
HO.
WHAT ARE YOU TWO DOING?
NOTHING.

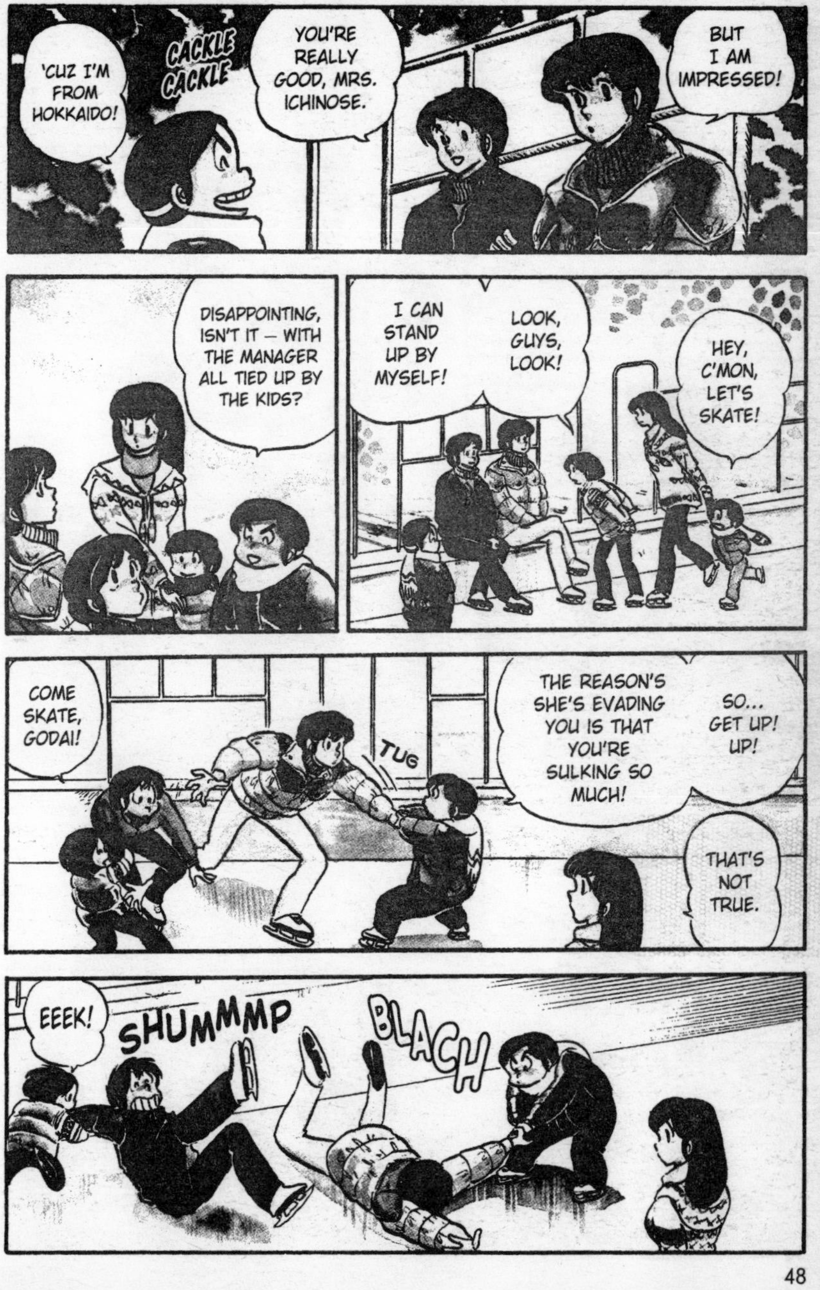
BUT I AM IMPRESSED!
YOU'RE REALLY GOOD, MRS. ICHINOSE.
CACKLE CACKLE
'CUZ I'M FROM HOKKAIDO!
HEY, C'MON, LET'S SKATE!
LOOK, GUYS, LOOK!
I CAN STAND UP BY MYSELF!
DISAPPOINTING, ISN'T IT — WITH THE MANAGER ALL TIED UP BY THE KIDS?
SO... GET UP! UP!
THE REASON'S SHE'S EVADING YOU IS THAT YOU'RE SULKING SO MUCH!
THAT'S NOT TRUE.
TUG
COME SKATE, GODAI!
BLACH
SHUMMMP
EEEK!

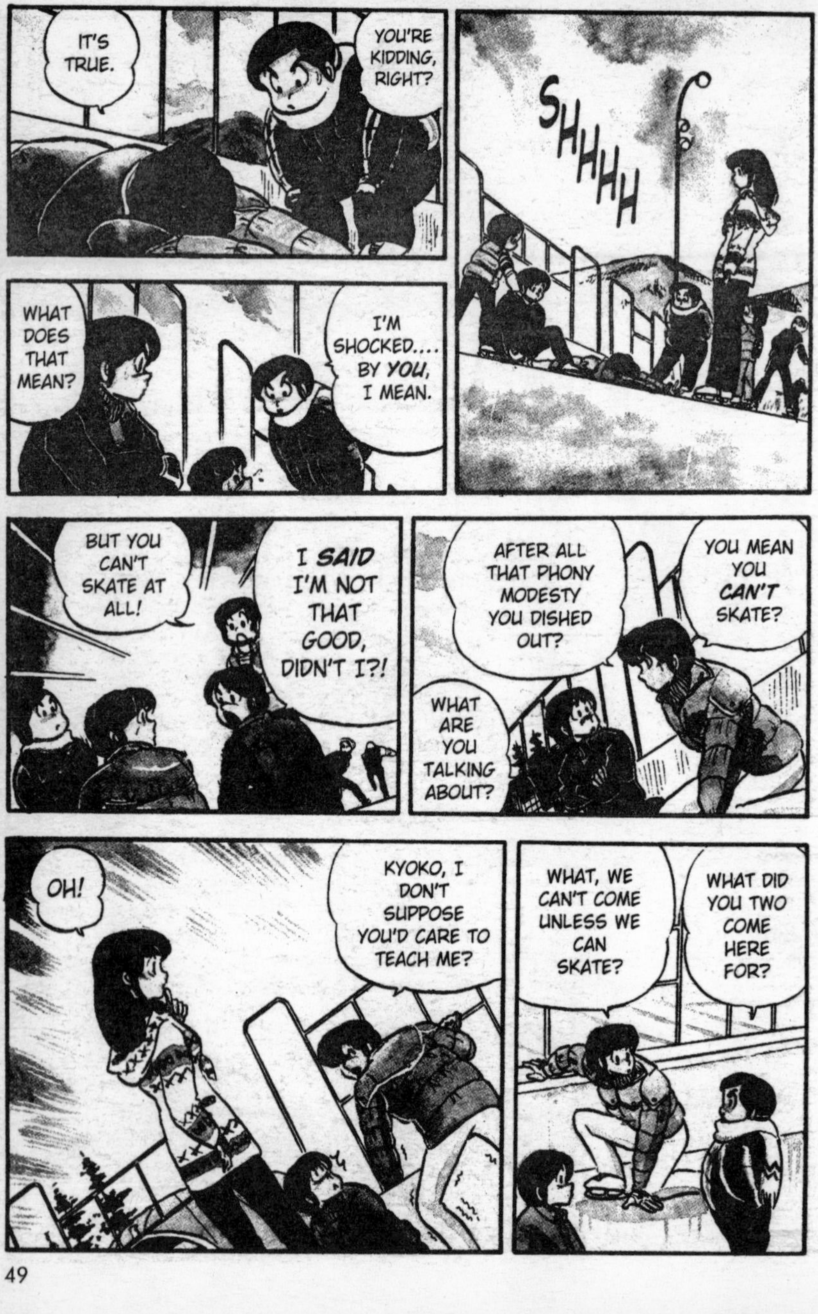
SHHHHH
YOU'RE KIDDING, RIGHT?
IT'S TRUE.
I'M SHOCKED.... BY YOU, I MEAN.
WHAT DOES THAT MEAN?
YOU MEAN YOU CAN'T SKATE?
AFTER ALL THAT PHONY MODESTY YOU DISHED OUT?
WHAT ARE YOU TALKING ABOUT?
I SAID I'M NOT THAT GOOD, DIDN'T I?!
BUT YOU CAN'T SKATE AT ALL!
WHAT DID YOU TWO COME HERE FOR?
WHAT, WE CAN'T COME UNLESS WE CAN SKATE?
KYOKO, I DON'T SUPPOSE YOU'D CARE TO TEACH ME?
OH!

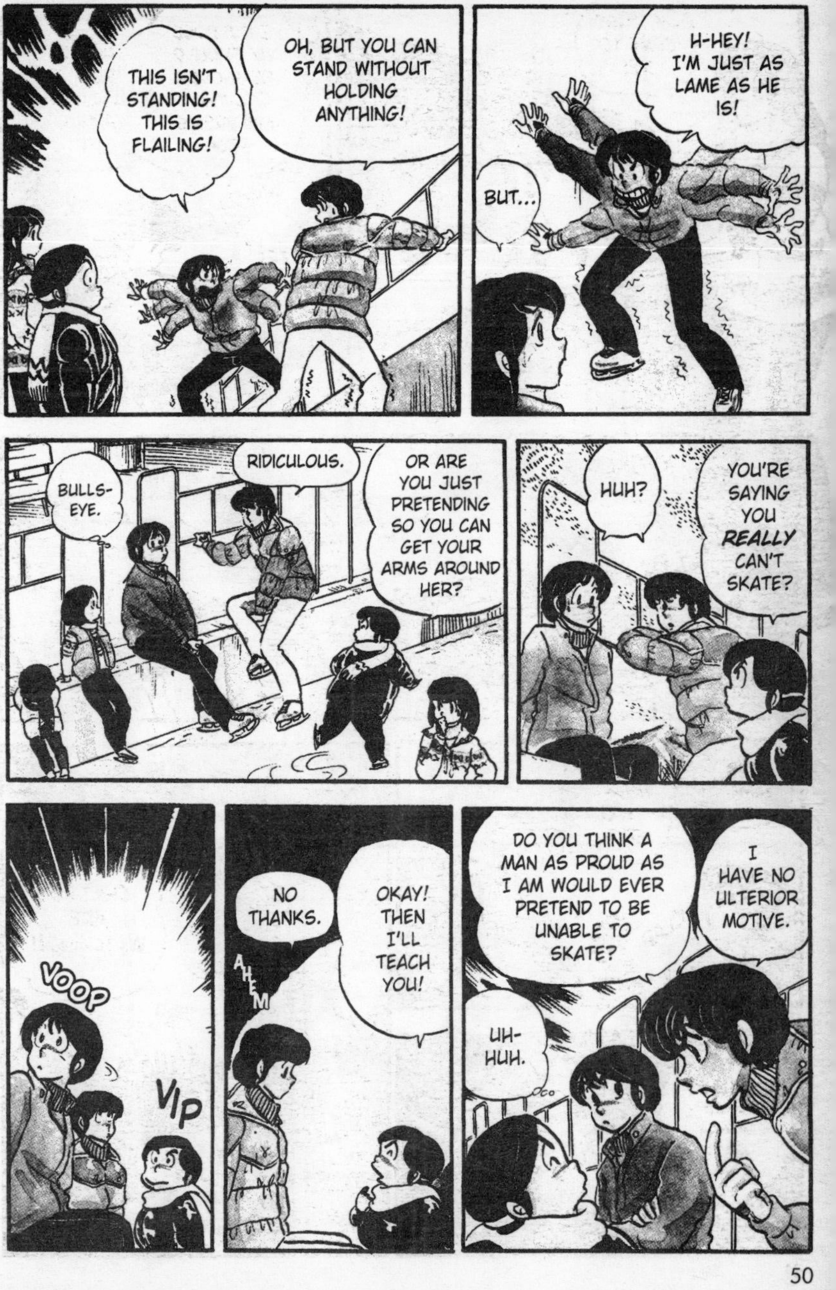
H-HEY! I'M JUST AS LAME AS HE IS!
BUT...
OH, BUT YOU CAN STAND WITHOUT HOLDING ANYTHING!
THIS ISN'T STANDING! THIS IS FLAILING!
YOU'RE SAYING YOU *REALLY* CAN'T SKATE?
HUH?
OR ARE YOU JUST PRETENDING SO YOU CAN GET YOUR ARMS AROUND HER?
RIDICULOUS.
BULLS-EYE.
I HAVE NO ULTERIOR MOTIVE.
DO YOU THINK A MAN AS PROUD AS I AM WOULD EVER PRETEND TO BE UNABLE TO SKATE?
UH-HUH.
OKAY! THEN I'LL TEACH YOU!
NO THANKS.
AHEM
VOOP
VIP

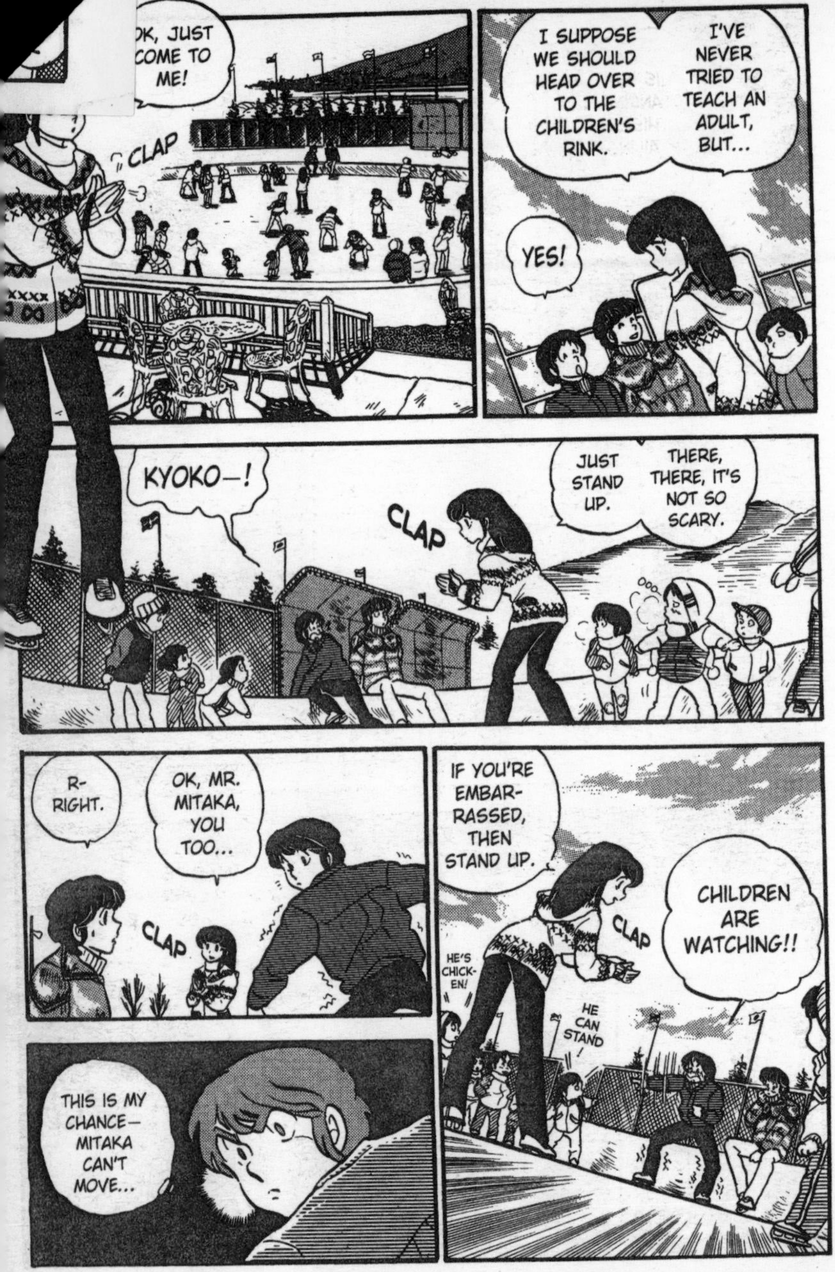
I'VE NEVER TRIED TO TEACH AN ADULT, BUT...
I SUPPOSE WE SHOULD HEAD OVER TO THE CHILDREN'S RINK.
YES!
OK, JUST COME TO ME!
CLAP
THERE, THERE, IT'S NOT SO SCARY.
JUST STAND UP.
CLAP
KYOKO—!
IF YOU'RE EMBARRASSED, THEN STAND UP.
CHILDREN ARE WATCHING!!
CLAP
HE'S CHICKEN!
HE CAN STAND!
OK, MR. MITAKA, YOU TOO...
R-RIGHT.
CLAP
THIS IS MY CHANCE— MITAKA CAN'T MOVE...

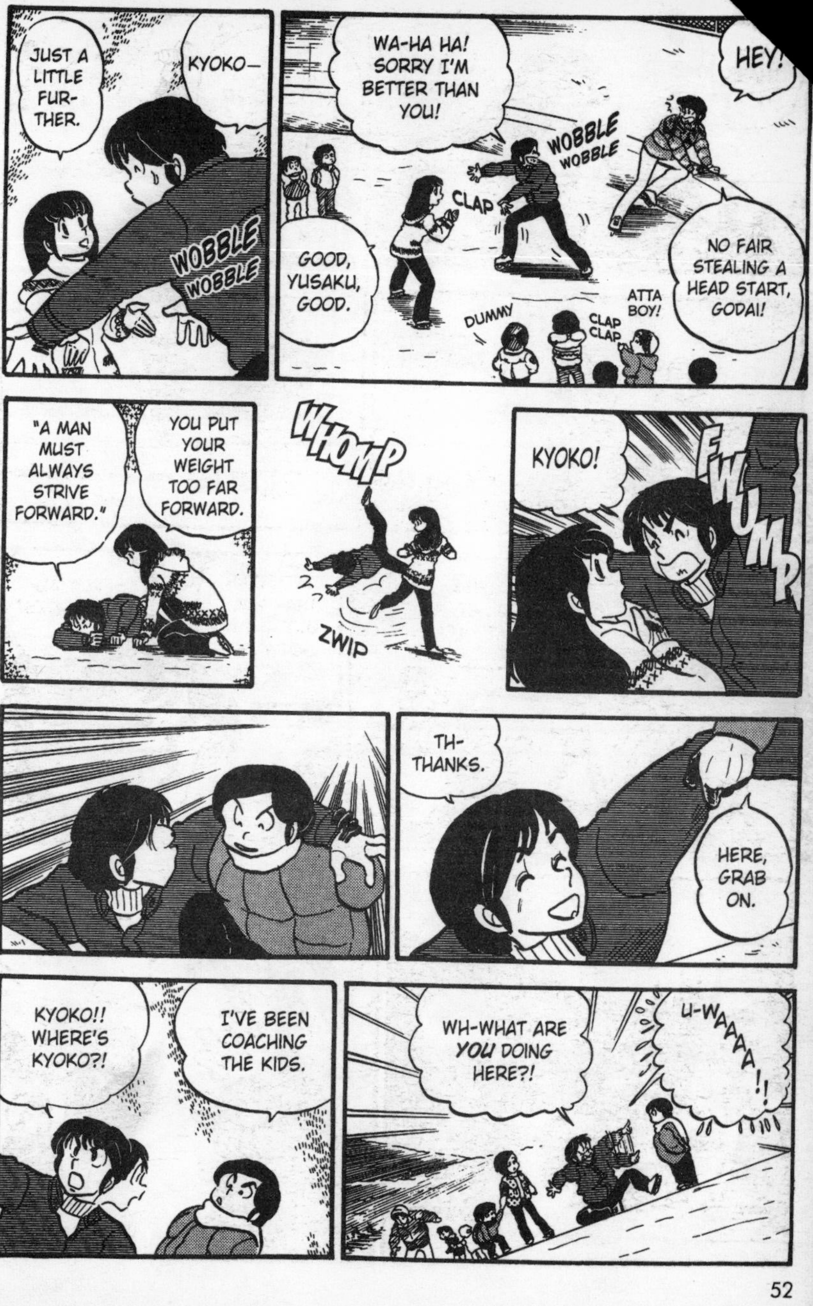
HEY!
WA-HA HA! SORRY I'M BETTER THAN YOU!
WOBBLE WOBBLE
CLAP
NO FAIR STEALING A HEAD START, GODAI!
GOOD, YUSAKU, GOOD.
ATTA BOY!
CLAP CLAP
DUMMY
KYOKO—
JUST A LITTLE FURTHER.
WOBBLE WOBBLE
KYOKO!
FWUMP
WHOMP
ZWIP
YOU PUT YOUR WEIGHT TOO FAR FORWARD.
"A MAN MUST ALWAYS STRIVE FORWARD."
HERE, GRAB ON.
TH-THANKS.
U-WAAAA!!
WH-WHAT ARE *YOU* DOING HERE?!
I'VE BEEN COACHING THE KIDS.
KYOKO!! WHERE'S KYOKO?!

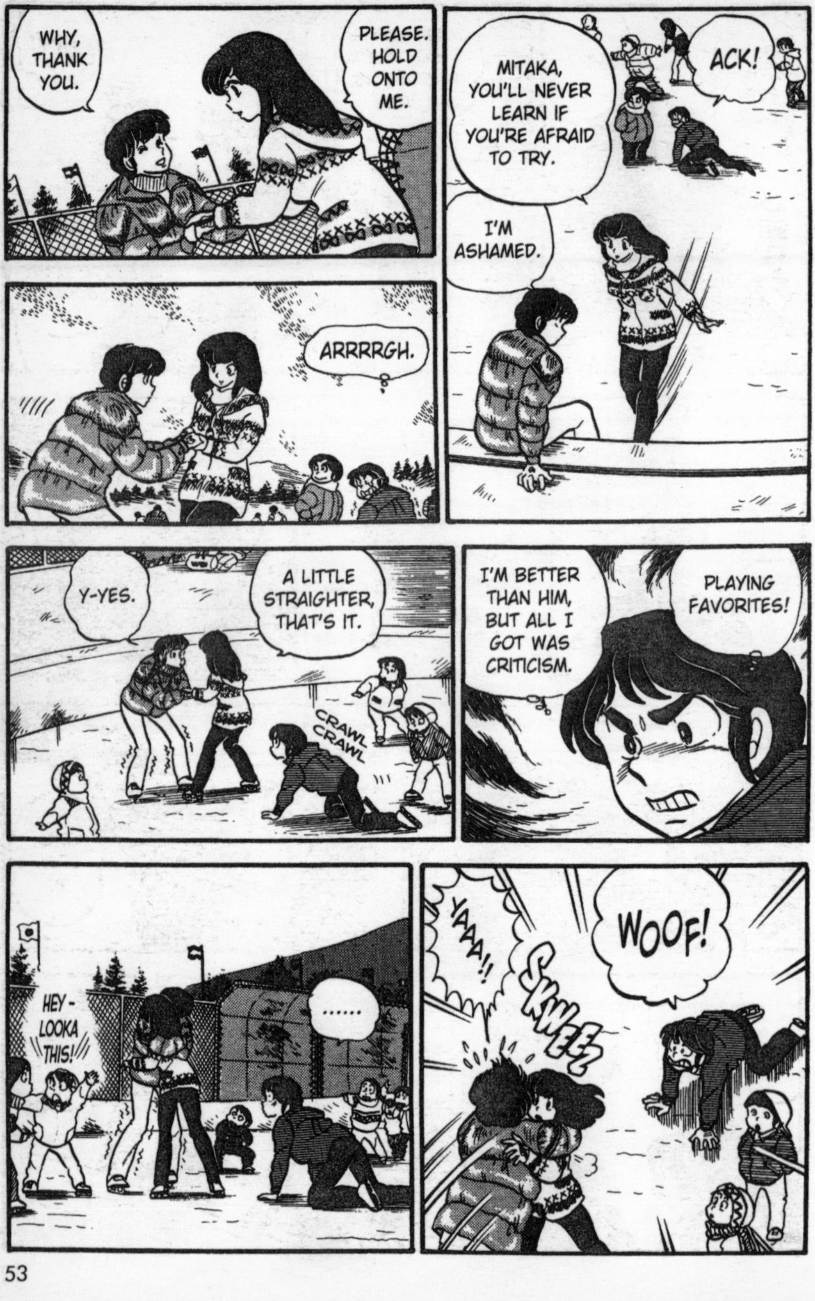
ACK!
MITAKA, YOU'LL NEVER LEARN IF YOU'RE AFRAID TO TRY.
I'M ASHAMED.
PLEASE. HOLD ONTO ME.
WHY, THANK YOU.
ARRRRGH.
PLAYING FAVORITES!
I'M BETTER THAN HIM, BUT ALL I GOT WAS CRITICISM.
A LITTLE STRAIGHTER, THAT'S IT.
Y-YES.
CRAWL CRAWL
WOOF!
SKWEEZ
YAAAA!!
......
HEY-LOOKA THIS!

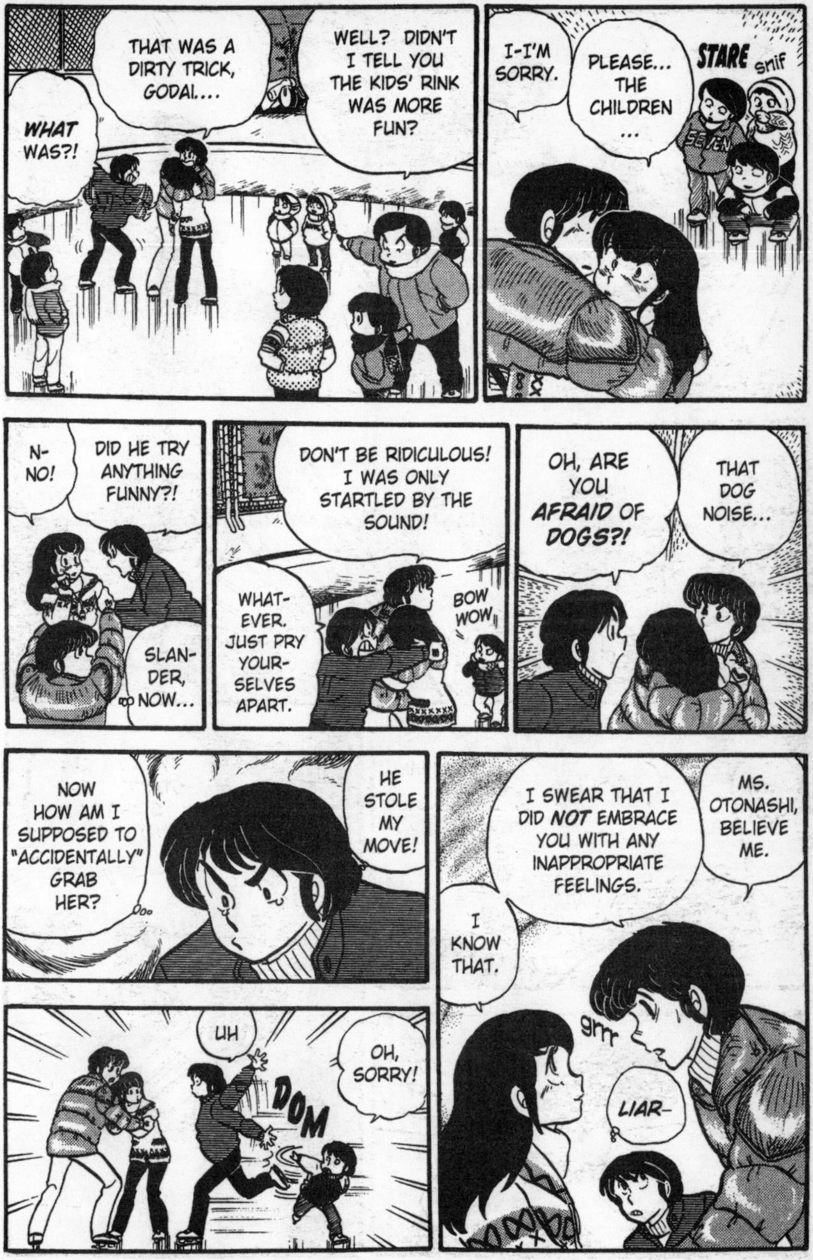
STARE
snif
PLEASE... THE CHILDREN ...
I-I'M SORRY.
WELL? DIDN'T I TELL YOU THE KIDS' RINK WAS MORE FUN?
THAT WAS A DIRTY TRICK, GODAI....
WHAT WAS?!
THAT DOG NOISE...
OH, ARE YOU AFRAID OF DOGS?!
DON'T BE RIDICULOUS! I WAS ONLY STARTLED BY THE SOUND!
BOW WOW
WHAT-EVER. JUST PRY YOUR-SELVES APART.
DID HE TRY ANYTHING FUNNY?!
N-NO!
SLAN-DER, NOW...
MS. OTONASHI, BELIEVE ME.
I SWEAR THAT I DID NOT EMBRACE YOU WITH ANY INAPPROPRIATE FEELINGS.
I KNOW THAT.
grrr
LIAR-
HE STOLE MY MOVE!
NOW HOW AM I SUPPOSED TO "ACCIDENTALLY" GRAB HER?
OH, SORRY!
UH
DOM

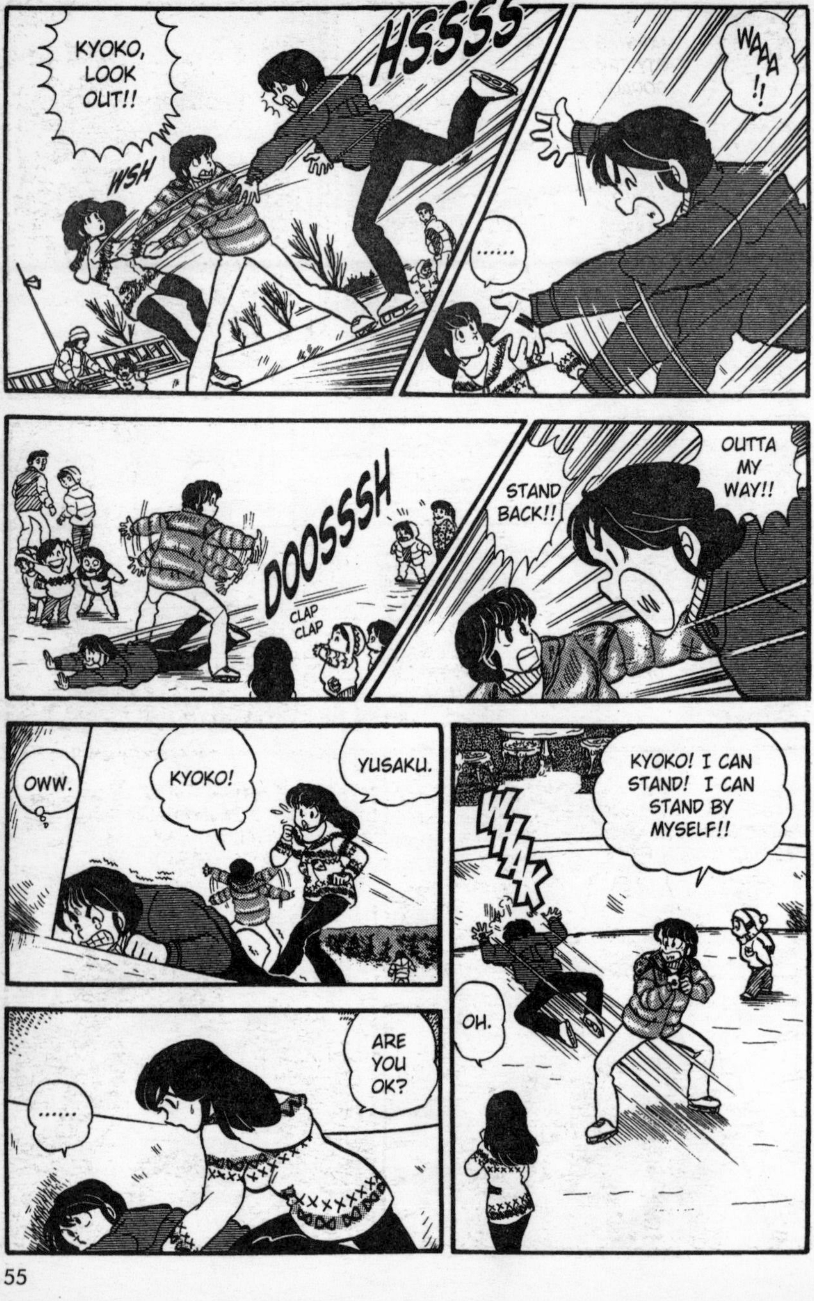
WAAA !!
......
KYOKO, LOOK OUT!!
HSSSS
WSH
OUTTA MY WAY!!
STAND BACK!!
DOOSSSH
CLAP CLAP
KYOKO! I CAN STAND! I CAN STAND BY MYSELF!!
WHAK
OH.
YUSAKU.
KYOKO!
OWW.
ARE YOU OK?
......

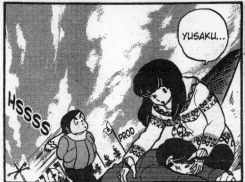

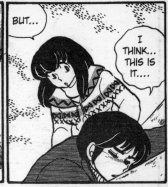

BUT...
I THINK... THIS IS IT....
YUSAKU...
PROD
HSSSS
JUST LEAVE 'IM ALONE FOR A WHILE.
WHAT?
BUT...
TREAT 'EM LIKE BABIES AND THEY'LL ACT LIKE BABIES.
MY FACE IS GOING TO FREEZE—
NO WAY
WANNA BET?
ARRGH!
H-HEY. HEY, STOP THAT.
HE'S DEAD
WOW!
POKE POKE
BWA HA HA
THAT'S NOT NICE.
POOR YOU, YUSAKU.
KRAK
WOW—YOUR CHEEKS ARE COLD—
AT LEAST YOU CARE, IKUKO.
SEE? YOU OWE ME 50 CENTS!
SHOOT.

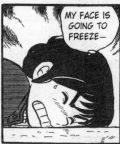

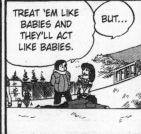

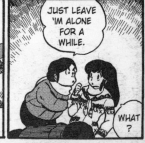

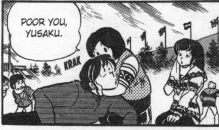

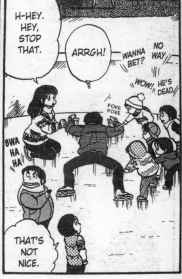

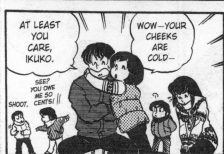

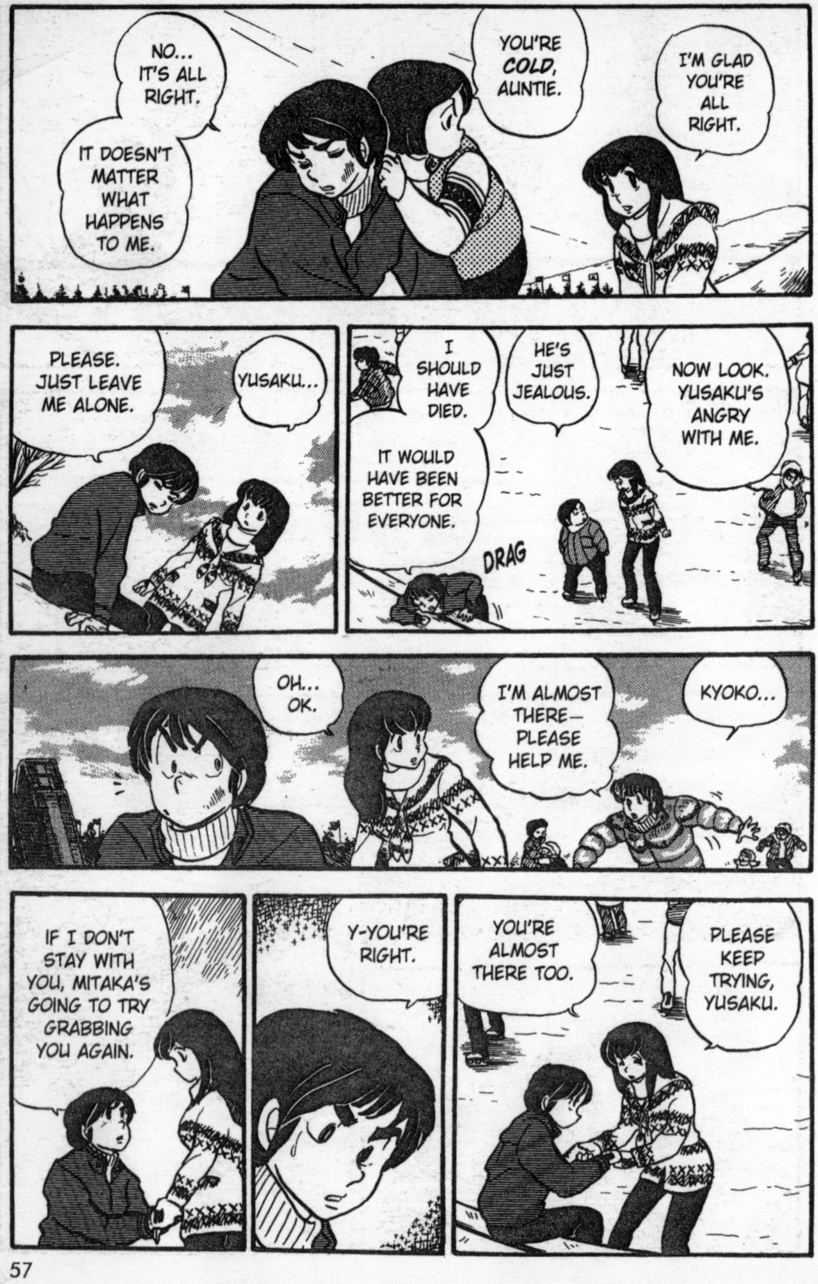
I'M GLAD YOU'RE ALL RIGHT.
YOU'RE COLD, AUNTIE.
NO... IT'S ALL RIGHT.
IT DOESN'T MATTER WHAT HAPPENS TO ME.
NOW LOOK. YUSAKU'S ANGRY WITH ME.
HE'S JUST JEALOUS.
I SHOULD HAVE DIED.
IT WOULD HAVE BEEN BETTER FOR EVERYONE.
DRAG
YUSAKU...
PLEASE. JUST LEAVE ME ALONE.
KYOKO...
I'M ALMOST THERE— PLEASE HELP ME.
OH... OK.
PLEASE KEEP TRYING, YUSAKU.
YOU'RE ALMOST THERE TOO.
Y-YOU'RE RIGHT.
IF I DON'T STAY WITH YOU, MITAKA'S GOING TO TRY GRABBING YOU AGAIN.

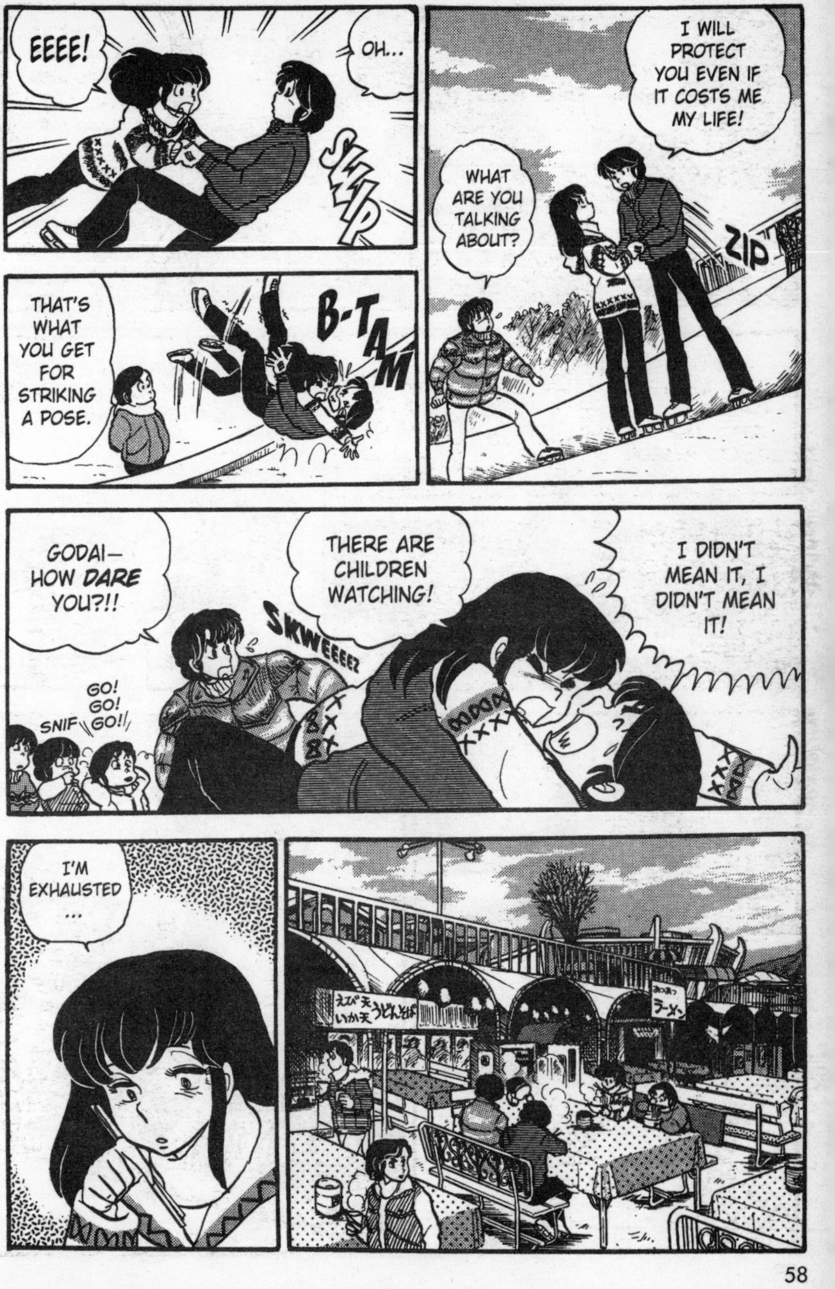
I WILL PROTECT YOU EVEN IF IT COSTS ME MY LIFE!
WHAT ARE YOU TALKING ABOUT?
ZIP
OH...
SWIP
EEEE!
B-TAM
THAT'S WHAT YOU GET FOR STRIKING A POSE.
I DIDN'T MEAN IT, I DIDN'T MEAN IT!
THERE ARE CHILDREN WATCHING!
SKWEEEEZ
GODAI— HOW *DARE* YOU?!!
GO! GO! GO!!
SNIF
I'M EXHAUSTED ...

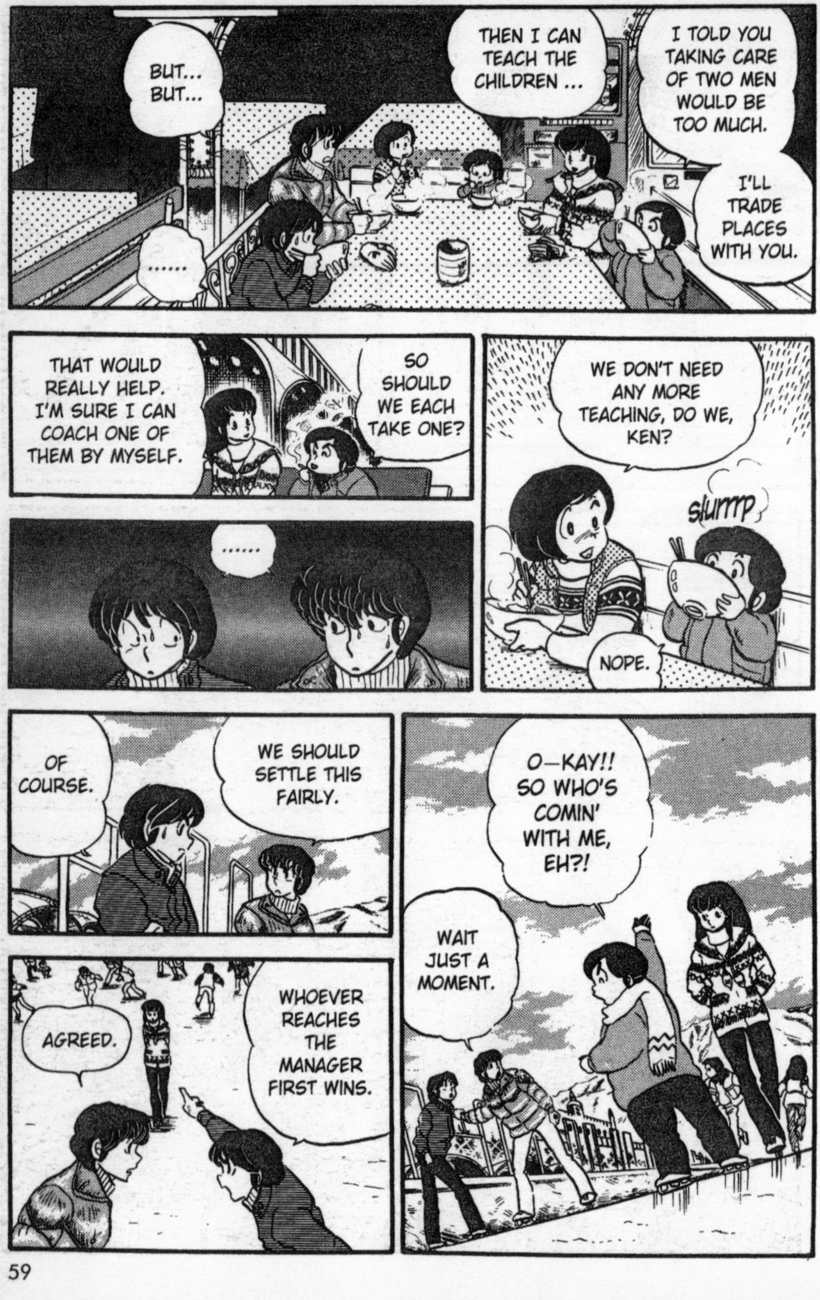
I TOLD YOU TAKING CARE OF TWO MEN WOULD BE TOO MUCH.
I'LL TRADE PLACES WITH YOU.
THEN I CAN TEACH THE CHILDREN ...
BUT... BUT...
......
WE DON'T NEED ANY MORE TEACHING, DO WE, KEN?
slurrp
NOPE.
SO SHOULD WE EACH TAKE ONE?
THAT WOULD REALLY HELP. I'M SURE I CAN COACH ONE OF THEM BY MYSELF.
......
O-KAY!! SO WHO'S COMIN' WITH ME, EH?!
WAIT JUST A MOMENT.
WE SHOULD SETTLE THIS FAIRLY.
OF COURSE.
WHOEVER REACHES THE MANAGER FIRST WINS.
AGREED.

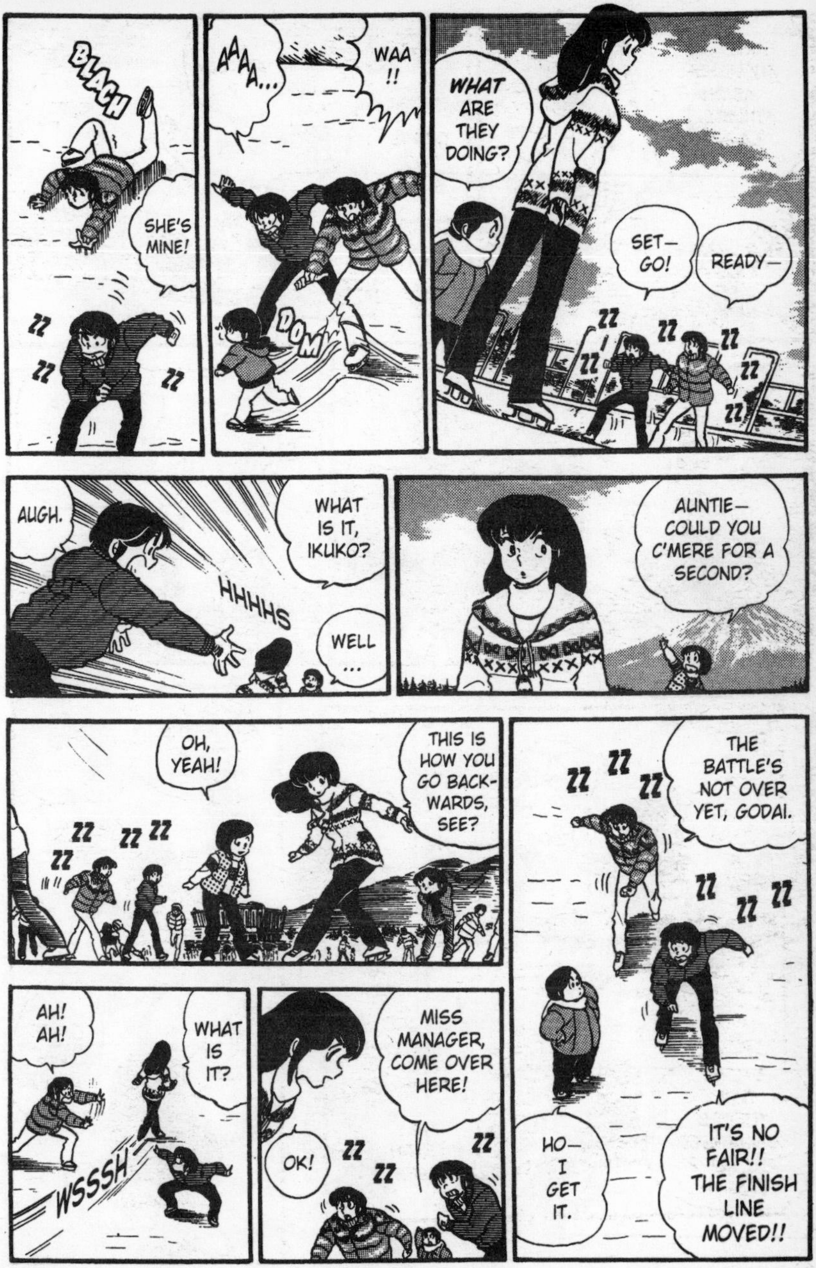
READY—
SET— GO!
ZZ
WHAT ARE THEY DOING?
WAA !!
AAAA...
DOM
BLACH
SHE'S MINE!
ZZ
AUNTIE— COULD YOU C'MERE FOR A SECOND?
WHAT IS IT, IKUKO?
WELL ...
AUGH.
HHHHS
THE BATTLE'S NOT OVER YET, GODAI.
ZZ
IT'S NO FAIR!! THE FINISH LINE MOVED!!
HO— I GET IT.
THIS IS HOW YOU GO BACK-WARDS, SEE?
OH, YEAH!
ZZ
MISS MANAGER, COME OVER HERE!
ZZ
OK!
WHAT IS IT?
AH! AH!
WSSSH

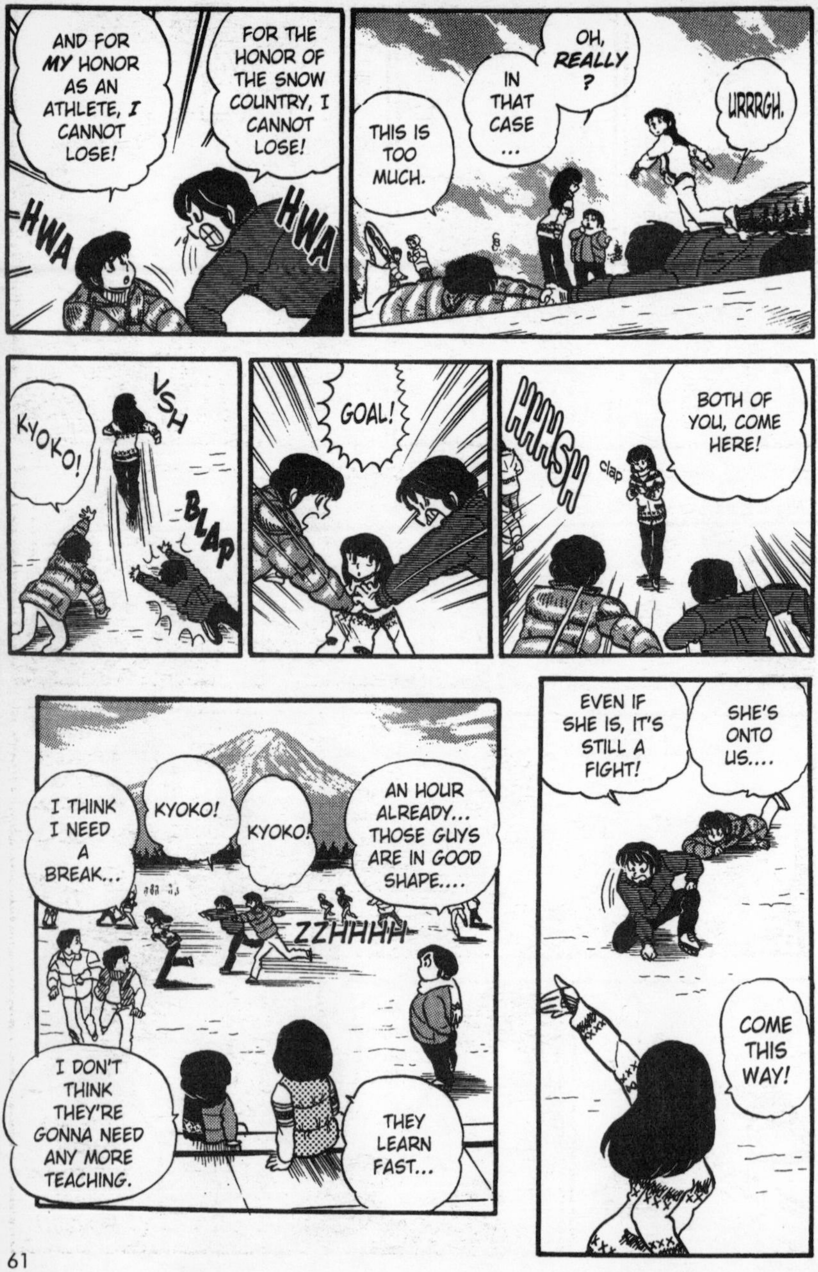
URRRGH.
OH, *REALLY*?
IN THAT CASE ...
THIS IS TOO MUCH.
FOR THE HONOR OF THE SNOW COUNTRY, I CANNOT LOSE!
AND FOR *MY* HONOR AS AN ATHLETE, *I* CANNOT LOSE!
HWA
HWA
BOTH OF YOU, COME HERE!
clap
CHHSH
GOAL!
VSH
KYOKO!
BLAP
SHE'S ONTO US....
EVEN IF SHE IS, IT'S STILL A FIGHT!
COME THIS WAY!
AN HOUR ALREADY... THOSE GUYS ARE IN GOOD SHAPE....
KYOKO!
KYOKO!
I THINK I NEED A BREAK...
ZZHHHH
THEY LEARN FAST...
I DON'T THINK THEY'RE GONNA NEED ANY MORE TEACHING.

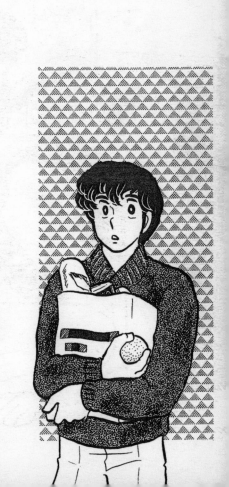

PART FOUR
KYOKO BABY AND MR. SOICHIRO

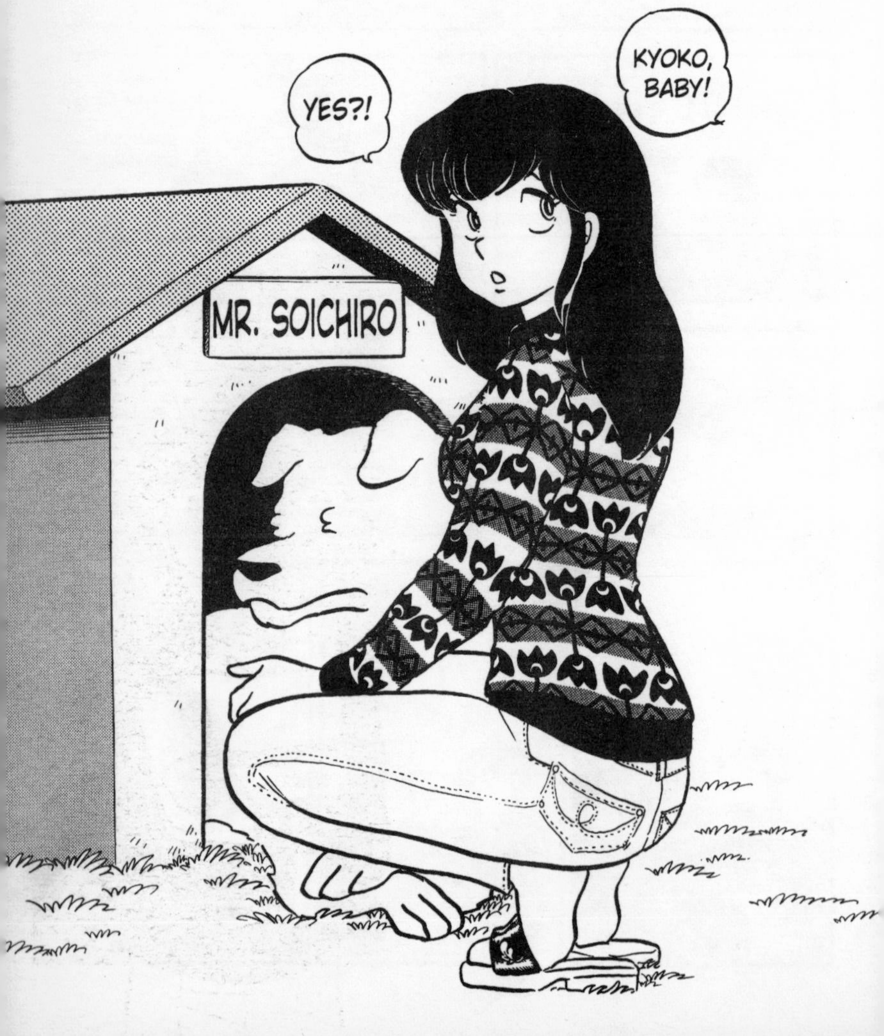
KYOKO, BABY!
YES?!
MR. SOICHIRO

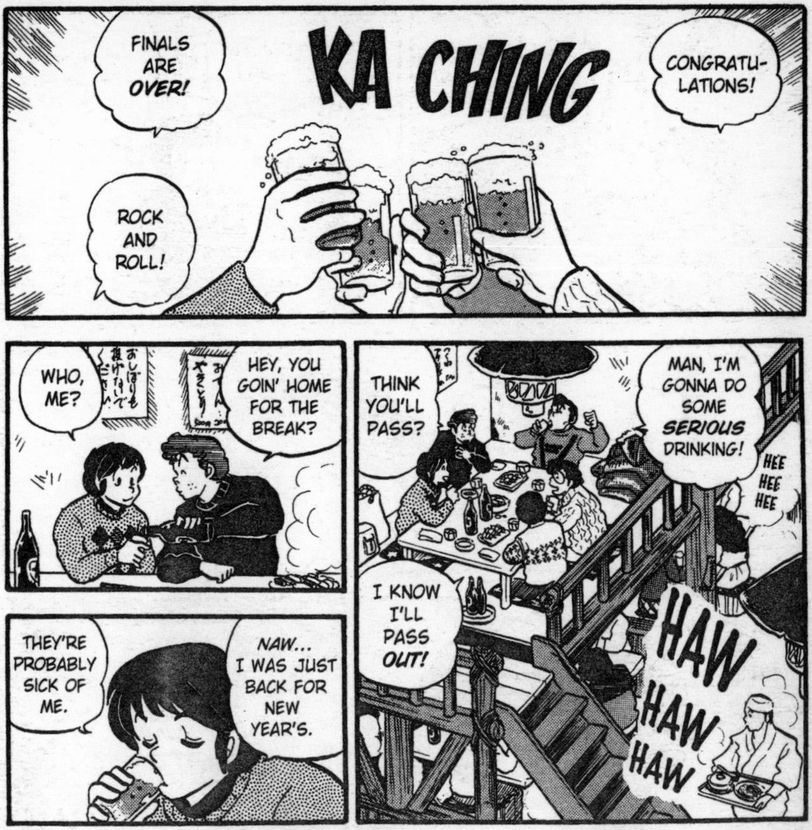
CONGRATULATIONS!
KA CHING
FINALS ARE OVER!
ROCK AND ROLL!
MAN, I'M GONNA DO SOME SERIOUS DRINKING!
HEE HEE HEE
THINK YOU'LL PASS?
I KNOW I'LL PASS OUT!
HAW HAW HAW
HEY, YOU GOIN' HOME FOR THE BREAK?
WHO, ME?
NAW... I WAS JUST BACK FOR NEW YEAR'S.
THEY'RE PROBABLY SICK OF ME.
NO KIDDIN'... HEY, DRINK UP!
HUH?
I'M GOING HOME... JUST FOR A WEEK OR SO, ANYWAY.
OH, YEAH?
C'MON—HAVE ANOTHER!
??

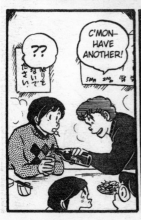

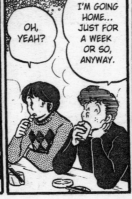

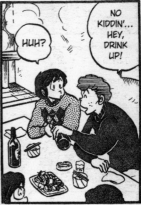

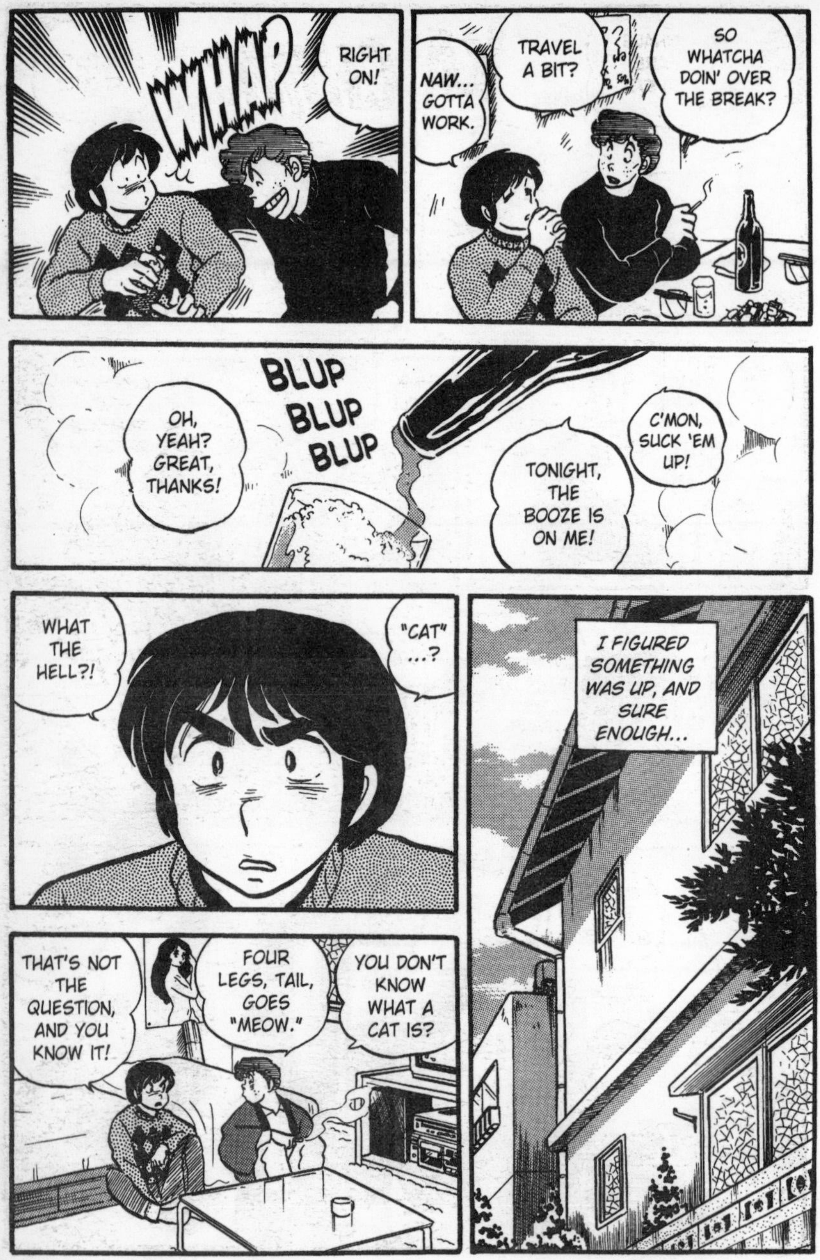
SO WHATCHA DOIN' OVER THE BREAK?
TRAVEL A BIT?
NAW... GOTTA WORK.
RIGHT ON!
WHAP
C'MON, SUCK 'EM UP!
TONIGHT, THE BOOZE IS ON ME!
BLUP BLUP BLUP
OH, YEAH? GREAT, THANKS!
I FIGURED SOMETHING WAS UP, AND SURE ENOUGH...
"CAT" ...?
WHAT THE HELL?!
YOU DON'T KNOW WHAT A CAT IS?
FOUR LEGS, TAIL, GOES "MEOW."
THAT'S NOT THE QUESTION, AND YOU KNOW IT!

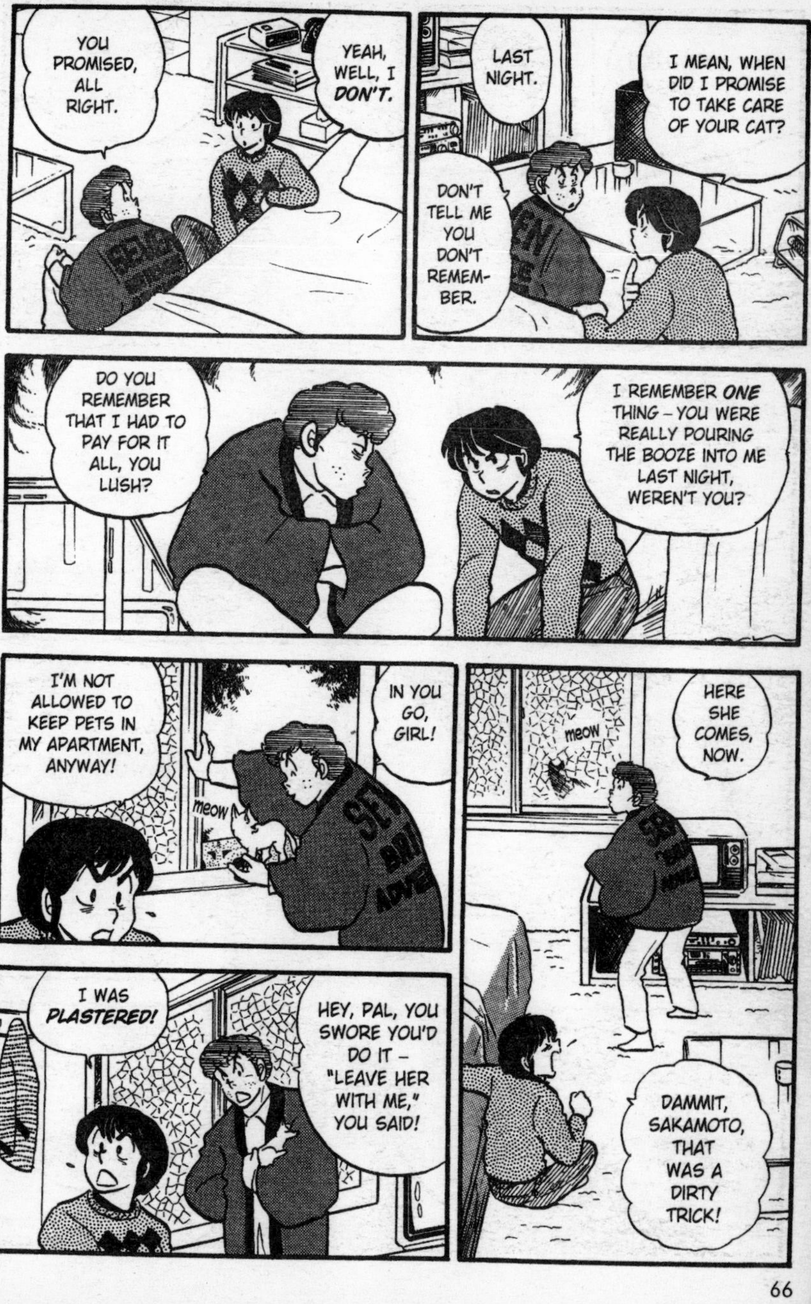
I MEAN, WHEN DID I PROMISE TO TAKE CARE OF YOUR CAT?
LAST NIGHT.
DON'T TELL ME YOU DON'T REMEMBER.
YEAH, WELL, I ***DON'T.***
YOU PROMISED, ALL RIGHT.
I REMEMBER ***ONE*** THING – YOU WERE REALLY POURING THE BOOZE INTO ME LAST NIGHT, WEREN'T YOU?
DO YOU REMEMBER THAT I HAD TO PAY FOR IT ALL, YOU LUSH?
HERE SHE COMES, NOW.
meow
DAMMIT, SAKAMOTO, THAT WAS A DIRTY TRICK!
IN YOU GO, GIRL!
I'M NOT ALLOWED TO KEEP PETS IN MY APARTMENT, ANYWAY!
meow
HEY, PAL, YOU SWORE YOU'D DO IT – "LEAVE HER WITH ME," YOU SAID!
I WAS ***PLASTERED!***

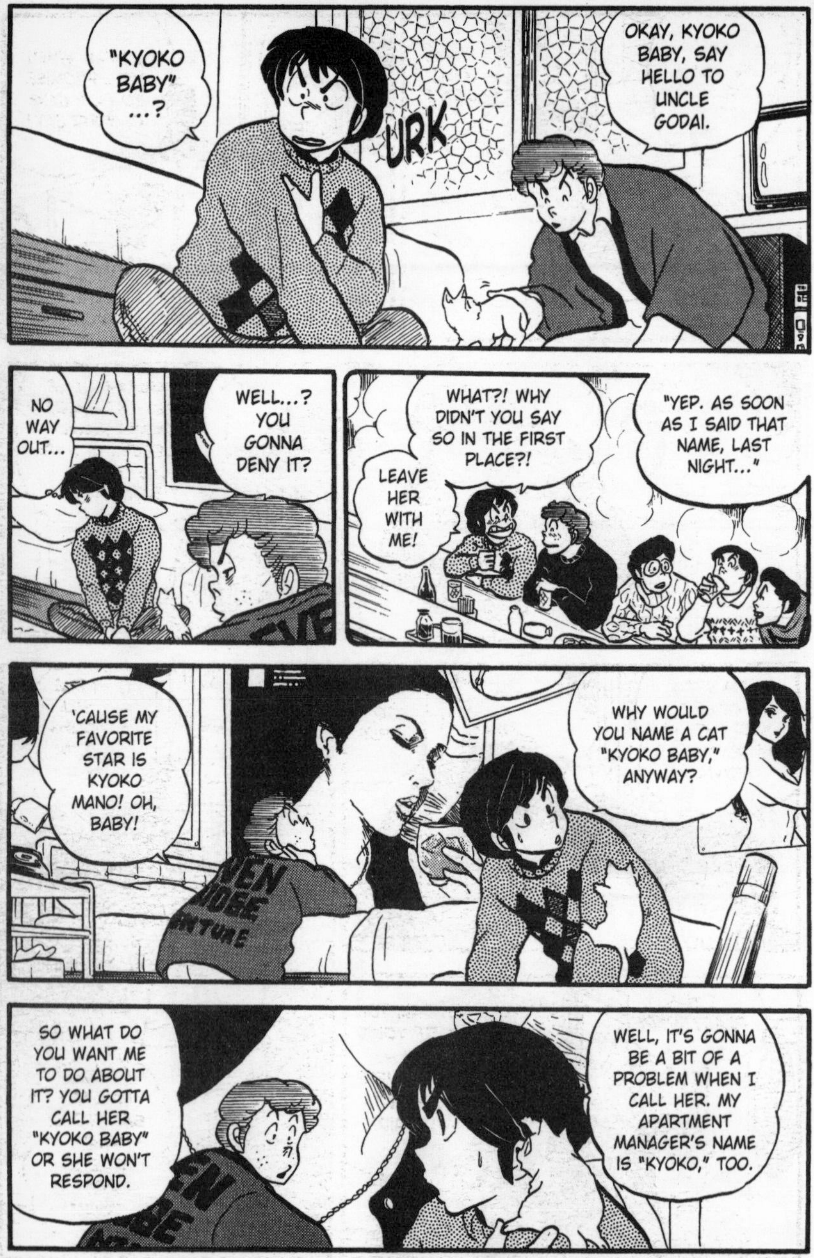
OKAY, KYOKO BABY, SAY HELLO TO UNCLE GODAI.
URK
"KYOKO BABY" ...?
"YEP. AS SOON AS I SAID THAT NAME, LAST NIGHT..."
WHAT?! WHY DIDN'T YOU SAY SO IN THE FIRST PLACE?!
LEAVE HER WITH ME!
WELL...? YOU GONNA DENY IT?
NO WAY OUT...
WHY WOULD YOU NAME A CAT "KYOKO BABY," ANYWAY?
'CAUSE MY FAVORITE STAR IS KYOKO MANO! OH, BABY!
WELL, IT'S GONNA BE A BIT OF A PROBLEM WHEN I CALL HER. MY APARTMENT MANAGER'S NAME IS "KYOKO," TOO.
SO WHAT DO YOU WANT ME TO DO ABOUT IT? YOU GOTTA CALL HER "KYOKO BABY" OR SHE WON'T RESPOND.

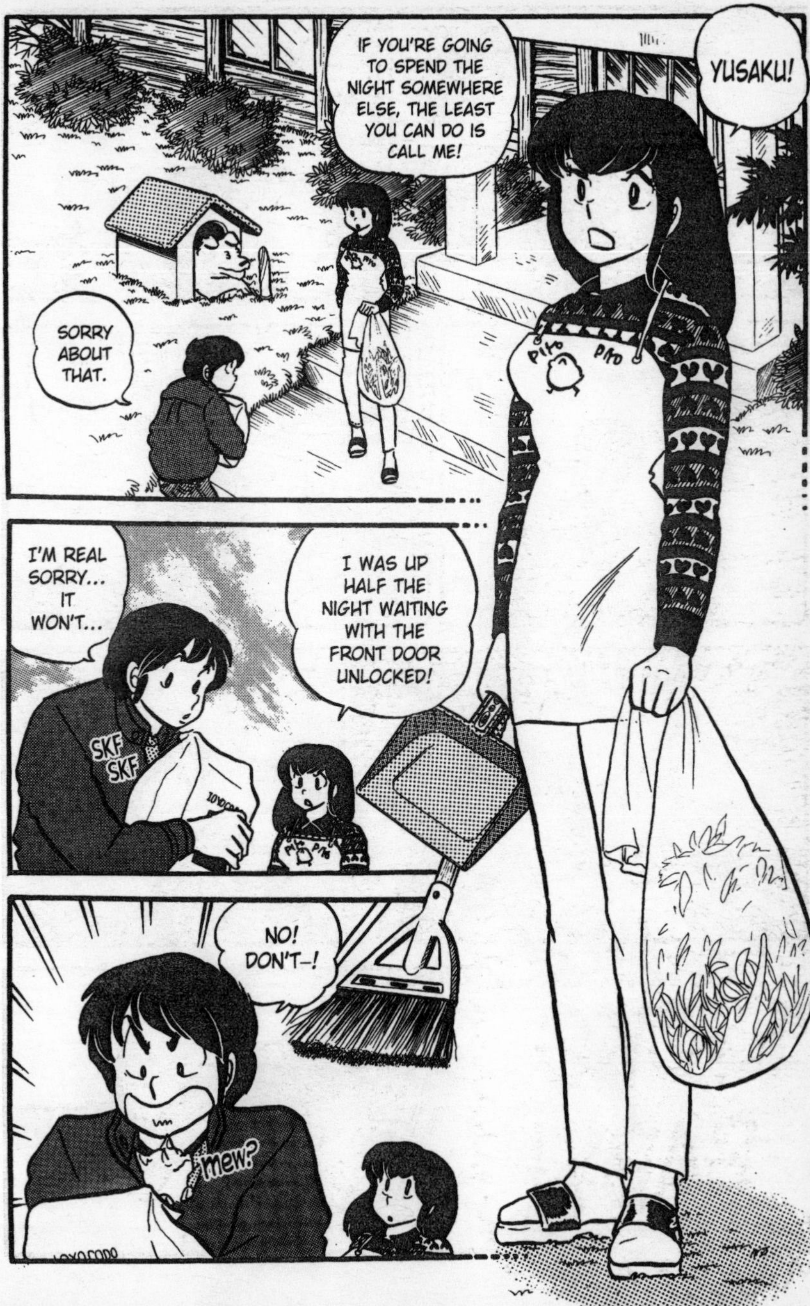
YUSAKU!
IF YOU'RE GOING TO SPEND THE NIGHT SOMEWHERE ELSE, THE LEAST YOU CAN DO IS CALL ME!
SORRY ABOUT THAT.
I WAS UP HALF THE NIGHT WAITING WITH THE FRONT DOOR UNLOCKED!
I'M REAL SORRY... IT WON'T...
SKF SKF
NO! DON'T-!
mew?

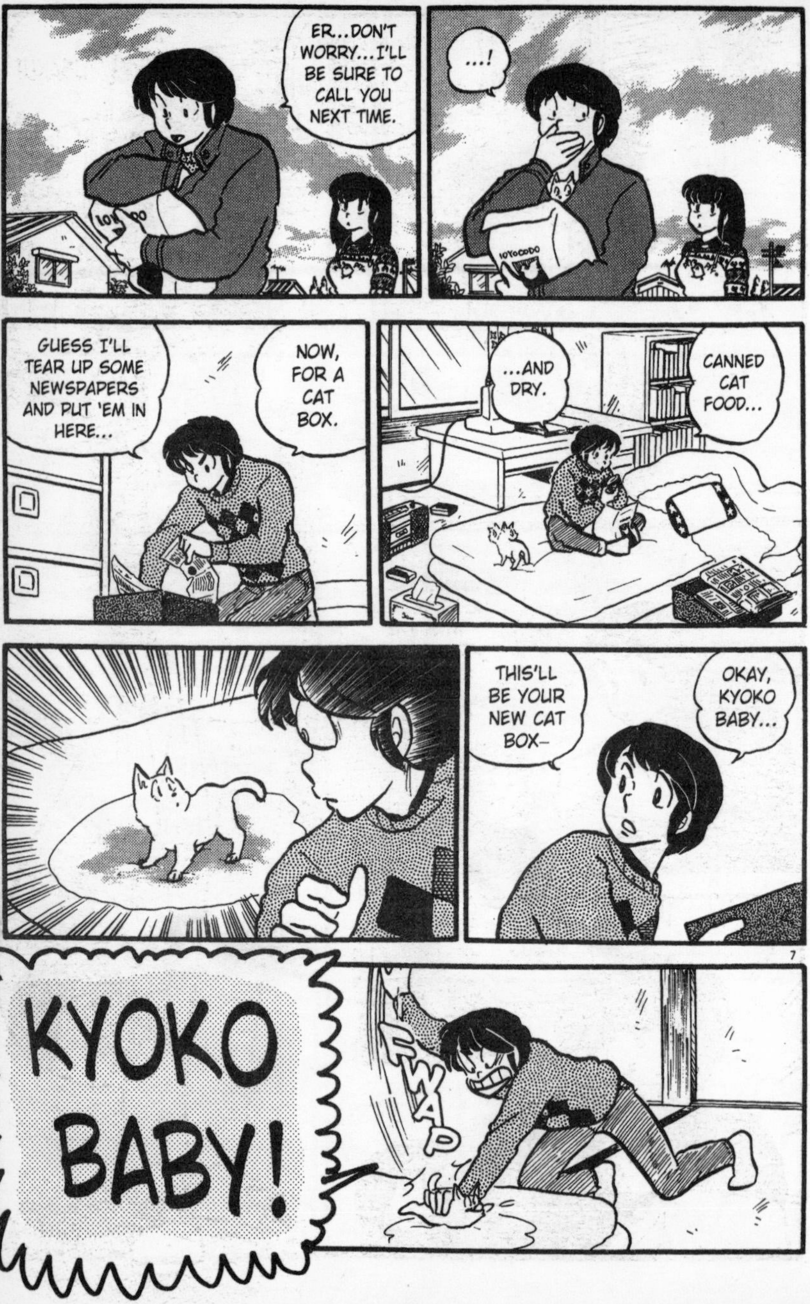
...!
ER...DON'T WORRY...I'LL BE SURE TO CALL YOU NEXT TIME.
CANNED CAT FOOD...
...AND DRY.
NOW, FOR A CAT BOX.
GUESS I'LL TEAR UP SOME NEWSPAPERS AND PUT 'EM IN HERE...
OKAY, KYOKO BABY...
THIS'LL BE YOUR NEW CAT BOX–
FWAP
KYOKO BABY!

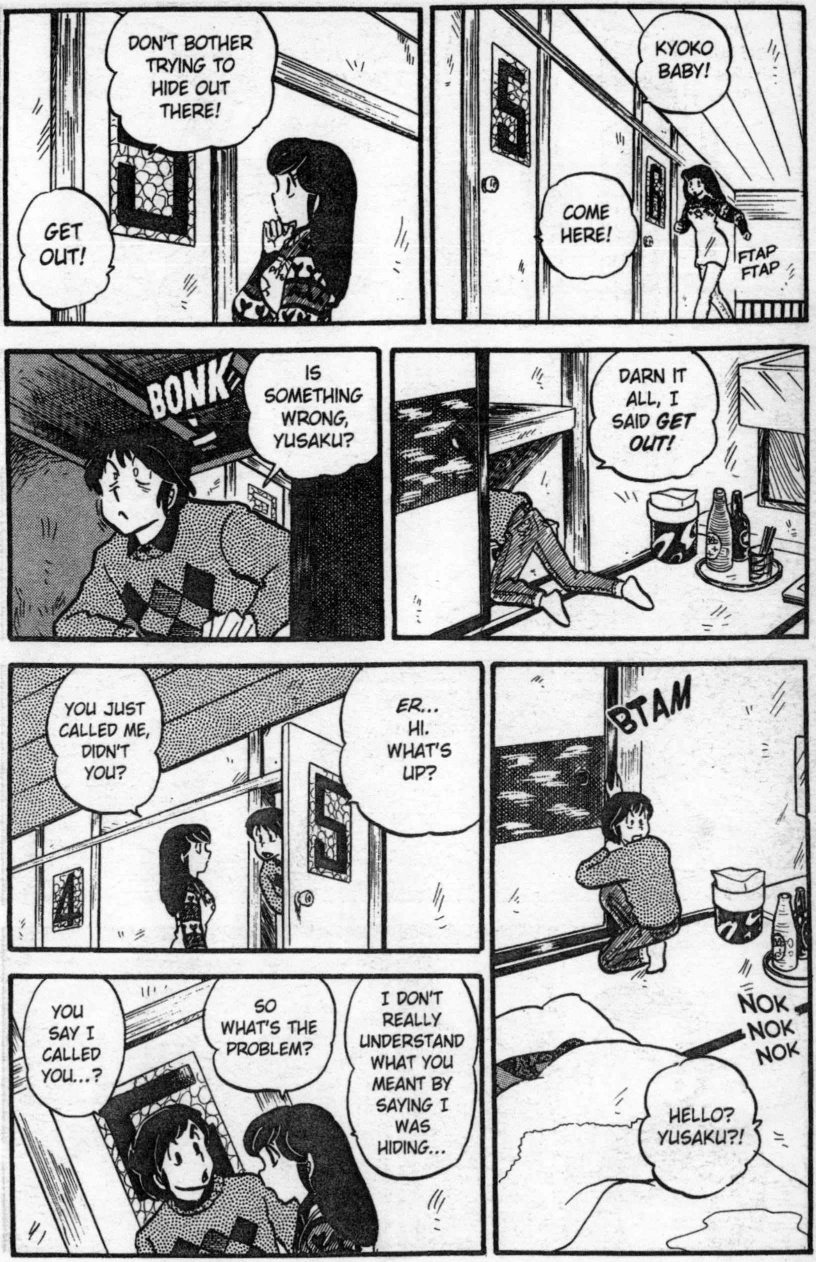
KYOKO BABY!
COME HERE!
FTAP FTAP
DON'T BOTHER TRYING TO HIDE OUT THERE!
GET OUT!
DARN IT ALL, I SAID *GET OUT!*
BONK
IS SOMETHING WRONG, YUSAKU?
BTAM
NOK NOK NOK
HELLO? YUSAKU?!
ER... HI. WHAT'S UP?
YOU JUST CALLED ME, DIDN'T YOU?
I DON'T REALLY UNDERSTAND WHAT YOU MEANT BY SAYING I WAS HIDING...
SO WHAT'S THE PROBLEM?
YOU SAY I CALLED YOU...?

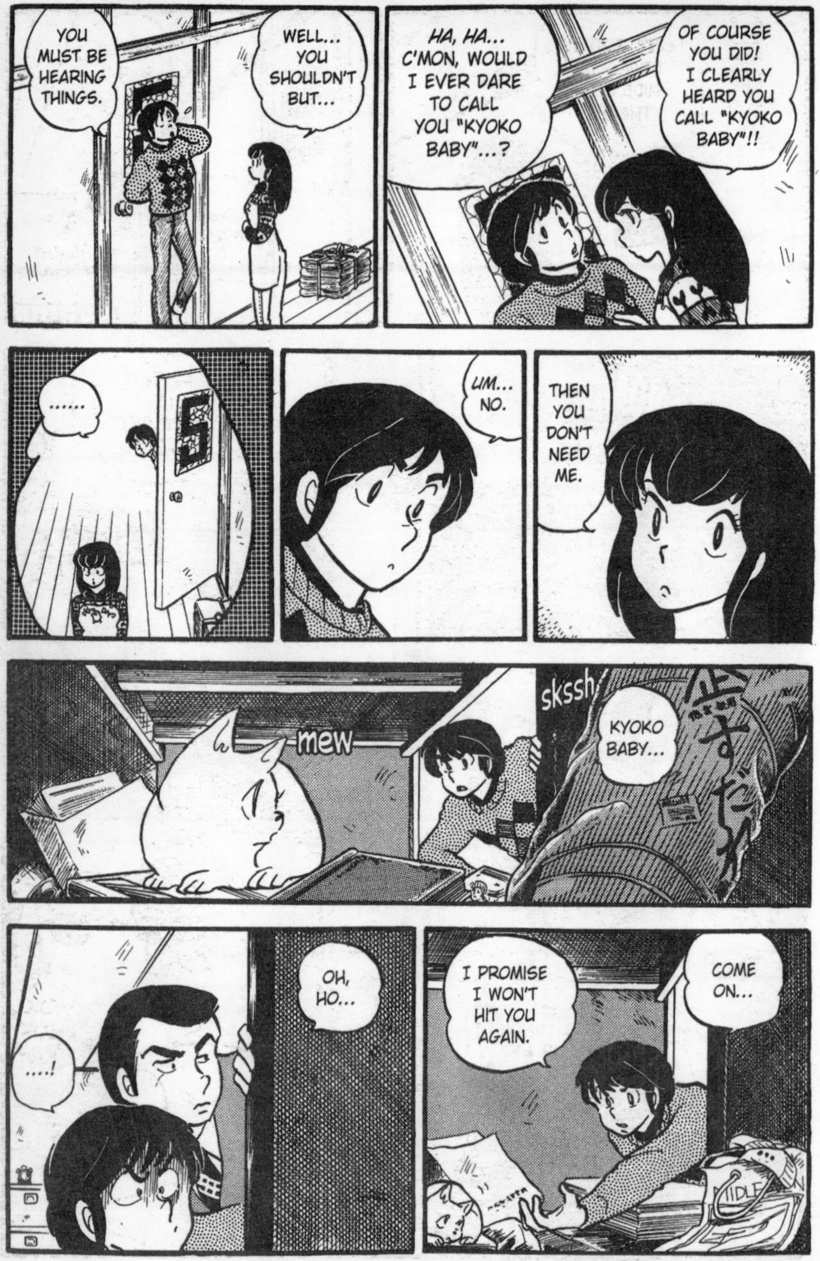
OF COURSE YOU DID! I CLEARLY HEARD YOU CALL "KYOKO BABY"!!
HA, HA... C'MON, WOULD I EVER DARE TO CALL YOU "KYOKO BABY"...?
WELL... YOU SHOULDN'T BUT...
YOU MUST BE HEARING THINGS.
THEN YOU DON'T NEED ME.
UM... NO.
......
sksssh
KYOKO BABY...
mew
COME ON...
I PROMISE I WON'T HIT YOU AGAIN.
OH, HO...
....!

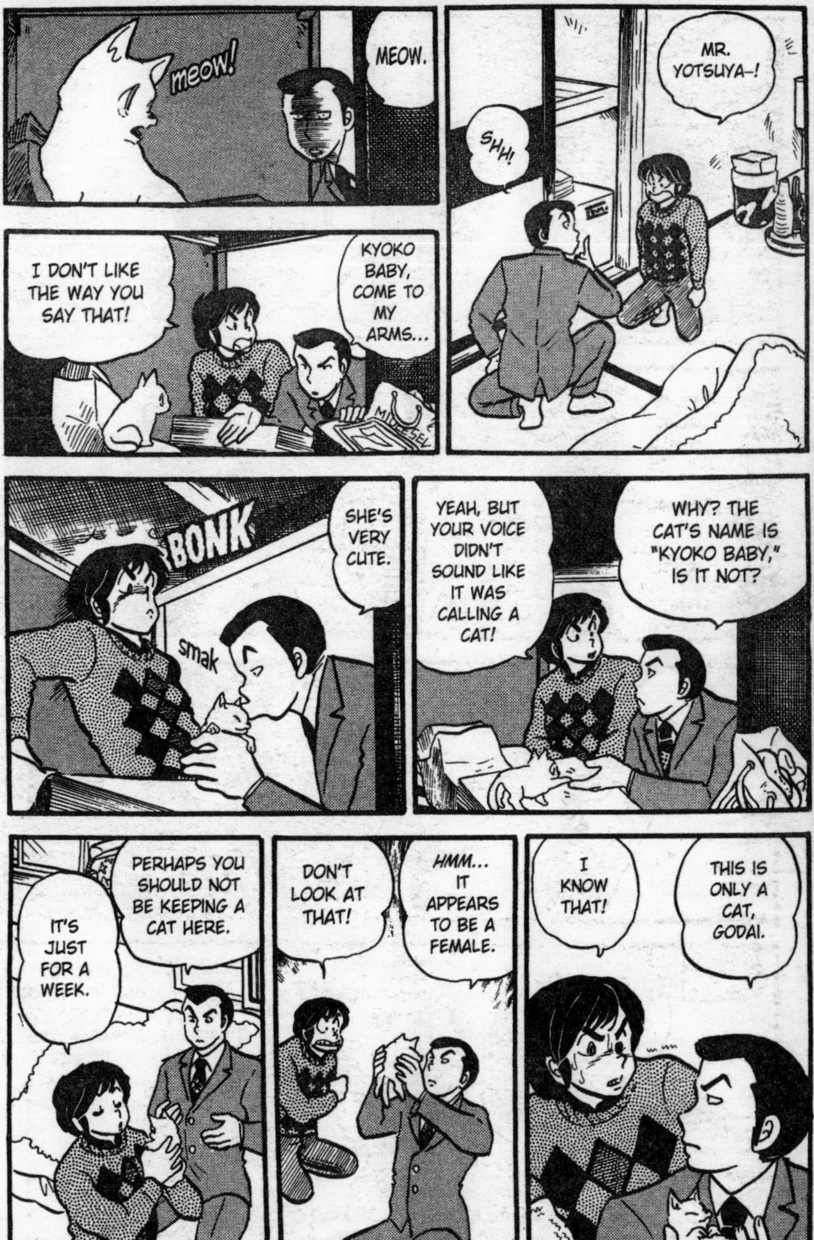
MR. YOTSUYA–!
SHH!
MEOW.
meow!
KYOKO BABY, COME TO MY ARMS...
I DON'T LIKE THE WAY YOU SAY THAT!
WHY? THE CAT'S NAME IS "KYOKO BABY," IS IT NOT?
YEAH, BUT YOUR VOICE DIDN'T SOUND LIKE IT WAS CALLING A CAT!
SHE'S VERY CUTE.
BONK
smak
THIS IS ONLY A CAT, GODAI.
I KNOW THAT!
HMM... IT APPEARS TO BE A FEMALE.
DON'T LOOK AT THAT!
PERHAPS YOU SHOULD NOT BE KEEPING A CAT HERE.
IT'S JUST FOR A WEEK.

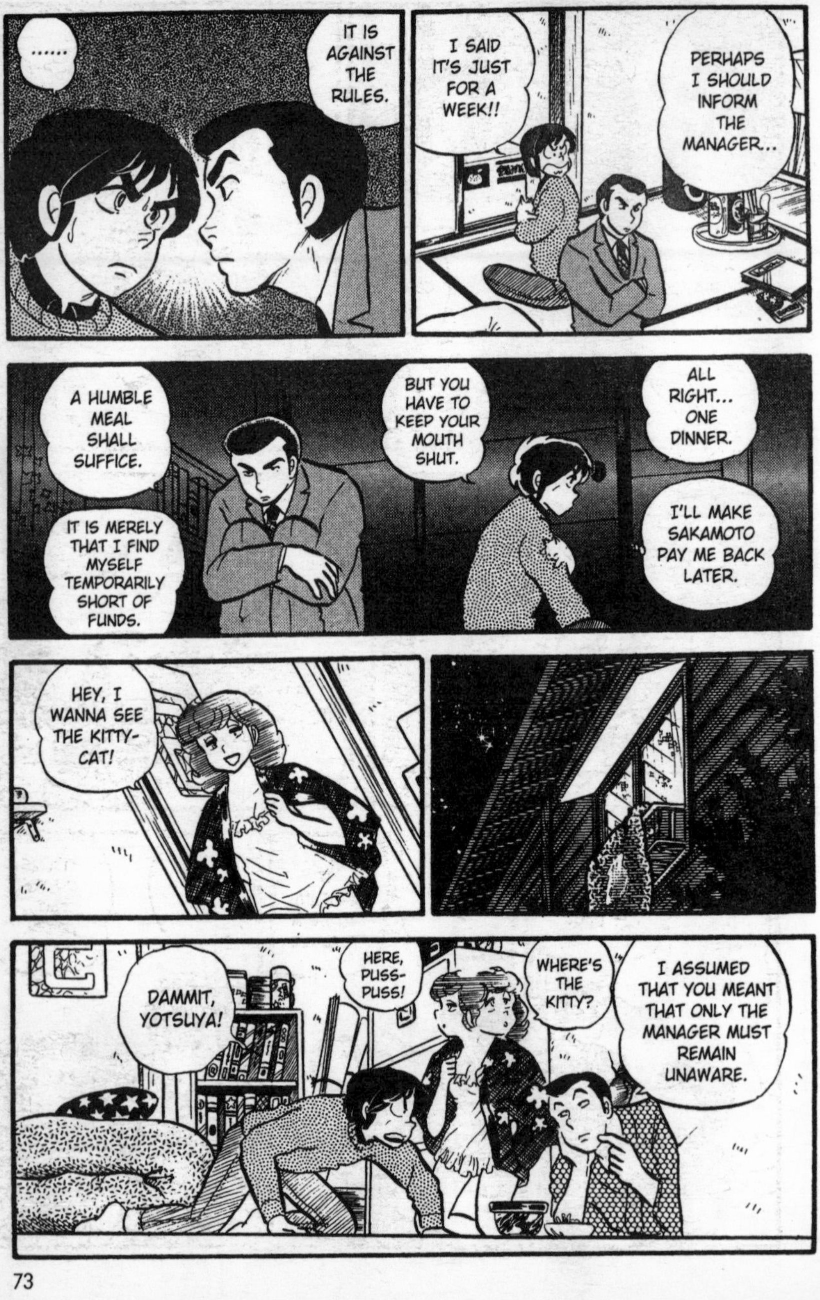

PERHAPS I SHOULD INFORM THE MANAGER...
I SAID IT'S JUST FOR A WEEK!!
IT IS AGAINST THE RULES.
......
ALL RIGHT... ONE DINNER.
I'LL MAKE SAKAMOTO PAY ME BACK LATER.
BUT YOU HAVE TO KEEP YOUR MOUTH SHUT.
A HUMBLE MEAL SHALL SUFFICE.
IT IS MERELY THAT I FIND MYSELF TEMPORARILY SHORT OF FUNDS.
HEY, I WANNA SEE THE KITTY-CAT!
I ASSUMED THAT YOU MEANT THAT ONLY THE MANAGER MUST REMAIN UNAWARE.
WHERE'S THE KITTY?
HERE, PUSS-PUSS!
DAMMIT, YOTSUYA!

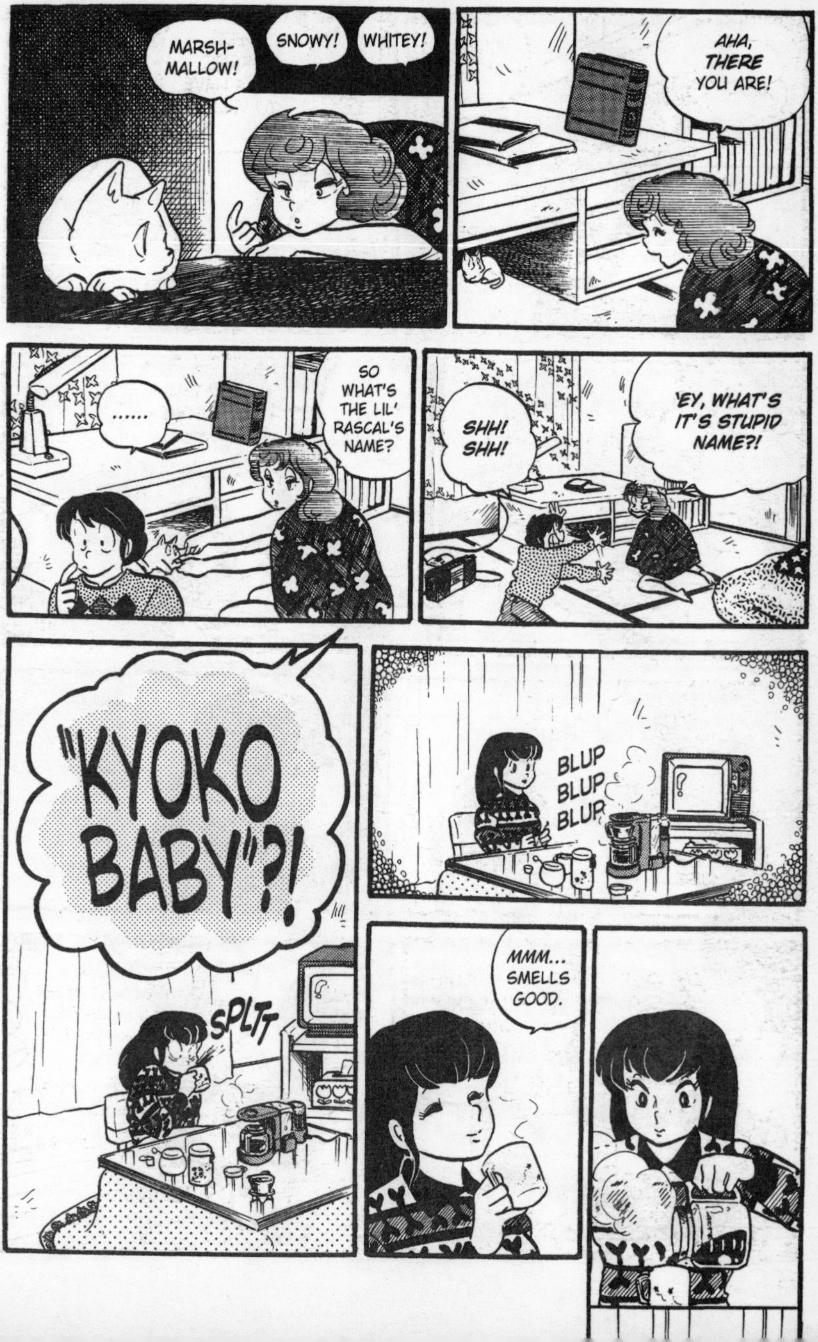
AHA, THERE YOU ARE!
WHITEY!
SNOWY!
MARSH-MALLOW!
'EY, WHAT'S IT'S STUPID NAME?!
SHH! SHH!
SO WHAT'S THE LIL' RASCAL'S NAME?
......
BLUP BLUP BLUP
MMM... SMELLS GOOD.
"KYOKO BABY"?!
SPLTT

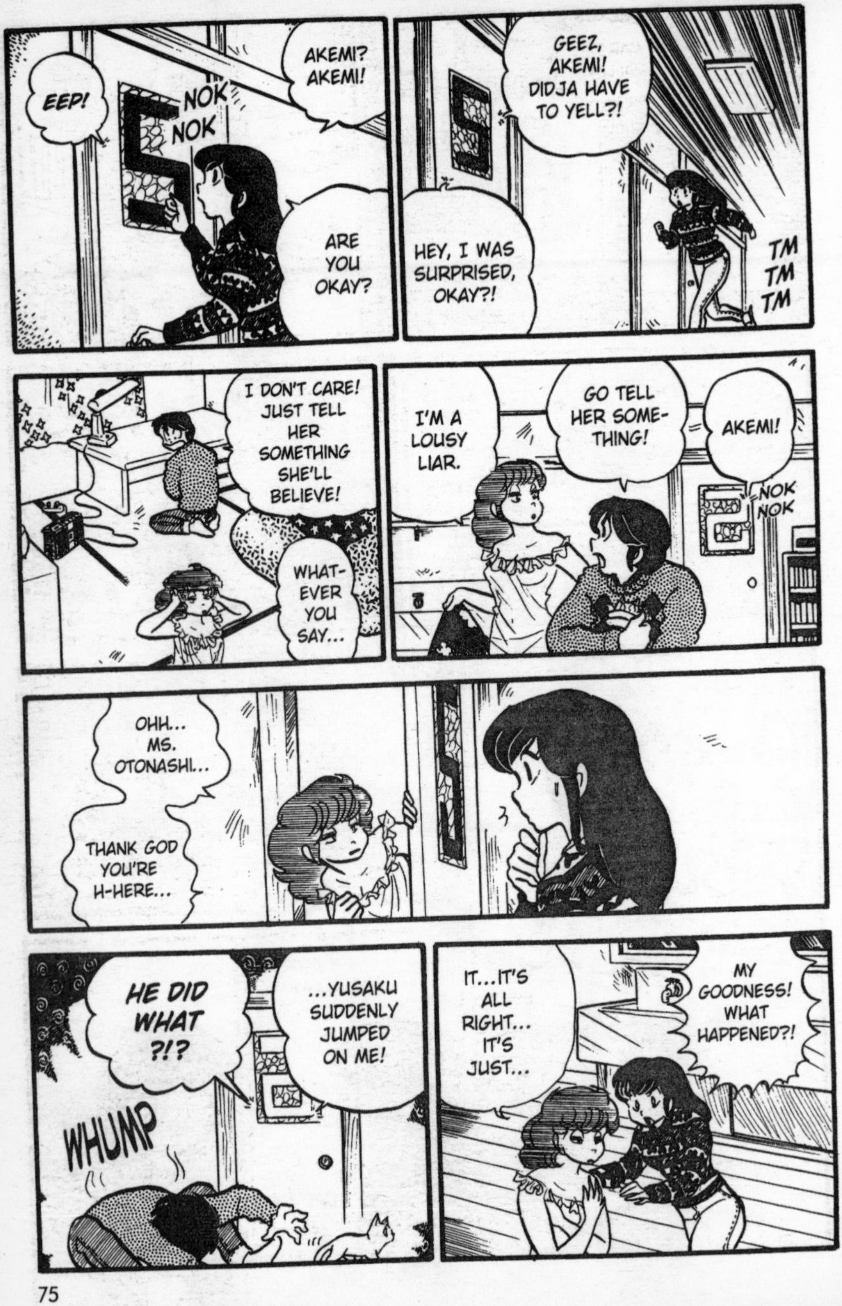
GEEZ, AKEMI! DIDJA HAVE TO YELL?!
HEY, I WAS SURPRISED, OKAY?!
TM TM TM
AKEMI? AKEMI!
NOK NOK
EEP!
ARE YOU OKAY?
AKEMI!
NOK NOK
GO TELL HER SOME-THING!
I'M A LOUSY LIAR.
I DON'T CARE! JUST TELL HER SOMETHING SHE'LL BELIEVE!
WHAT-EVER YOU SAY...
OHH... MS. OTONASHI...
THANK GOD YOU'RE H-HERE...
MY GOODNESS! WHAT HAPPENED?!
IT...IT'S ALL RIGHT... IT'S JUST...
...YUSAKU SUDDENLY JUMPED ON ME!
HE DID WHAT ?!?
WHUMP

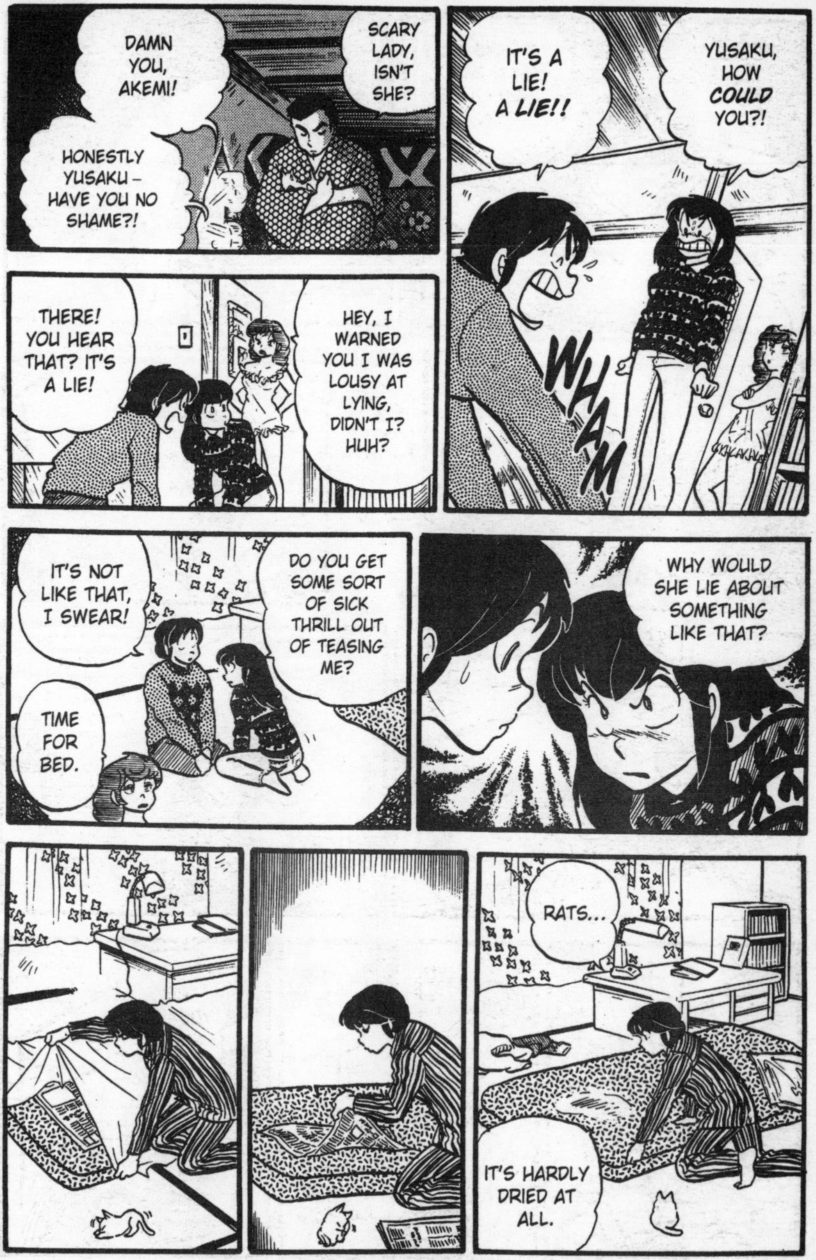
YUSAKU, HOW COULD YOU?!
IT'S A LIE! A LIE!!
WHAM
SCARY LADY, ISN'T SHE?
DAMN YOU, AKEMI!
HONESTLY YUSAKU – HAVE YOU NO SHAME?!
HEY, I WARNED YOU I WAS LOUSY AT LYING, DIDN'T I? HUH?
THERE! YOU HEAR THAT? IT'S A LIE!
WHY WOULD SHE LIE ABOUT SOMETHING LIKE THAT?
DO YOU GET SOME SORT OF SICK THRILL OUT OF TEASING ME?
IT'S NOT LIKE THAT, I SWEAR!
TIME FOR BED.
RATS...
IT'S HARDLY DRIED AT ALL.

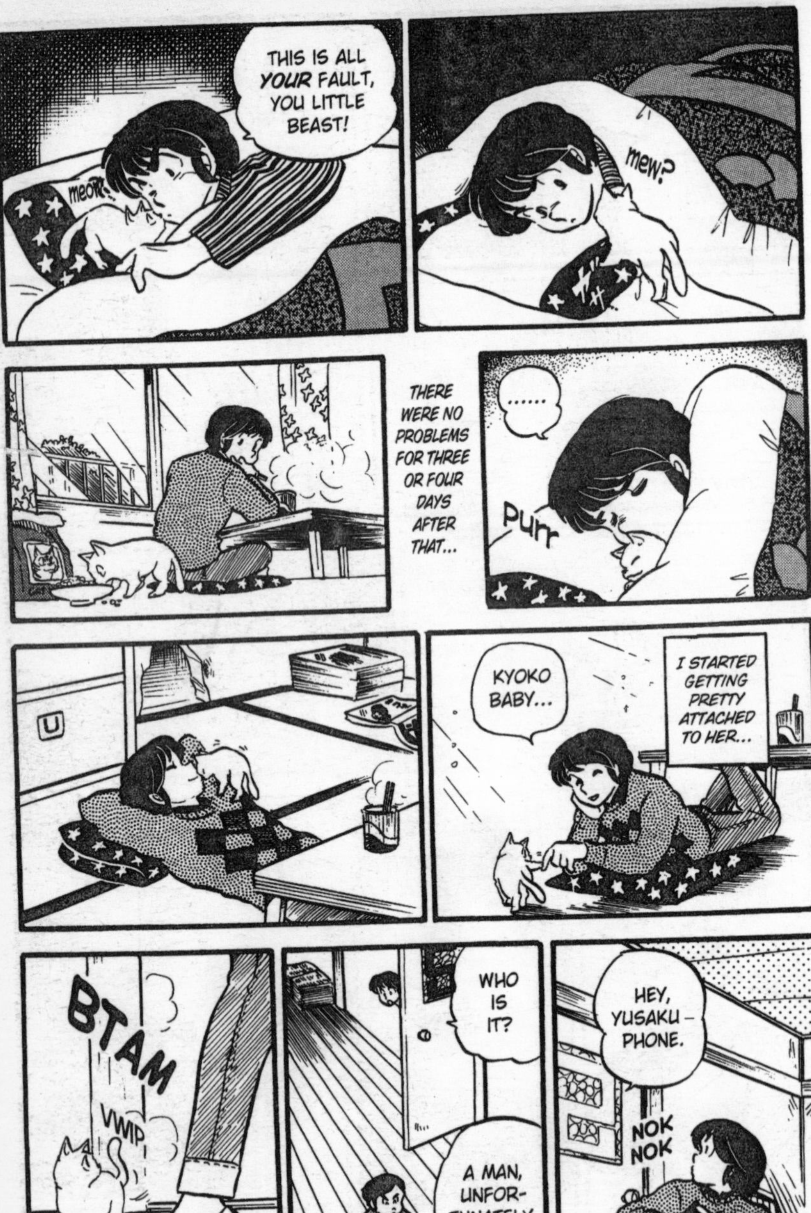
mew?
THIS IS ALL YOUR FAULT, YOU LITTLE BEAST!
meow
......
Purr
THERE WERE NO PROBLEMS FOR THREE OR FOUR DAYS AFTER THAT...
I STARTED GETTING PRETTY ATTACHED TO HER...
KYOKO BABY...
HEY, YUSAKU-PHONE.
NOK NOK
WHO IS IT?
A MAN, UNFORTUNATELY.
BTAM
VWIP

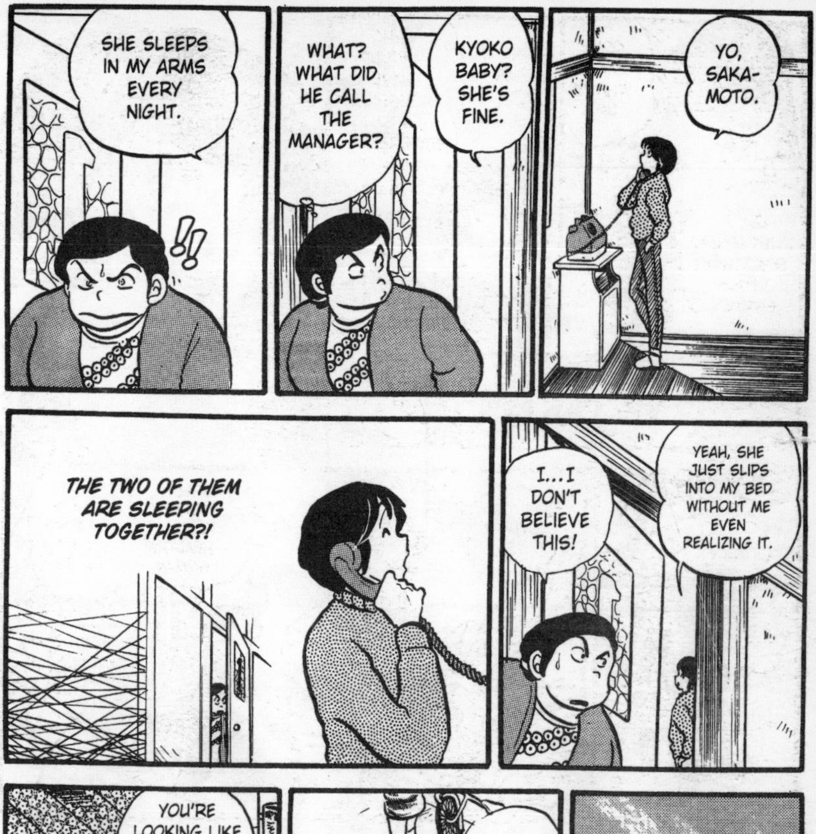
YO, SAKA-MOTO.
KYOKO BABY? SHE'S FINE.
WHAT? WHAT DID HE CALL THE MANAGER?
SHE SLEEPS IN MY ARMS EVERY NIGHT.
!!
YEAH, SHE JUST SLIPS INTO MY BED WITHOUT ME EVEN REALIZING IT.
I...I DON'T BELIEVE THIS!
THE TWO OF THEM ARE SLEEPING TOGETHER?!
時計
KYOKO!
OH, MRS. ICHINOSE.
YOU'RE LOOKING LIKE THE CAT THAT ATE THE CANARY... WHY?

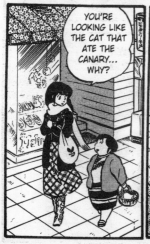

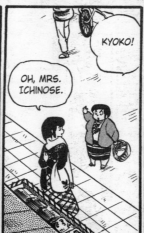

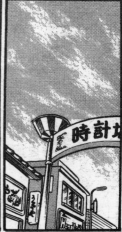

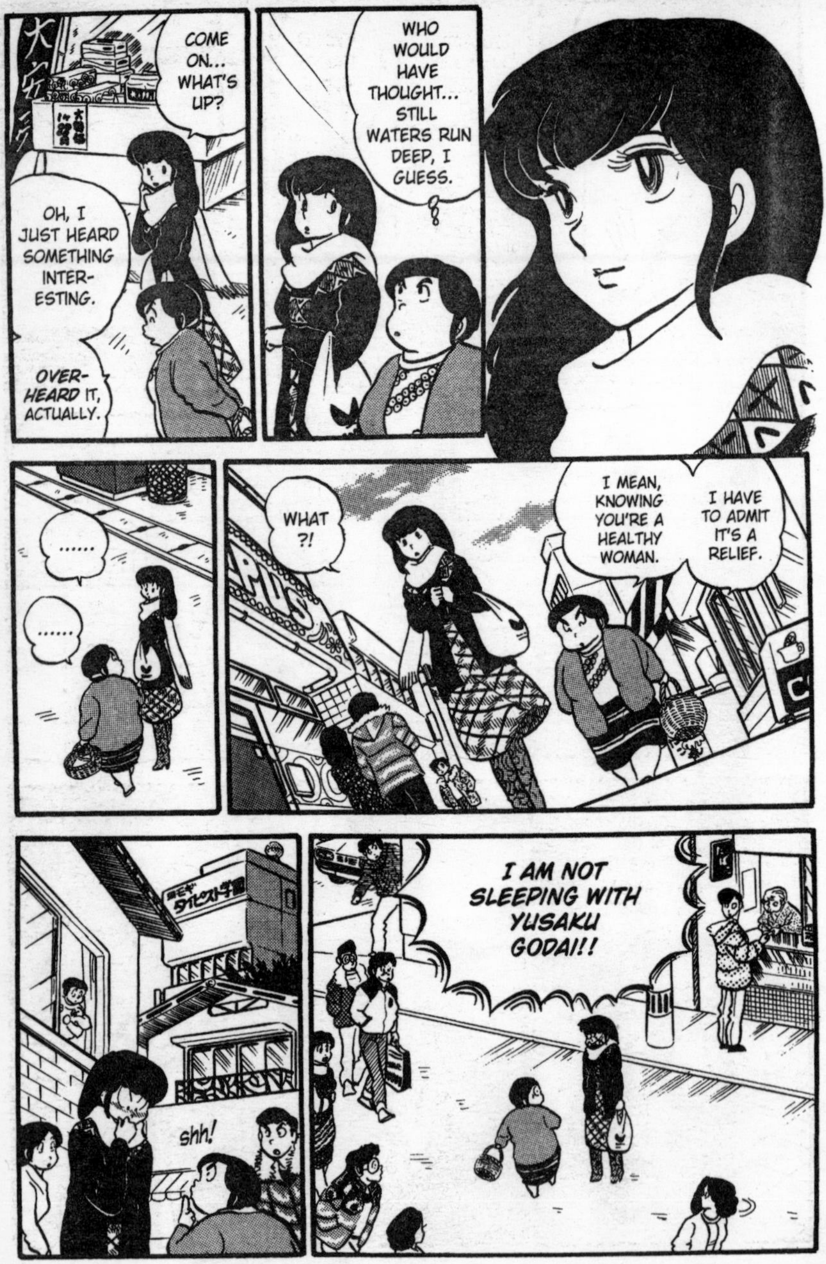
WHO WOULD HAVE THOUGHT... STILL WATERS RUN DEEP, I GUESS.
COME ON... WHAT'S UP?
OH, I JUST HEARD SOMETHING INTER-ESTING.
OVER-HEARD IT, ACTUALLY.
I HAVE TO ADMIT IT'S A RELIEF.
I MEAN, KNOWING YOU'RE A HEALTHY WOMAN.
WHAT ?!
......
......
I AM NOT SLEEPING WITH YUSAKU GODAI!!
shh!

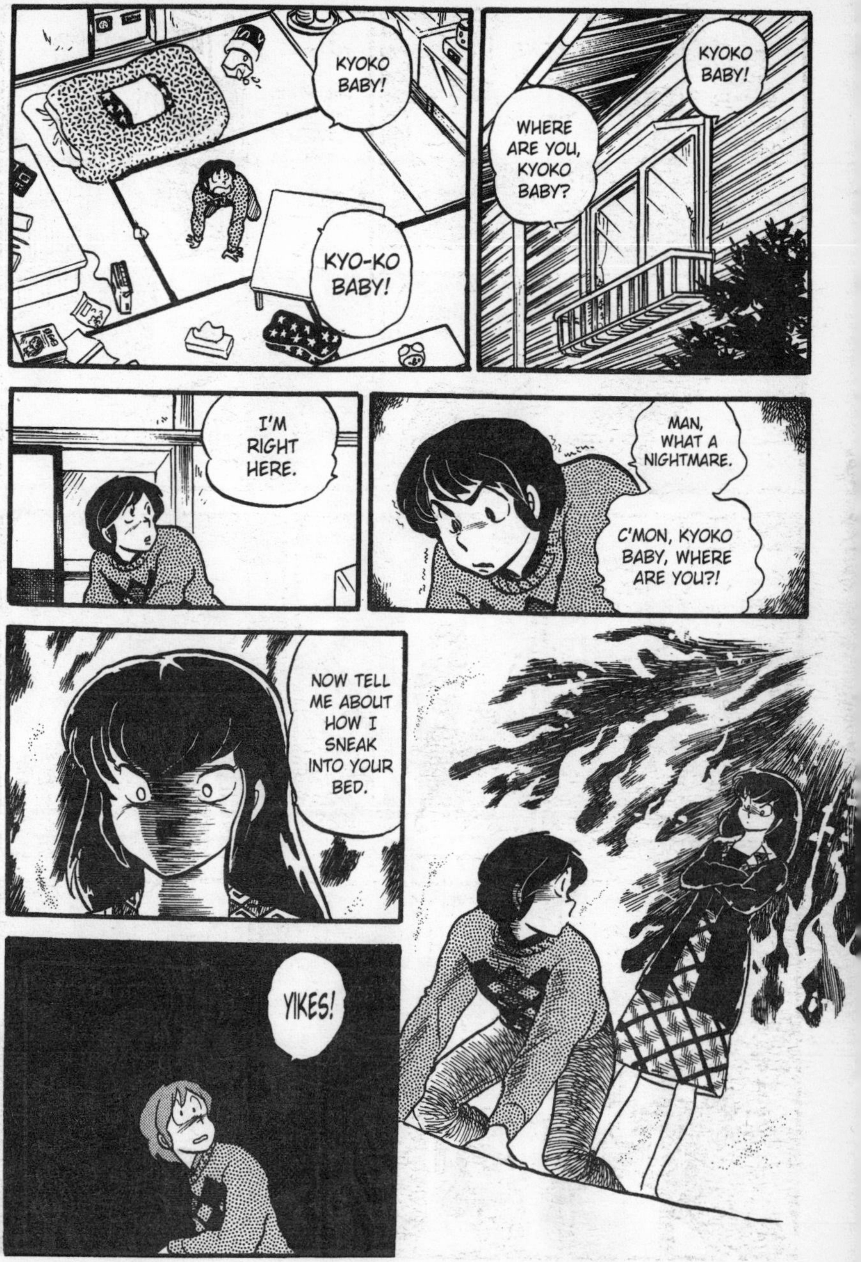
KYOKO BABY!
WHERE ARE YOU, KYOKO BABY?
KYOKO BABY!
KYO-KO BABY!
MAN, WHAT A NIGHTMARE.
C'MON, KYOKO BABY, WHERE ARE YOU?!
I'M RIGHT HERE.
NOW TELL ME ABOUT HOW I SNEAK INTO YOUR BED.
YIKES!

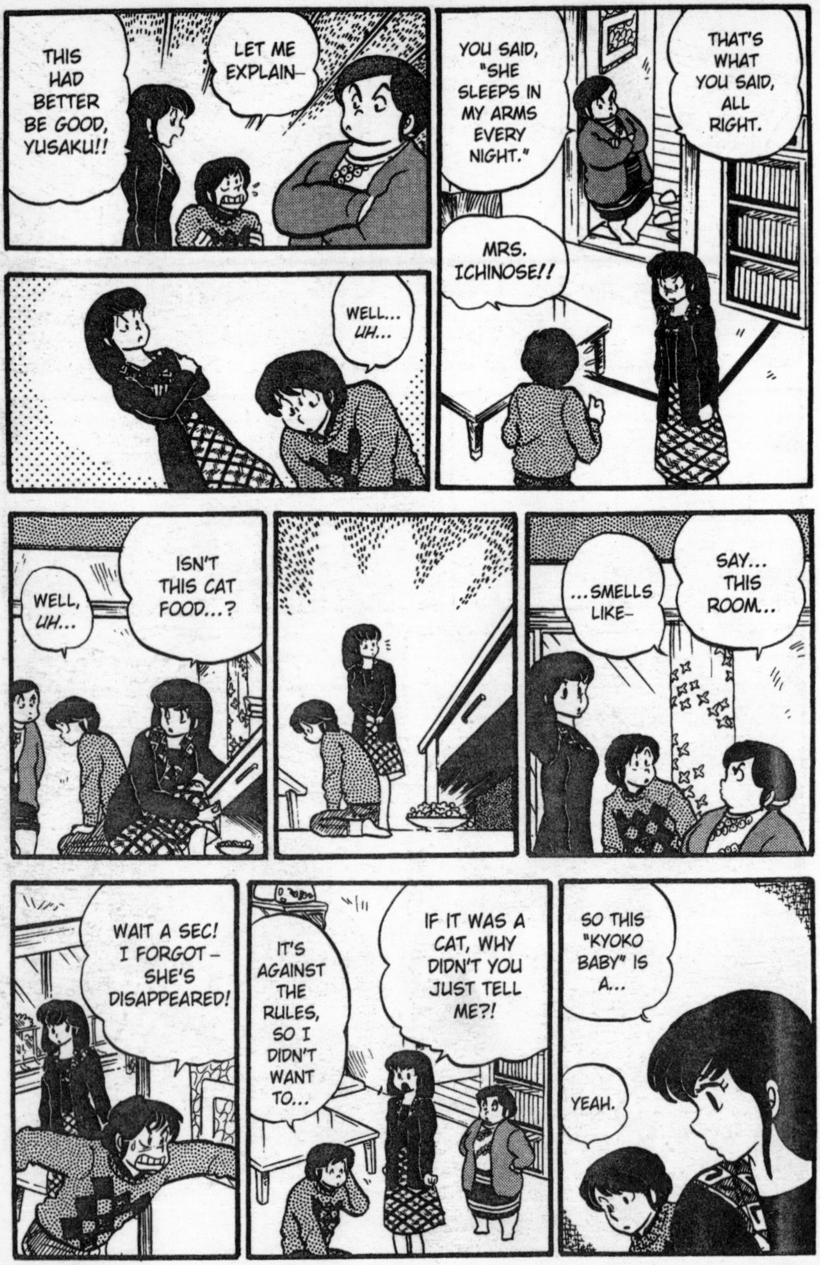
THAT'S WHAT YOU SAID, ALL RIGHT.
YOU SAID, "SHE SLEEPS IN MY ARMS EVERY NIGHT."
MRS. ICHINOSE!!
LET ME EXPLAIN–
THIS HAD BETTER BE GOOD, YUSAKU!!
WELL... UH...
SAY... THIS ROOM...
...SMELLS LIKE–
ISN'T THIS CAT FOOD...?
WELL, UH...
SO THIS "KYOKO BABY" IS A...
YEAH.
IF IT WAS A CAT, WHY DIDN'T YOU JUST TELL ME?!
IT'S AGAINST THE RULES, SO I DIDN'T WANT TO...
WAIT A SEC! I FORGOT – SHE'S DISAPPEARED!

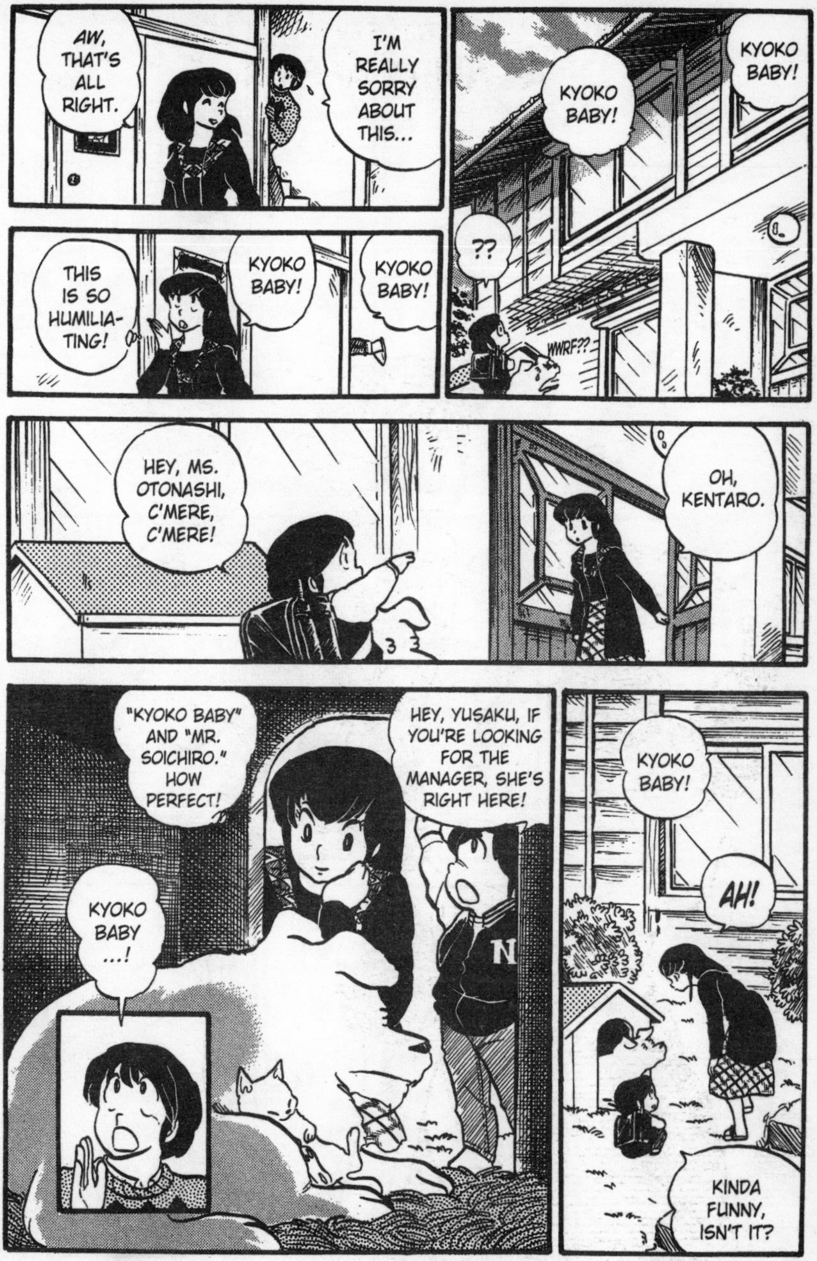
KYOKO BABY!
KYOKO BABY!
??
WWRF??
I'M REALLY SORRY ABOUT THIS...
AW, THAT'S ALL RIGHT.
KYOKO BABY!
KYOKO BABY!
THIS IS SO HUMILIA-TING!
OH, KENTARO.
HEY, MS. OTONASHI, C'MERE, C'MERE!
KYOKO BABY!
AH!
KINDA FUNNY, ISN'T IT?
HEY, YUSAKU, IF YOU'RE LOOKING FOR THE MANAGER, SHE'S RIGHT HERE!
"KYOKO BABY" AND "MR. SOICHIRO." HOW PERFECT!
KYOKO BABY ...!

PART FIVE

A FAMILY AFFAIR

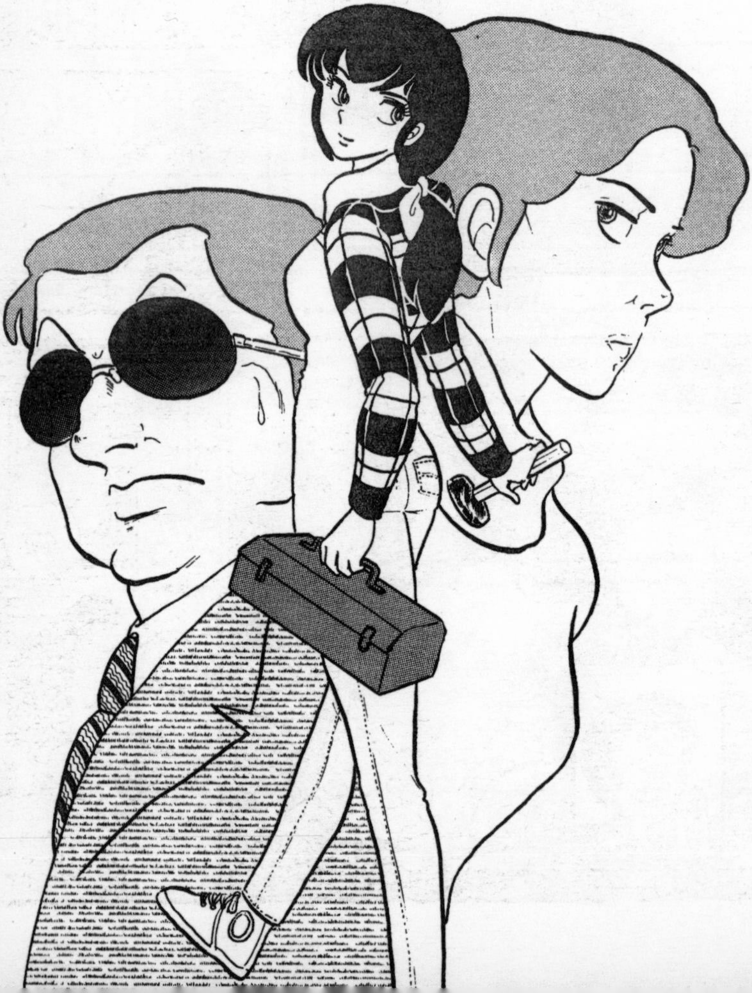

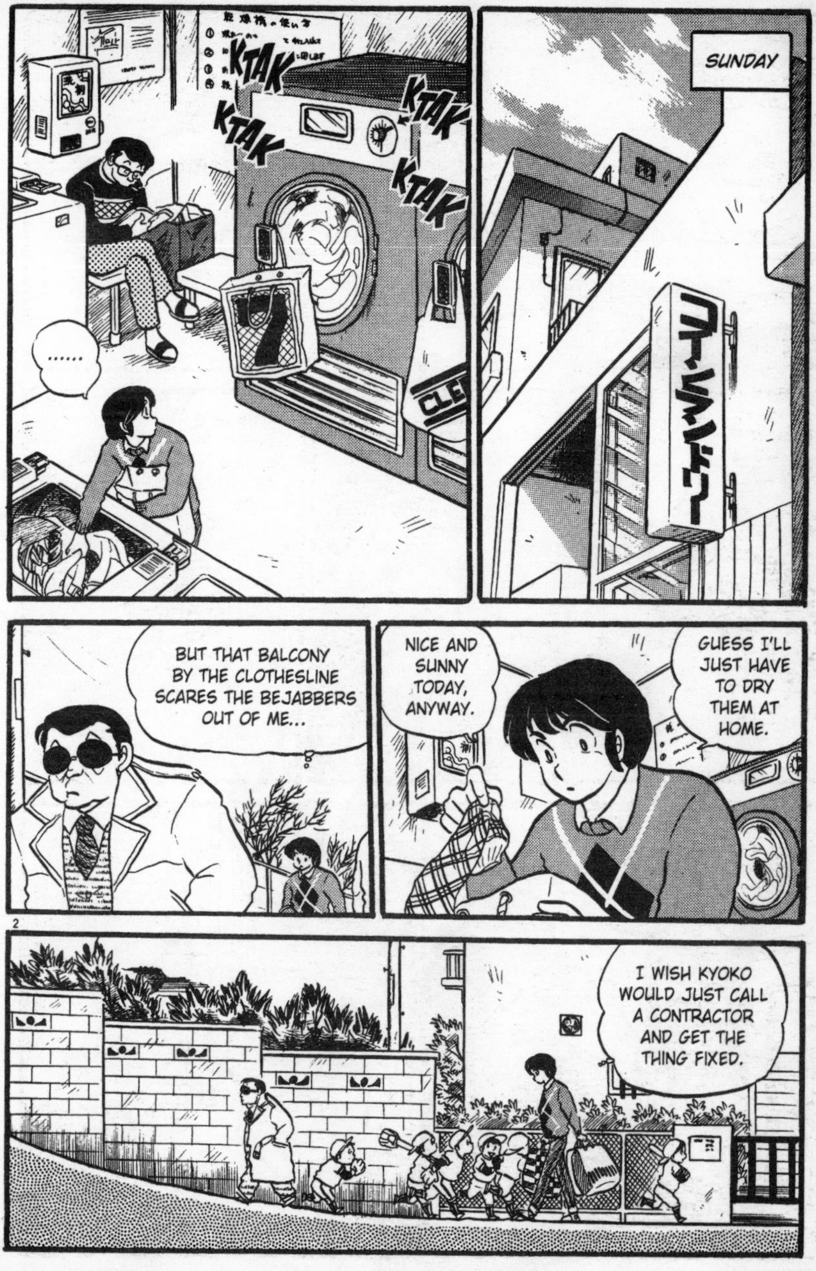

SUNDAY
コイン・ランドリー
KTAK
KTAK
KTAK
KTAK
……
GUESS I'LL JUST HAVE TO DRY THEM AT HOME.
NICE AND SUNNY TODAY, ANYWAY.
BUT THAT BALCONY BY THE CLOTHESLINE SCARES THE BEJABBERS OUT OF ME…
I WISH KYOKO WOULD JUST CALL A CONTRACTOR AND GET THE THING FIXED.

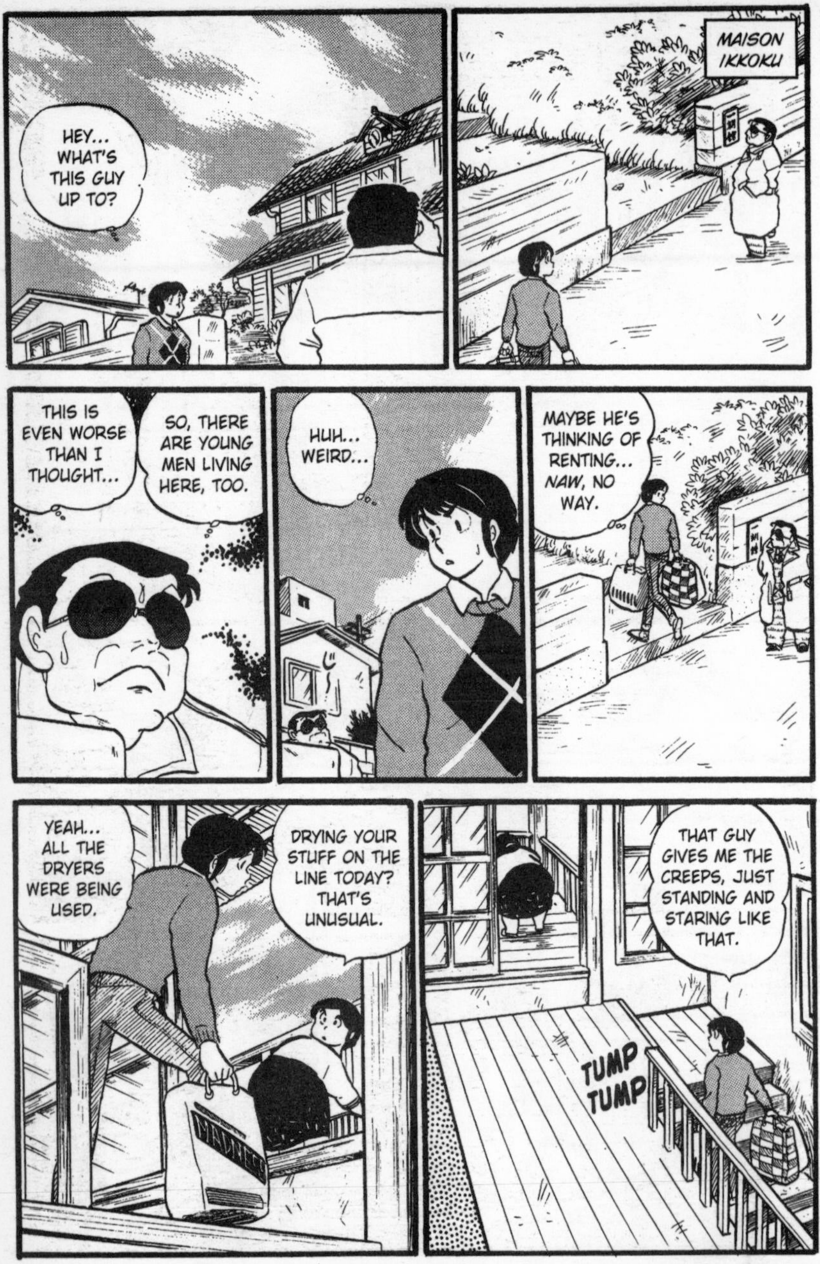
MAISON IKKOKU
HEY... WHAT'S THIS GUY UP TO?
MAYBE HE'S THINKING OF RENTING... *NAW*, NO WAY.
HUH... WEIRD...
SO, THERE ARE YOUNG MEN LIVING HERE, TOO.
THIS IS EVEN WORSE THAN I THOUGHT...
THAT GUY GIVES ME THE CREEPS, JUST STANDING AND STARING LIKE THAT.
TUMP TUMP
DRYING YOUR STUFF ON THE LINE TODAY? THAT'S UNUSUAL.
YEAH... ALL THE DRYERS WERE BEING USED.

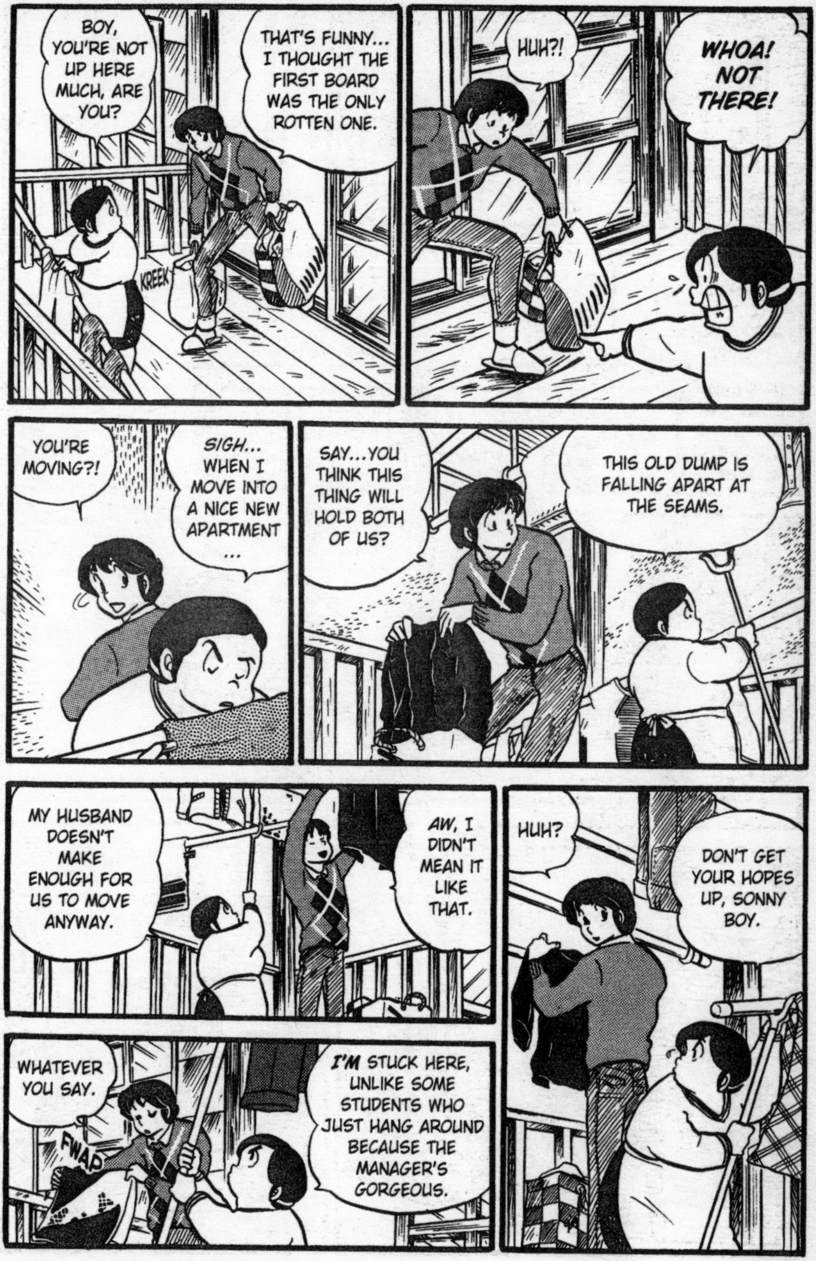
WHOA! NOT THERE!
HUH?!
THAT'S FUNNY... I THOUGHT THE FIRST BOARD WAS THE ONLY ROTTEN ONE.
BOY, YOU'RE NOT UP HERE MUCH, ARE YOU?
KREEK
THIS OLD DUMP IS FALLING APART AT THE SEAMS.
SAY...YOU THINK THIS THING WILL HOLD BOTH OF US?
SIGH... WHEN I MOVE INTO A NICE NEW APARTMENT ...
YOU'RE MOVING?!
DON'T GET YOUR HOPES UP, SONNY BOY.
HUH?
AW, I DIDN'T MEAN IT LIKE THAT.
MY HUSBAND DOESN'T MAKE ENOUGH FOR US TO MOVE ANYWAY.
I'M STUCK HERE, UNLIKE SOME STUDENTS WHO JUST HANG AROUND BECAUSE THE MANAGER'S GORGEOUS.
WHATEVER YOU SAY.
FWAP

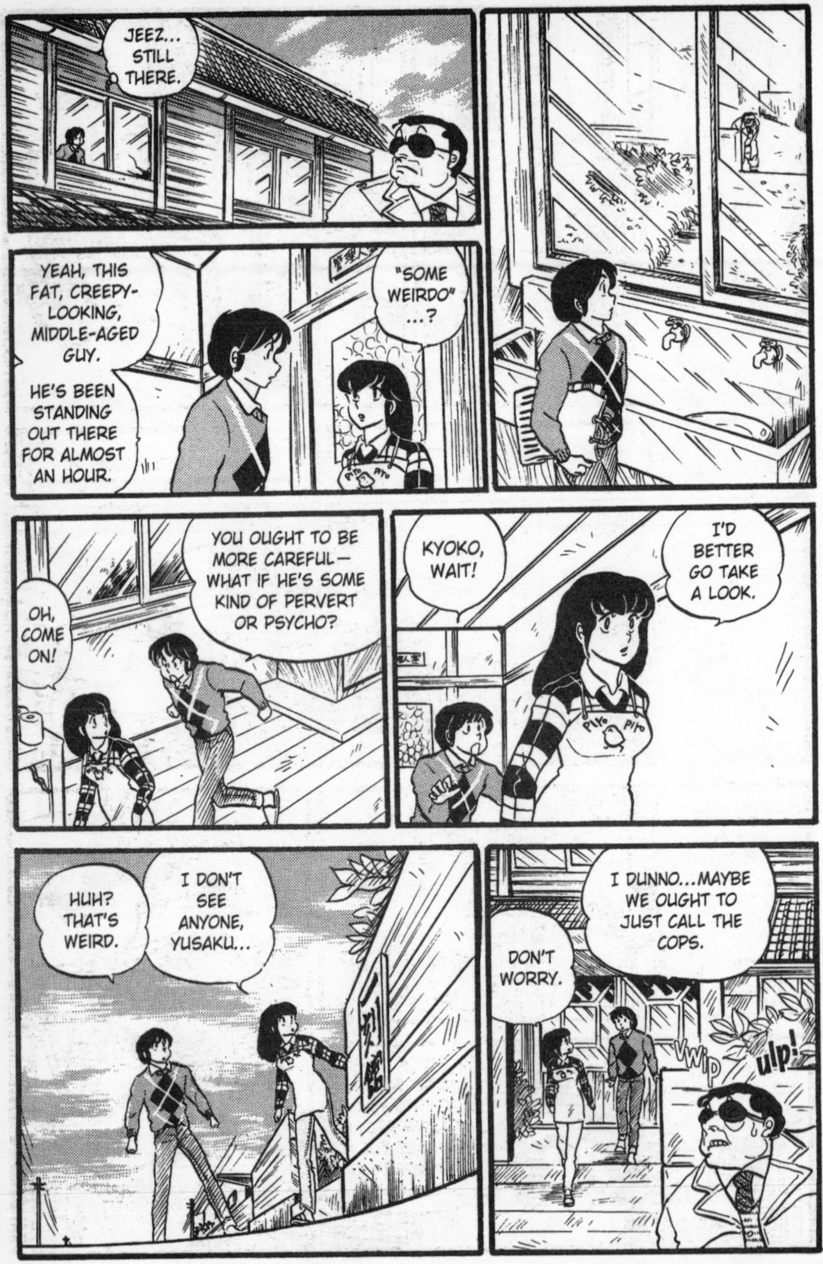
JEEZ... STILL THERE.
"SOME WEIRDO" ...?
YEAH, THIS FAT, CREEPY-LOOKING, MIDDLE-AGED GUY.
HE'S BEEN STANDING OUT THERE FOR ALMOST AN HOUR.
I'D BETTER GO TAKE A LOOK.
KYOKO, WAIT!
YOU OUGHT TO BE MORE CAREFUL—WHAT IF HE'S SOME KIND OF PERVERT OR PSYCHO?
OH, COME ON!
I DUNNO...MAYBE WE OUGHT TO JUST CALL THE COPS.
DON'T WORRY.
ulp!
VWip
I DON'T SEE ANYONE, YUSAKU...
HUH? THAT'S WEIRD.

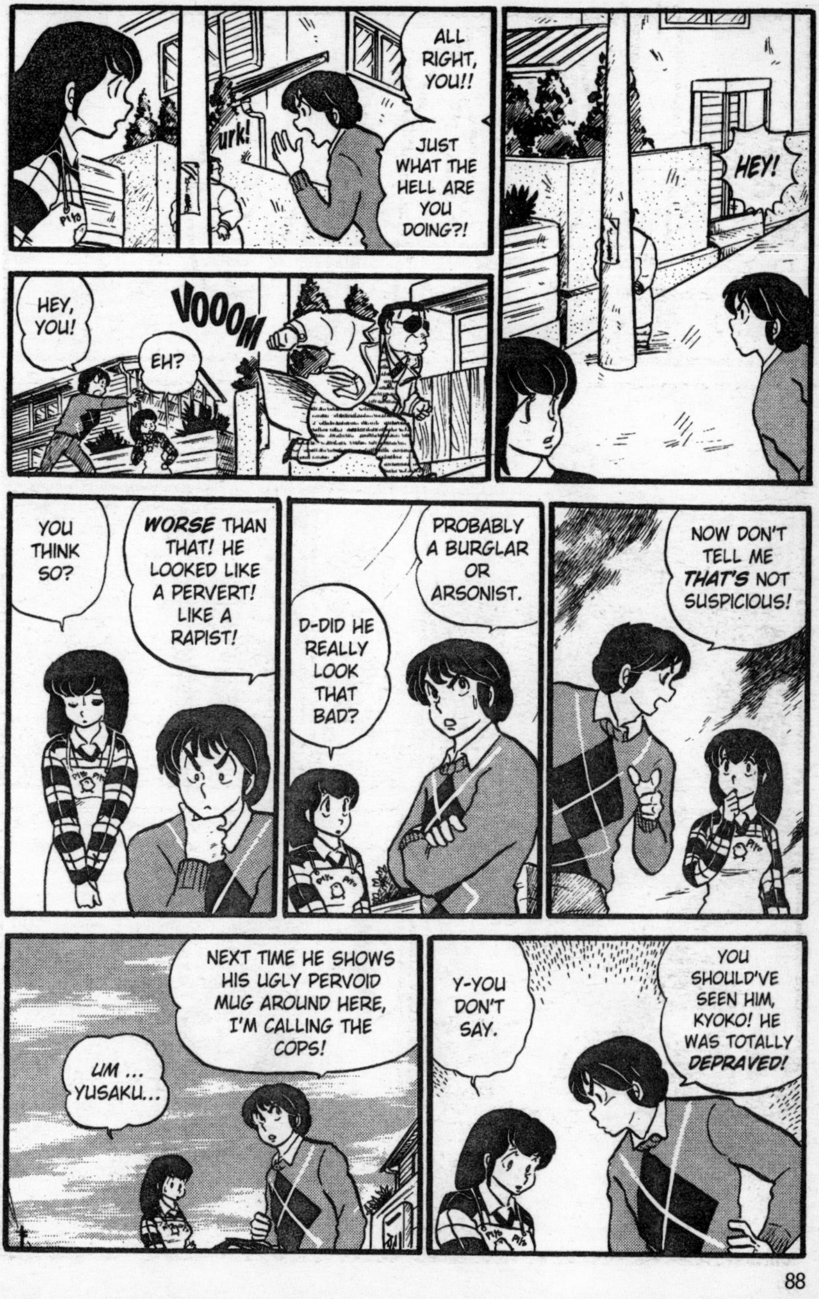
HEY!
ALL RIGHT, YOU!!
JUST WHAT THE HELL ARE YOU DOING?!
urk!
VOOOM
HEY, YOU!
EH?
NOW DON'T TELL ME *THAT'S* NOT SUSPICIOUS!
PROBABLY A BURGLAR OR ARSONIST.
D-DID HE REALLY LOOK THAT BAD?
WORSE THAN THAT! HE LOOKED LIKE A PERVERT! LIKE A RAPIST!
YOU THINK SO?
YOU SHOULD'VE SEEN HIM, KYOKO! HE WAS TOTALLY *DEPRAVED!*
Y-YOU DON'T SAY.
NEXT TIME HE SHOWS HIS UGLY PERVOID MUG AROUND HERE, I'M CALLING THE COPS!
UM ... YUSAKU...

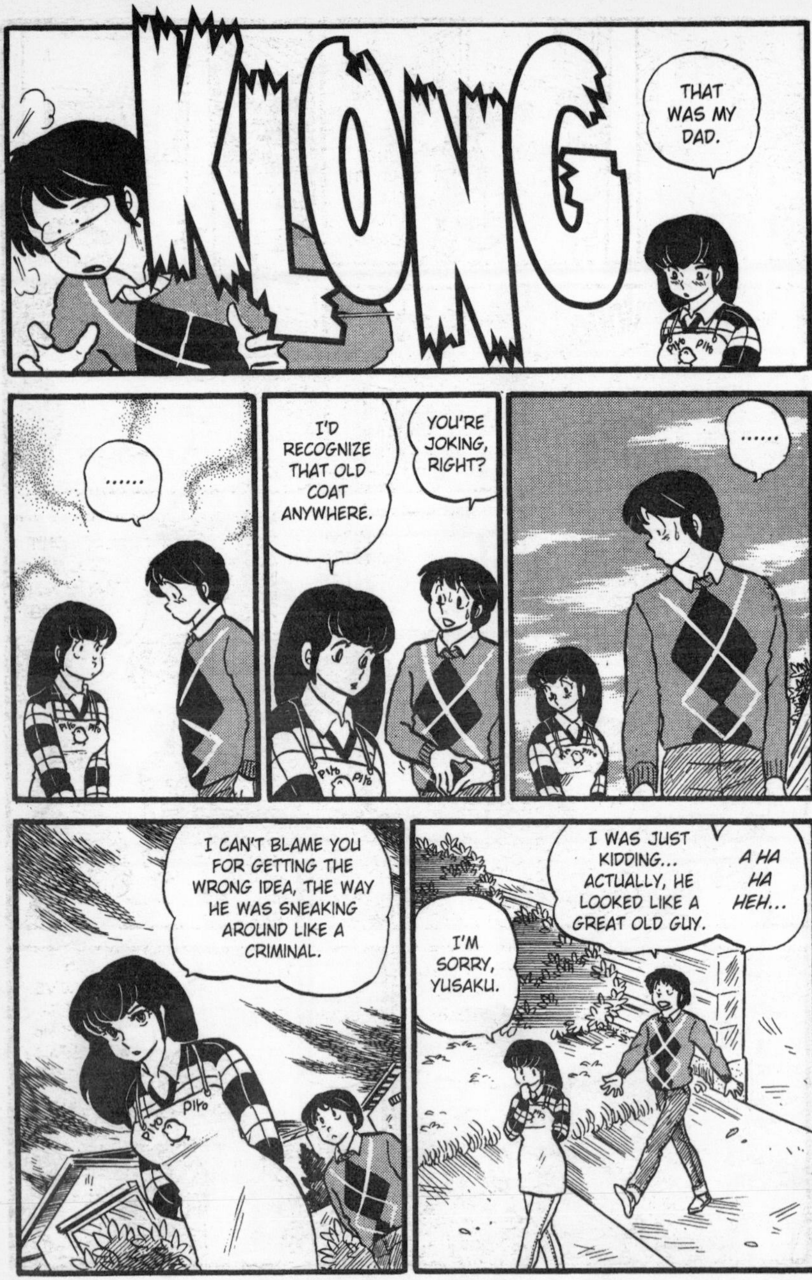
KLONG
THAT WAS MY DAD.
......
YOU'RE JOKING, RIGHT?
I'D RECOGNIZE THAT OLD COAT ANYWHERE.
......
A HA HA HEH...
I WAS JUST KIDDING... ACTUALLY, HE LOOKED LIKE A GREAT OLD GUY.
I'M SORRY, YUSAKU.
I CAN'T BLAME YOU FOR GETTING THE WRONG IDEA, THE WAY HE WAS SNEAKING AROUND LIKE A CRIMINAL.

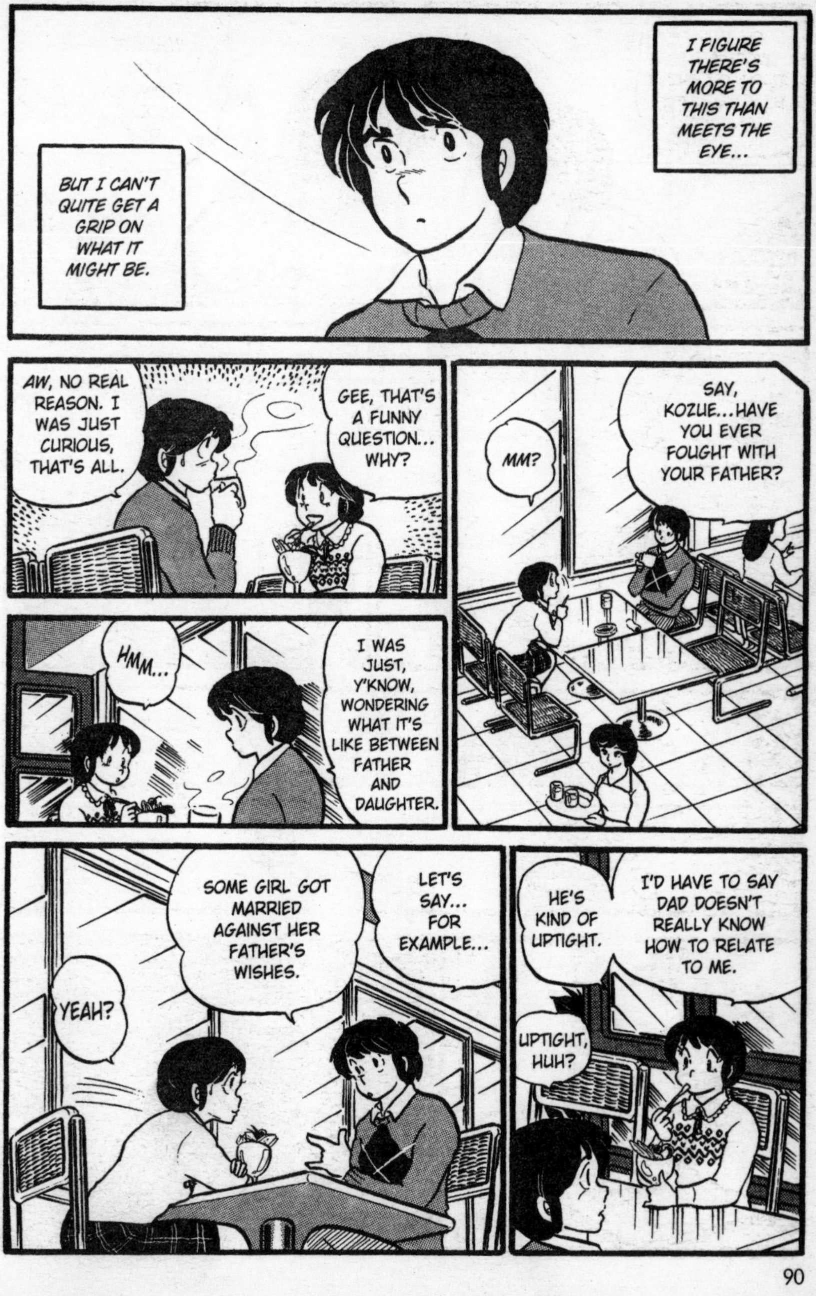
I FIGURE THERE'S MORE TO THIS THAN MEETS THE EYE...
BUT I CAN'T QUITE GET A GRIP ON WHAT IT MIGHT BE.
SAY, KOZUE...HAVE YOU EVER FOUGHT WITH YOUR FATHER?
MM?
GEE, THAT'S A FUNNY QUESTION... WHY?
AW, NO REAL REASON. I WAS JUST CURIOUS, THAT'S ALL.
I WAS JUST, Y'KNOW, WONDERING WHAT IT'S LIKE BETWEEN FATHER AND DAUGHTER.
HMM...
I'D HAVE TO SAY DAD DOESN'T REALLY KNOW HOW TO RELATE TO ME.
HE'S KIND OF UPTIGHT.
UPTIGHT, HUH?
LET'S SAY... FOR EXAMPLE...
SOME GIRL GOT MARRIED AGAINST HER FATHER'S WISHES.
YEAH?

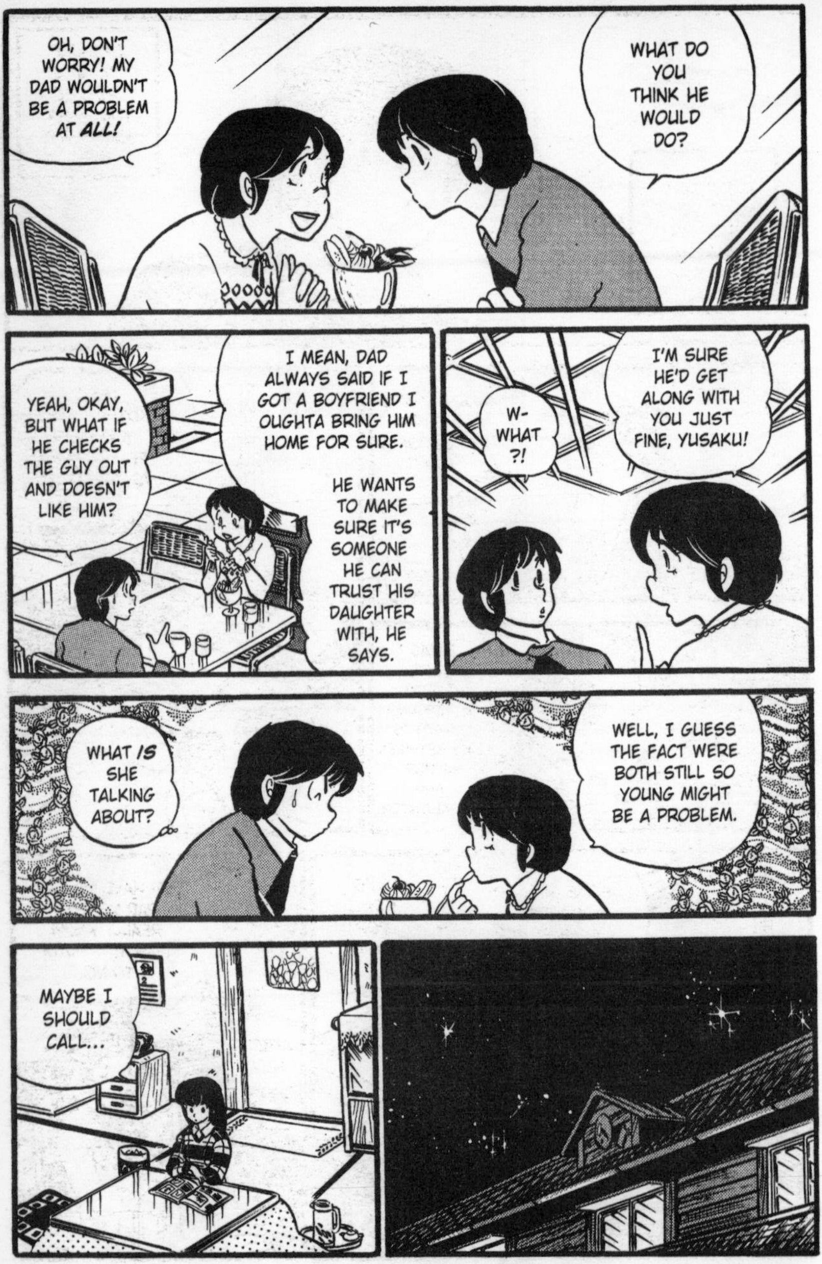
WHAT DO YOU THINK HE WOULD DO?
OH, DON'T WORRY! MY DAD WOULDN'T BE A PROBLEM AT *ALL!*
I'M SURE HE'D GET ALONG WITH YOU JUST FINE, YUSAKU!
W-WHAT?!
I MEAN, DAD ALWAYS SAID IF I GOT A BOYFRIEND I OUGHTA BRING HIM HOME FOR SURE.
HE WANTS TO MAKE SURE IT'S SOMEONE HE CAN TRUST HIS DAUGHTER WITH, HE SAYS.
YEAH, OKAY, BUT WHAT IF HE CHECKS THE GUY OUT AND DOESN'T LIKE HIM?
WELL, I GUESS THE FACT WERE BOTH STILL SO YOUNG MIGHT BE A PROBLEM.
WHAT *IS* SHE TALKING ABOUT?
MAYBE I SHOULD CALL...

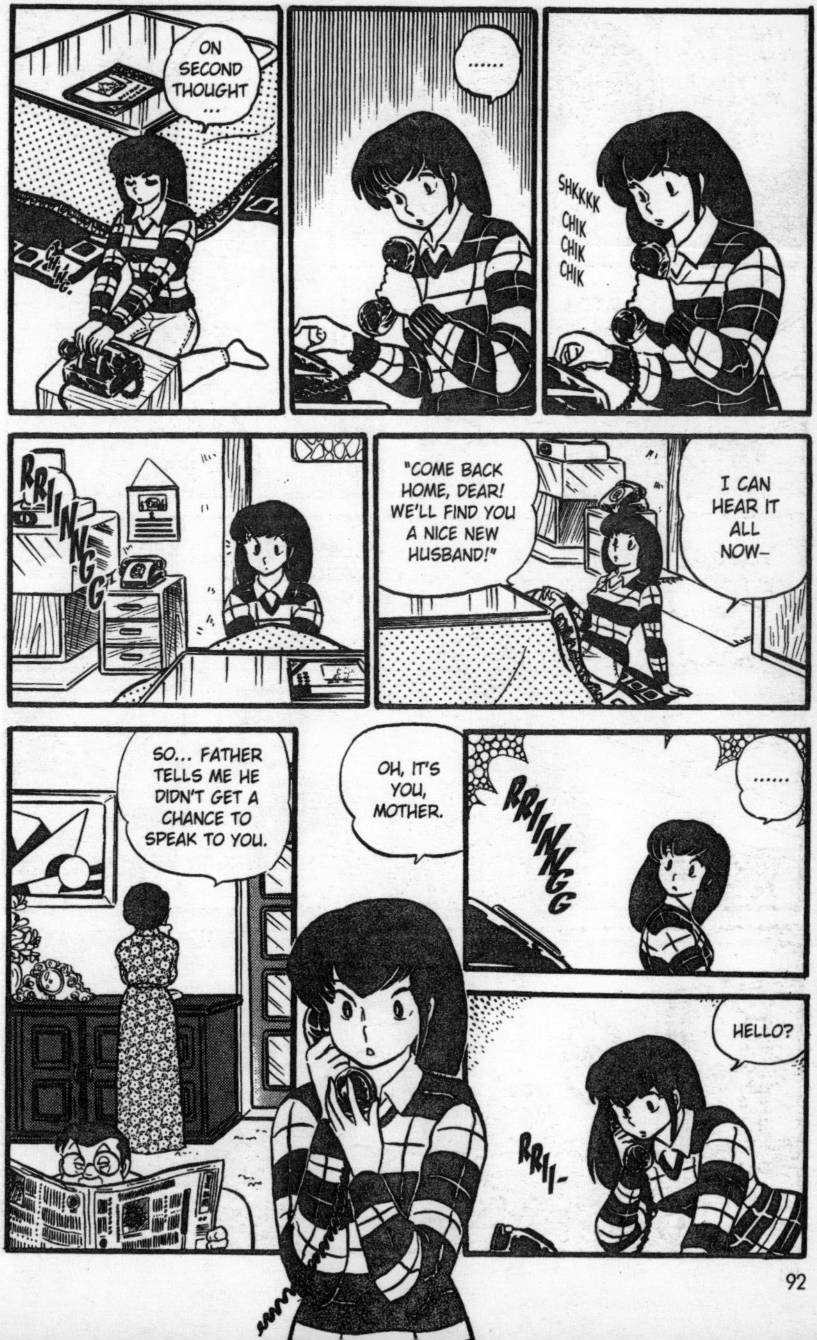
SHKKKK
CHIK
CHIK
CHIK
......
ON SECOND THOUGHT ...
CHING
I CAN HEAR IT ALL NOW–
"COME BACK HOME, DEAR! WE'LL FIND YOU A NICE NEW HUSBAND!"
RRIINNGG
......
RRIINNGG
HELLO?
RRII-
OH, IT'S YOU, MOTHER.
SO... FATHER TELLS ME HE DIDN'T GET A CHANCE TO SPEAK TO YOU.

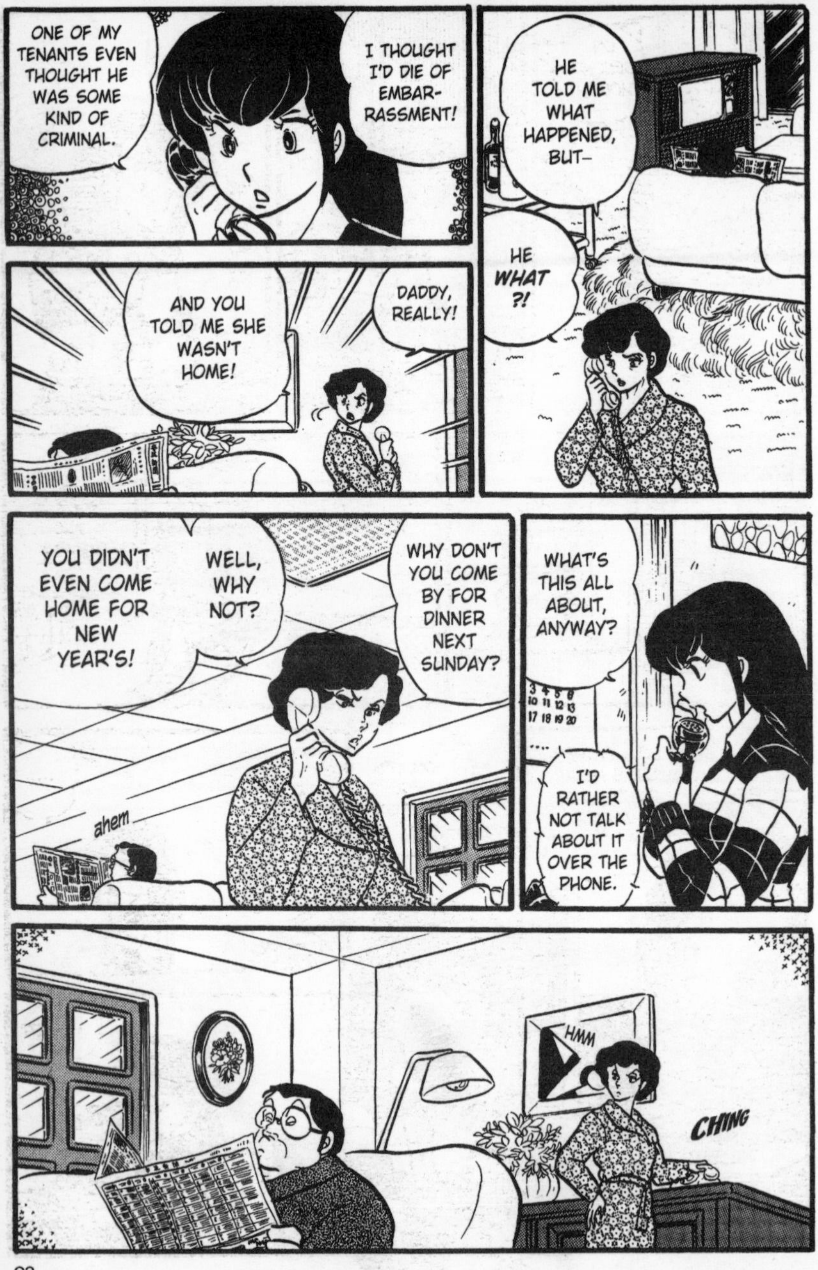
HE TOLD ME WHAT HAPPENED, BUT–
HE WHAT?!
I THOUGHT I'D DIE OF EMBARRASSMENT!
ONE OF MY TENANTS EVEN THOUGHT HE WAS SOME KIND OF CRIMINAL.
DADDY, REALLY!
AND YOU TOLD ME SHE WASN'T HOME!
WHAT'S THIS ALL ABOUT, ANYWAY?
I'D RATHER NOT TALK ABOUT IT OVER THE PHONE.
WHY DON'T YOU COME BY FOR DINNER NEXT SUNDAY?
WELL, WHY NOT?
YOU DIDN'T EVEN COME HOME FOR NEW YEAR'S!
ahem
HMM
CHING

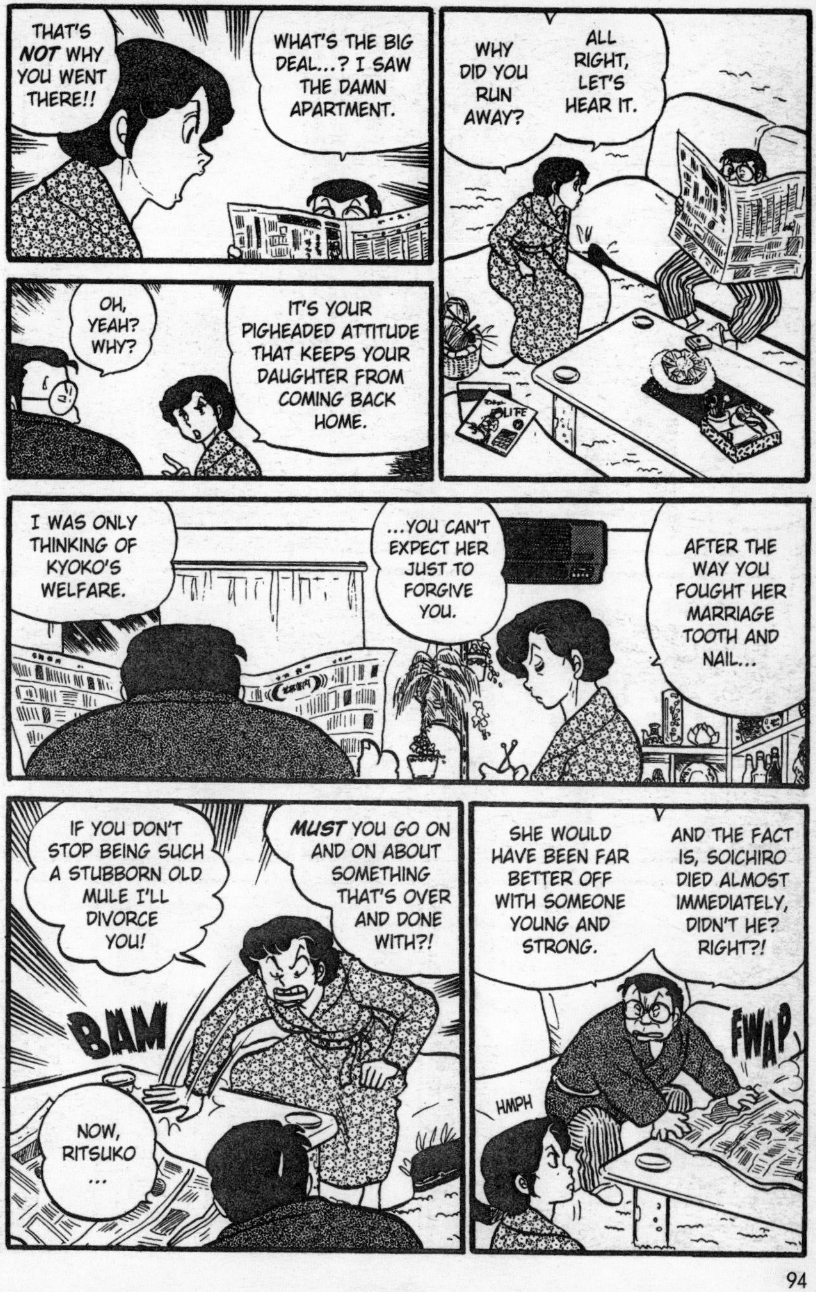
ALL RIGHT, LET'S HEAR IT.
WHY DID YOU RUN AWAY?
WHAT'S THE BIG DEAL...? I SAW THE DAMN APARTMENT.
THAT'S **NOT** WHY YOU WENT THERE!!
IT'S YOUR PIGHEADED ATTITUDE THAT KEEPS YOUR DAUGHTER FROM COMING BACK HOME.
OH, YEAH? WHY?
AFTER THE WAY YOU FOUGHT HER MARRIAGE TOOTH AND NAIL...
...YOU CAN'T EXPECT HER JUST TO FORGIVE YOU.
I WAS ONLY THINKING OF KYOKO'S WELFARE.
AND THE FACT IS, SOICHIRO DIED ALMOST IMMEDIATELY, DIDN'T HE? RIGHT?!
SHE WOULD HAVE BEEN FAR BETTER OFF WITH SOMEONE YOUNG AND STRONG.
FWAP
HMPH
MUST YOU GO ON AND ON ABOUT SOMETHING THAT'S OVER AND DONE WITH?!
IF YOU DON'T STOP BEING SUCH A STUBBORN OLD MULE I'LL DIVORCE YOU!
BAM
NOW, RITSUKO ...

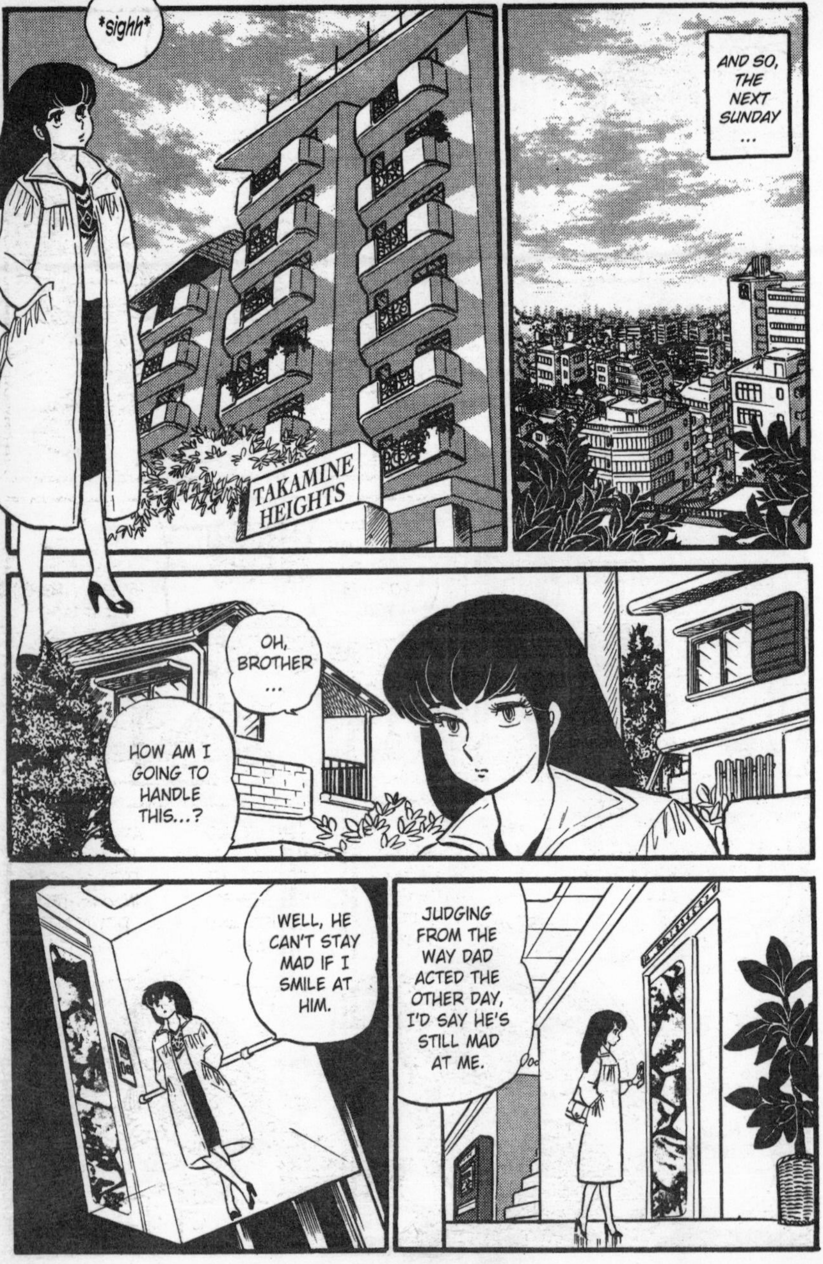
AND SO, THE NEXT SUNDAY ...
sighh
TAKAMINE HEIGHTS
OH, BROTHER ...
HOW AM I GOING TO HANDLE THIS...?
JUDGING FROM THE WAY DAD ACTED THE OTHER DAY, I'D SAY HE'S STILL MAD AT ME.
WELL, HE CAN'T STAY MAD IF I SMILE AT HIM.

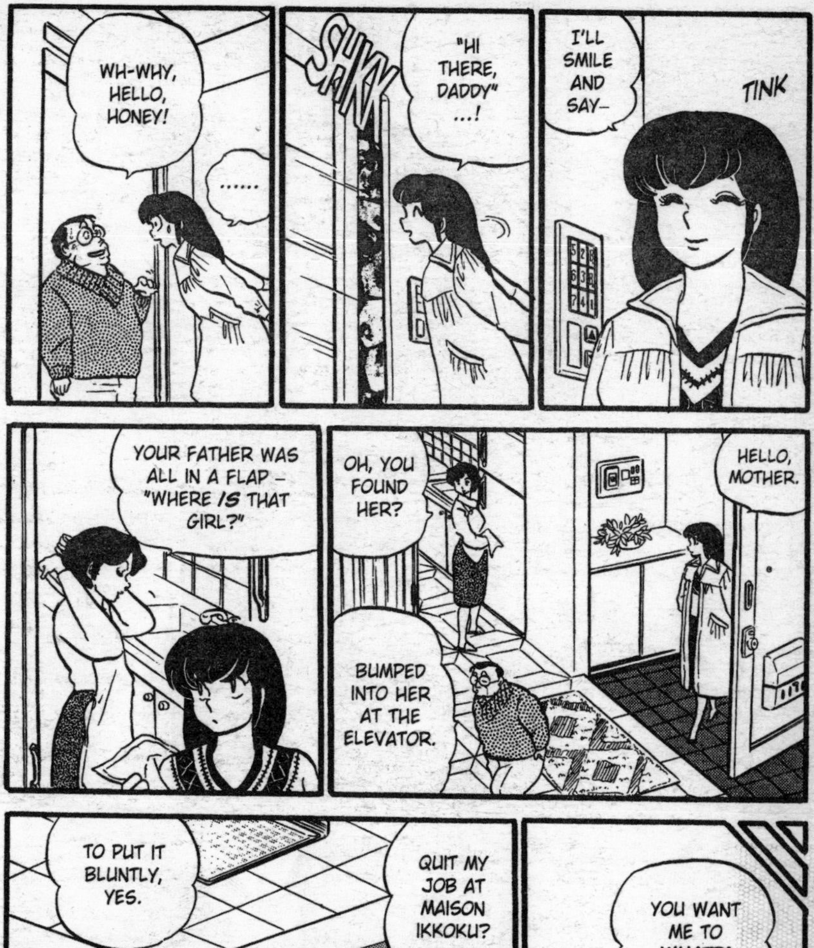
I'LL SMILE AND SAY–
TINK
"HI THERE, DADDY" ...!
WH-WHY, HELLO, HONEY!
......
HELLO, MOTHER.
OH, YOU FOUND HER?
BUMPED INTO HER AT THE ELEVATOR.
YOUR FATHER WAS ALL IN A FLAP – "WHERE *IS* THAT GIRL?"
YOU WANT ME TO **WHAT?!**
QUIT MY JOB AT MAISON IKKOKU?
TO PUT IT BLUNTLY, YES.
CHIK

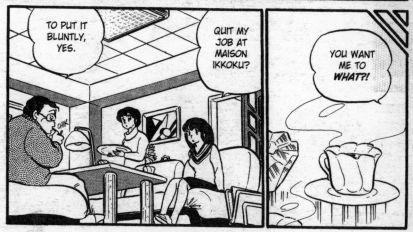

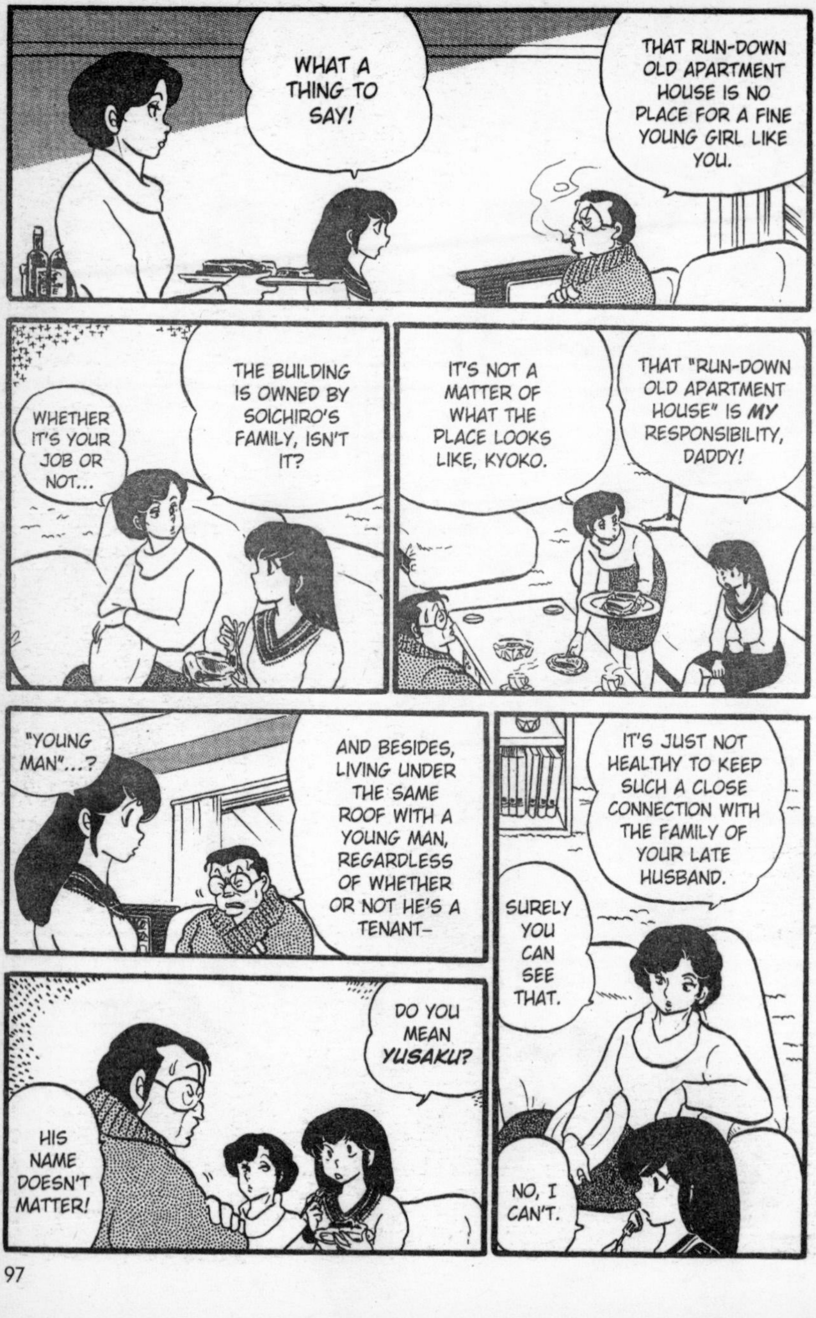
THAT RUN-DOWN OLD APARTMENT HOUSE IS NO PLACE FOR A FINE YOUNG GIRL LIKE YOU.
WHAT A THING TO SAY!
THAT "RUN-DOWN OLD APARTMENT HOUSE" IS *MY* RESPONSIBILITY, DADDY!
IT'S NOT A MATTER OF WHAT THE PLACE LOOKS LIKE, KYOKO.
THE BUILDING IS OWNED BY SOICHIRO'S FAMILY, ISN'T IT?
WHETHER IT'S YOUR JOB OR NOT...
IT'S JUST NOT HEALTHY TO KEEP SUCH A CLOSE CONNECTION WITH THE FAMILY OF YOUR LATE HUSBAND.
SURELY YOU CAN SEE THAT.
NO, I CAN'T.
AND BESIDES, LIVING UNDER THE SAME ROOF WITH A YOUNG MAN, REGARDLESS OF WHETHER OR NOT HE'S A TENANT–
"YOUNG MAN"...?
DO YOU MEAN *YUSAKU?*
HIS NAME DOESN'T MATTER!

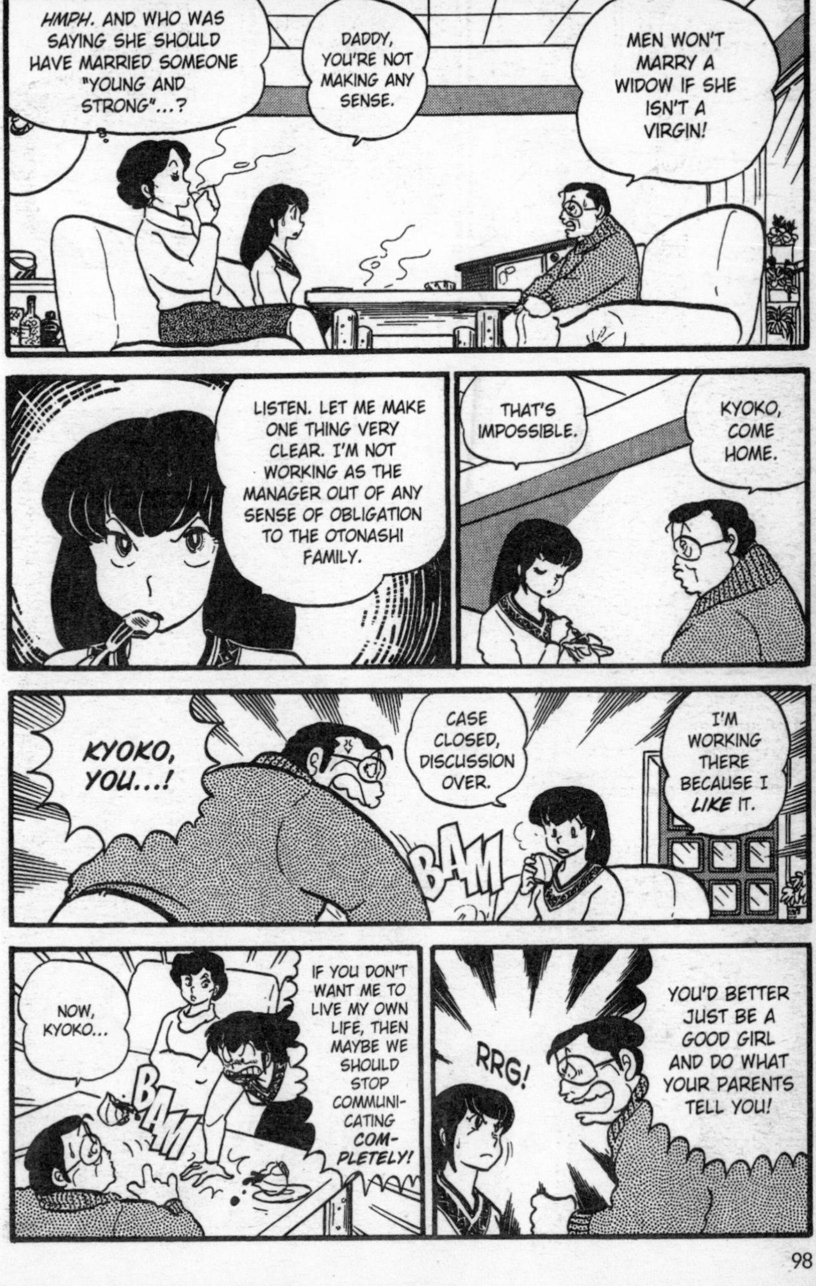
MEN WON'T MARRY A WIDOW IF SHE ISN'T A VIRGIN!
DADDY, YOU'RE NOT MAKING ANY SENSE.
HMPH. AND WHO WAS SAYING SHE SHOULD HAVE MARRIED SOMEONE "YOUNG AND STRONG"...?
KYOKO, COME HOME.
THAT'S IMPOSSIBLE.
LISTEN. LET ME MAKE ONE THING VERY CLEAR. I'M NOT WORKING AS THE MANAGER OUT OF ANY SENSE OF OBLIGATION TO THE OTONASHI FAMILY.
I'M WORKING THERE BECAUSE I *LIKE* IT.
CASE CLOSED, DISCUSSION OVER.
BAM
KYOKO, YOU...!
YOU'D BETTER JUST BE A GOOD GIRL AND DO WHAT YOUR PARENTS TELL YOU!
RRG!
IF YOU DON'T WANT ME TO LIVE MY OWN LIFE, THEN MAYBE WE SHOULD STOP COMMUNI-CATING COM-PLETELY!
BAM
NOW, KYOKO...

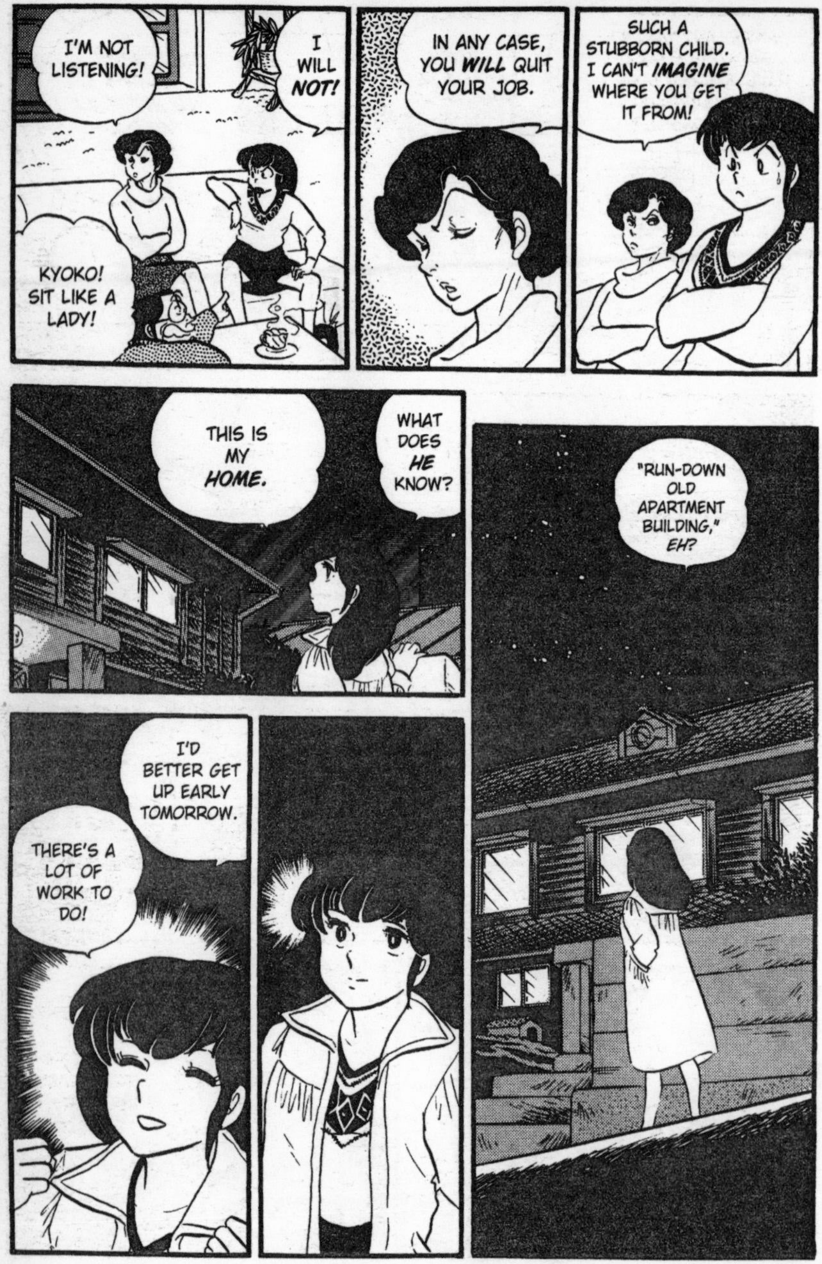
SUCH A STUBBORN CHILD. I CAN'T *IMAGINE* WHERE YOU GET IT FROM!
IN ANY CASE, YOU *WILL* QUIT YOUR JOB.
I WILL *NOT!*
I'M NOT LISTENING!
KYOKO! SIT LIKE A LADY!
"RUN-DOWN OLD APARTMENT BUILDING," *EH?*
WHAT DOES *HE* KNOW?
THIS IS MY *HOME.*
I'D BETTER GET UP EARLY TOMORROW.
THERE'S A LOT OF WORK TO DO!

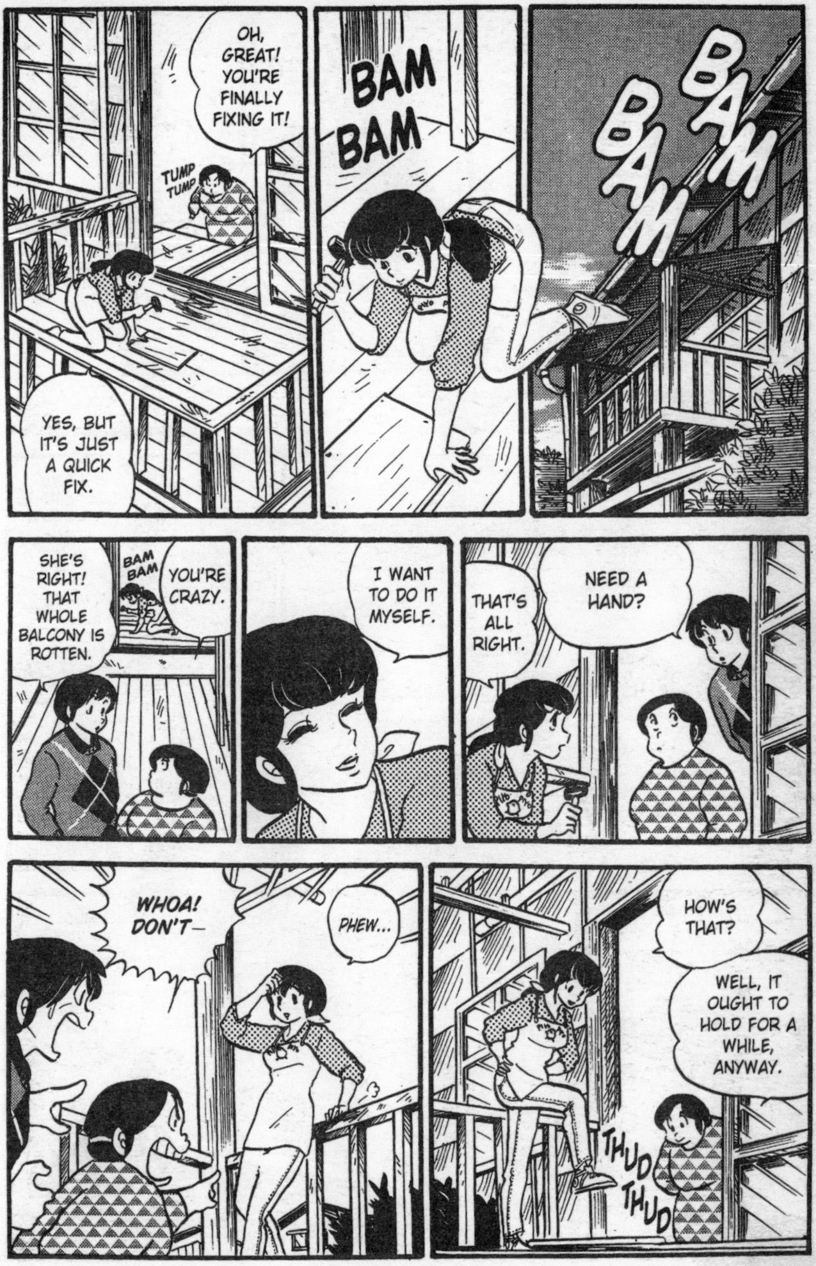
BAM
BAM
BAM
BAM
BAM
OH, GREAT! YOU'RE FINALLY FIXING IT!
TUMP TUMP
YES, BUT IT'S JUST A QUICK FIX.
NEED A HAND?
THAT'S ALL RIGHT.
I WANT TO DO IT MYSELF.
YOU'RE CRAZY.
BAM BAM
SHE'S RIGHT! THAT WHOLE BALCONY IS ROTTEN.
HOW'S THAT?
WELL, IT OUGHT TO HOLD FOR A WHILE, ANYWAY.
THUD THUD
PHEW...
WHOA! DON'T—

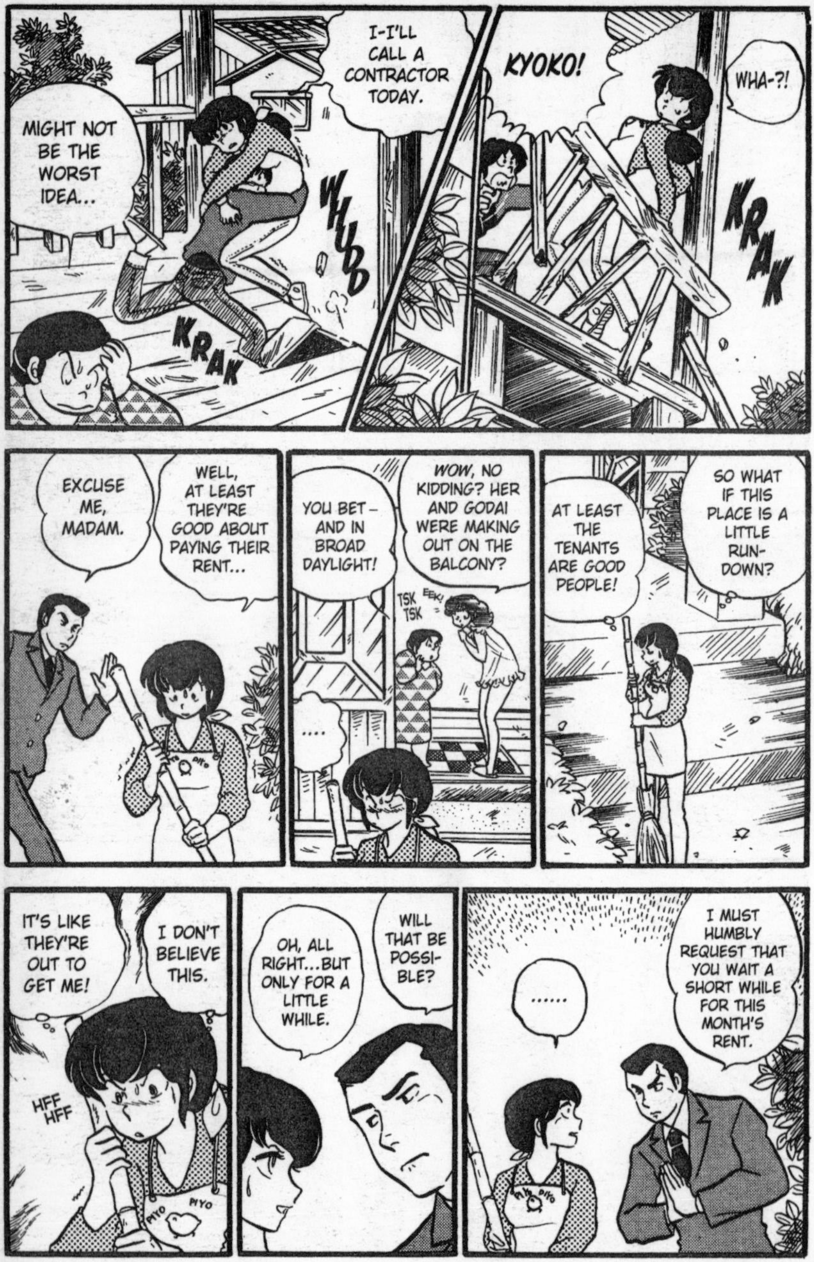
WHA-?!
KYOKO!
KRAK
I-I'LL CALL A CONTRACTOR TODAY.
MIGHT NOT BE THE WORST IDEA...
WHUDD
KRAK
SO WHAT IF THIS PLACE IS A LITTLE RUN-DOWN?
AT LEAST THE TENANTS ARE GOOD PEOPLE!
WOW, NO KIDDING? HER AND GODAI WERE MAKING OUT ON THE BALCONY?
YOU BET – AND IN BROAD DAYLIGHT!
EEK!
TSK TSK
....
WELL, AT LEAST THEY'RE GOOD ABOUT PAYING THEIR RENT...
EXCUSE ME, MADAM.
I MUST HUMBLY REQUEST THAT YOU WAIT A SHORT WHILE FOR THIS MONTH'S RENT.
......
WILL THAT BE POSSI-BLE?
OH, ALL RIGHT...BUT ONLY FOR A LITTLE WHILE.
I DON'T BELIEVE THIS.
IT'S LIKE THEY'RE OUT TO GET ME!
HFF HFF

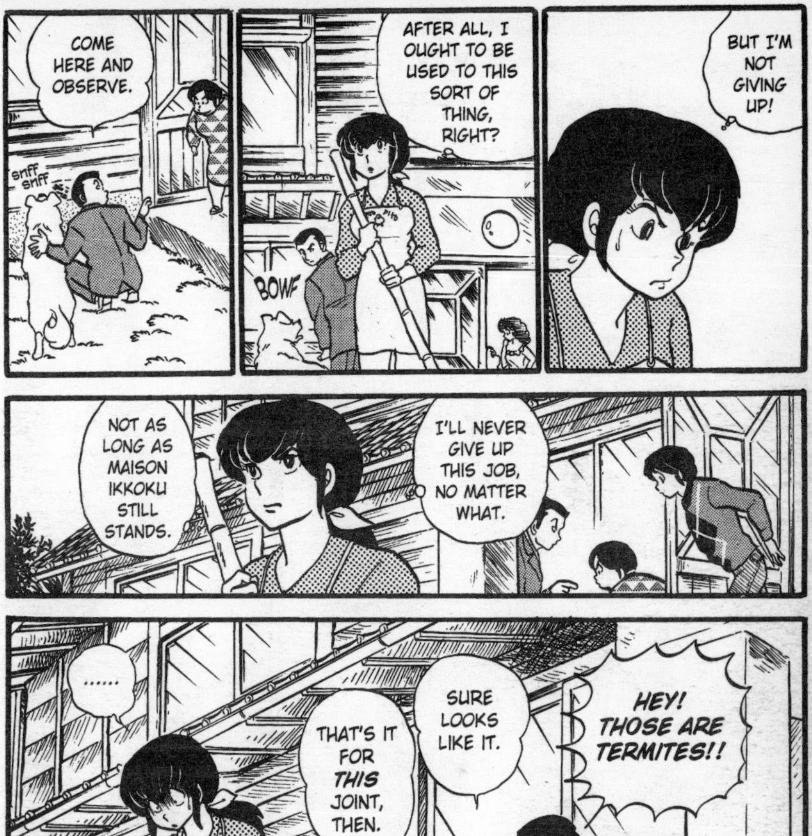
BUT I'M NOT GIVING UP!
AFTER ALL, I OUGHT TO BE USED TO THIS SORT OF THING, RIGHT?
BOWF
COME HERE AND OBSERVE.
sniff sniff
I'LL NEVER GIVE UP THIS JOB, NO MATTER WHAT.
NOT AS LONG AS MAISON IKKOKU STILL STANDS.
HEY! THOSE ARE TERMITES!!
SURE LOOKS LIKE IT.
THAT'S IT FOR *THIS* JOINT, THEN.
......
KTONK

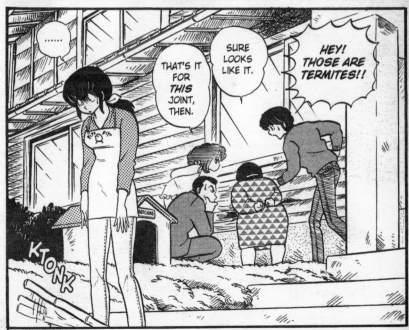

PART SIX

THE BIG ANNOUNCEMENT

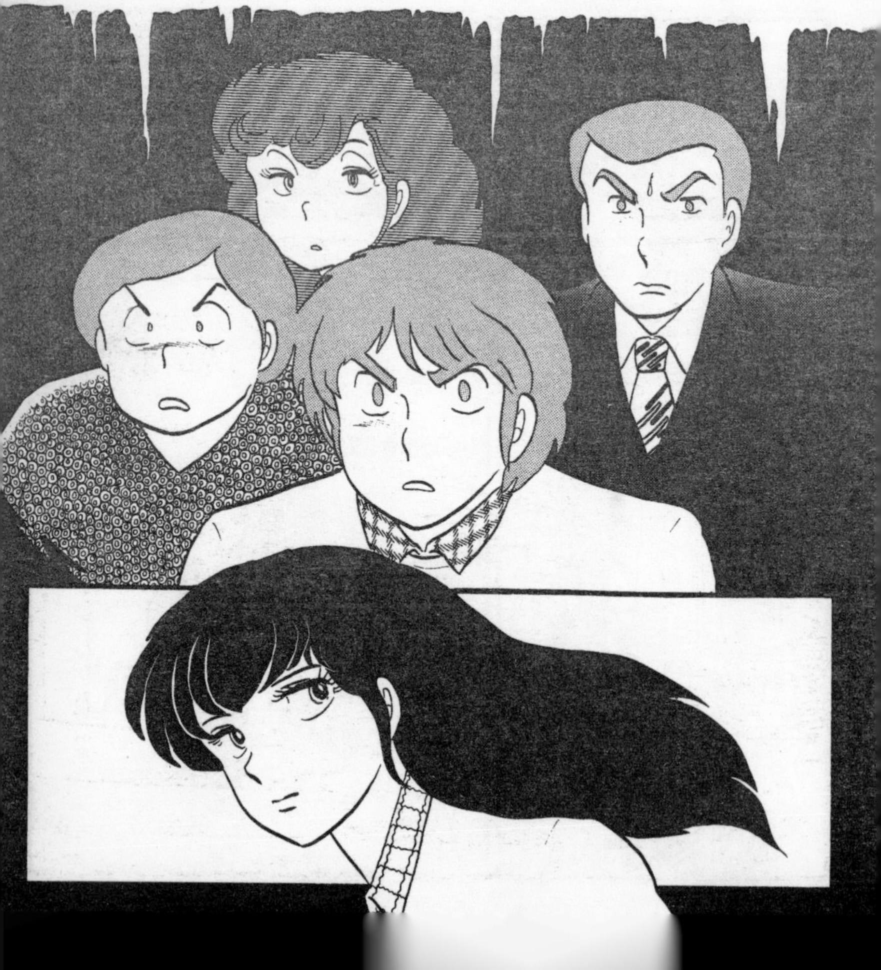

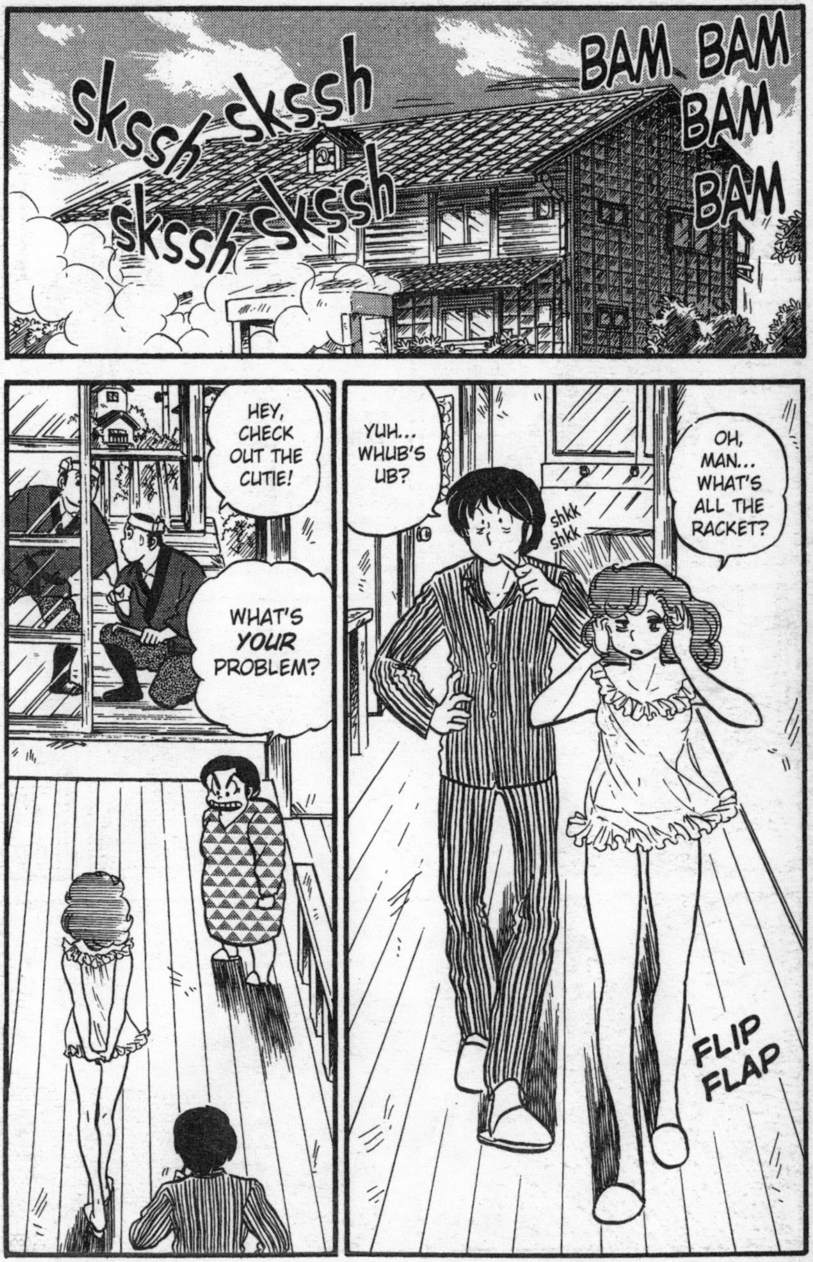
BAM BAM BAM BAM
sksssh sksssh sksssh sksssh
OH, MAN... WHAT'S ALL THE RACKET?
shkk shkk
YUH... WHUB'S UB?
FLIP FLAP
HEY, CHECK OUT THE CUTIE!
WHAT'S *YOUR* PROBLEM?

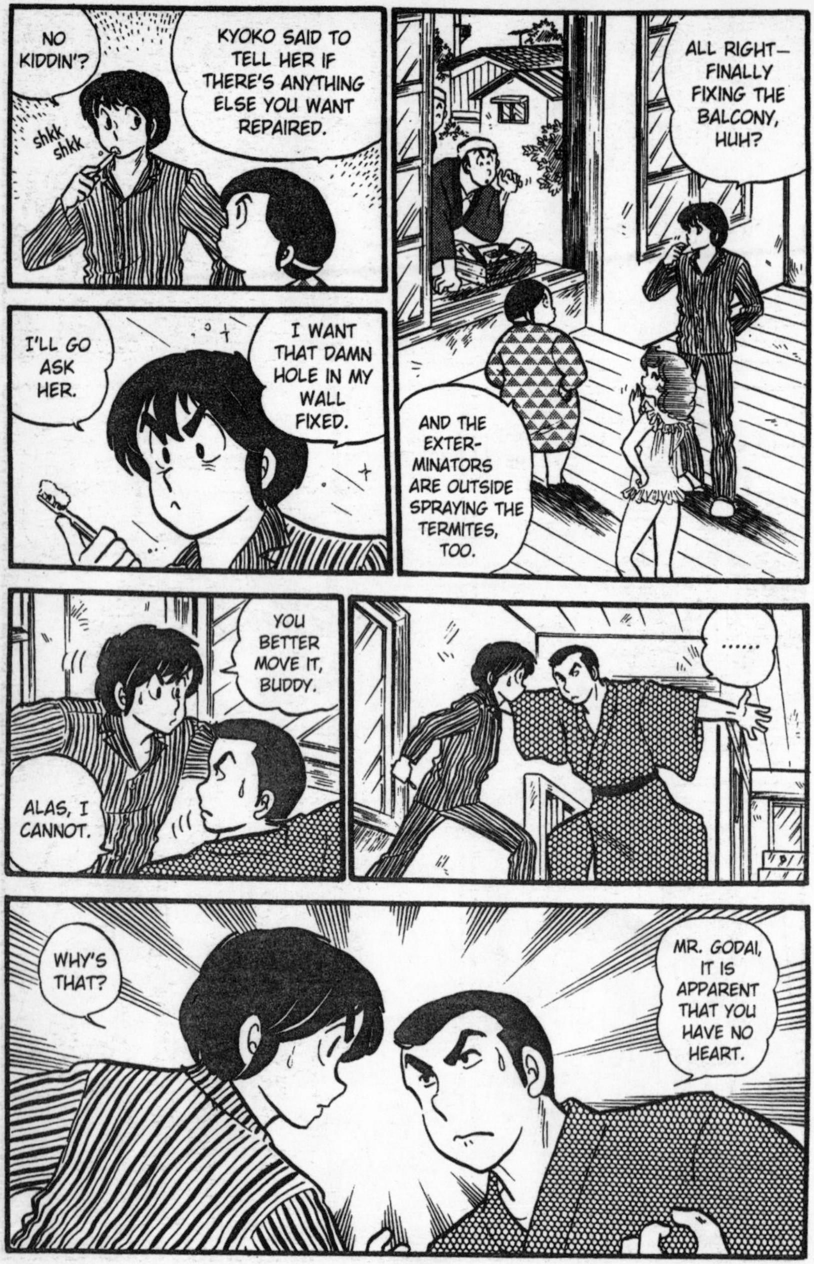
ALL RIGHT—FINALLY FIXING THE BALCONY, HUH?
AND THE EXTERMINATORS ARE OUTSIDE SPRAYING THE TERMITES, TOO.
KYOKO SAID TO TELL HER IF THERE'S ANYTHING ELSE YOU WANT REPAIRED.
NO KIDDIN'?
shkk shkk
I WANT THAT DAMN HOLE IN MY WALL FIXED.
I'LL GO ASK HER.
......
YOU BETTER MOVE IT, BUDDY.
ALAS, I CANNOT.
MR. GODAI, IT IS APPARENT THAT YOU HAVE NO HEART.
WHY'S THAT?

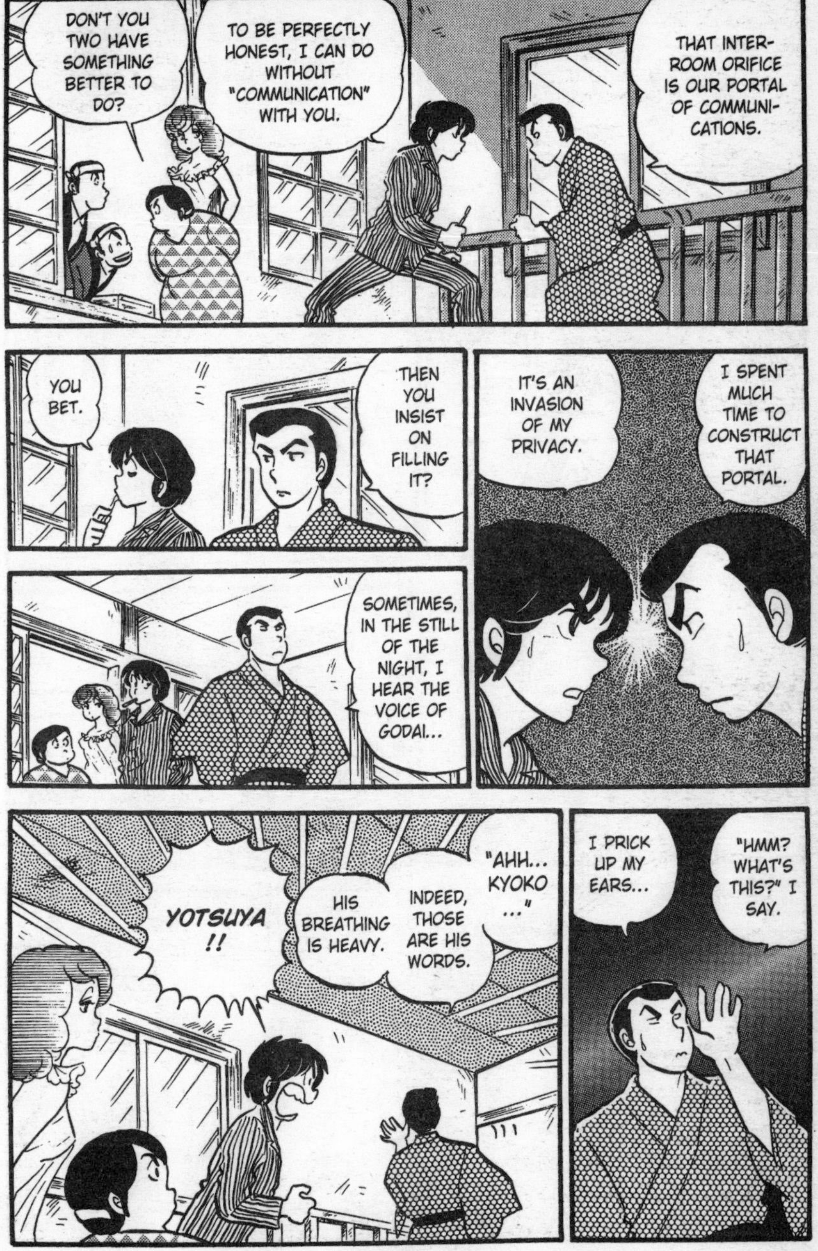
THAT INTER-ROOM ORIFICE IS OUR PORTAL OF COMMUNICATIONS.
TO BE PERFECTLY HONEST, I CAN DO WITHOUT "COMMUNICATION" WITH YOU.
DON'T YOU TWO HAVE SOMETHING BETTER TO DO?
I SPENT MUCH TIME TO CONSTRUCT THAT PORTAL.
IT'S AN INVASION OF MY PRIVACY.
THEN YOU INSIST ON FILLING IT?
YOU BET.
SOMETIMES, IN THE STILL OF THE NIGHT, I HEAR THE VOICE OF GODAI...
"HMM? WHAT'S THIS?" I SAY.
I PRICK UP MY EARS...
"AHH... KYOKO ..."
INDEED, THOSE ARE HIS WORDS.
HIS BREATHING IS HEAVY.
YOTSUYA !!

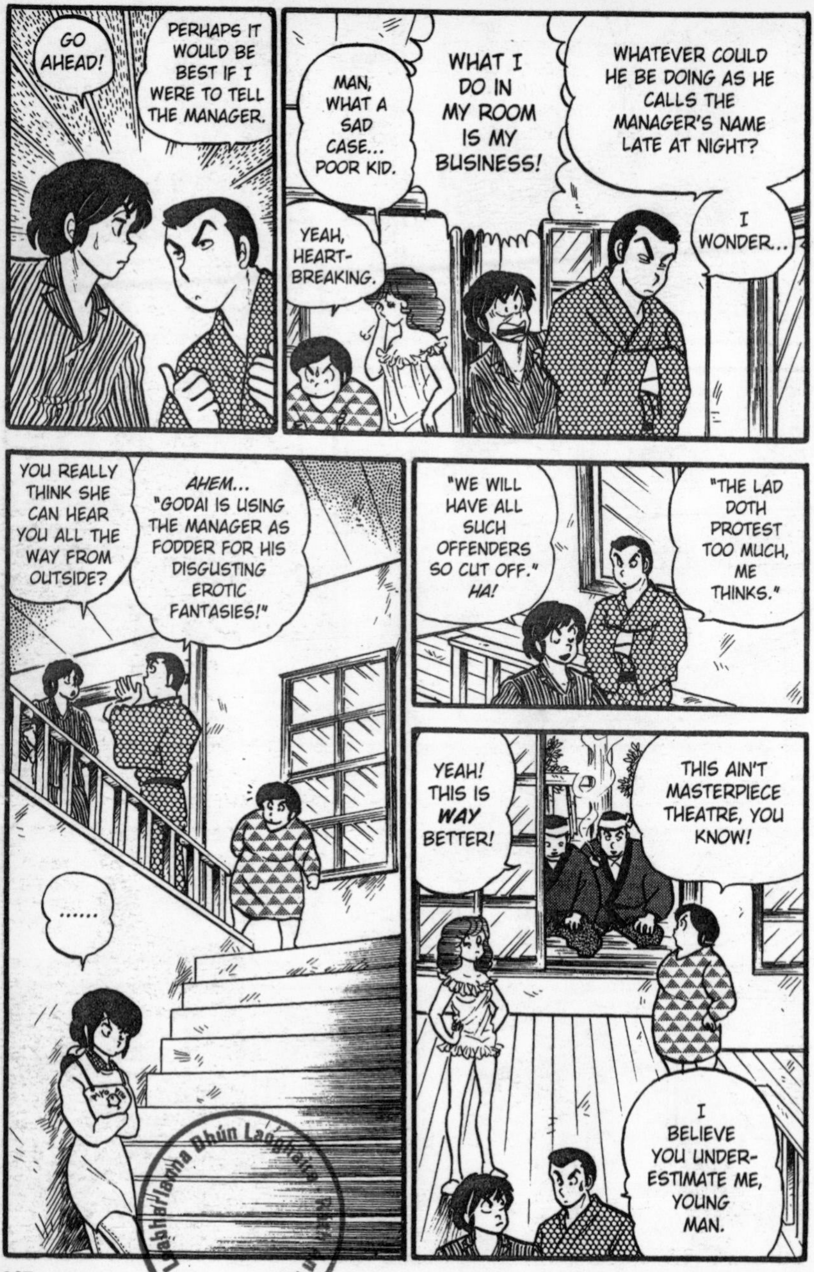

WHATEVER COULD HE BE DOING AS HE CALLS THE MANAGER'S NAME LATE AT NIGHT?
I WONDER...
WHAT I DO IN MY ROOM IS MY BUSINESS!
MAN, WHAT A SAD CASE... POOR KID.
YEAH, HEART-BREAKING.
PERHAPS IT WOULD BE BEST IF I WERE TO TELL THE MANAGER.
GO AHEAD!
"THE LAD DOTH PROTEST TOO MUCH, ME THINKS."
"WE WILL HAVE ALL SUCH OFFENDERS SO CUT OFF." *HA!*
THIS AIN'T MASTERPIECE THEATRE, YOU KNOW!
YEAH! THIS IS *WAY* BETTER!
I BELIEVE YOU UNDER-ESTIMATE ME, YOUNG MAN.
AHEM... "GODAI IS USING THE MANAGER AS FODDER FOR HIS DISGUSTING EROTIC FANTASIES!"
YOU REALLY THINK SHE CAN HEAR YOU ALL THE WAY FROM OUTSIDE?
......

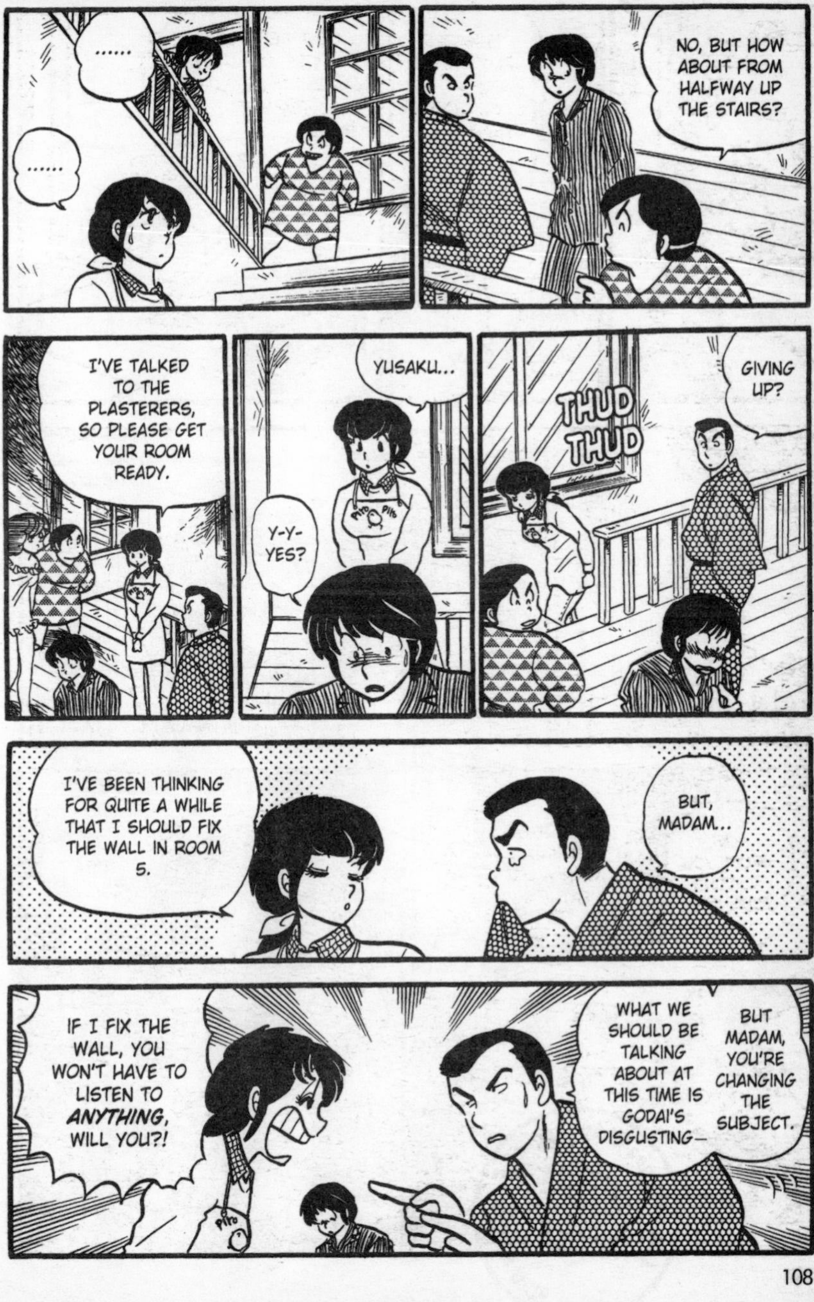
NO, BUT HOW ABOUT FROM HALFWAY UP THE STAIRS?
......
......
GIVING UP?
THUD THUD
YUSAKU...
Y-Y-YES?
I'VE TALKED TO THE PLASTERERS, SO PLEASE GET YOUR ROOM READY.
BUT, MADAM...
I'VE BEEN THINKING FOR QUITE A WHILE THAT I SHOULD FIX THE WALL IN ROOM 5.
BUT MADAM, YOU'RE CHANGING THE SUBJECT.
WHAT WE SHOULD BE TALKING ABOUT AT THIS TIME IS GODAI'S DISGUSTING—
IF I FIX THE WALL, YOU WON'T HAVE TO LISTEN TO *ANYTHING*, WILL YOU?!

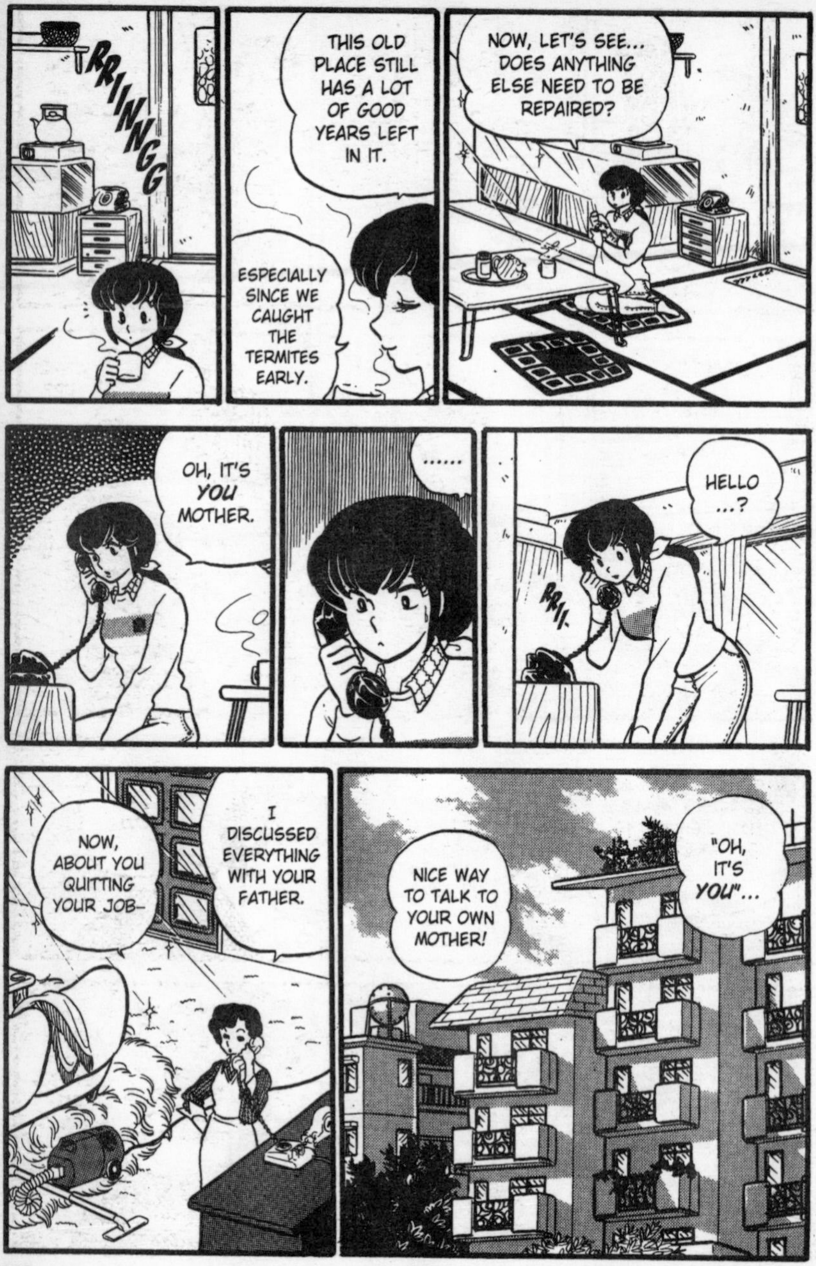
NOW, LET'S SEE... DOES ANYTHING ELSE NEED TO BE REPAIRED?
THIS OLD PLACE STILL HAS A LOT OF GOOD YEARS LEFT IN IT.
ESPECIALLY SINCE WE CAUGHT THE TERMITES EARLY.
RRIINNGG
HELLO ...?
RRII-
......
OH, IT'S *YOU* MOTHER.
"OH, IT'S *YOU*"...
NICE WAY TO TALK TO YOUR OWN MOTHER!
I DISCUSSED EVERYTHING WITH YOUR FATHER.
NOW, ABOUT YOU QUITTING YOUR JOB–

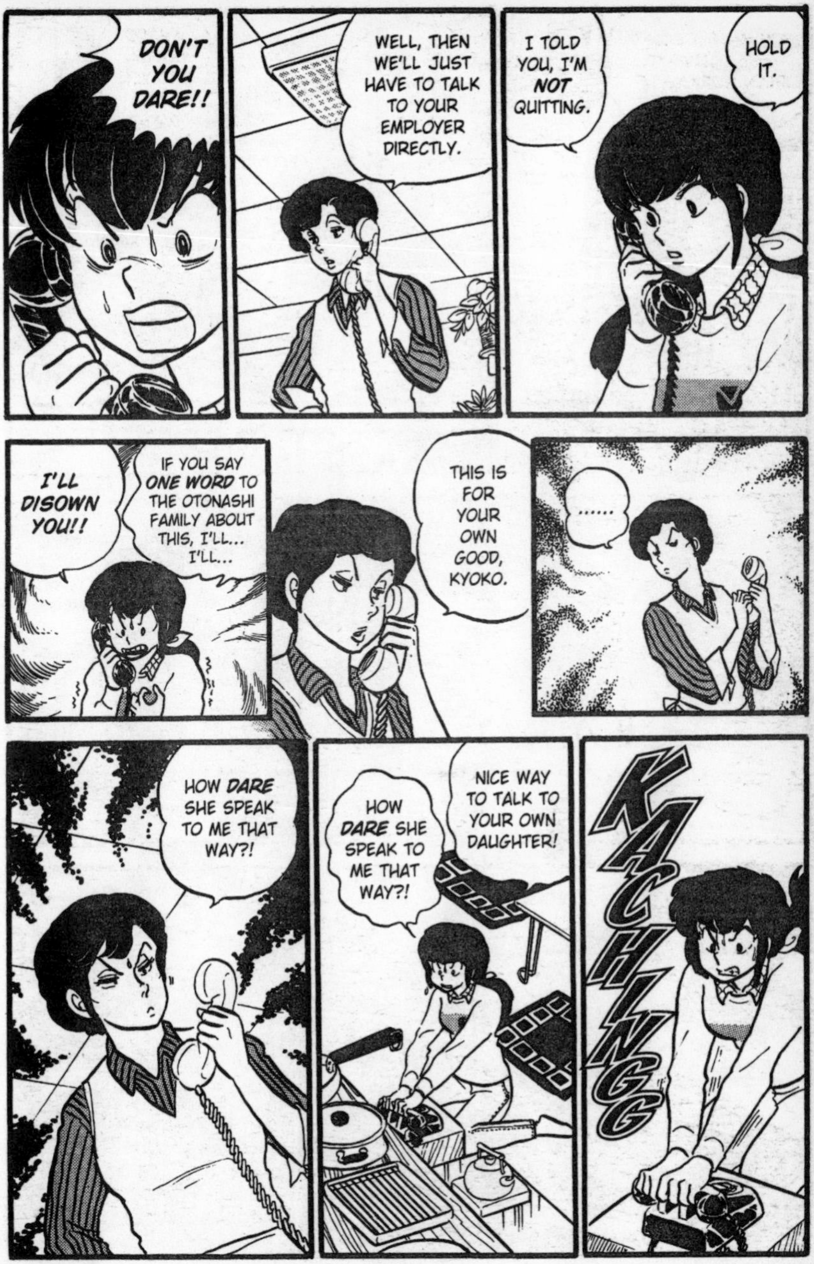
HOLD IT.
I TOLD YOU, I'M NOT QUITTING.
WELL, THEN WE'LL JUST HAVE TO TALK TO YOUR EMPLOYER DIRECTLY.
DON'T YOU DARE!!
......
THIS IS FOR YOUR OWN GOOD, KYOKO.
IF YOU SAY ONE WORD TO THE OTONASHI FAMILY ABOUT THIS, I'LL... I'LL...
I'LL DISOWN YOU!!
KACHINGG
NICE WAY TO TALK TO YOUR OWN DAUGHTER!
HOW DARE SHE SPEAK TO ME THAT WAY?!
HOW DARE SHE SPEAK TO ME THAT WAY?!

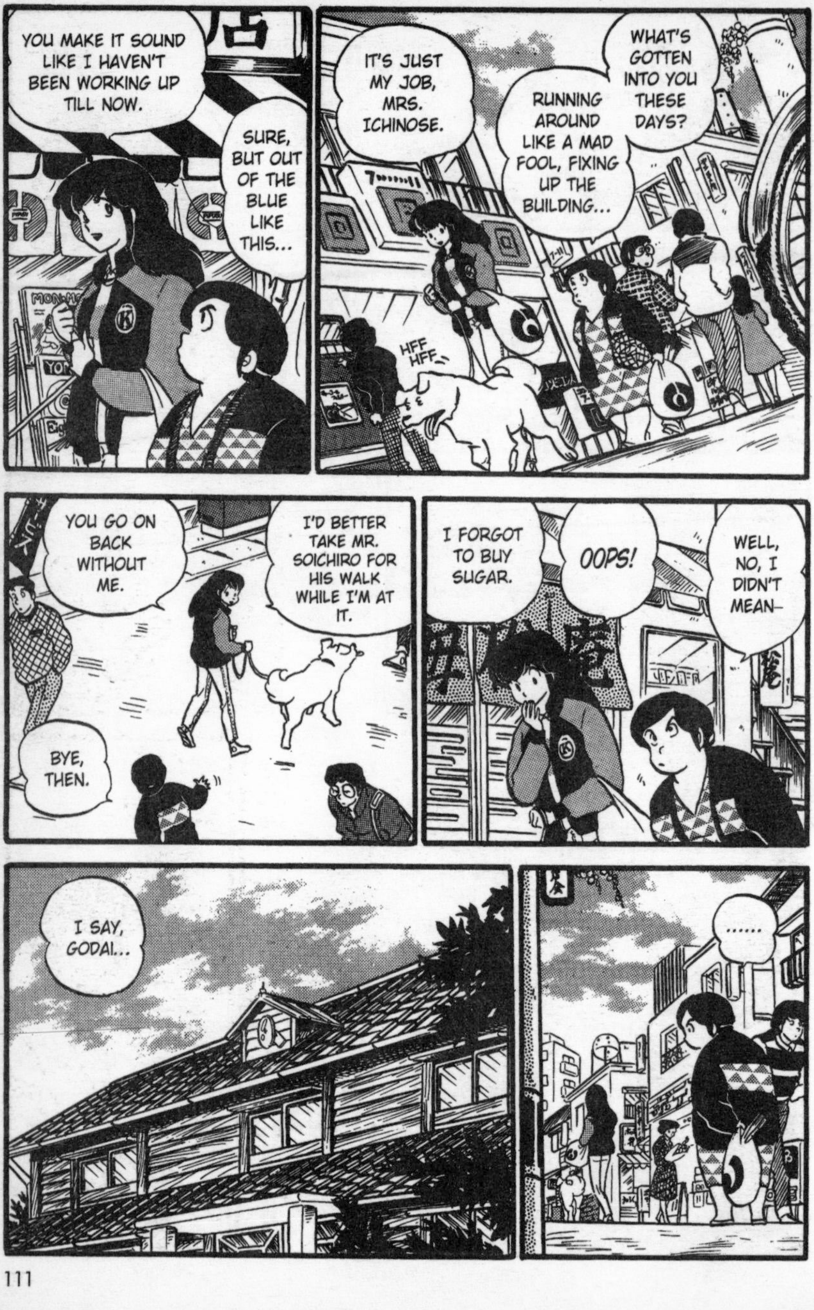
WHAT'S GOTTEN INTO YOU THESE DAYS?
RUNNING AROUND LIKE A MAD FOOL, FIXING UP THE BUILDING...
IT'S JUST MY JOB, MRS. ICHINOSE.
HFF HFF
SURE, BUT OUT OF THE BLUE LIKE THIS...
YOU MAKE IT SOUND LIKE I HAVEN'T BEEN WORKING UP TILL NOW.
WELL, NO, I DIDN'T MEAN—
OOPS!
I FORGOT TO BUY SUGAR.
I'D BETTER TAKE MR. SOICHIRO FOR HIS WALK WHILE I'M AT IT.
YOU GO ON BACK WITHOUT ME.
BYE, THEN.
......
I SAY, GODAI...

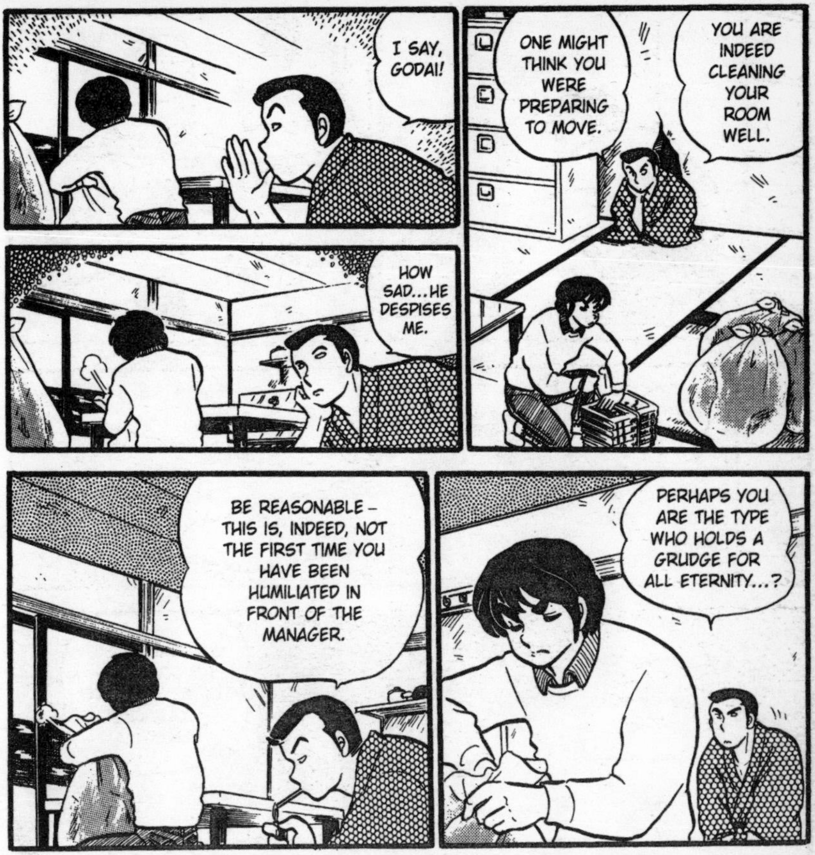
YOU ARE INDEED CLEANING YOUR ROOM WELL.
ONE MIGHT THINK YOU WERE PREPARING TO MOVE.
I SAY, GODAI!
HOW SAD...HE DESPISES ME.
PERHAPS YOU ARE THE TYPE WHO HOLDS A GRUDGE FOR ALL ETERNITY...?
BE REASONABLE – THIS IS, INDEED, NOT THE FIRST TIME YOU HAVE BEEN HUMILIATED IN FRONT OF THE MANAGER.
.....
SURELY YOU REMEMBER HOW TO SPEAK.
I AM FINDING IT DIFFICULT TO CARRY BOTH SIDES OF THIS CONVERSATION.

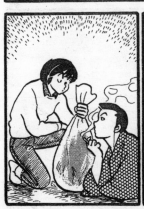

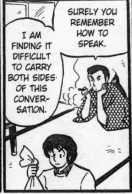

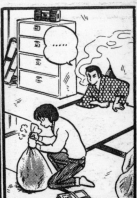

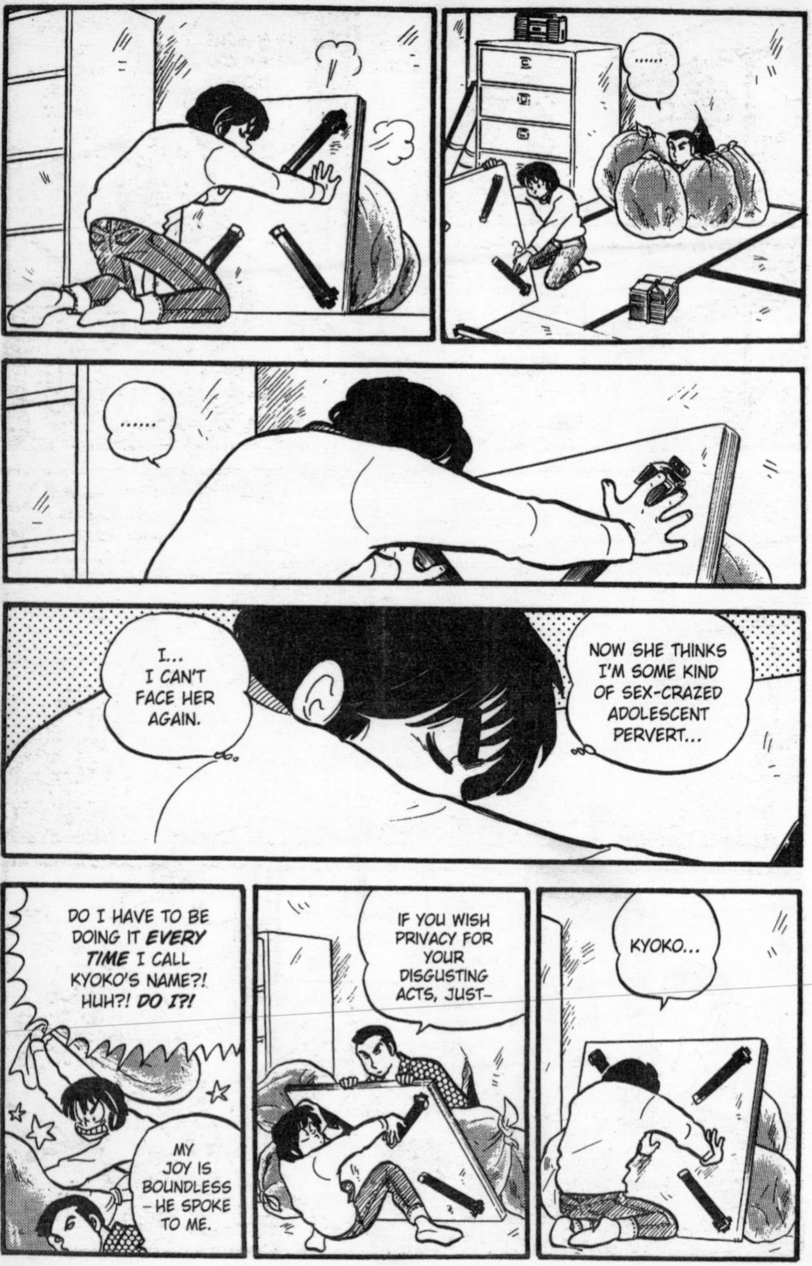

......
......
NOW SHE THINKS I'M SOME KIND OF SEX-CRAZED ADOLESCENT PERVERT...
I... I CAN'T FACE HER AGAIN.
KYOKO...
IF YOU WISH PRIVACY FOR YOUR DISGUSTING ACTS, JUST-
DO I HAVE TO BE DOING IT EVERY TIME I CALL KYOKO'S NAME?! HUH?! DO I?!
MY JOY IS BOUNDLESS – HE SPOKE TO ME.

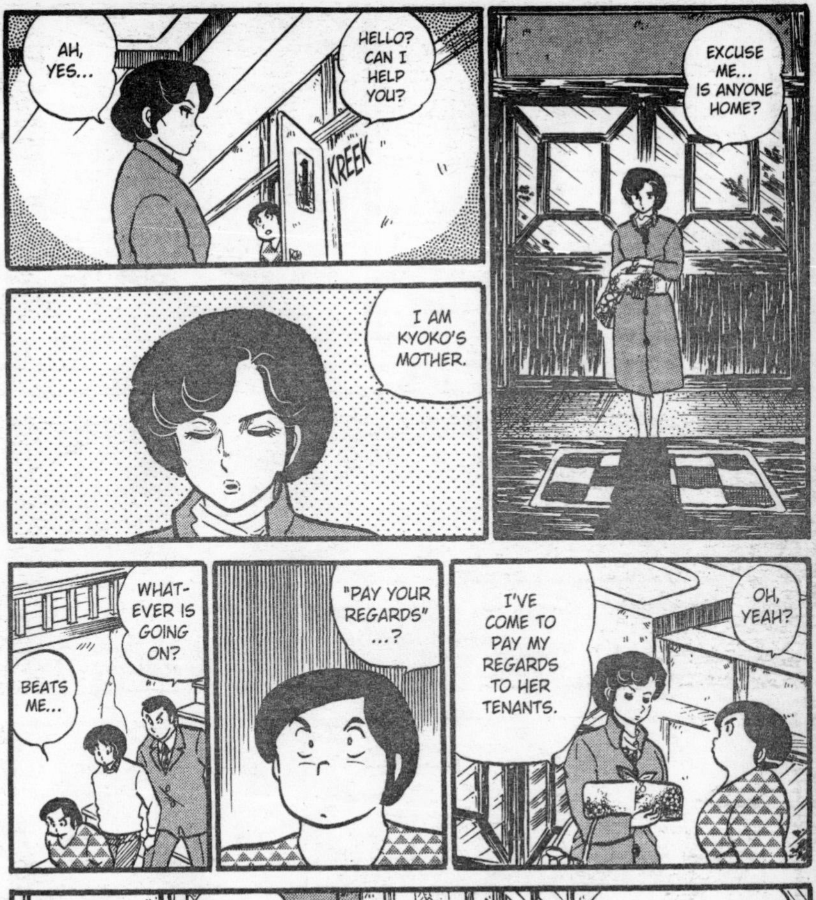
EXCUSE ME... IS ANYONE HOME?
HELLO? CAN I HELP YOU?
AH, YES...
KREEK
I AM KYOKO'S MOTHER.
OH, YEAH?
I'VE COME TO PAY MY REGARDS TO HER TENANTS.
"PAY YOUR REGARDS" ...?
WHAT-EVER IS GOING ON?
BEATS ME...
I WOULD LIKE TO THANK YOU ALL FOR BEING SO KIND TO MY DAUGHTER FOR ALL THESE YEARS.
IT WAS NOTHING.

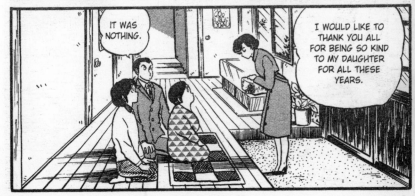

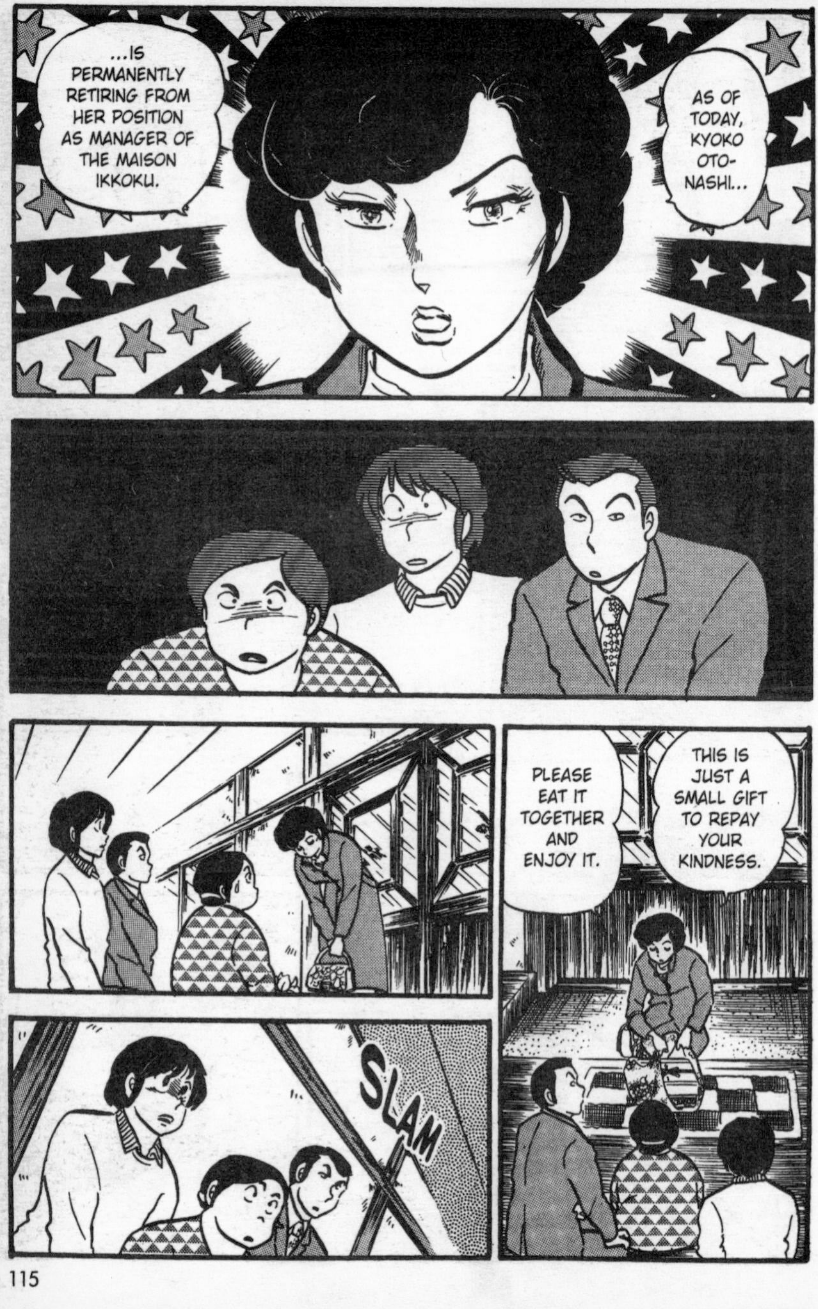
AS OF TODAY, KYOKO OTO-NASHI...
...IS PERMANENTLY RETIRING FROM HER POSITION AS MANAGER OF THE MAISON IKKOKU.
THIS IS JUST A SMALL GIFT TO REPAY YOUR KINDNESS.
PLEASE EAT IT TOGETHER AND ENJOY IT.
SLAM

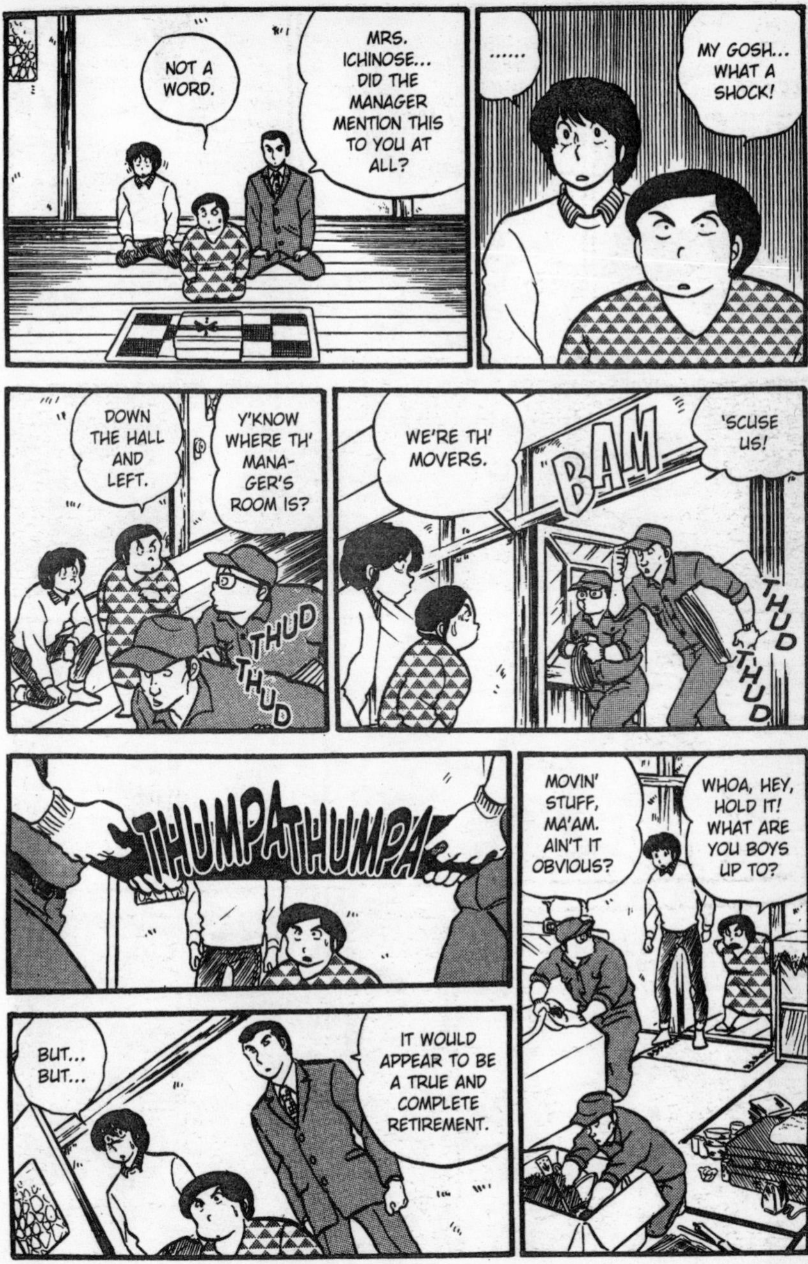
MY GOSH... WHAT A SHOCK!
......
MRS. ICHINOSE... DID THE MANAGER MENTION THIS TO YOU AT ALL?
NOT A WORD.
'SCUSE US!
BAM
WE'RE TH' MOVERS.
THUD THUD
Y'KNOW WHERE TH' MANA-GER'S ROOM IS?
DOWN THE HALL AND LEFT.
THUD THUD
WHOA, HEY, HOLD IT! WHAT ARE YOU BOYS UP TO?
MOVIN' STUFF, MA'AM. AIN'T IT OBVIOUS?
THUMPATHUMPA
IT WOULD APPEAR TO BE A TRUE AND COMPLETE RETIREMENT.
BUT... BUT...

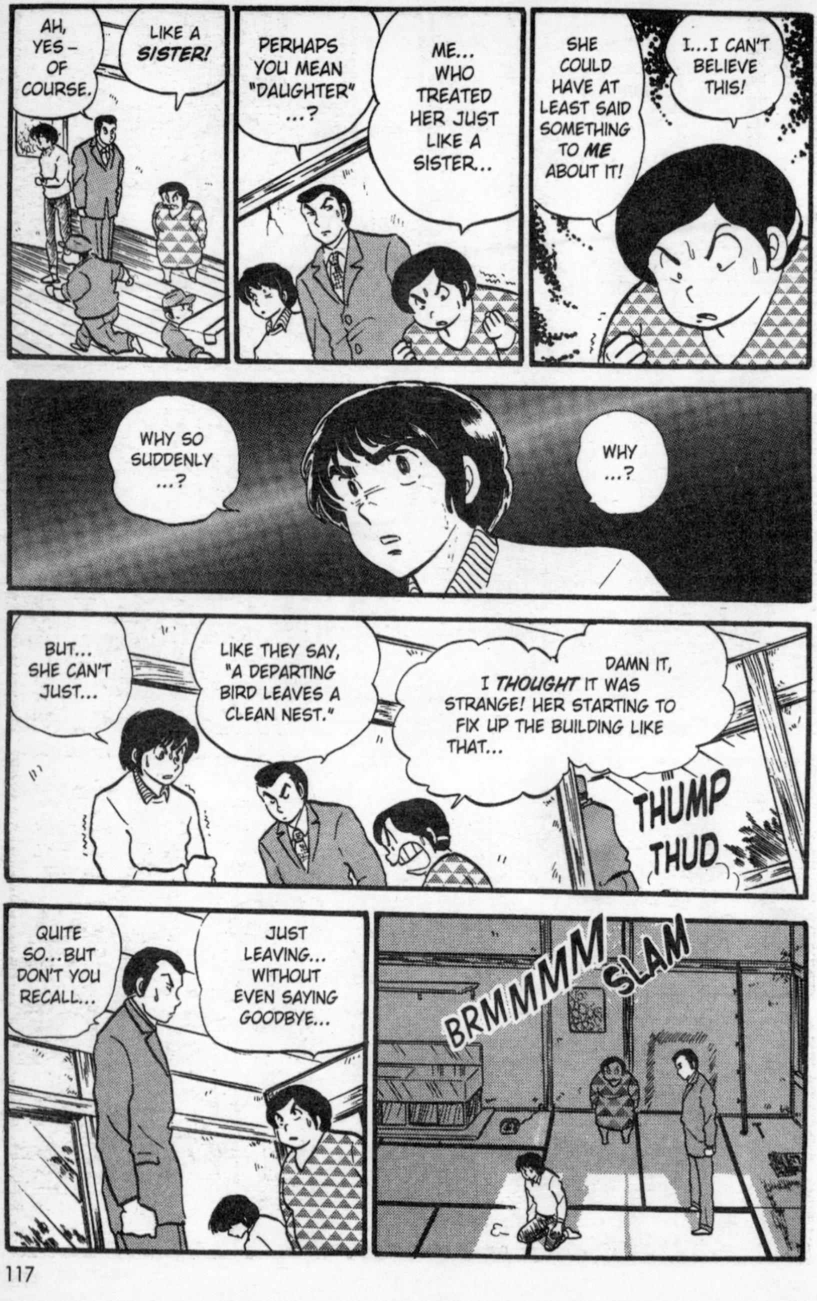
I...I CAN'T BELIEVE THIS!
SHE COULD HAVE AT LEAST SAID SOMETHING TO *ME* ABOUT IT!
ME... WHO TREATED HER JUST LIKE A SISTER...
PERHAPS YOU MEAN "DAUGHTER" ...?
LIKE A *SISTER!*
AH, YES – OF COURSE.
WHY ...?
WHY SO SUDDENLY ...?
DAMN IT, I *THOUGHT* IT WAS STRANGE! HER STARTING TO FIX UP THE BUILDING LIKE THAT...
THUMP
THUD
LIKE THEY SAY, "A DEPARTING BIRD LEAVES A CLEAN NEST."
BUT... SHE CAN'T JUST...
BRMMMM
SLAM
JUST LEAVING... WITHOUT EVEN SAYING GOODBYE...
QUITE SO...BUT DON'T YOU RECALL...

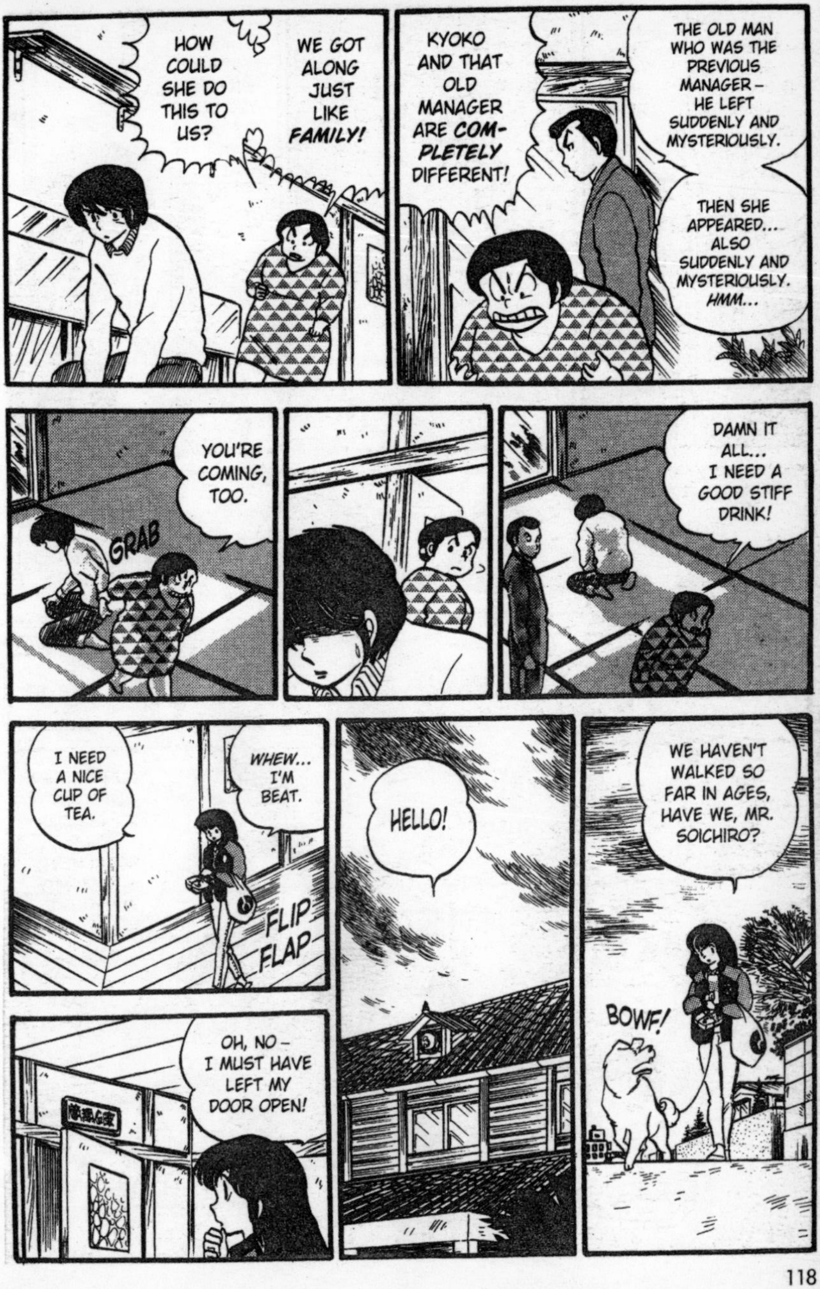
THE OLD MAN WHO WAS THE PREVIOUS MANAGER – HE LEFT SUDDENLY AND MYSTERIOUSLY.
KYOKO AND THAT OLD MANAGER ARE ***COMPLETELY*** DIFFERENT!
THEN SHE APPEARED... ALSO SUDDENLY AND MYSTERIOUSLY. ***HMM...***
WE GOT ALONG JUST LIKE ***FAMILY!***
HOW COULD SHE DO THIS TO US?
DAMN IT ALL... I NEED A GOOD STIFF DRINK!
YOU'RE COMING, TOO.
GRAB
WE HAVEN'T WALKED SO FAR IN AGES, HAVE WE, MR. SOICHIRO?
BOWF!
HELLO!
WHEW... I'M BEAT.
I NEED A NICE CUP OF TEA.
FLIP FLAP
OH, NO – I MUST HAVE LEFT MY DOOR OPEN!

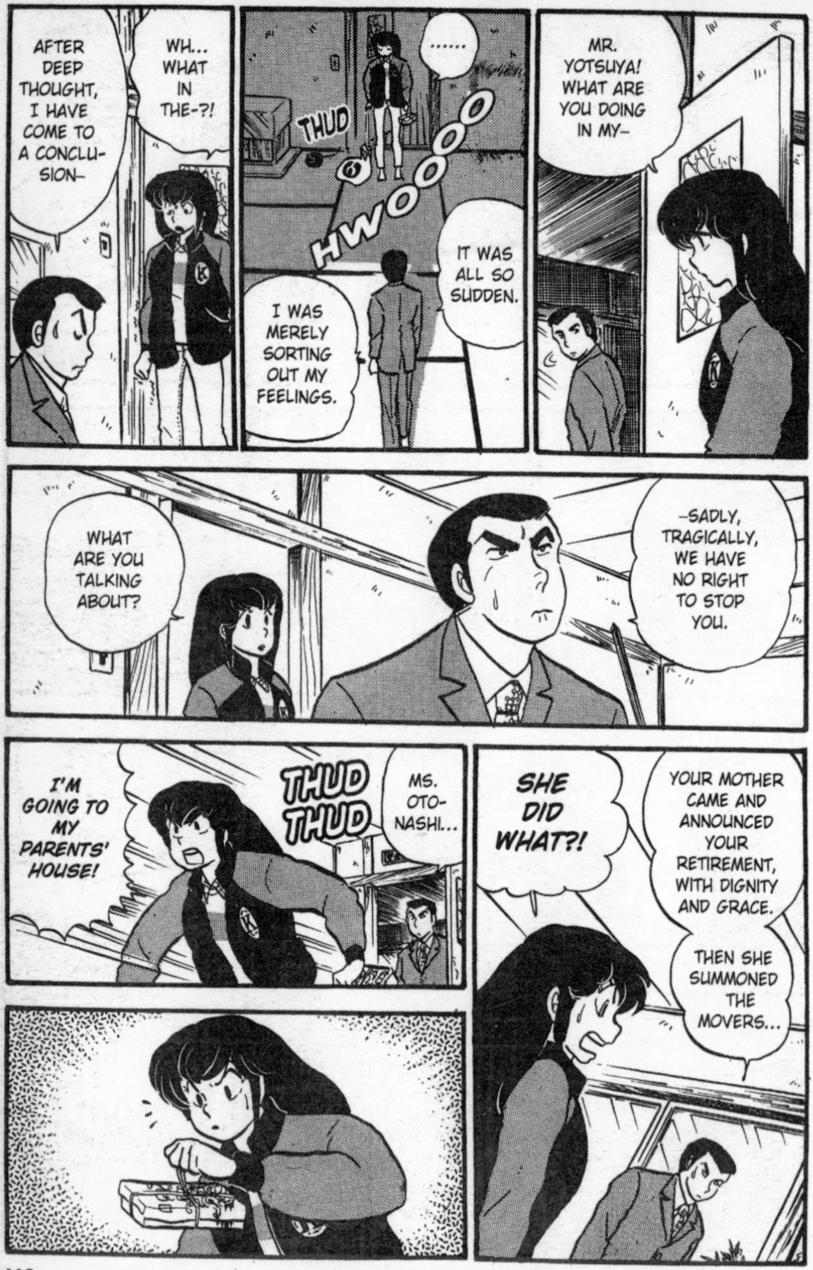
MR. YOTSUYA! WHAT ARE YOU DOING IN MY–
......
THUD
HWOOOOO
IT WAS ALL SO SUDDEN.
I WAS MERELY SORTING OUT MY FEELINGS.
WH... WHAT IN THE-?!
AFTER DEEP THOUGHT, I HAVE COME TO A CONCLUSION–
–SADLY, TRAGICALLY, WE HAVE NO RIGHT TO STOP YOU.
WHAT ARE YOU TALKING ABOUT?
YOUR MOTHER CAME AND ANNOUNCED YOUR RETIREMENT, WITH DIGNITY AND GRACE.
THEN SHE SUMMONED THE MOVERS...
SHE DID WHAT?!
MS. OTO-NASHI...
THUD THUD
I'M GOING TO MY PARENTS' HOUSE!

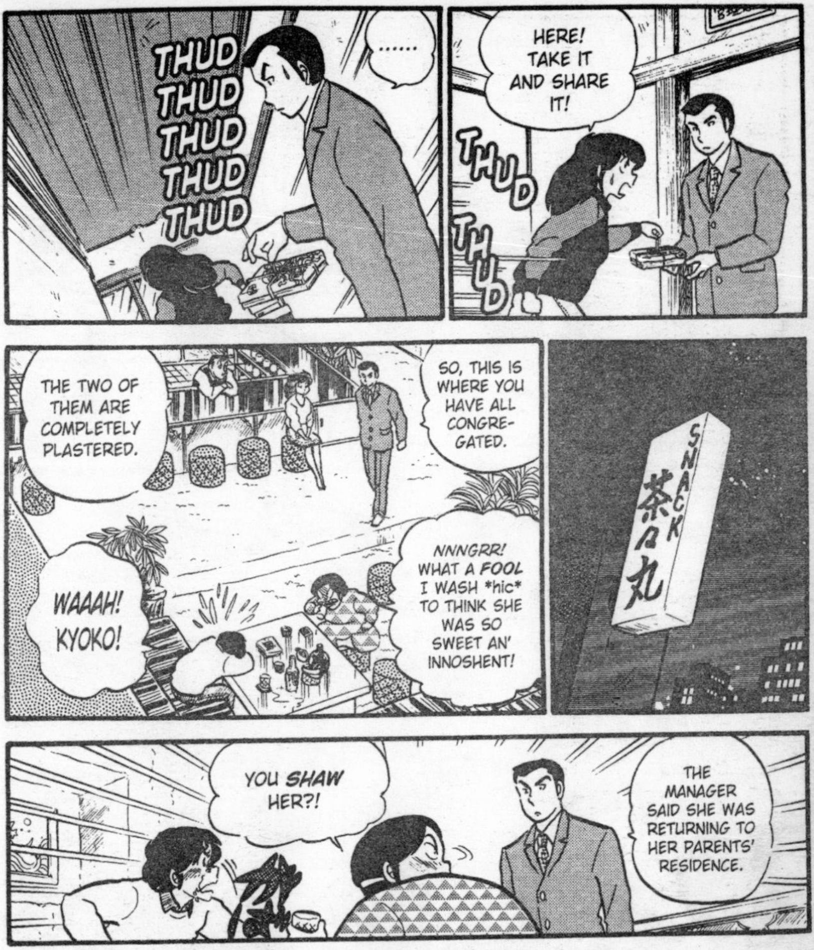
HERE! TAKE IT AND SHARE IT!
THUD THUD
......
THUD THUD THUD THUD THUD
SNACK 茶々丸
SO, THIS IS WHERE YOU HAVE ALL CONGREGATED.
THE TWO OF THEM ARE COMPLETELY PLASTERED.
NNNGRR! WHAT A FOOL I WASH *hic* TO THINK SHE WAS SO SWEET AN' INNOSHENT!
WAAAH! KYOKO!
THE MANAGER SAID SHE WAS RETURNING TO HER PARENTS' RESIDENCE.
YOU SHAW HER?!
THIS WAS OFFERED AS A GOING-AWAY GIFT.
WHUZZAT?
HUH? CAKES?
DOESH SHE THINK SHE CAN BUY US OFF WITH SOME STINKIN' CAKESH?!
sniff *sob*

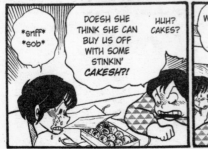

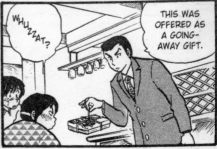

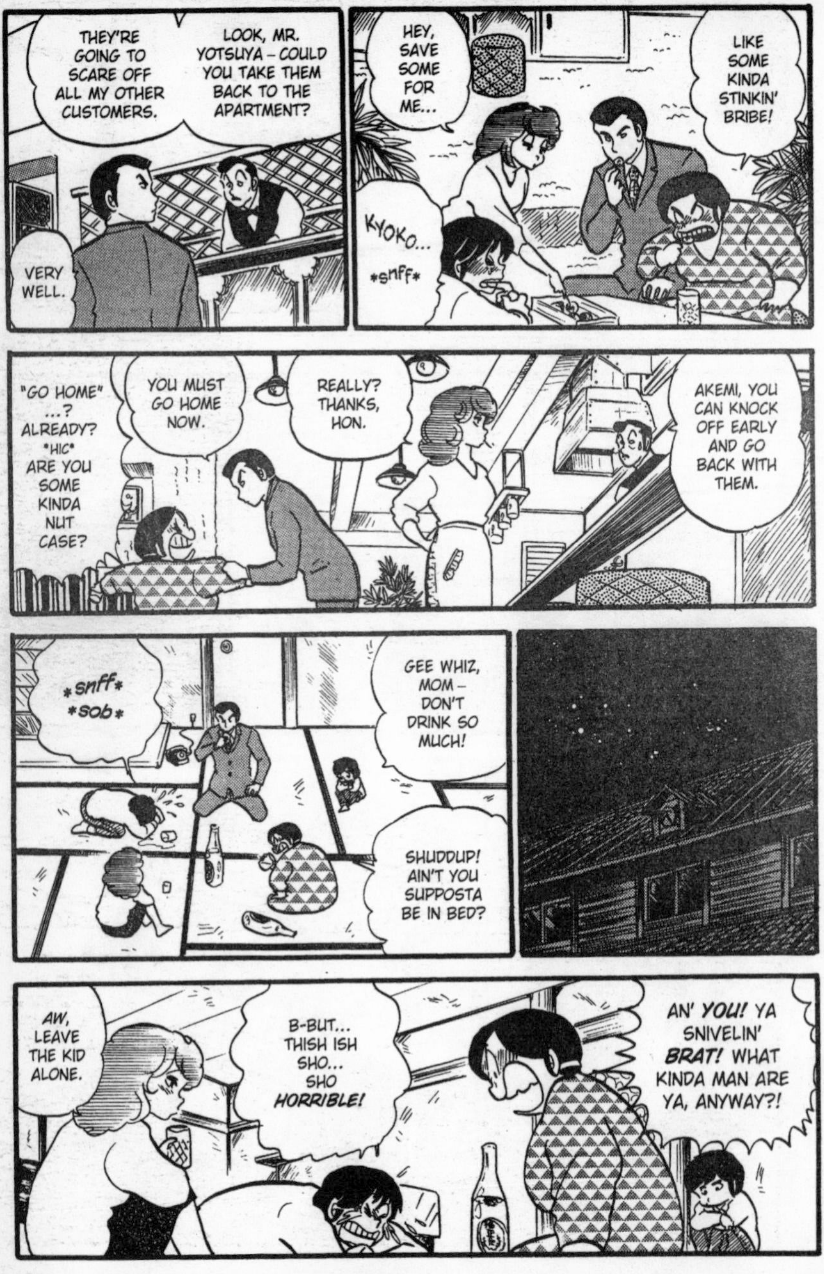
LIKE SOME KINDA STINKIN' BRIBE!
HEY, SAVE SOME FOR ME...
KYOKO... *snff*
LOOK, MR. YOTSUYA – COULD YOU TAKE THEM BACK TO THE APARTMENT?
THEY'RE GOING TO SCARE OFF ALL MY OTHER CUSTOMERS.
VERY WELL.
AKEMI, YOU CAN KNOCK OFF EARLY AND GO BACK WITH THEM.
REALLY? THANKS, HON.
YOU MUST GO HOME NOW.
"GO HOME" ...? ALREADY? *HIC* ARE YOU SOME KINDA NUT CASE?
GEE WHIZ, MOM – DON'T DRINK SO MUCH!
SHUDDUP! AIN'T YOU SUPPOSTA BE IN BED?
snff *sob*
AN' YOU! YA SNIVELIN' BRAT! WHAT KINDA MAN ARE YA, ANYWAY?!
B-BUT... THISH ISH SHO... SHO HORRIBLE!
AW, LEAVE THE KID ALONE.

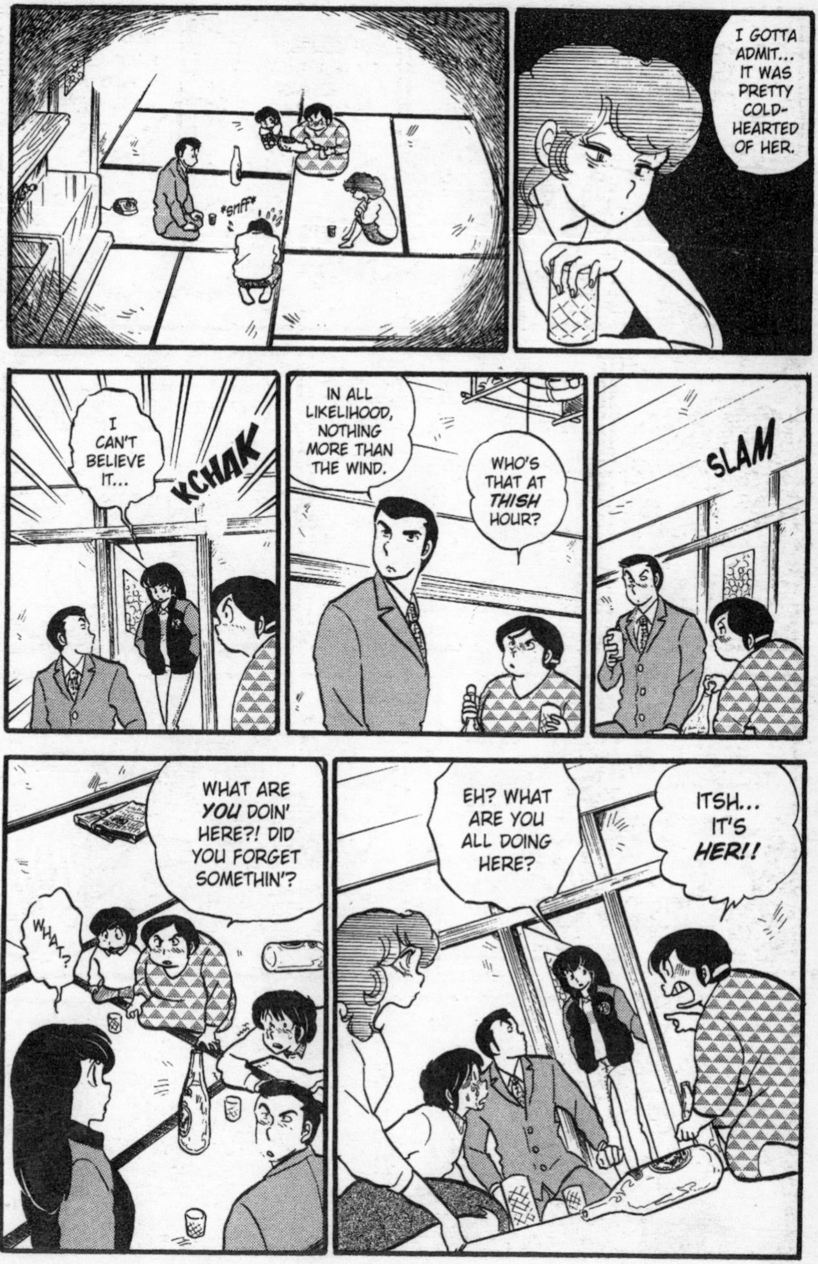
I GOTTA ADMIT... IT WAS PRETTY COLD-HEARTED OF HER.
sniff
SLAM
WHO'S THAT AT *THISH* HOUR?
IN ALL LIKELIHOOD, NOTHING MORE THAN THE WIND.
KCHAK
I CAN'T BELIEVE IT...
ITSH... IT'S *HER!!*
EH? WHAT ARE YOU ALL DOING HERE?
WHAT ARE *YOU* DOIN' HERE?! DID YOU FORGET SOMETHIN'?
WHAT?

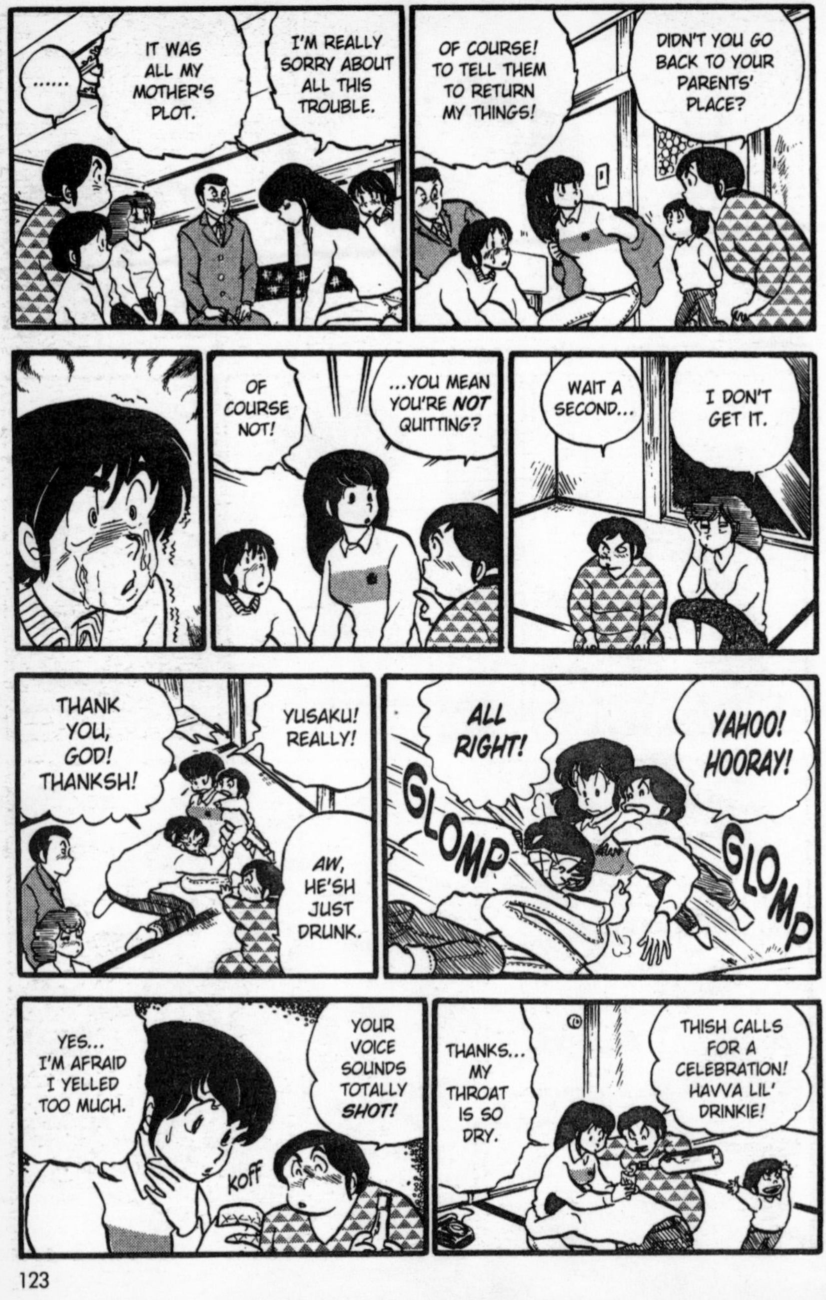
DIDN'T YOU GO BACK TO YOUR PARENTS' PLACE?
OF COURSE! TO TELL THEM TO RETURN MY THINGS!
I'M REALLY SORRY ABOUT ALL THIS TROUBLE.
IT WAS ALL MY MOTHER'S PLOT.
......
I DON'T GET IT.
WAIT A SECOND...
...YOU MEAN YOU'RE NOT QUITTING?
OF COURSE NOT!
YAHOO! HOORAY!
ALL RIGHT!
GLOMP
GLOMP
YUSAKU! REALLY!
THANK YOU, GOD! THANKSH!
AW, HE'SH JUST DRUNK.
THISH CALLS FOR A CELEBRATION! HAVVA LIL' DRINKIE!
THANKS... MY THROAT IS SO DRY.
YOUR VOICE SOUNDS TOTALLY SHOT!
KOFF
YES... I'M AFRAID I YELLED TOO MUCH.

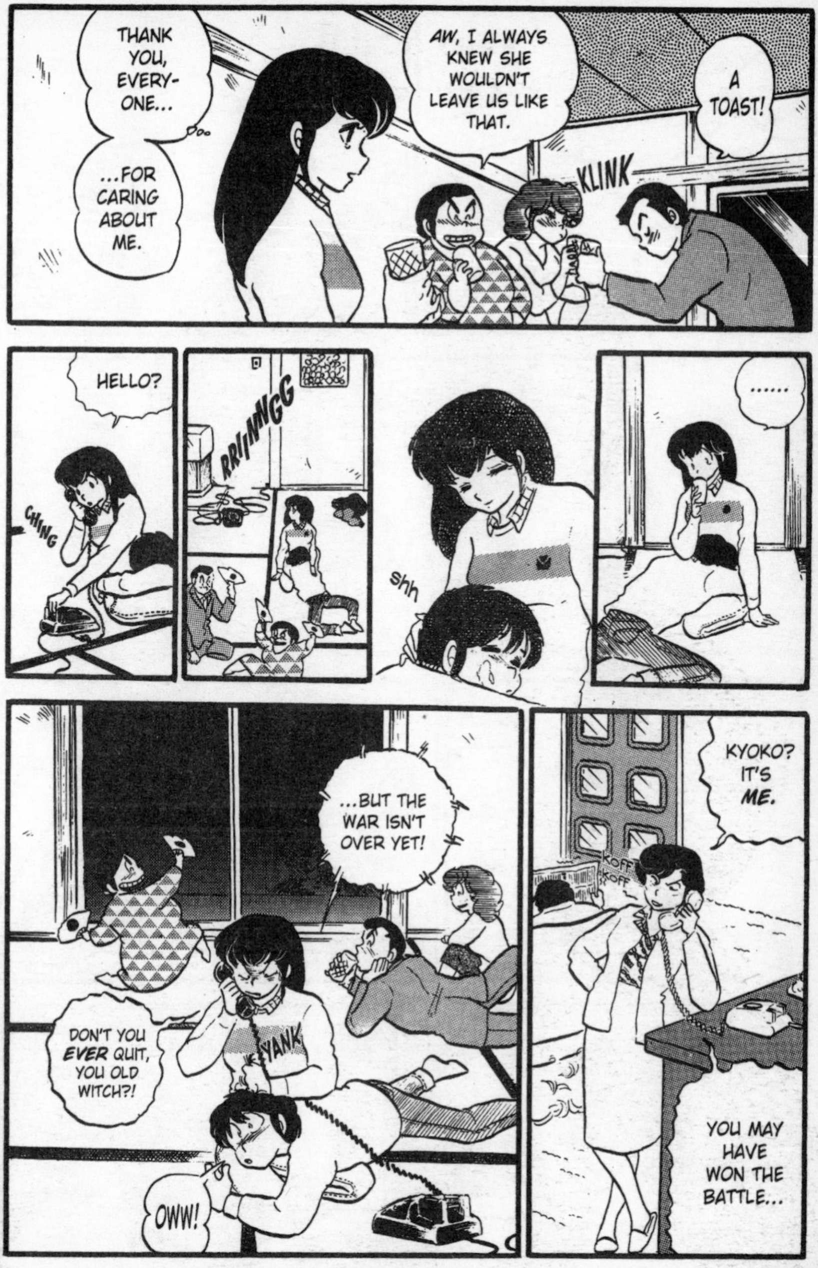
A TOAST!
KLINK
AW, I ALWAYS KNEW SHE WOULDN'T LEAVE US LIKE THAT.
THANK YOU, EVERY-ONE...
...FOR CARING ABOUT ME.
......
shh
RRIIINNGG
HELLO?
CHING
KYOKO? IT'S **ME.**
KOFF KOFF
YOU MAY HAVE WON THE BATTLE...
...BUT THE WAR ISN'T OVER YET!
DON'T YOU **EVER** QUIT, YOU OLD WITCH?!
YANK
OWW!

PART SEVEN
I'M CONVINCED

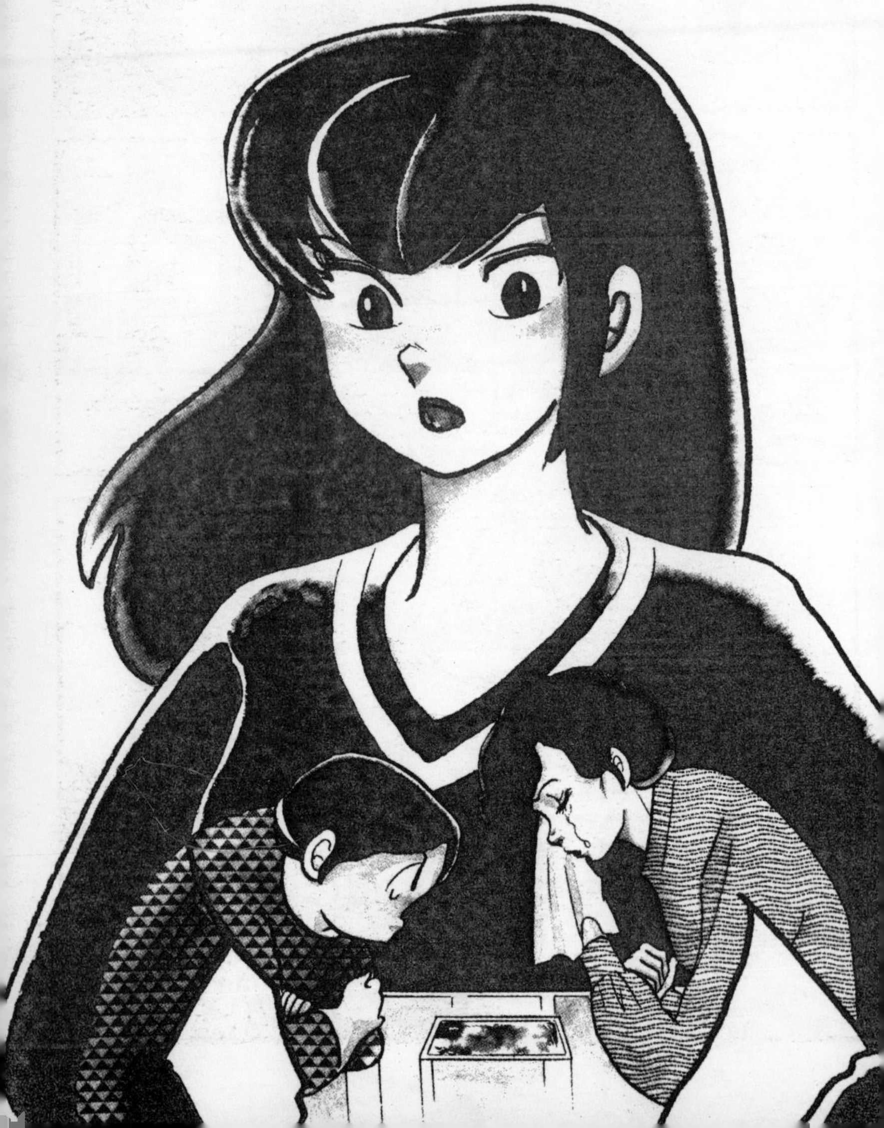

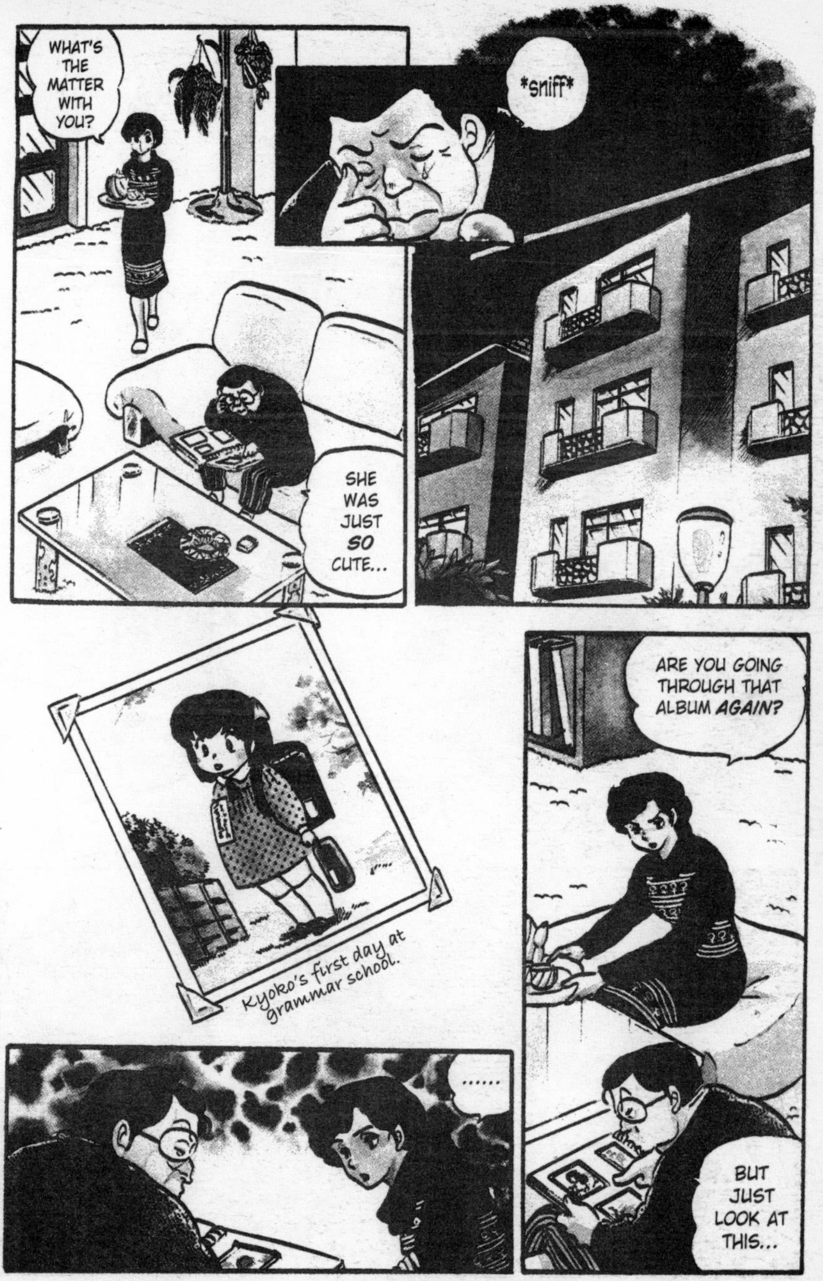
sniff
WHAT'S THE MATTER WITH YOU?
SHE WAS JUST **SO** CUTE...
ARE YOU GOING THROUGH THAT ALBUM ***AGAIN?***
BUT JUST LOOK AT THIS...
Kyoko's first day at grammar school.
......

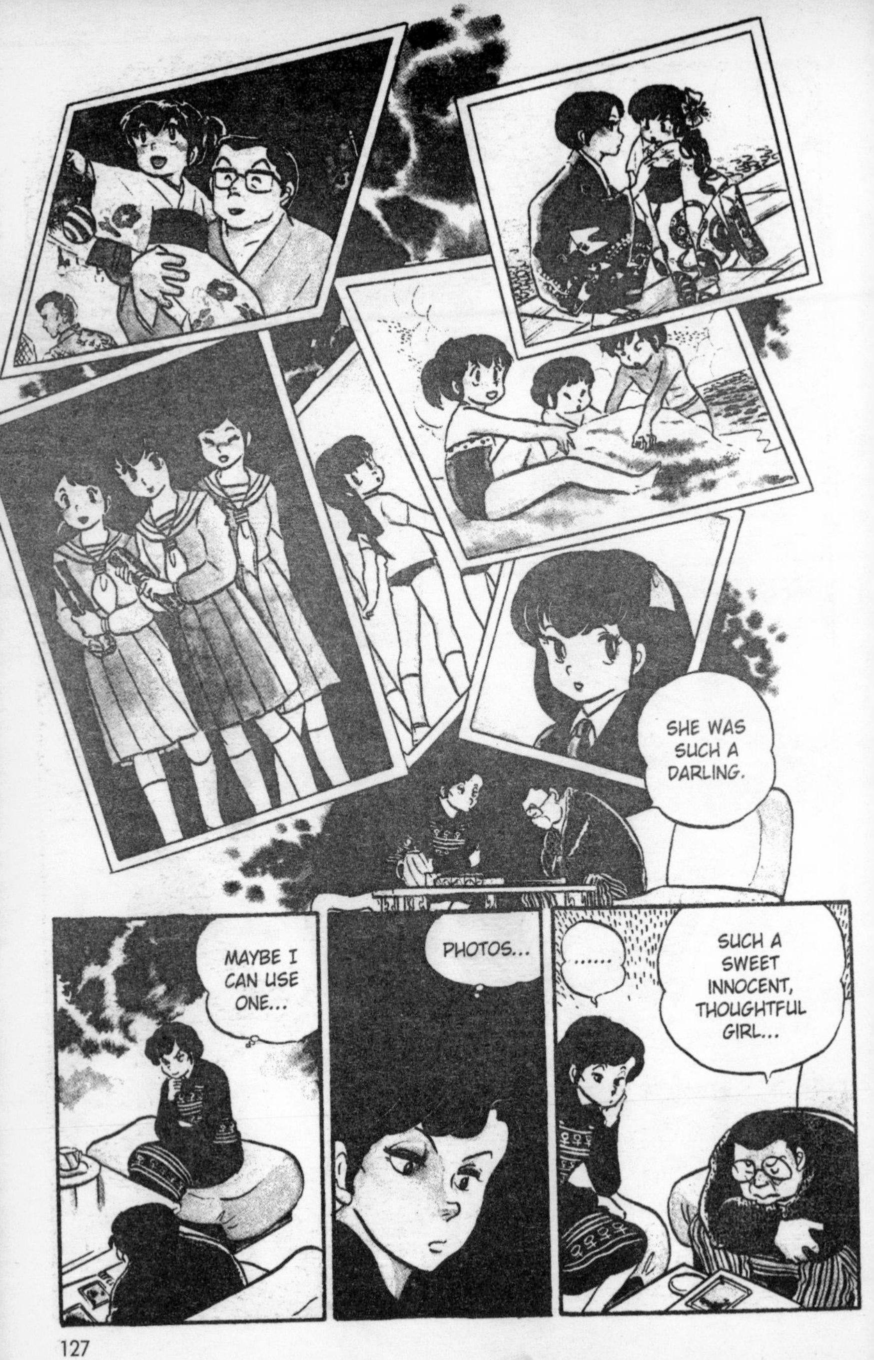
SHE WAS SUCH A DARLING.
SUCH A SWEET INNOCENT, THOUGHTFUL GIRL...
......
PHOTOS...
MAYBE I CAN USE ONE...

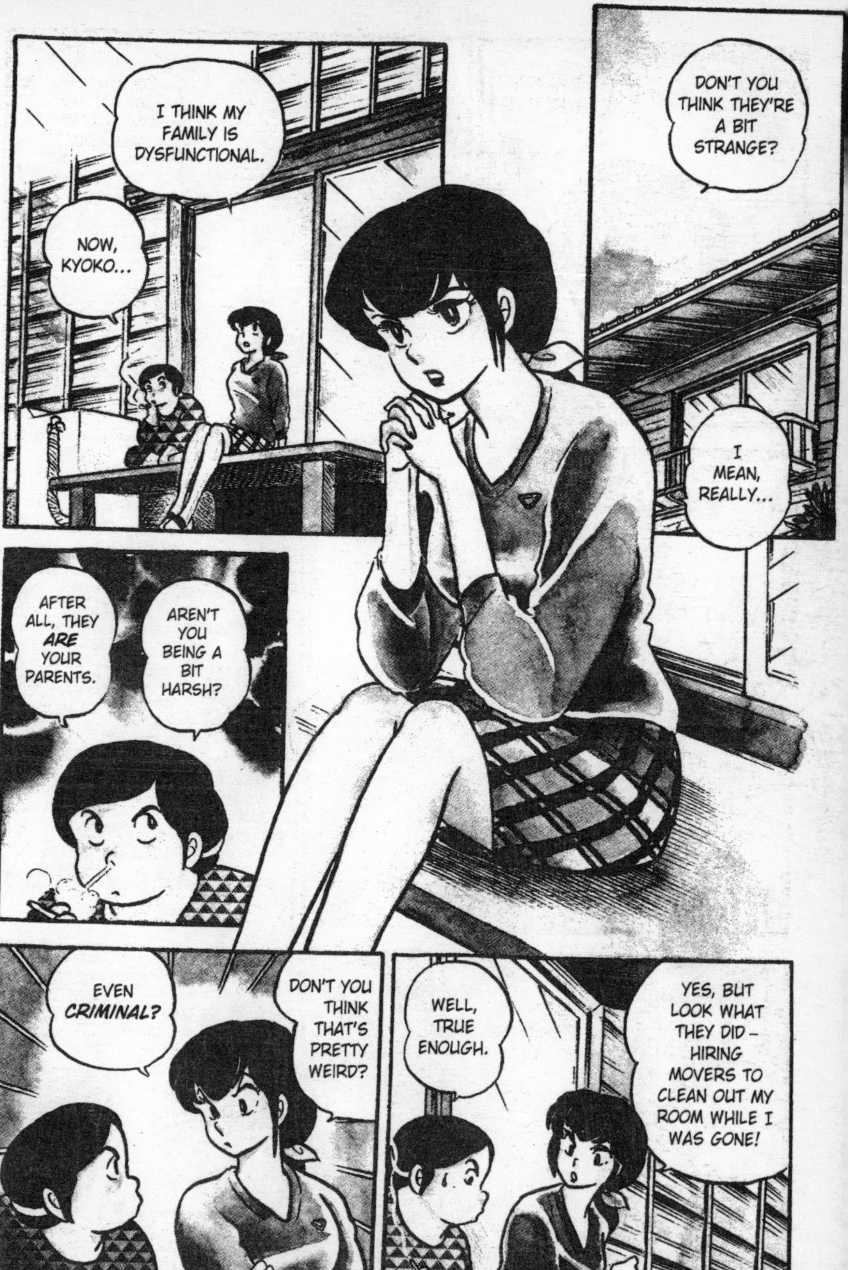
DON'T YOU THINK THEY'RE A BIT STRANGE?
I MEAN, REALLY...
I THINK MY FAMILY IS DYSFUNCTIONAL.
NOW, KYOKO...
AREN'T YOU BEING A BIT HARSH?
AFTER ALL, THEY *ARE* YOUR PARENTS.
YES, BUT LOOK WHAT THEY DID— HIRING MOVERS TO CLEAN OUT MY ROOM WHILE I WAS GONE!
WELL, TRUE ENOUGH.
DON'T YOU THINK THAT'S PRETTY WEIRD?
EVEN *CRIMINAL?*

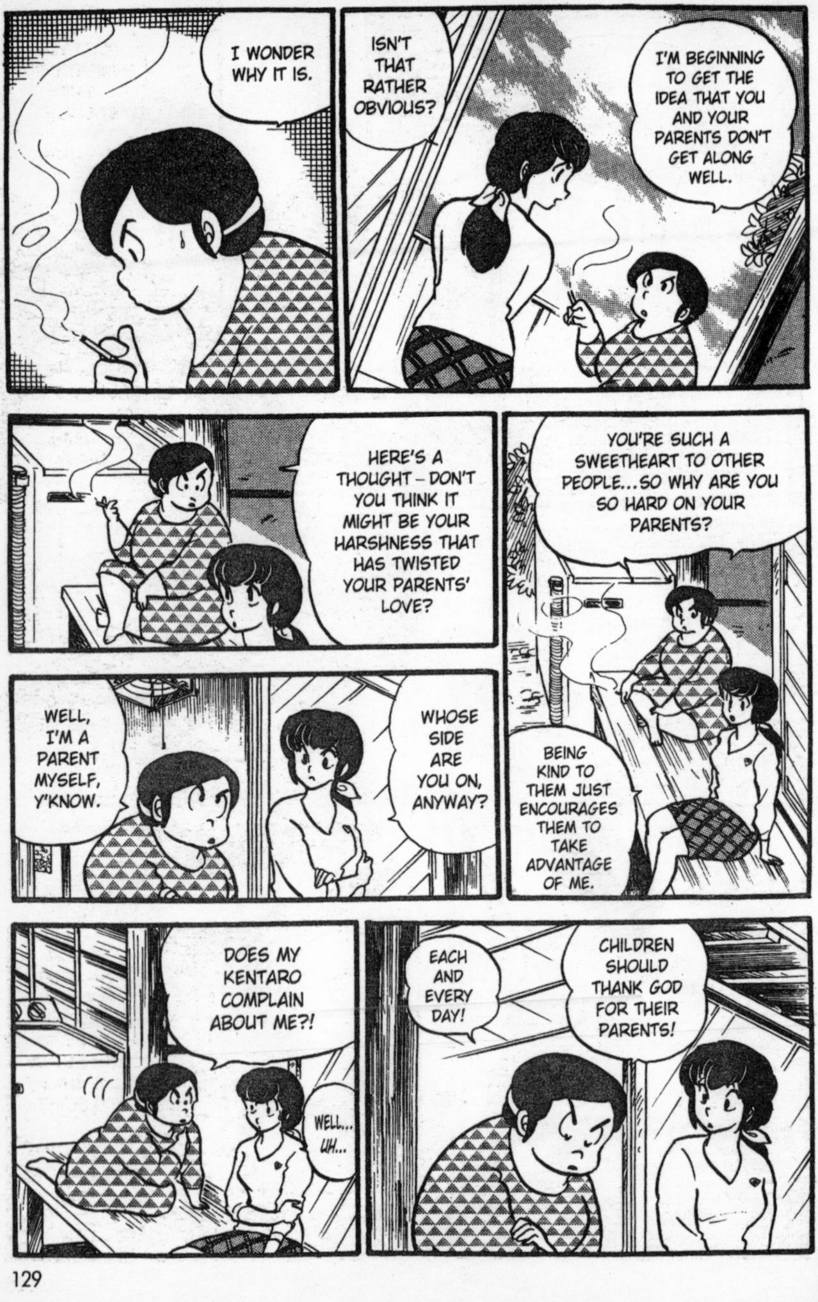

I'M BEGINNING TO GET THE IDEA THAT YOU AND YOUR PARENTS DON'T GET ALONG WELL.
ISN'T THAT RATHER OBVIOUS?
I WONDER WHY IT IS.
YOU'RE SUCH A SWEETHEART TO OTHER PEOPLE...SO WHY ARE YOU SO HARD ON YOUR PARENTS?
BEING KIND TO THEM JUST ENCOURAGES THEM TO TAKE ADVANTAGE OF ME.
HERE'S A THOUGHT – DON'T YOU THINK IT MIGHT BE YOUR HARSHNESS THAT HAS TWISTED YOUR PARENTS' LOVE?
WHOSE SIDE ARE YOU ON, ANYWAY?
WELL, I'M A PARENT MYSELF, Y'KNOW.
CHILDREN SHOULD THANK GOD FOR THEIR PARENTS!
EACH AND EVERY DAY!
DOES MY KENTARO COMPLAIN ABOUT ME?!
WELL... UH...

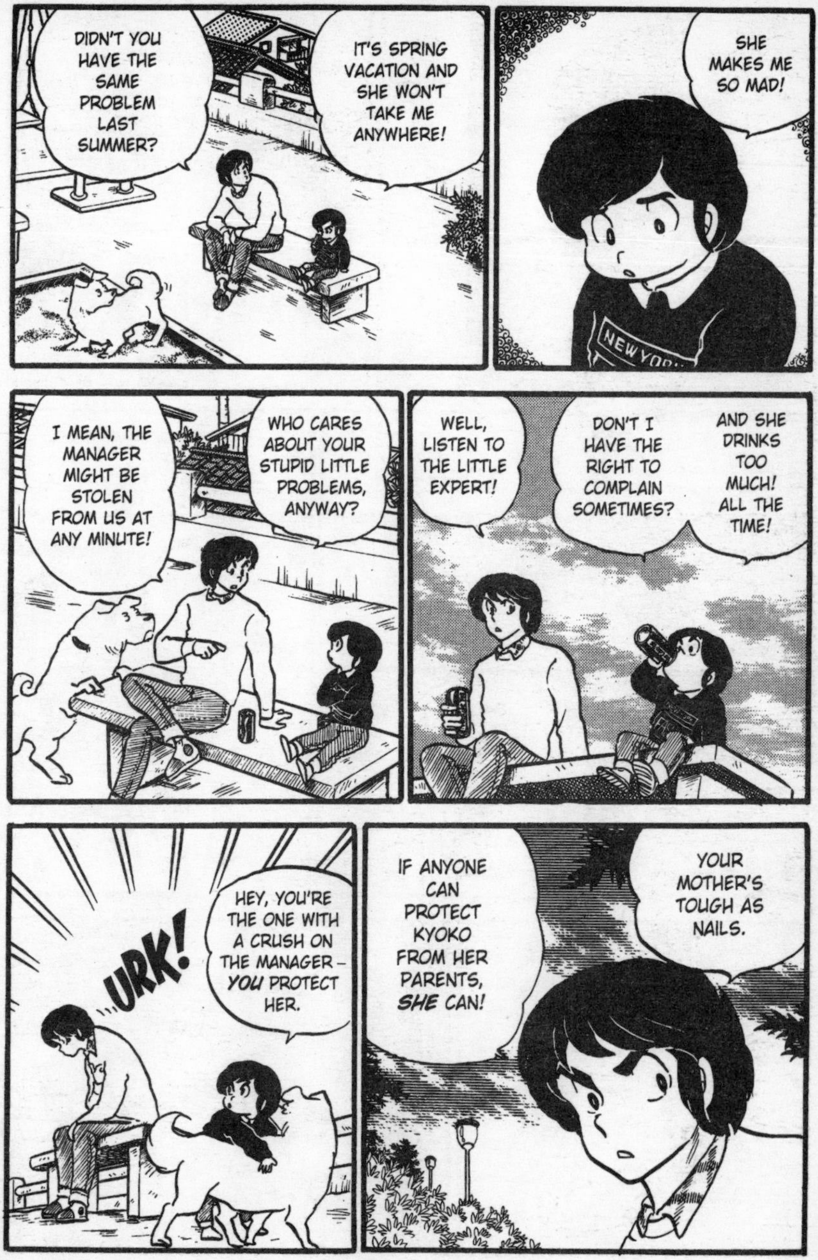
SHE MAKES ME SO MAD!
IT'S SPRING VACATION AND SHE WON'T TAKE ME ANYWHERE!
DIDN'T YOU HAVE THE SAME PROBLEM LAST SUMMER?
AND SHE DRINKS TOO MUCH! ALL THE TIME!
DON'T I HAVE THE RIGHT TO COMPLAIN SOMETIMES?
WELL, LISTEN TO THE LITTLE EXPERT!
WHO CARES ABOUT YOUR STUPID LITTLE PROBLEMS, ANYWAY?
I MEAN, THE MANAGER MIGHT BE STOLEN FROM US AT ANY MINUTE!
YOUR MOTHER'S TOUGH AS NAILS.
IF ANYONE CAN PROTECT KYOKO FROM HER PARENTS, *SHE* CAN!
HEY, YOU'RE THE ONE WITH A CRUSH ON THE MANAGER–*YOU* PROTECT HER.
URK!

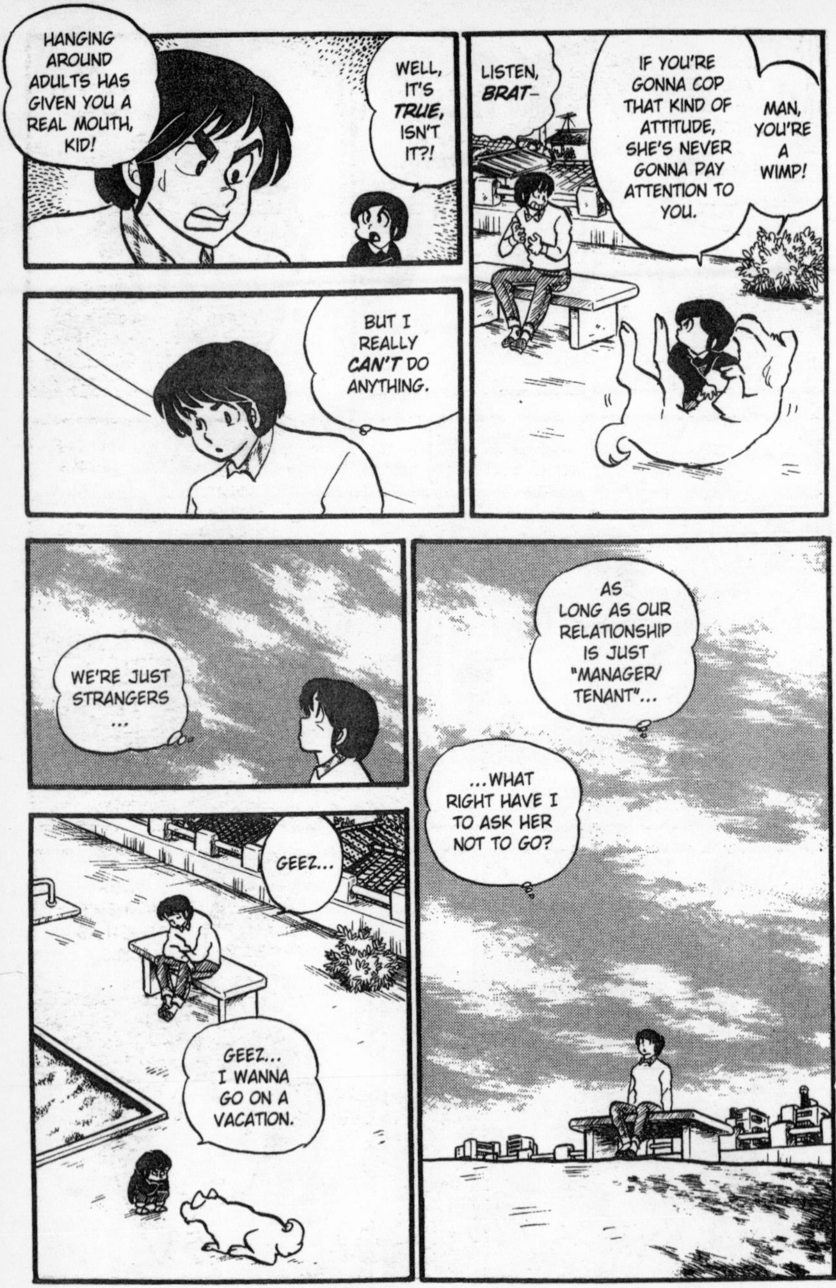
MAN, YOU'RE A WIMP!
IF YOU'RE GONNA COP THAT KIND OF ATTITUDE, SHE'S NEVER GONNA PAY ATTENTION TO YOU.
LISTEN, *BRAT*–
WELL, IT'S *TRUE*, ISN'T IT?!
HANGING AROUND ADULTS HAS GIVEN YOU A REAL MOUTH, KID!
BUT I REALLY *CAN'T* DO ANYTHING.
AS LONG AS OUR RELATIONSHIP IS JUST "MANAGER/TENANT"...
...WHAT RIGHT HAVE I TO ASK HER NOT TO GO?
WE'RE JUST STRANGERS ...
GEEZ...
GEEZ... I WANNA GO ON A VACATION.

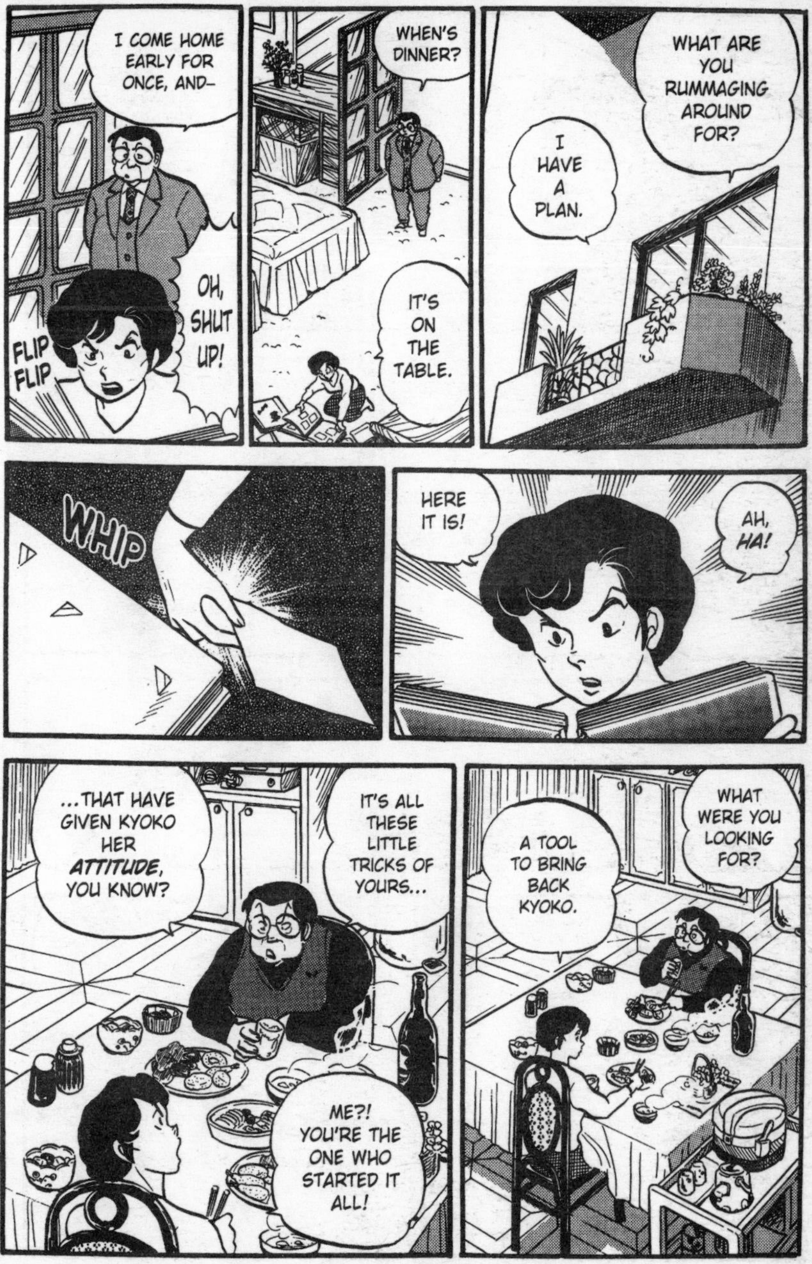

WHAT ARE YOU RUMMAGING AROUND FOR?
I HAVE A PLAN.
WHEN'S DINNER?
IT'S ON THE TABLE.
I COME HOME EARLY FOR ONCE, AND–
OH, SHUT UP!
FLIP FLIP
AH, HA!
HERE IT IS!
WHIP
WHAT WERE YOU LOOKING FOR?
A TOOL TO BRING BACK KYOKO.
IT'S ALL THESE LITTLE TRICKS OF YOURS...
...THAT HAVE GIVEN KYOKO HER *ATTITUDE*, YOU KNOW?
ME?! YOU'RE THE ONE WHO STARTED IT ALL!

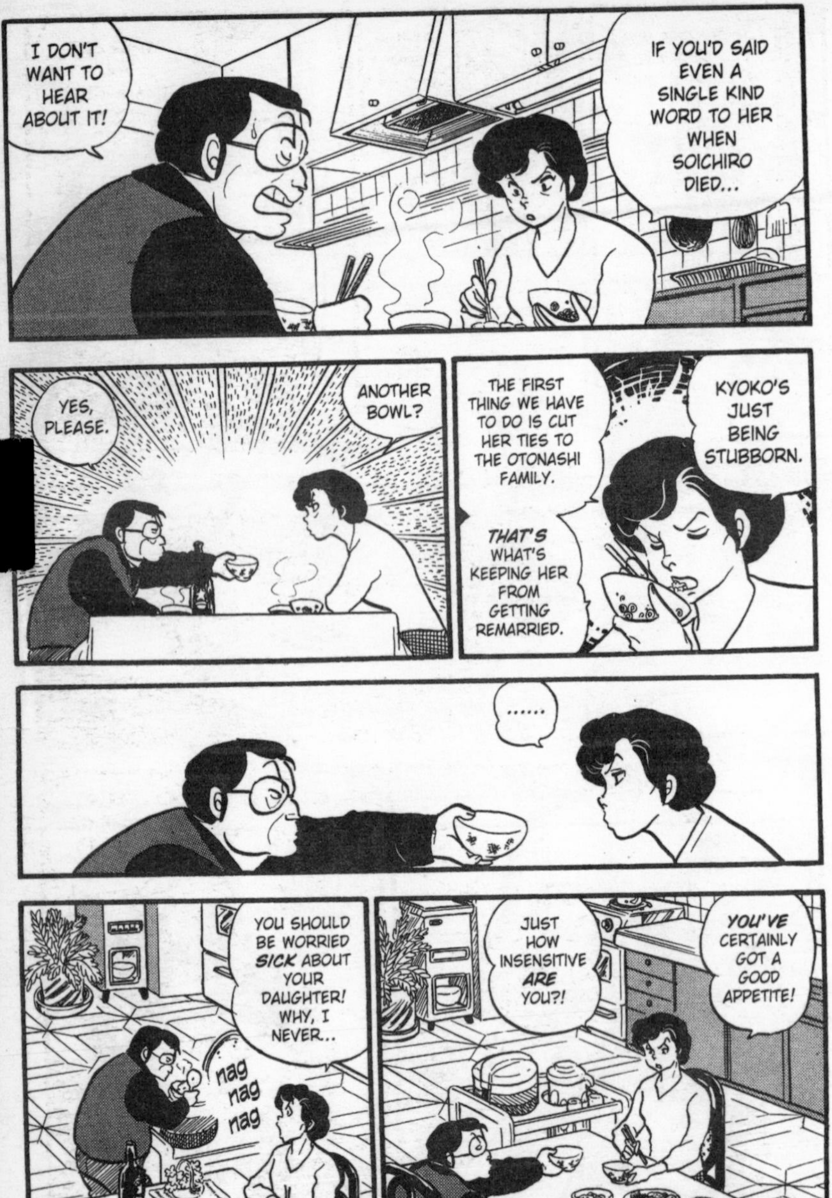
IF YOU'D SAID EVEN A SINGLE KIND WORD TO HER WHEN SOICHIRO DIED...
I DON'T WANT TO HEAR ABOUT IT!
KYOKO'S JUST BEING STUBBORN.
THE FIRST THING WE HAVE TO DO IS CUT HER TIES TO THE OTONASHI FAMILY.
THAT'S WHAT'S KEEPING HER FROM GETTING REMARRIED.
ANOTHER BOWL?
YES, PLEASE.
......
YOU'VE CERTAINLY GOT A GOOD APPETITE!
JUST HOW INSENSITIVE *ARE* YOU?!
YOU SHOULD BE WORRIED *SICK* ABOUT YOUR DAUGHTER! WHY, I NEVER...
nag nag nag

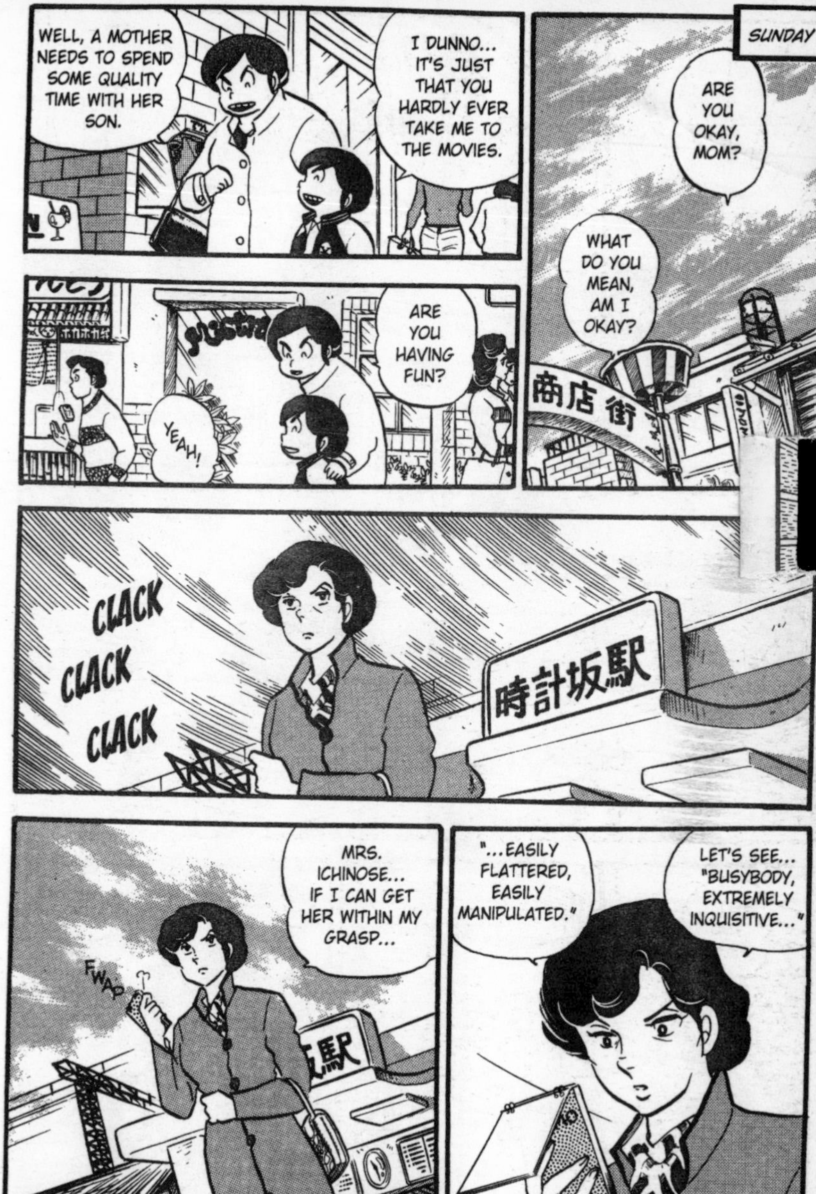
SUNDAY
ARE YOU OKAY, MOM?
WHAT DO YOU MEAN, AM I OKAY?
商店街
I DUNNO... IT'S JUST THAT YOU HARDLY EVER TAKE ME TO THE MOVIES.
WELL, A MOTHER NEEDS TO SPEND SOME QUALITY TIME WITH HER SON.
ARE YOU HAVING FUN?
YEAH!
CLACK
CLACK
CLACK
時計坂駅
LET'S SEE... "BUSYBODY, EXTREMELY INQUISITIVE..."
"...EASILY FLATTERED, EASILY MANIPULATED."
MRS. ICHINOSE... IF I CAN GET HER WITHIN MY GRASP...
FWAP

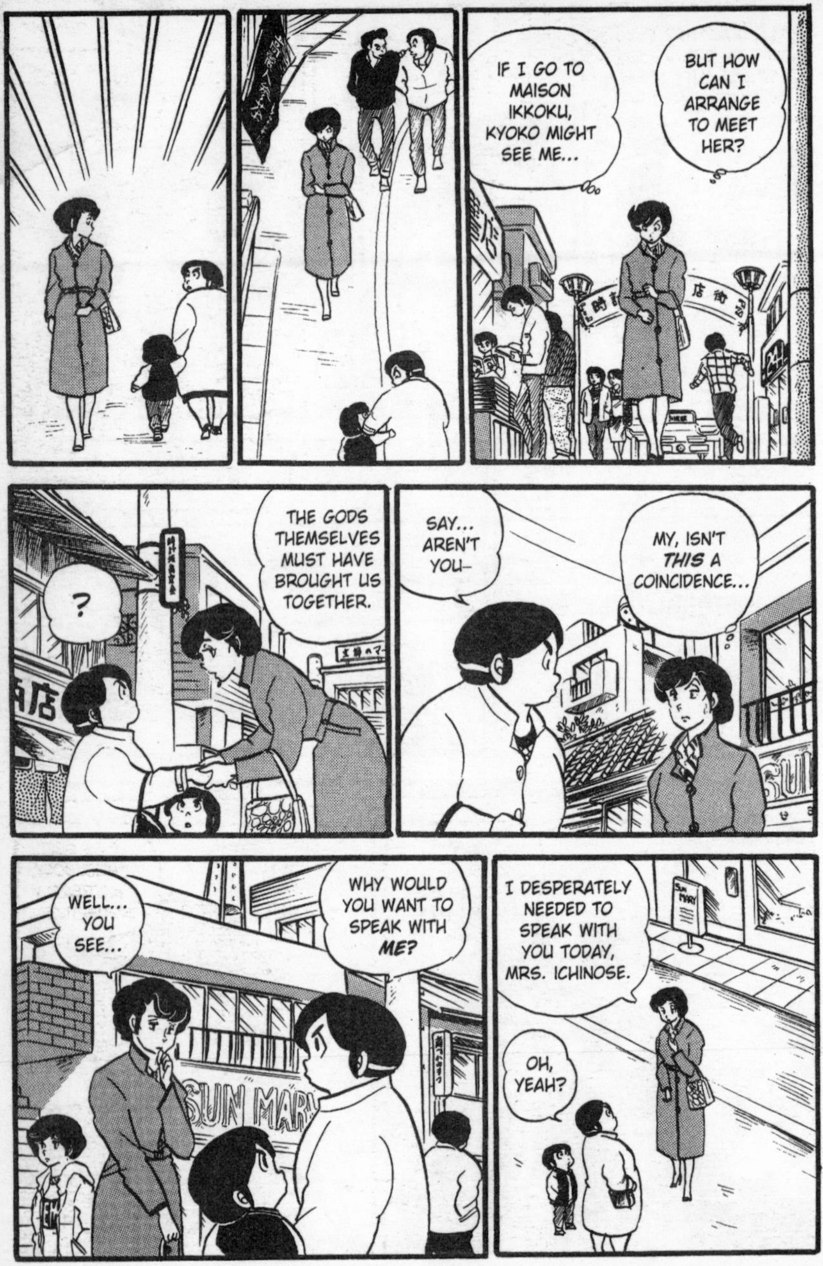
BUT HOW CAN I ARRANGE TO MEET HER?
IF I GO TO MAISON IKKOKU, KYOKO MIGHT SEE ME...
MY, ISN'T *THIS* A COINCIDENCE...
SAY... AREN'T YOU–
THE GODS THEMSELVES MUST HAVE BROUGHT US TOGETHER.
?
I DESPERATELY NEEDED TO SPEAK WITH YOU TODAY, MRS. ICHINOSE.
OH, YEAH?
WHY WOULD YOU WANT TO SPEAK WITH *ME?*
WELL... YOU SEE...

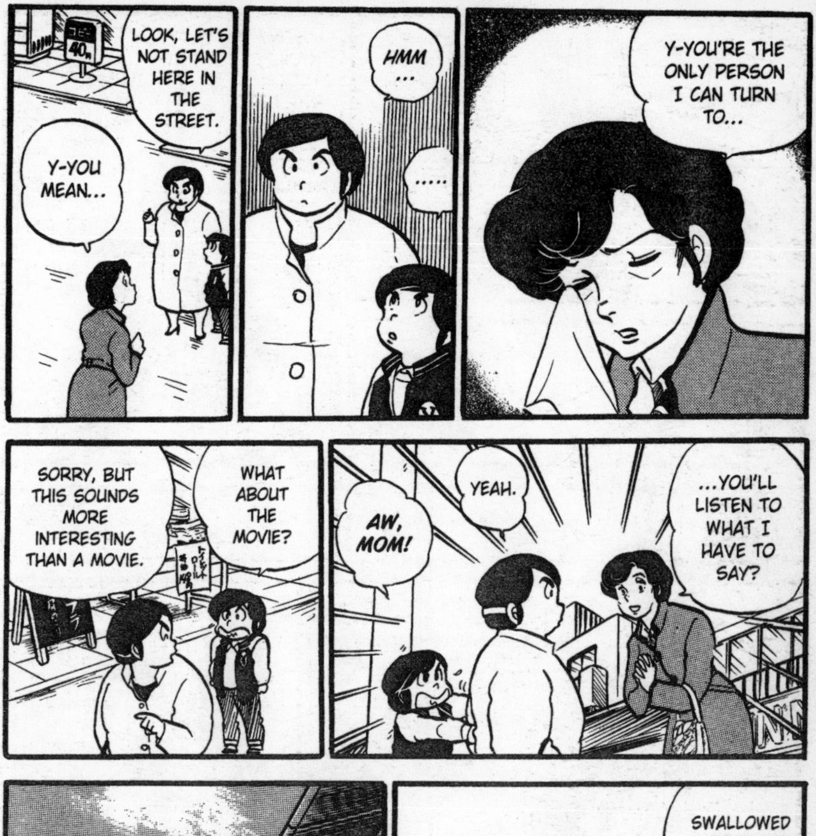
Y-YOU'RE THE ONLY PERSON I CAN TURN TO...
HMM...
.....
LOOK, LET'S NOT STAND HERE IN THE STREET.
Y-YOU MEAN...
...YOU'LL LISTEN TO WHAT I HAVE TO SAY?
YEAH.
AW, MOM!
WHAT ABOUT THE MOVIE?
SORRY, BUT THIS SOUNDS MORE INTERESTING THAN A MOVIE.
SWALLOWED HOOK, LINE, AND SINKER.
OH, DON'T COMPLAIN. I'LL BUY YOU SOMETHING YUMMY TO EAT INSTEAD.
YOU KEEP TREATING ME LIKE THIS AND I'M GOING TO JOIN A GANG!
NO KIDDING? MRS. ICHINOSE TOOK KENTARO TO A MOVIE?

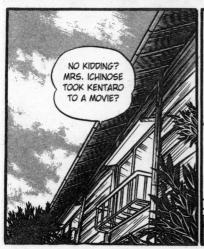

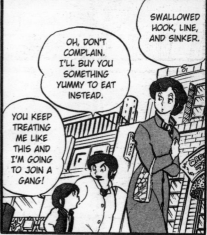

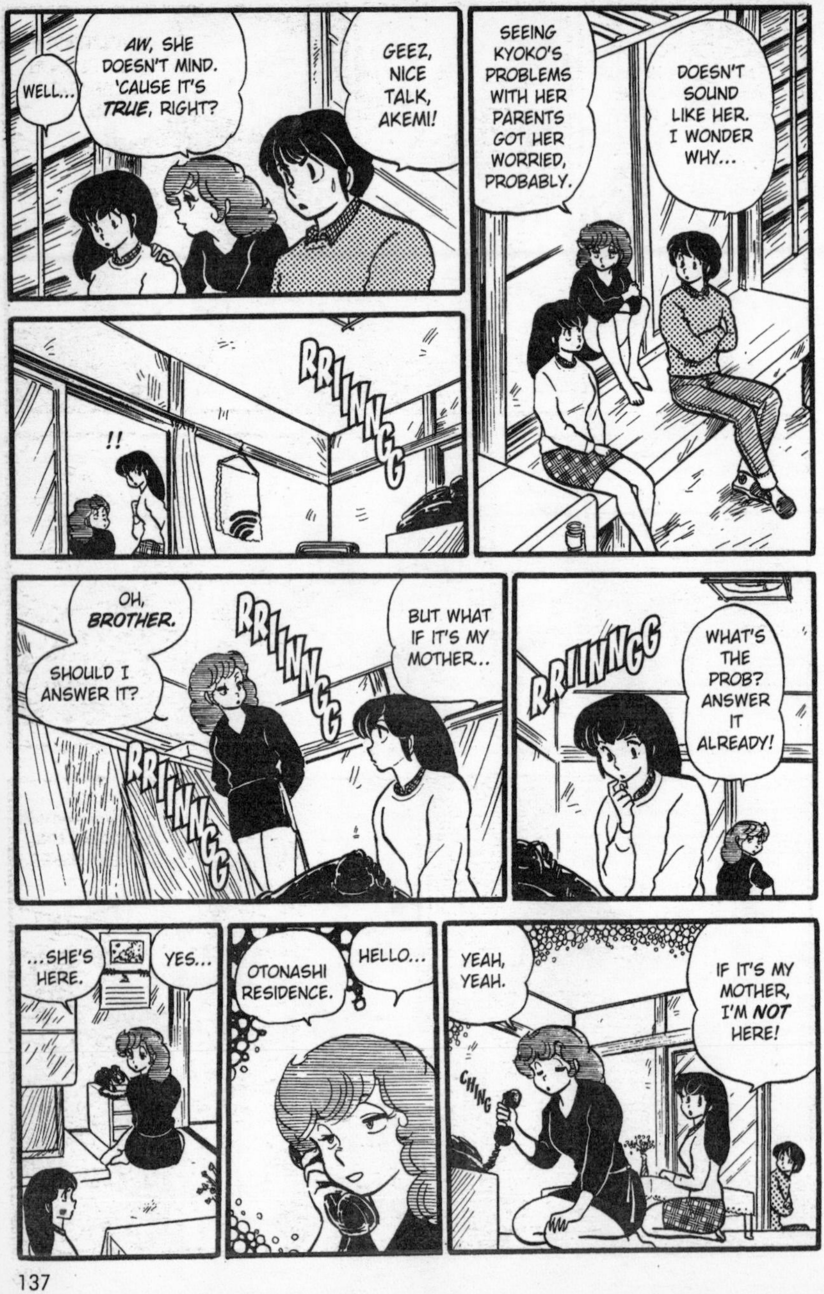
DOESN'T SOUND LIKE HER. I WONDER WHY...
SEEING KYOKO'S PROBLEMS WITH HER PARENTS GOT HER WORRIED, PROBABLY.
GEEZ, NICE TALK, AKEMI!
AW, SHE DOESN'T MIND. 'CAUSE IT'S TRUE, RIGHT?
WELL...
RRIINNGG
!!
WHAT'S THE PROB? ANSWER IT ALREADY!
RRIINNGG
BUT WHAT IF IT'S MY MOTHER...
RRIINNGG
OH, BROTHER.
SHOULD I ANSWER IT?
RRIINNGG
IF IT'S MY MOTHER, I'M NOT HERE!
YEAH, YEAH.
CHING
HELLO...
OTONASHI RESIDENCE.
YES...
...SHE'S HERE.

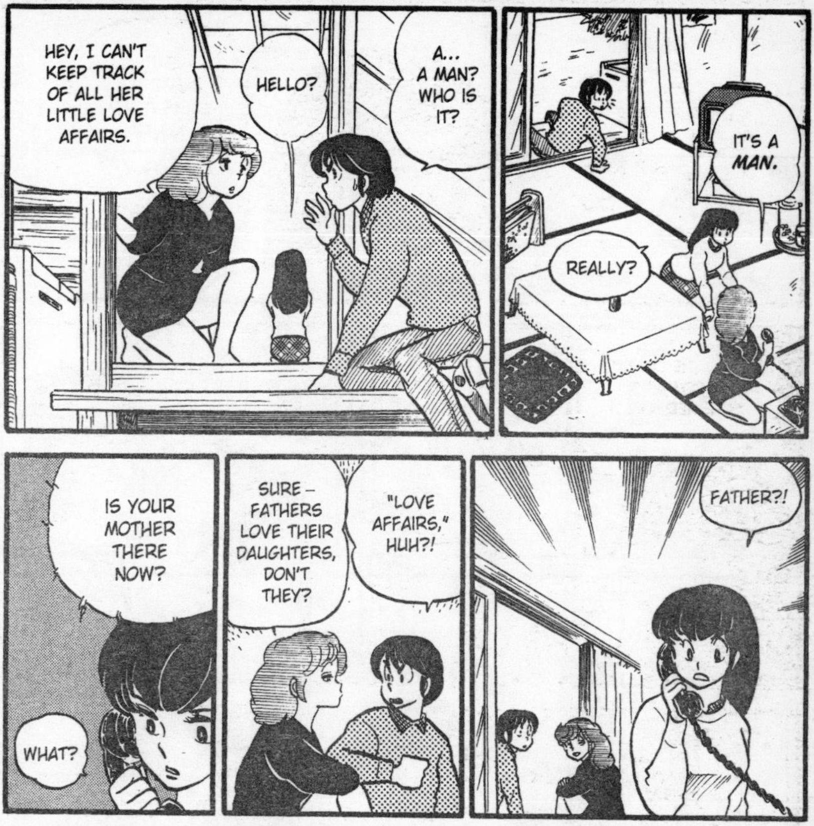
IT'S A *MAN.*
REALLY?
A... A MAN? WHO IS IT?
HELLO?
HEY, I CAN'T KEEP TRACK OF ALL HER LITTLE LOVE AFFAIRS.
FATHER?!
"LOVE AFFAIRS," HUH?!
SURE – FATHERS LOVE THEIR DAUGHTERS, DON'T THEY?
IS YOUR MOTHER THERE NOW?
WHAT?
NO, SHE'S NOT.
WHY DO YOU ASK?
WELL, IT'S JUST THAT...
...I REALLY WANT TO TALK WITH YOU ALONE.
UM...
THINGS ALWAYS GET MIXED UP WHEN YOUR MOTHER IS THERE.

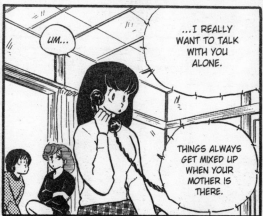

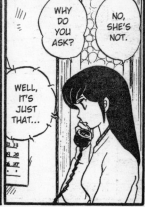

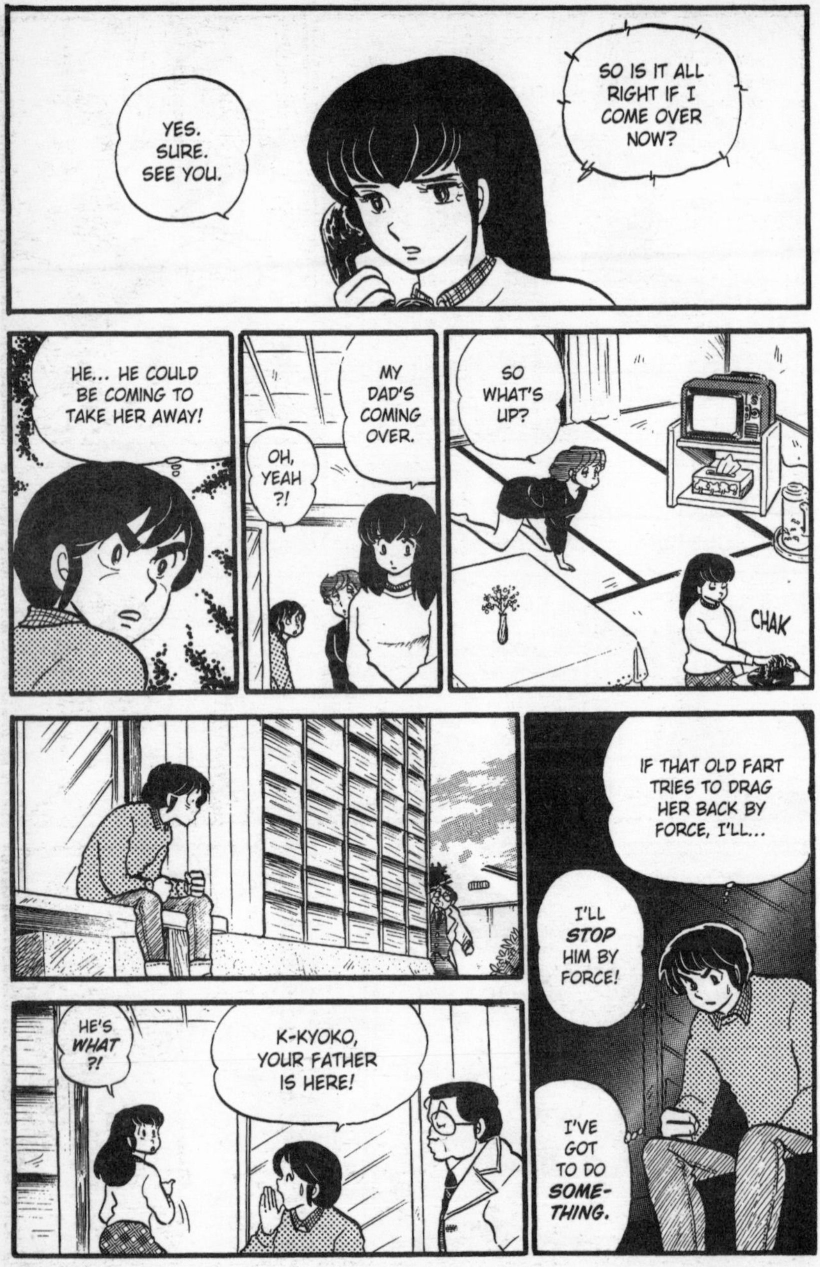
SO IS IT ALL RIGHT IF I COME OVER NOW?
YES. SURE. SEE YOU.
SO WHAT'S UP?
CHAK
MY DAD'S COMING OVER.
OH, YEAH ?!
HE... HE COULD BE COMING TO TAKE HER AWAY!
IF THAT OLD FART TRIES TO DRAG HER BACK BY FORCE, I'LL...
I'LL *STOP* HIM BY FORCE!
I'VE GOT TO DO *SOME-THING.*
K-KYOKO, YOUR FATHER IS HERE!
HE'S *WHAT* ?!

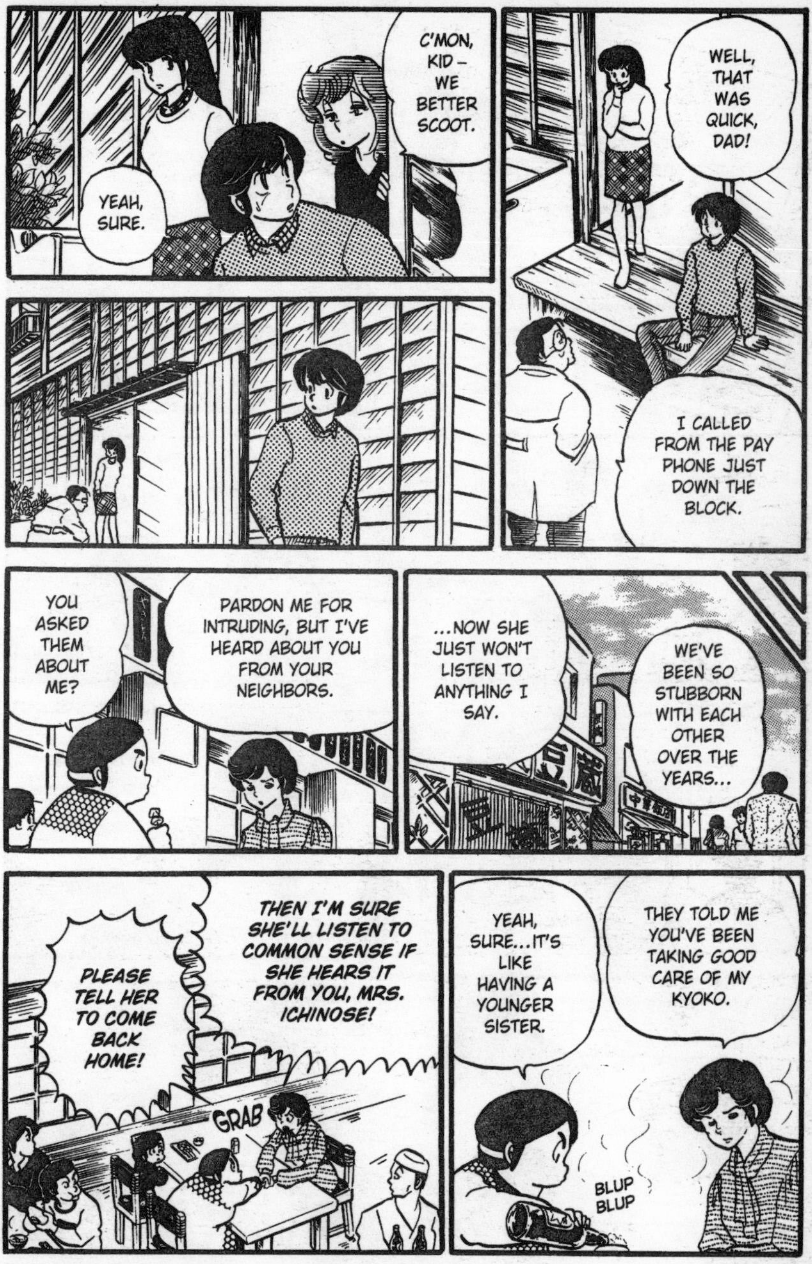
WELL, THAT WAS QUICK, DAD!
I CALLED FROM THE PAY PHONE JUST DOWN THE BLOCK.
C'MON, KID – WE BETTER SCOOT.
YEAH, SURE.
WE'VE BEEN SO STUBBORN WITH EACH OTHER OVER THE YEARS...
...NOW SHE JUST WON'T LISTEN TO ANYTHING I SAY.
PARDON ME FOR INTRUDING, BUT I'VE HEARD ABOUT YOU FROM YOUR NEIGHBORS.
YOU ASKED THEM ABOUT ME?
THEY TOLD ME YOU'VE BEEN TAKING GOOD CARE OF MY KYOKO.
YEAH, SURE...IT'S LIKE HAVING A YOUNGER SISTER.
BLUP BLUP
THEN I'M SURE SHE'LL LISTEN TO COMMON SENSE IF SHE HEARS IT FROM YOU, MRS. ICHINOSE!
PLEASE TELL HER TO COME BACK HOME!
GRAB

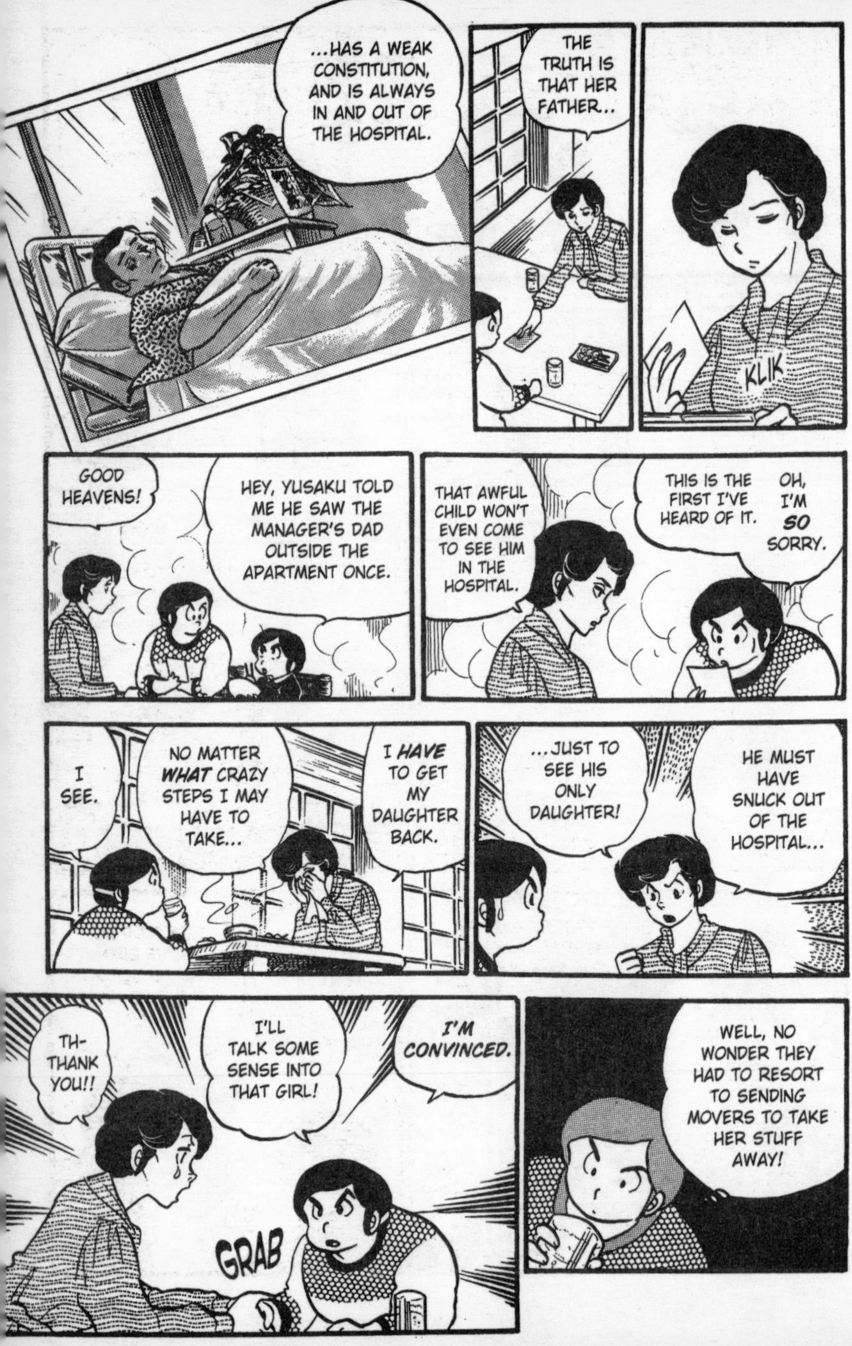
KLIK
THE TRUTH IS THAT HER FATHER...
...HAS A WEAK CONSTITUTION, AND IS ALWAYS IN AND OUT OF THE HOSPITAL.
OH, I'M SO SORRY.
THIS IS THE FIRST I'VE HEARD OF IT.
THAT AWFUL CHILD WON'T EVEN COME TO SEE HIM IN THE HOSPITAL.
HEY, YUSAKU TOLD ME HE SAW THE MANAGER'S DAD OUTSIDE THE APARTMENT ONCE.
GOOD HEAVENS!
HE MUST HAVE SNUCK OUT OF THE HOSPITAL...
...JUST TO SEE HIS ONLY DAUGHTER!
I HAVE TO GET MY DAUGHTER BACK.
NO MATTER WHAT CRAZY STEPS I MAY HAVE TO TAKE...
I SEE.
WELL, NO WONDER THEY HAD TO RESORT TO SENDING MOVERS TO TAKE HER STUFF AWAY!
I'M CONVINCED.
I'LL TALK SOME SENSE INTO THAT GIRL!
GRAB
TH-THANK YOU!!

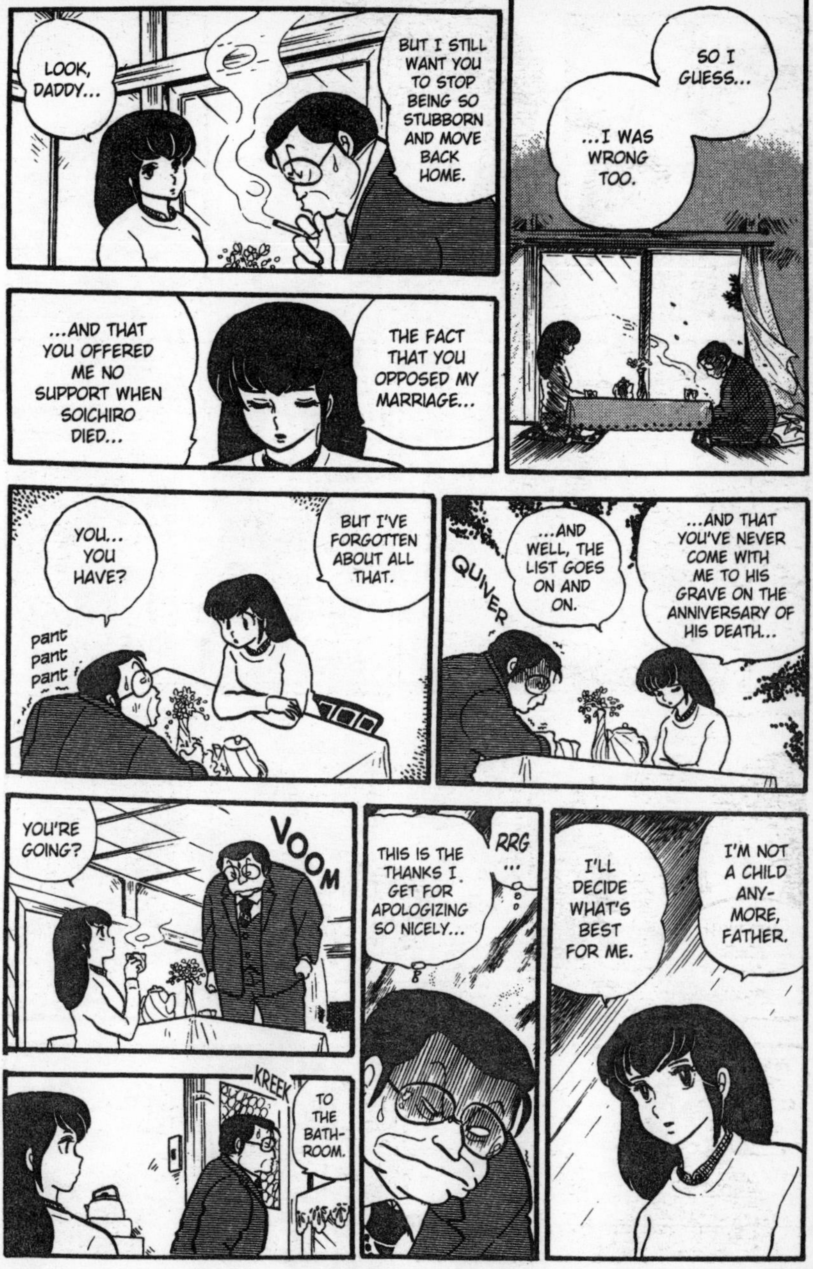
SO I GUESS...
...I WAS WRONG TOO.
BUT I STILL WANT YOU TO STOP BEING SO STUBBORN AND MOVE BACK HOME.
LOOK, DADDY...
THE FACT THAT YOU OPPOSED MY MARRIAGE...
...AND THAT YOU OFFERED ME NO SUPPORT WHEN SOICHIRO DIED...
...AND THAT YOU'VE NEVER COME WITH ME TO HIS GRAVE ON THE ANNIVERSARY OF HIS DEATH...
...AND WELL, THE LIST GOES ON AND ON.
QUIVER
BUT I'VE FORGOTTEN ABOUT ALL THAT.
YOU... YOU HAVE?
pant pant pant
I'M NOT A CHILD ANY-MORE, FATHER.
I'LL DECIDE WHAT'S BEST FOR ME.
RRG...
THIS IS THE THANKS I GET FOR APOLOGIZING SO NICELY...
VOOM
YOU'RE GOING?
KREEK
TO THE BATH-ROOM.

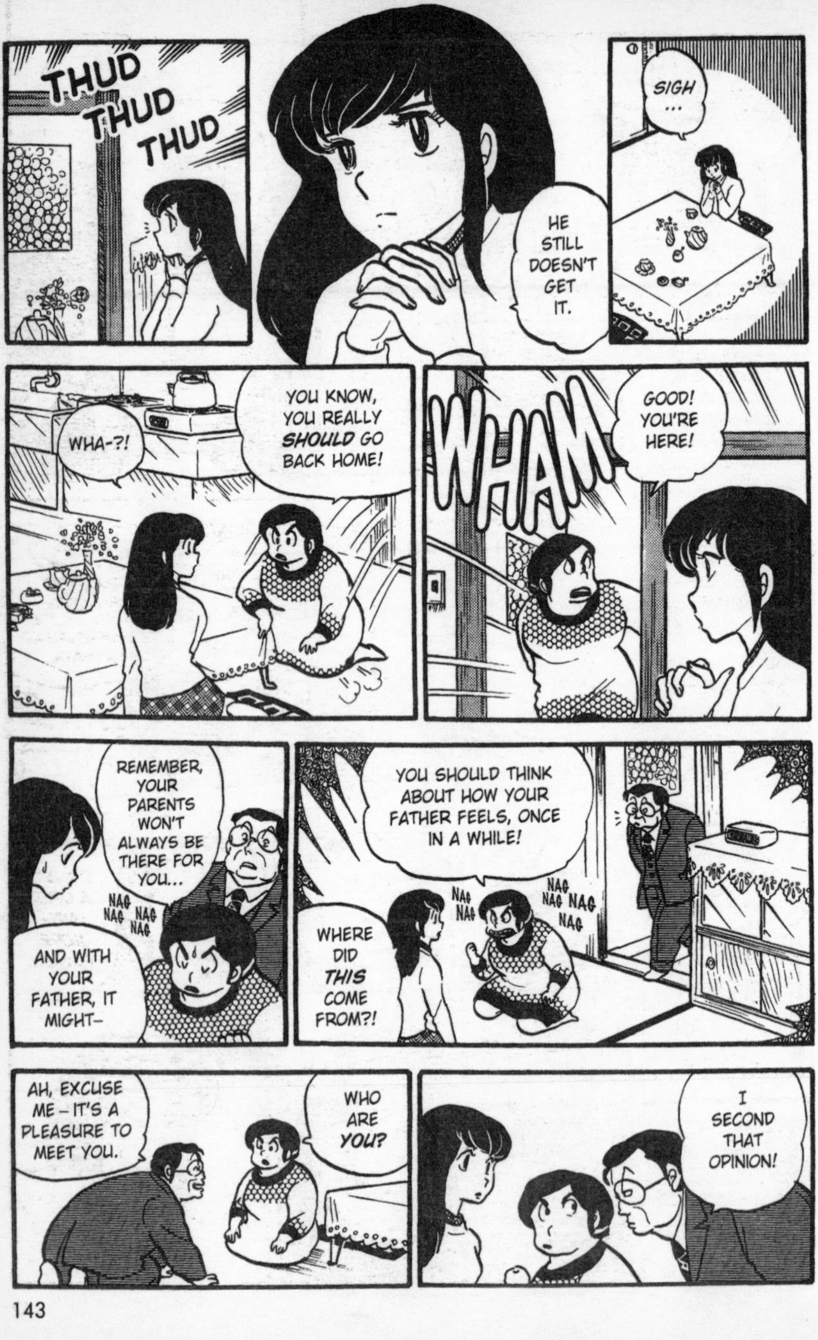
SIGH ...
HE STILL DOESN'T GET IT.
THUD THUD THUD
GOOD! YOU'RE HERE!
WHAM
YOU KNOW, YOU REALLY SHOULD GO BACK HOME!
WHA-?!
YOU SHOULD THINK ABOUT HOW YOUR FATHER FEELS, ONCE IN A WHILE!
NAG NAG NAG NAG
NAG NAG
WHERE DID THIS COME FROM?!
REMEMBER, YOUR PARENTS WON'T ALWAYS BE THERE FOR YOU...
NAG NAG NAG NAG
AND WITH YOUR FATHER, IT MIGHT–
I SECOND THAT OPINION!
WHO ARE YOU?
AH, EXCUSE ME – IT'S A PLEASURE TO MEET YOU.

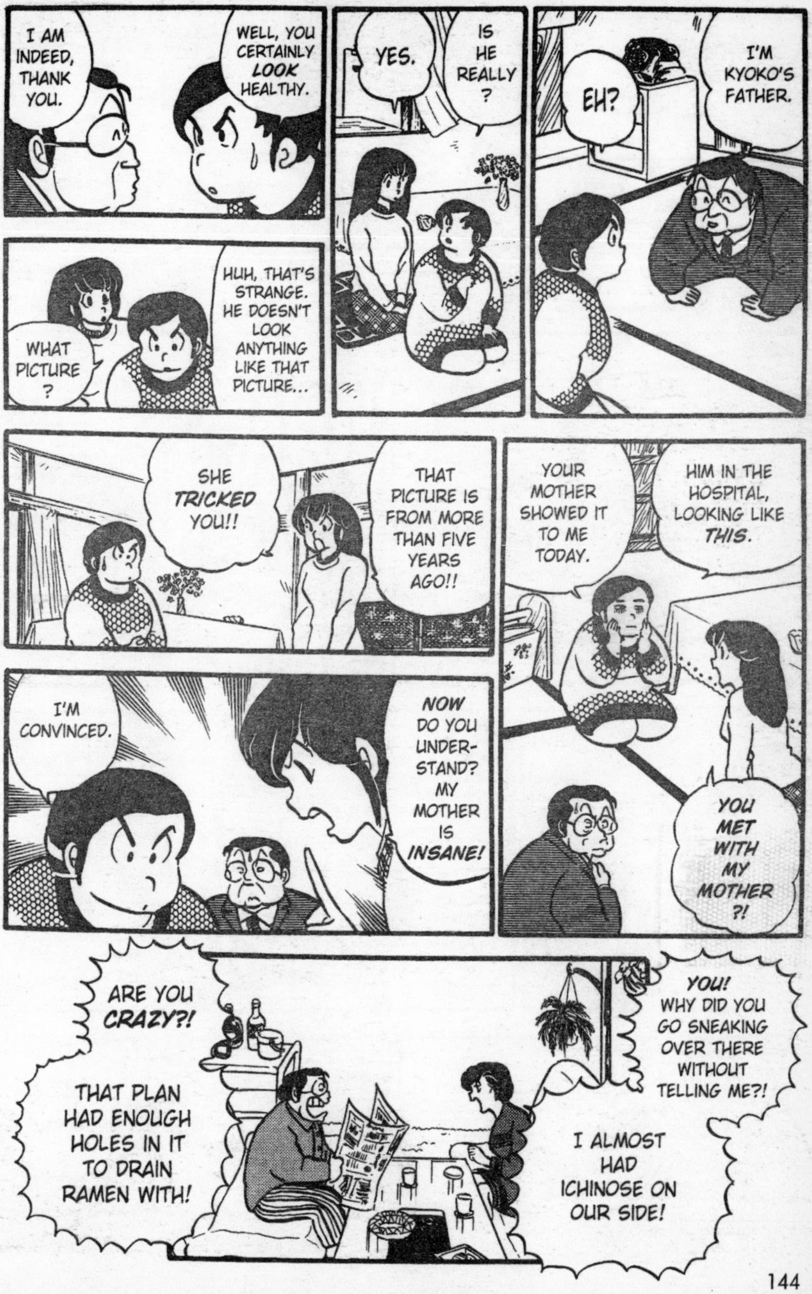
I'M KYOKO'S FATHER.
EH?
IS HE REALLY?
YES.
WELL, YOU CERTAINLY LOOK HEALTHY.
I AM INDEED, THANK YOU.
HUH, THAT'S STRANGE. HE DOESN'T LOOK ANYTHING LIKE THAT PICTURE...
WHAT PICTURE?
HIM IN THE HOSPITAL, LOOKING LIKE THIS.
YOUR MOTHER SHOWED IT TO ME TODAY.
YOU MET WITH MY MOTHER?!
THAT PICTURE IS FROM MORE THAN FIVE YEARS AGO!!
SHE TRICKED YOU!!
NOW DO YOU UNDERSTAND? MY MOTHER IS INSANE!
I'M CONVINCED.
YOU! WHY DID YOU GO SNEAKING OVER THERE WITHOUT TELLING ME?!
I ALMOST HAD ICHINOSE ON OUR SIDE!
ARE YOU CRAZY?!
THAT PLAN HAD ENOUGH HOLES IN IT TO DRAIN RAMEN WITH!

PART EIGHT

I'LL NEVER GIVE UP!

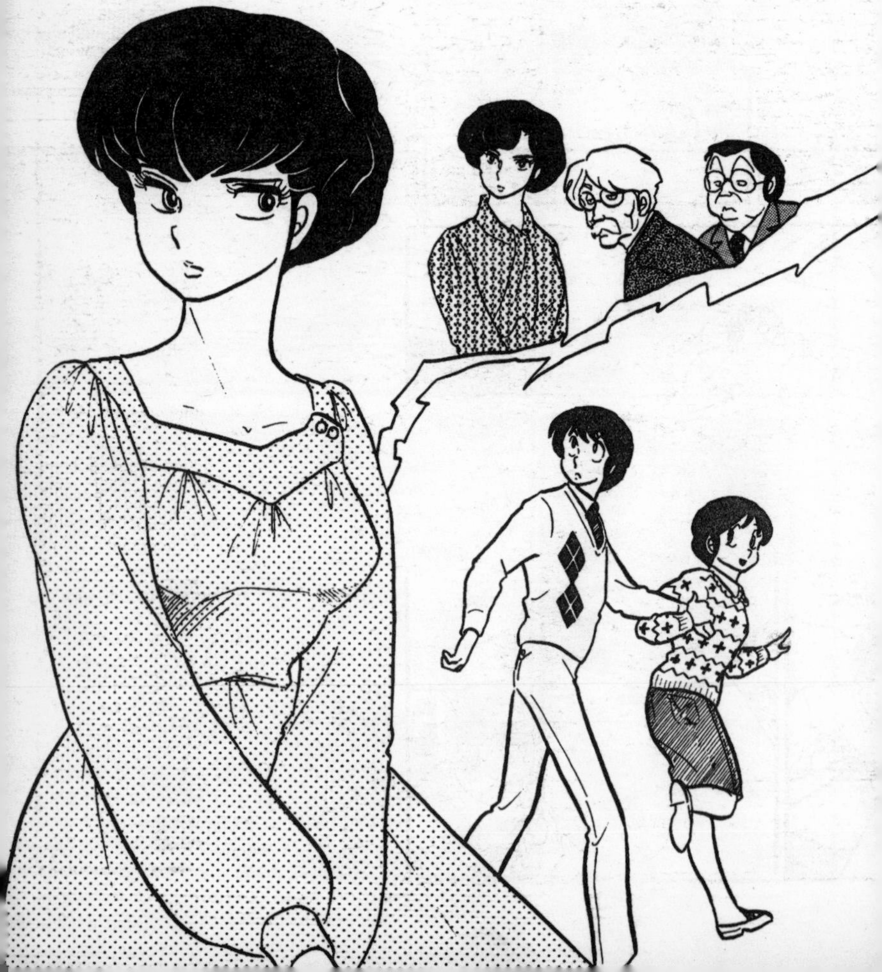

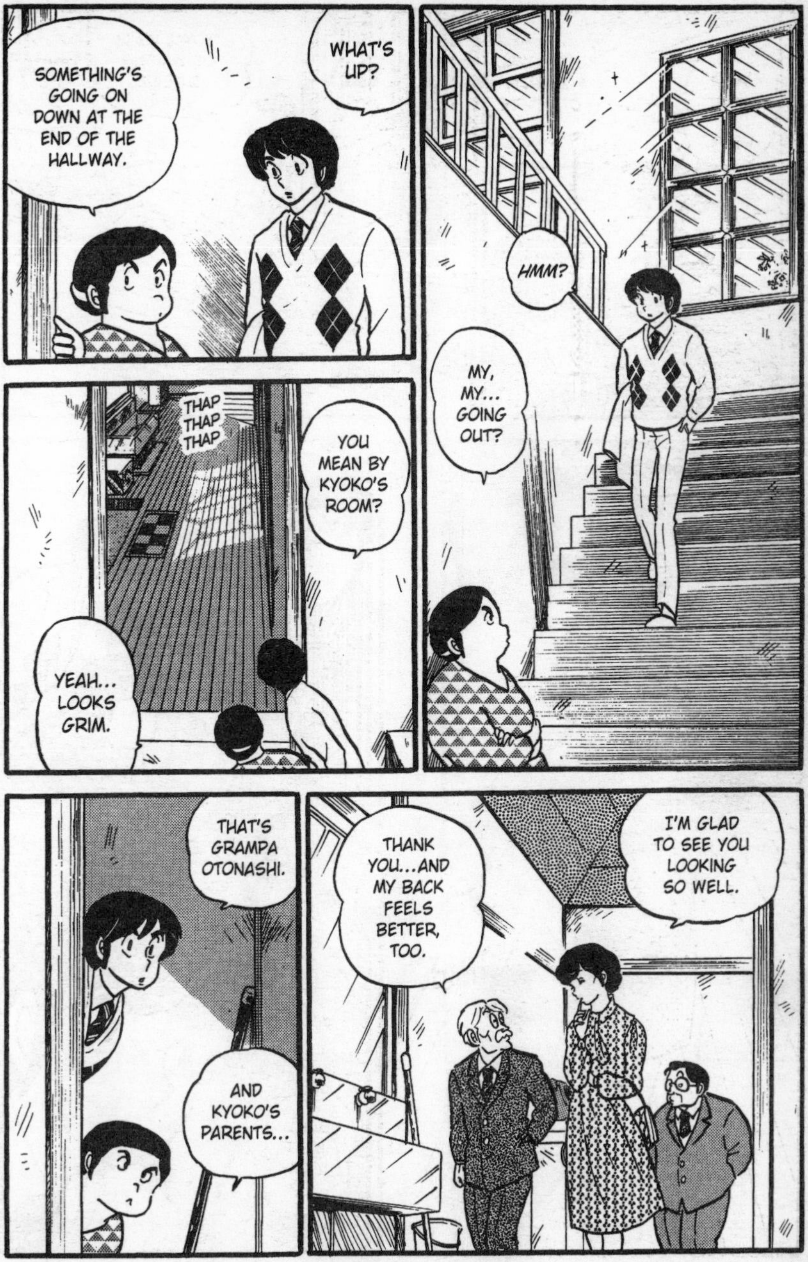
HMM?
MY, MY... GOING OUT?
WHAT'S UP?
SOMETHING'S GOING ON DOWN AT THE END OF THE HALLWAY.
YOU MEAN BY KYOKO'S ROOM?
THAP THAP THAP
YEAH... LOOKS GRIM.
I'M GLAD TO SEE YOU LOOKING SO WELL.
THANK YOU...AND MY BACK FEELS BETTER, TOO.
THAT'S GRAMPA OTONASHI.
AND KYOKO'S PARENTS...

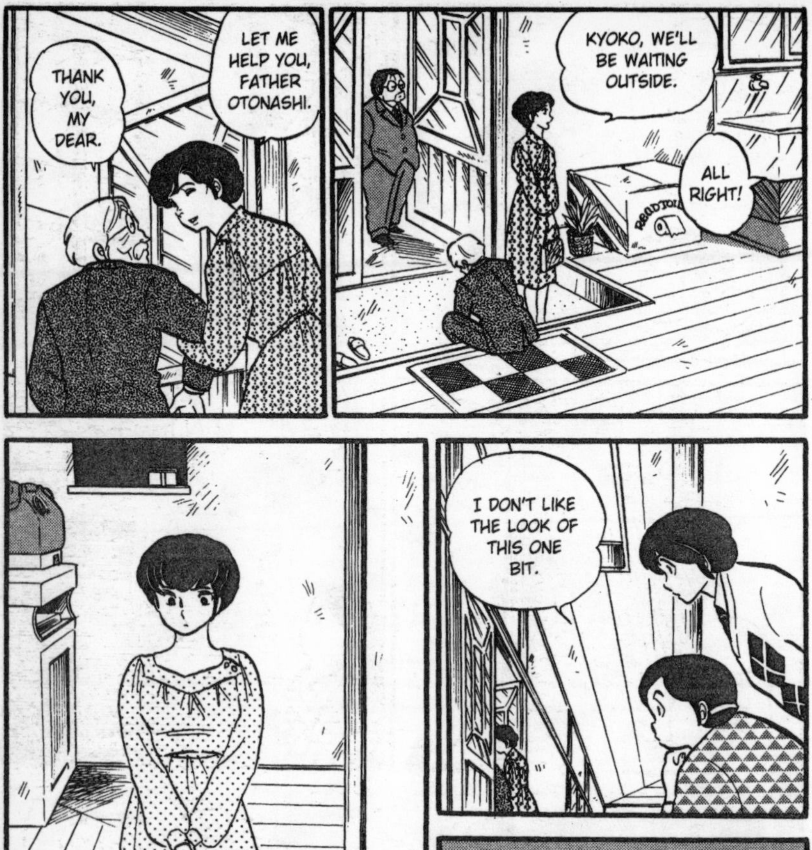
KYOKO, WE'LL BE WAITING OUTSIDE.
ALL RIGHT!
LET ME HELP YOU, FATHER OTONASHI.
THANK YOU, MY DEAR.
I DON'T LIKE THE LOOK OF THIS ONE BIT.
ME, EITHER!
SAY... ISN'T TODAY ...?
THAP
THAP
THAP

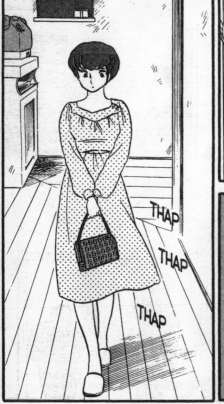

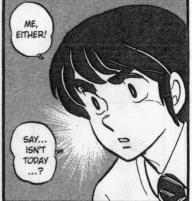

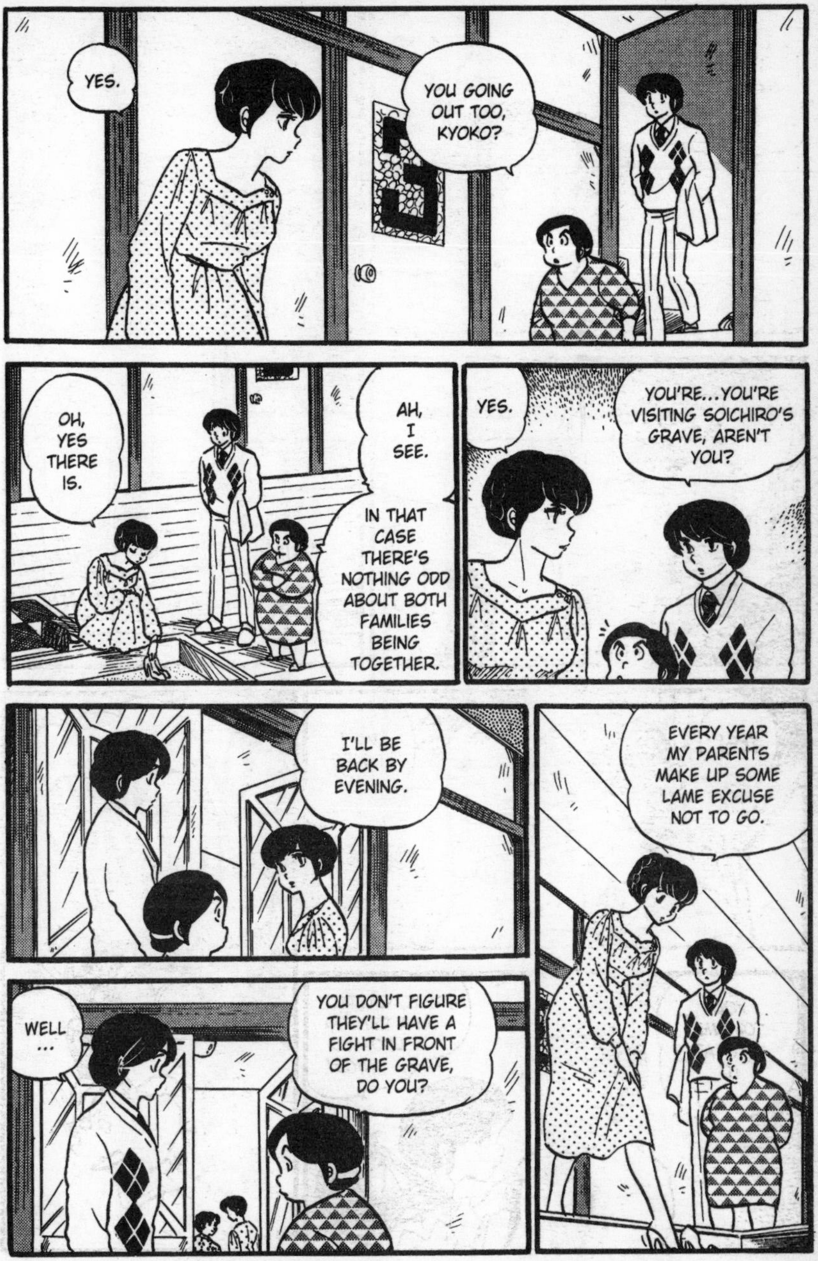
YOU GOING OUT TOO, KYOKO?
YES.
YOU'RE...YOU'RE VISITING SOICHIRO'S GRAVE, AREN'T YOU?
YES.
AH, I SEE.
IN THAT CASE THERE'S NOTHING ODD ABOUT BOTH FAMILIES BEING TOGETHER.
OH, YES THERE IS.
EVERY YEAR MY PARENTS MAKE UP SOME LAME EXCUSE NOT TO GO.
I'LL BE BACK BY EVENING.
YOU DON'T FIGURE THEY'LL HAVE A FIGHT IN FRONT OF THE GRAVE, DO YOU?
WELL ...

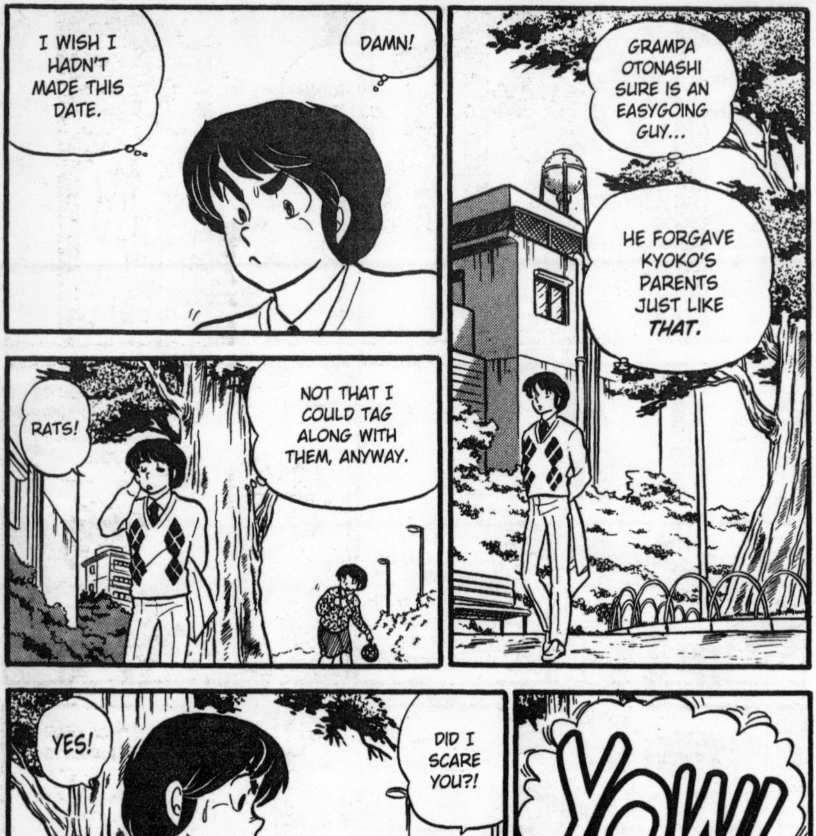
GRAMPA OTONASHI SURE IS AN EASYGOING GUY...
HE FORGAVE KYOKO'S PARENTS JUST LIKE *THAT.*
DAMN!
I WISH I HADN'T MADE THIS DATE.
NOT THAT I COULD TAG ALONG WITH THEM, ANYWAY.
RATS!
YOW!
DID I SCARE YOU?!
YES!
GREAT, YOU PUT ON A TIE! YOU LOOK SO *NICE!*
YOU TOLD ME TO WEAR IT!

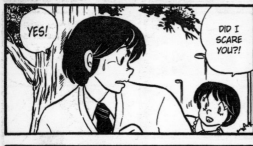

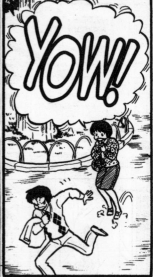

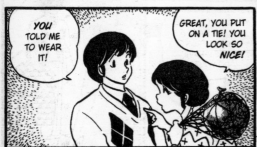

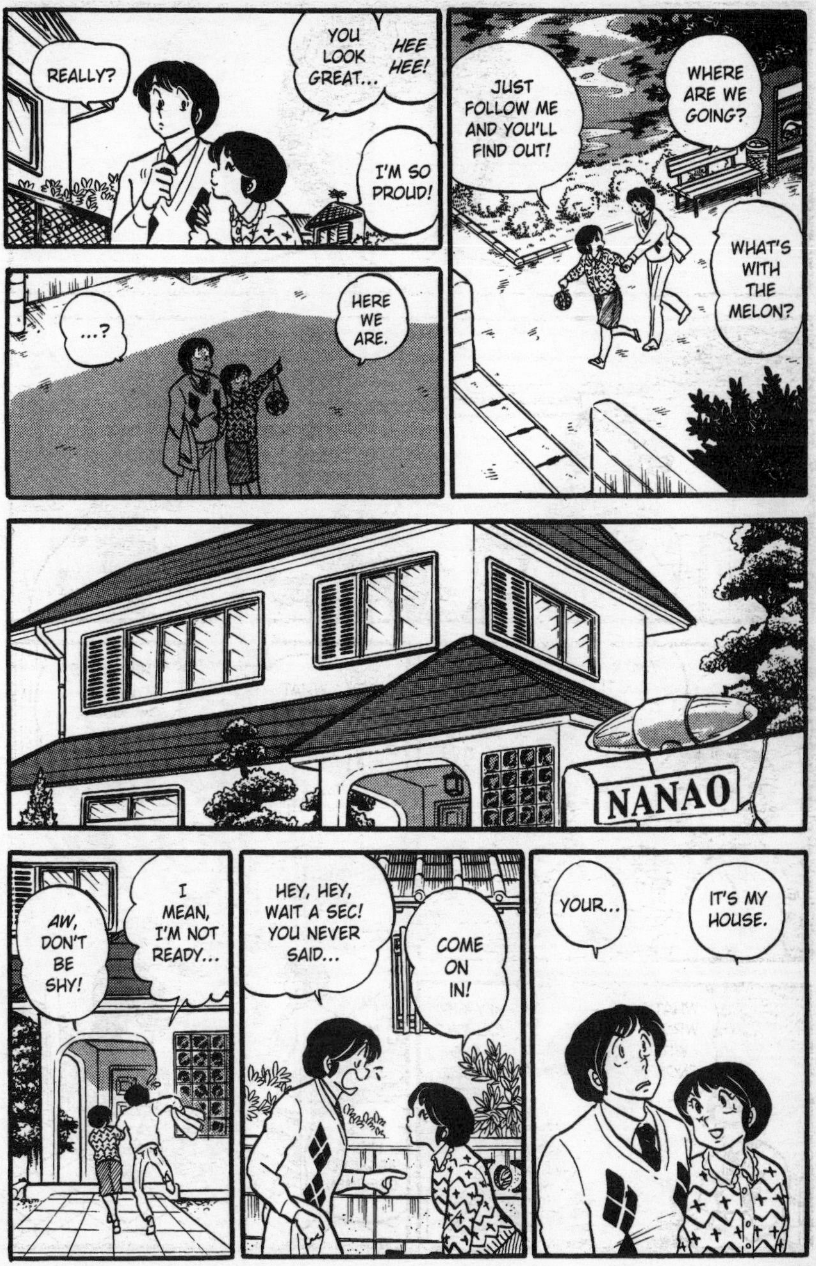
WHERE ARE WE GOING?
JUST FOLLOW ME AND YOU'LL FIND OUT!
WHAT'S WITH THE MELON?
YOU LOOK GREAT...
HEE HEE!
I'M SO PROUD!
REALLY?
HERE WE ARE.
...?
NANAO
IT'S MY HOUSE.
YOUR...
COME ON IN!
HEY, HEY, WAIT A SEC! YOU NEVER SAID...
I MEAN, I'M NOT READY...
AW, DON'T BE SHY!

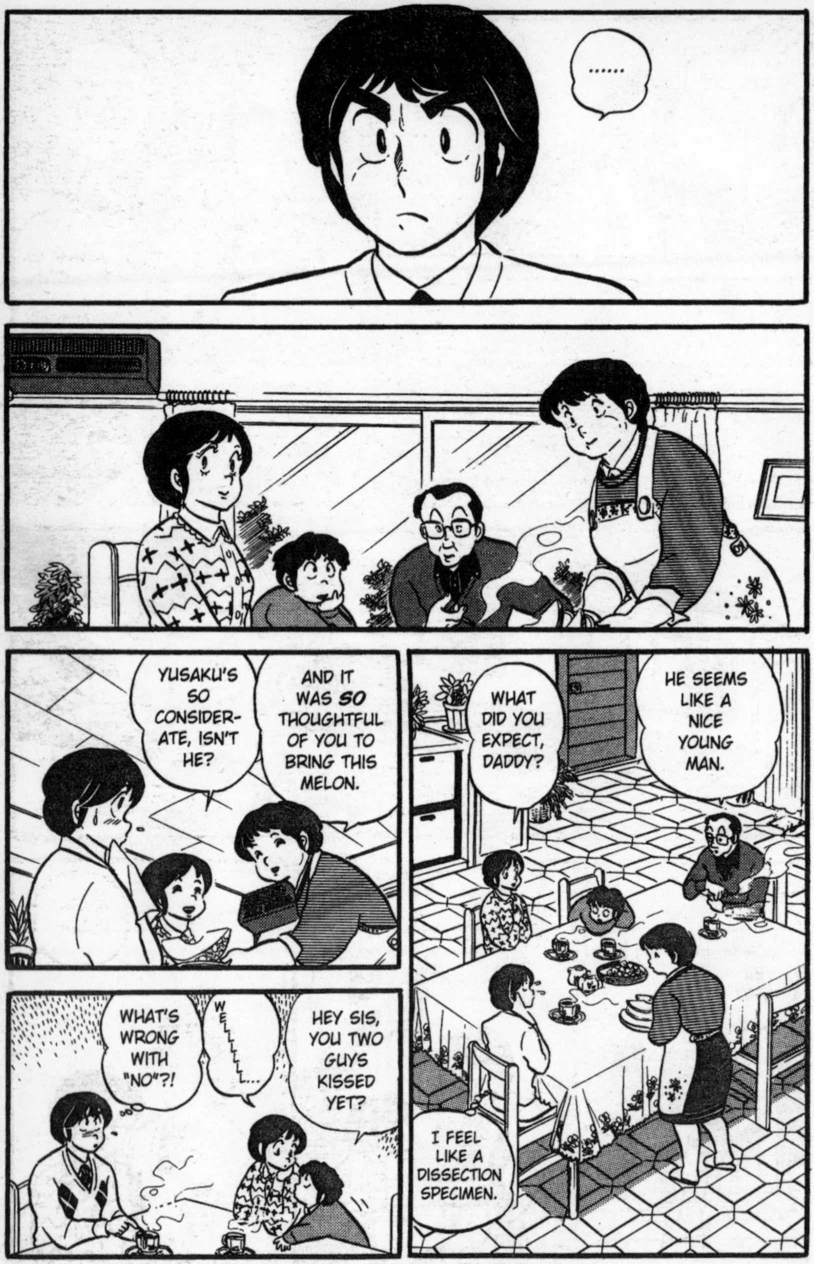
......
HE SEEMS LIKE A NICE YOUNG MAN.
WHAT DID YOU EXPECT, DADDY?
I FEEL LIKE A DISSECTION SPECIMEN.
AND IT WAS ***SO*** THOUGHTFUL OF YOU TO BRING THIS MELON.
YUSAKU'S SO CONSIDER-ATE, ISN'T HE?
HEY SIS, YOU TWO GUYS KISSED YET?
WELLLLLL...
WHAT'S WRONG WITH "NO"?!

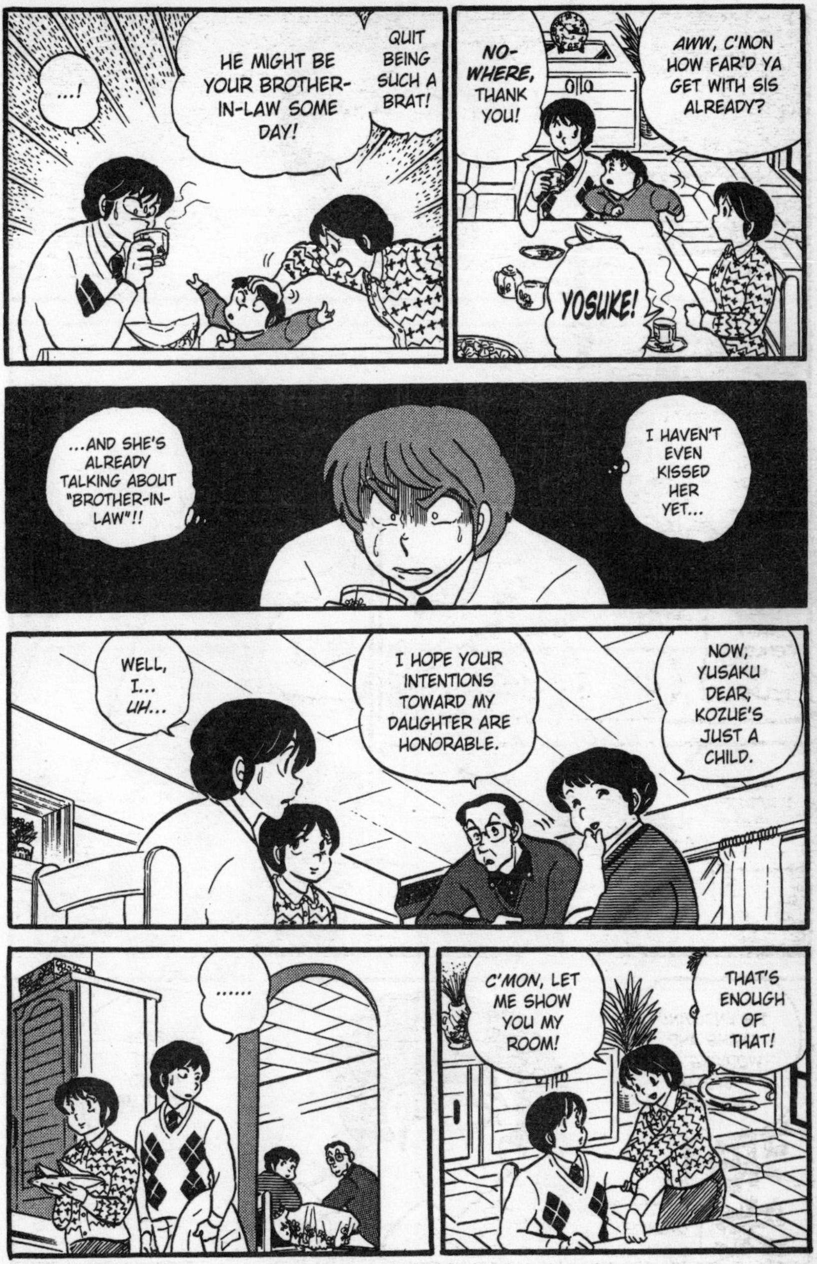
AWW, C'MON HOW FAR'D YA GET WITH SIS ALREADY?
NO-WHERE, THANK YOU!
YOSUKE!
QUIT BEING SUCH A BRAT!
HE MIGHT BE YOUR BROTHER-IN-LAW SOME DAY!
...!
I HAVEN'T EVEN KISSED HER YET...
...AND SHE'S ALREADY TALKING ABOUT "BROTHER-IN-LAW"!!
NOW, YUSAKU DEAR, KOZUE'S JUST A CHILD.
I HOPE YOUR INTENTIONS TOWARD MY DAUGHTER ARE HONORABLE.
WELL, I... UH...
THAT'S ENOUGH OF THAT!
C'MON, LET ME SHOW YOU MY ROOM!
......

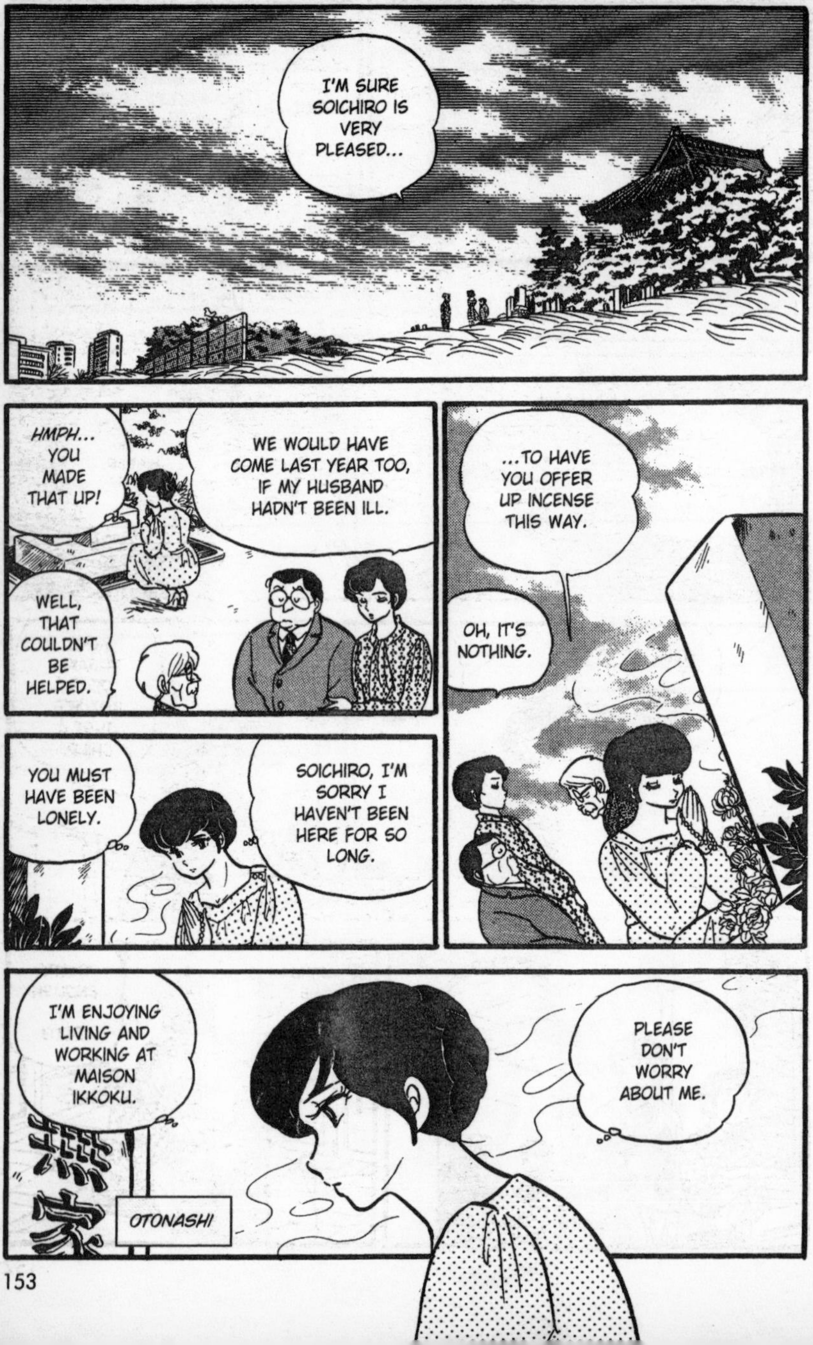

I'M SURE SOICHIRO IS VERY PLEASED...
...TO HAVE YOU OFFER UP INCENSE THIS WAY.
OH, IT'S NOTHING.
WE WOULD HAVE COME LAST YEAR TOO, IF MY HUSBAND HADN'T BEEN ILL.
HMPH... YOU MADE THAT UP!
WELL, THAT COULDN'T BE HELPED.
SOICHIRO, I'M SORRY I HAVEN'T BEEN HERE FOR SO LONG.
YOU MUST HAVE BEEN LONELY.
PLEASE DON'T WORRY ABOUT ME.
I'M ENJOYING LIVING AND WORKING AT MAISON IKKOKU.
OTONASHI

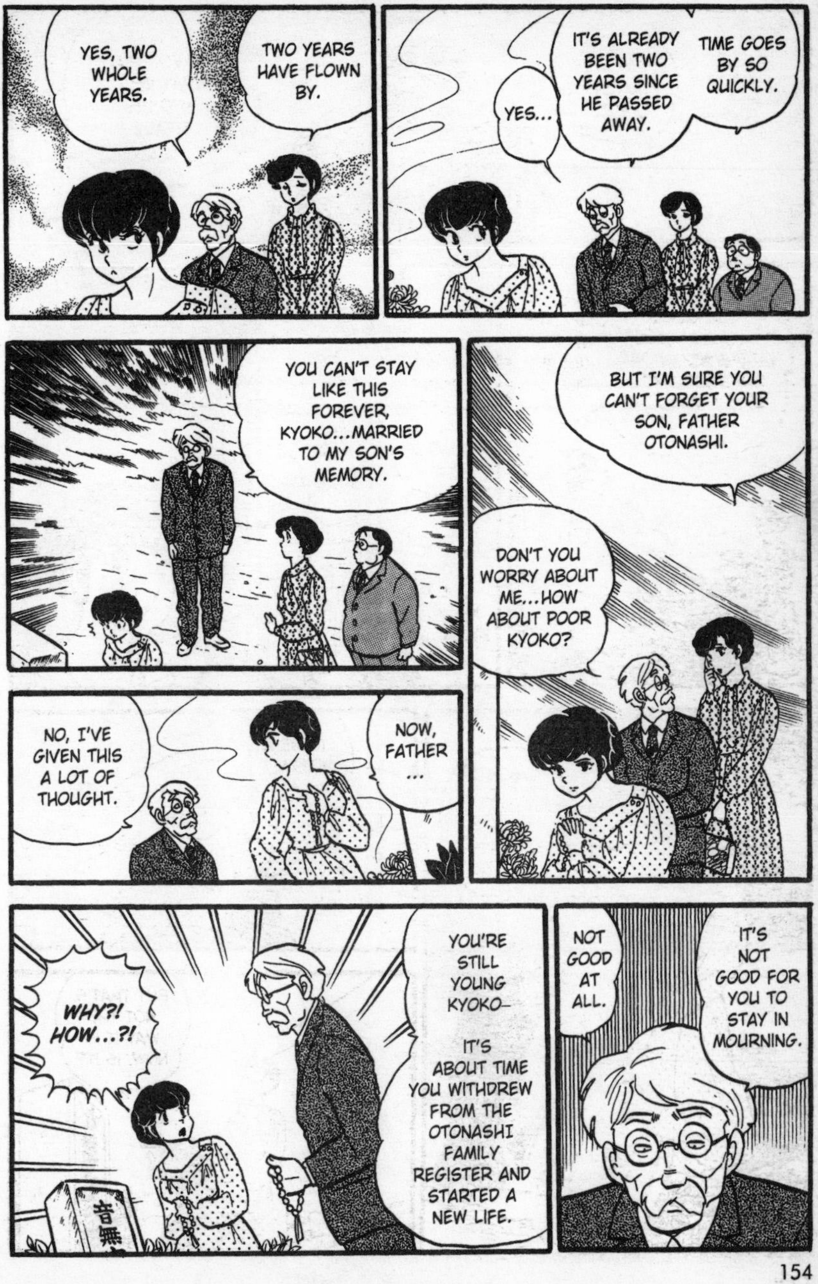
TIME GOES BY SO QUICKLY.
IT'S ALREADY BEEN TWO YEARS SINCE HE PASSED AWAY.
YES...
TWO YEARS HAVE FLOWN BY.
YES, TWO WHOLE YEARS.
BUT I'M SURE YOU CAN'T FORGET YOUR SON, FATHER OTONASHI.
DON'T YOU WORRY ABOUT ME...HOW ABOUT POOR KYOKO?
YOU CAN'T STAY LIKE THIS FOREVER, KYOKO...MARRIED TO MY SON'S MEMORY.
NOW, FATHER ...
NO, I'VE GIVEN THIS A LOT OF THOUGHT.
IT'S NOT GOOD FOR YOU TO STAY IN MOURNING.
NOT GOOD AT ALL.
YOU'RE STILL YOUNG KYOKO—
IT'S ABOUT TIME YOU WITHDREW FROM THE OTONASHI FAMILY REGISTER AND STARTED A NEW LIFE.
WHY?! HOW...?!

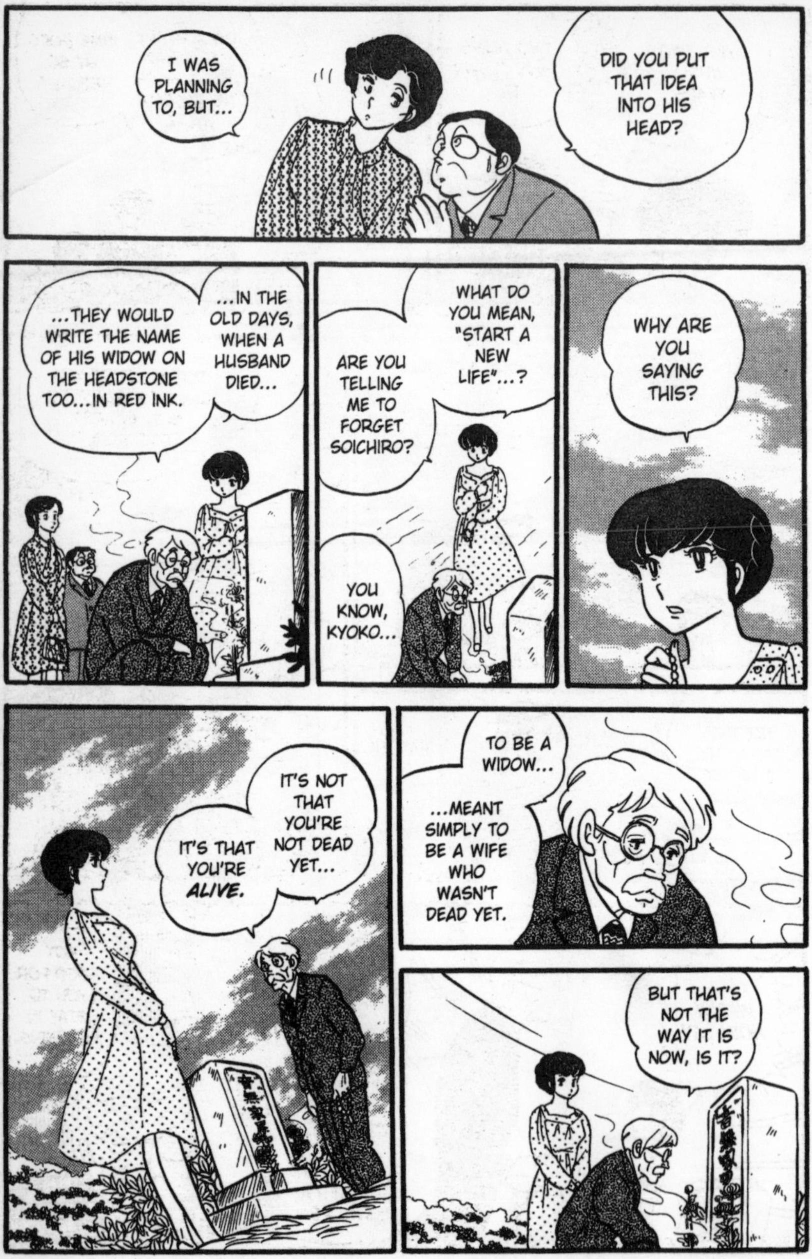
DID YOU PUT THAT IDEA INTO HIS HEAD?
I WAS PLANNING TO, BUT...
WHY ARE YOU SAYING THIS?
WHAT DO YOU MEAN, "START A NEW LIFE"...?
ARE YOU TELLING ME TO FORGET SOICHIRO?
YOU KNOW, KYOKO...
...IN THE OLD DAYS, WHEN A HUSBAND DIED...
...THEY WOULD WRITE THE NAME OF HIS WIDOW ON THE HEADSTONE TOO...IN RED INK.
TO BE A WIDOW...
...MEANT SIMPLY TO BE A WIFE WHO WASN'T DEAD YET.
BUT THAT'S NOT THE WAY IT IS NOW, IS IT?
IT'S NOT THAT YOU'RE NOT DEAD YET...
IT'S THAT YOU'RE *ALIVE.*

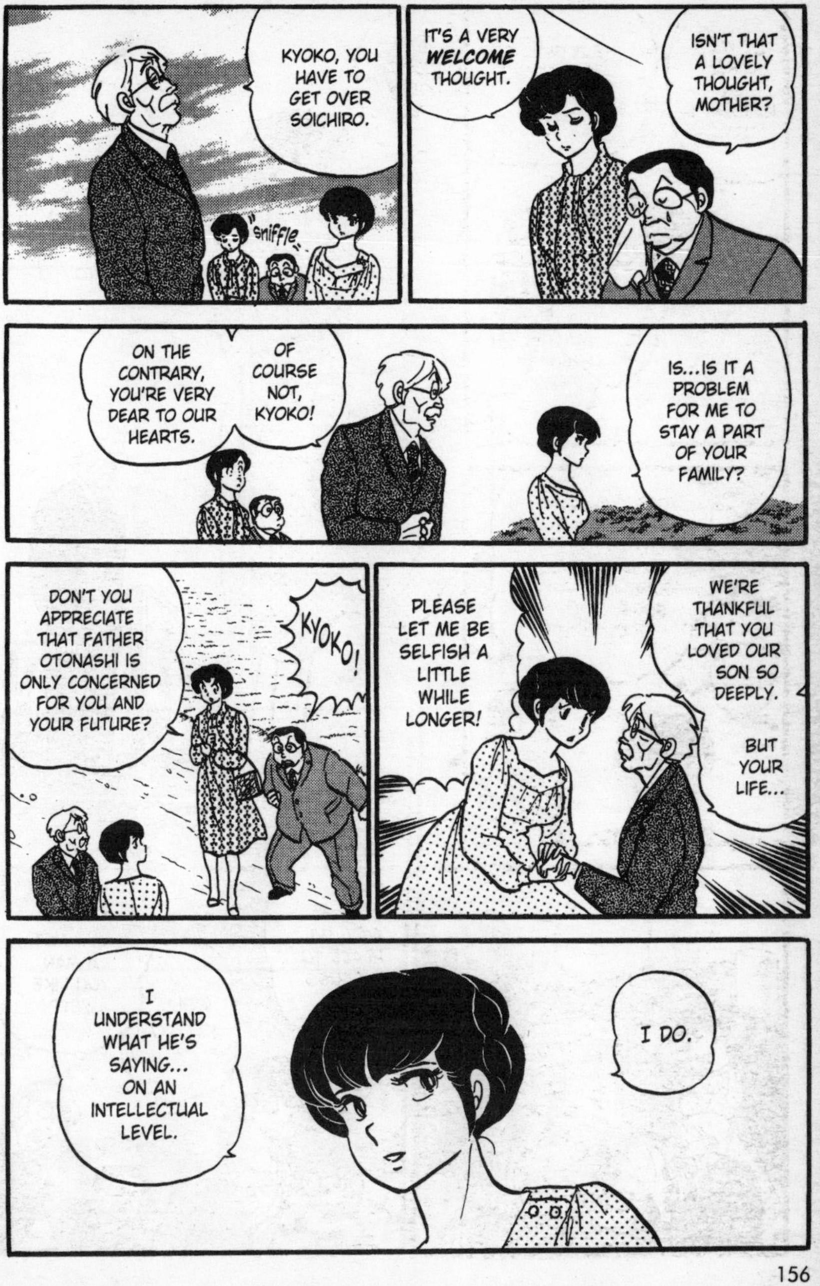
ISN'T THAT A LOVELY THOUGHT, MOTHER?
IT'S A VERY ***WELCOME*** THOUGHT.
KYOKO, YOU HAVE TO GET OVER SOICHIRO.
sniffle
IS...IS IT A PROBLEM FOR ME TO STAY A PART OF YOUR FAMILY?
OF COURSE NOT, KYOKO!
ON THE CONTRARY, YOU'RE VERY DEAR TO OUR HEARTS.
WE'RE THANKFUL THAT YOU LOVED OUR SON SO DEEPLY.
BUT YOUR LIFE...
PLEASE LET ME BE SELFISH A LITTLE WHILE LONGER!
KYOKO!
DON'T YOU APPRECIATE THAT FATHER OTONASHI IS ONLY CONCERNED FOR YOU AND YOUR FUTURE?
I DO.
I UNDERSTAND WHAT HE'S SAYING... ON AN INTELLECTUAL LEVEL.

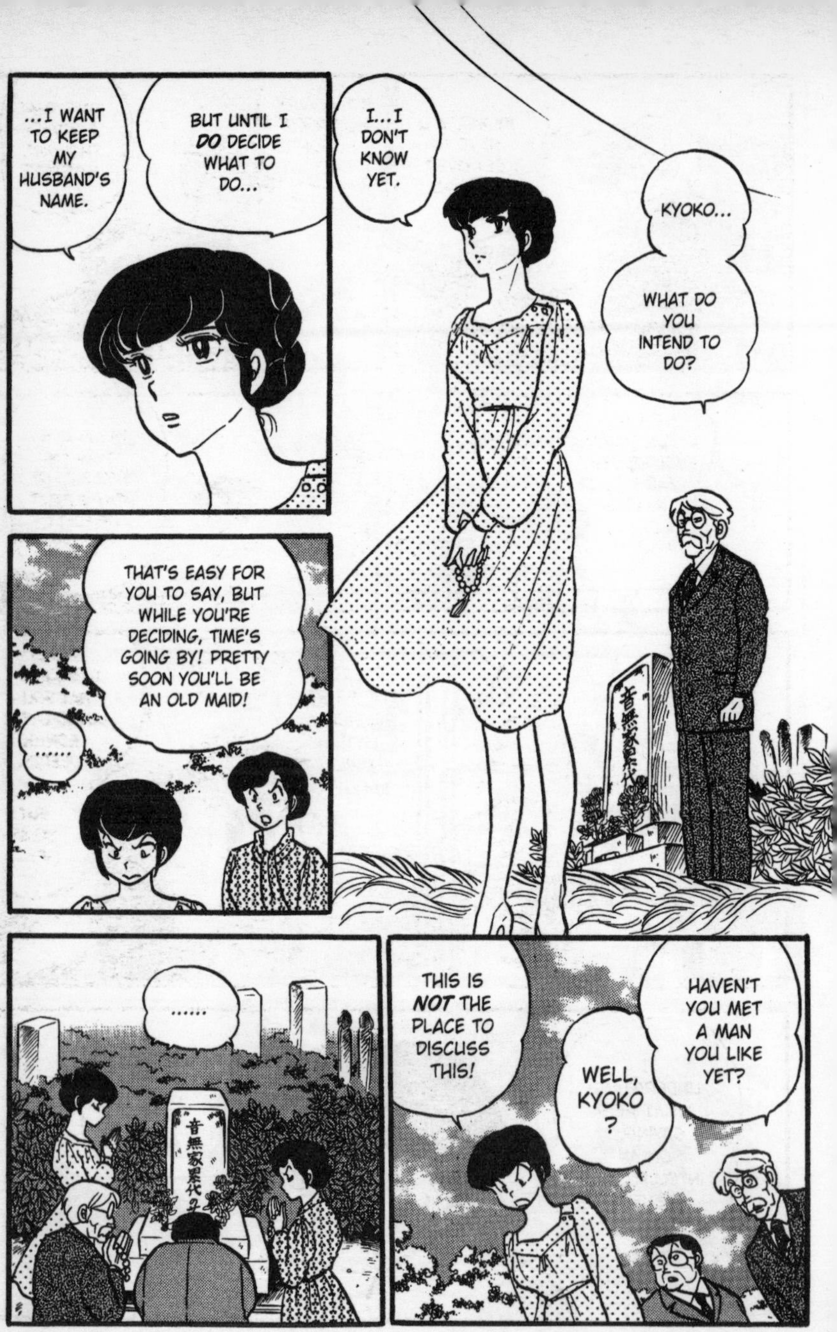
KYOKO...
WHAT DO YOU INTEND TO DO?
I...I DON'T KNOW YET.
BUT UNTIL I *DO* DECIDE WHAT TO DO...
...I WANT TO KEEP MY HUSBAND'S NAME.
THAT'S EASY FOR YOU TO SAY, BUT WHILE YOU'RE DECIDING, TIME'S GOING BY! PRETTY SOON YOU'LL BE AN OLD MAID!
......
HAVEN'T YOU MET A MAN YOU LIKE YET?
WELL, KYOKO?
THIS IS *NOT* THE PLACE TO DISCUSS THIS!
......

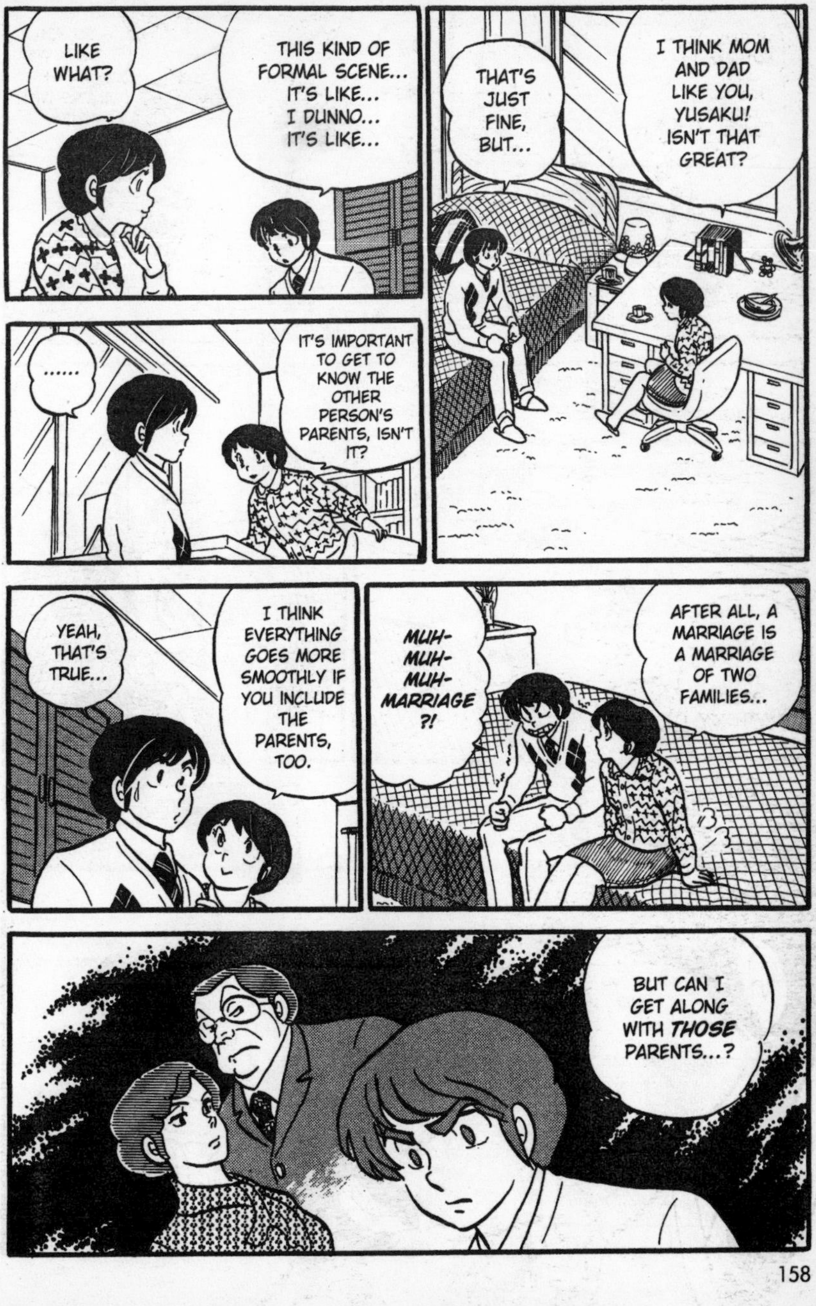
I THINK MOM AND DAD LIKE YOU, YUSAKU! ISN'T THAT GREAT?
THAT'S JUST FINE, BUT...
THIS KIND OF FORMAL SCENE... IT'S LIKE... I DUNNO... IT'S LIKE...
LIKE WHAT?
IT'S IMPORTANT TO GET TO KNOW THE OTHER PERSON'S PARENTS, ISN'T IT?
......
AFTER ALL, A MARRIAGE IS A MARRIAGE OF TWO FAMILIES...
MUH-MUH-MUH-MARRIAGE?!
I THINK EVERYTHING GOES MORE SMOOTHLY IF YOU INCLUDE THE PARENTS, TOO.
YEAH, THAT'S TRUE...
BUT CAN I GET ALONG WITH *THOSE* PARENTS...?

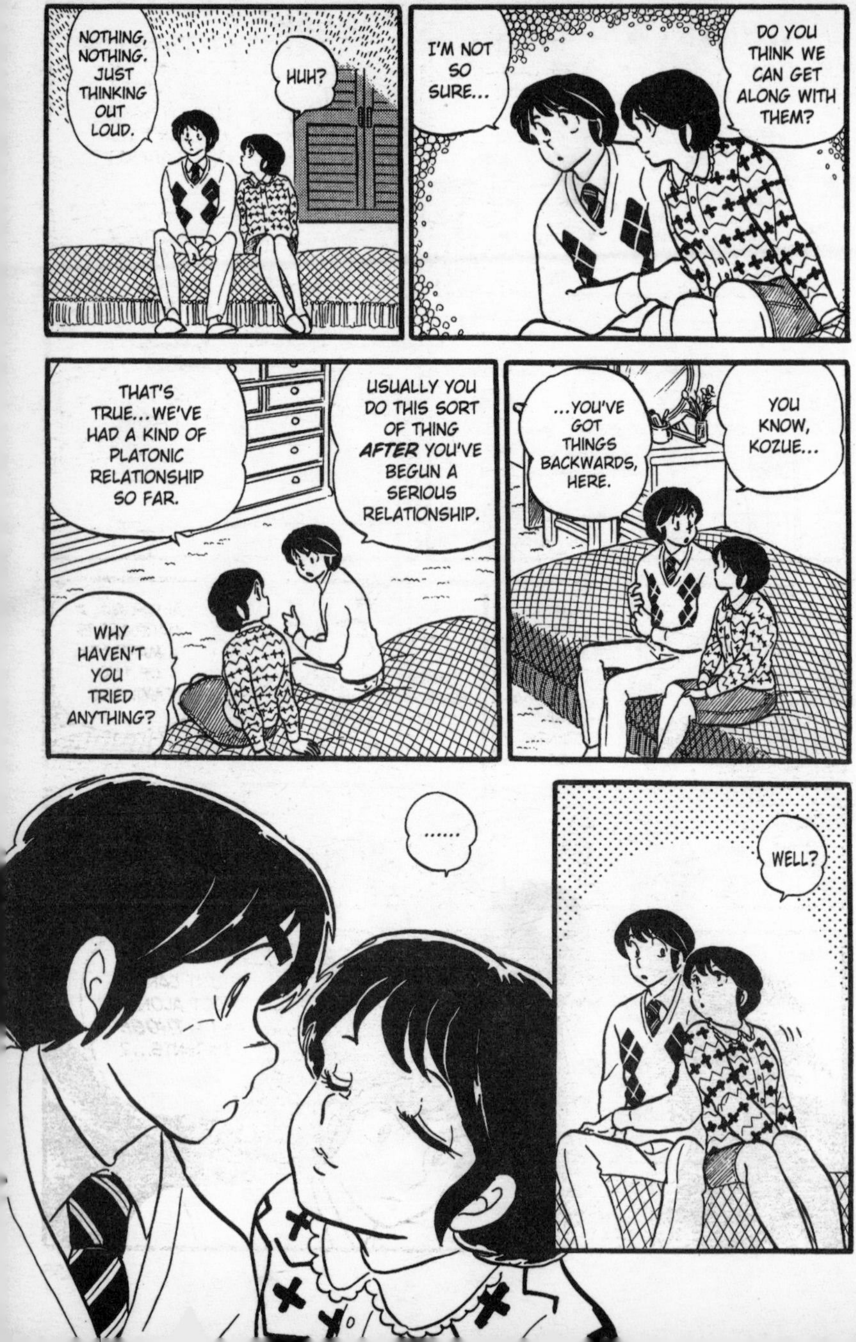
DO YOU THINK WE CAN GET ALONG WITH THEM?
I'M NOT SO SURE...
HUH?
NOTHING, NOTHING. JUST THINKING OUT LOUD.
YOU KNOW, KOZUE...
...YOU'VE GOT THINGS BACKWARDS, HERE.
USUALLY YOU DO THIS SORT OF THING *AFTER* YOU'VE BEGUN A SERIOUS RELATIONSHIP.
THAT'S TRUE...WE'VE HAD A KIND OF PLATONIC RELATIONSHIP SO FAR.
WHY HAVEN'T YOU TRIED ANYTHING?
WELL?
......

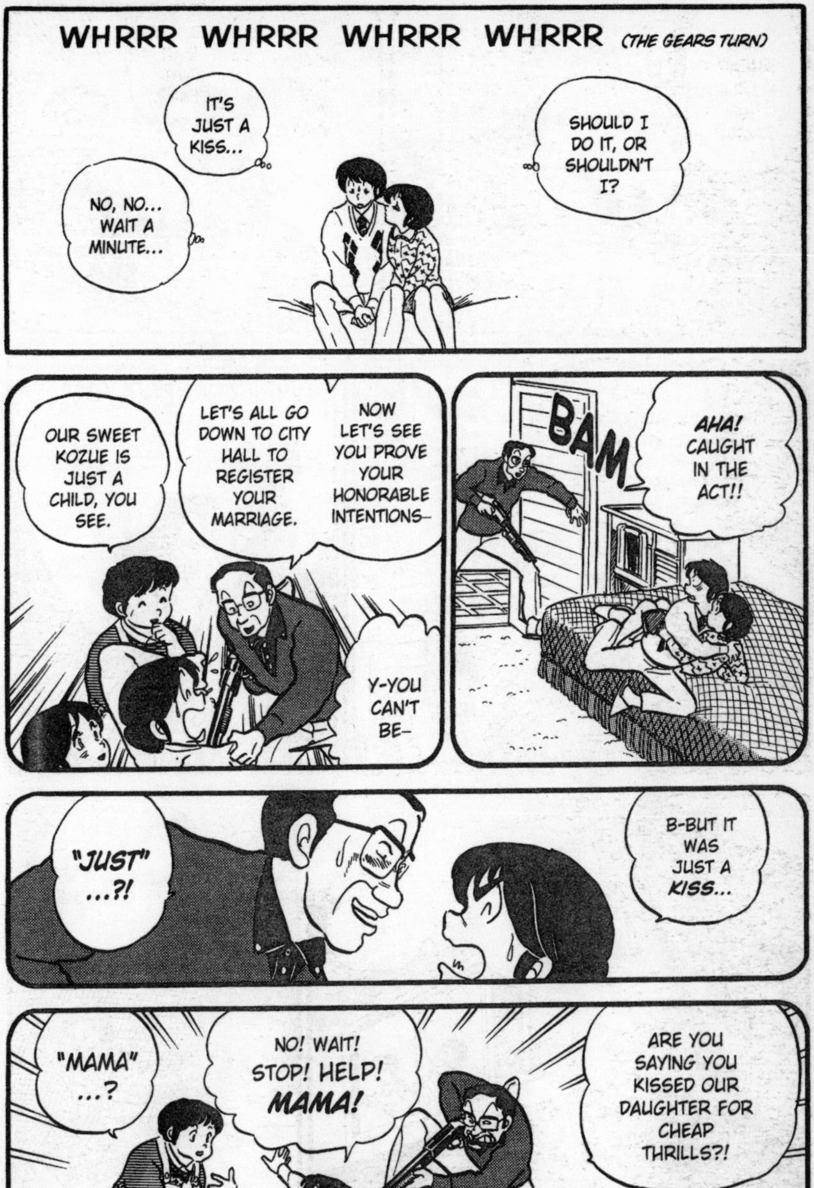
WHRRR WHRRR WHRRR WHRRR (THE GEARS TURN)
SHOULD I DO IT, OR SHOULDN'T I?
IT'S JUST A KISS...
NO, NO... WAIT A MINUTE...
BAM
AHA! CAUGHT IN THE ACT!!
NOW LET'S SEE YOU PROVE YOUR HONORABLE INTENTIONS–
LET'S ALL GO DOWN TO CITY HALL TO REGISTER YOUR MARRIAGE.
OUR SWEET KOZUE IS JUST A CHILD, YOU SEE.
Y-YOU CAN'T BE–
B-BUT IT WAS JUST A KISS...
"JUST" ...?!
ARE YOU SAYING YOU KISSED OUR DAUGHTER FOR CHEAP THRILLS?!
NO! WAIT! STOP! HELP! MAMA!
"MAMA" ...?

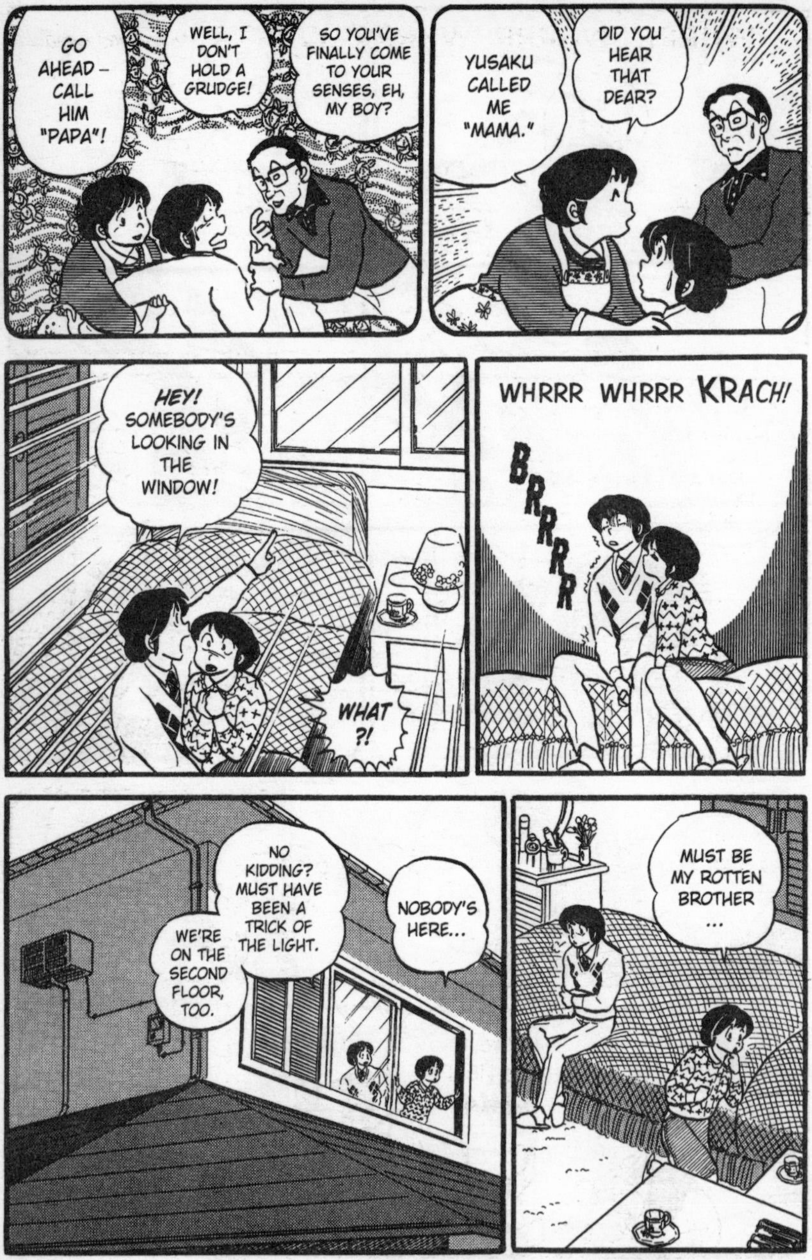
DID YOU HEAR THAT DEAR?
YUSAKU CALLED ME "MAMA."
SO YOU'VE FINALLY COME TO YOUR SENSES, EH, MY BOY?
WELL, I DON'T HOLD A GRUDGE!
GO AHEAD – CALL HIM "PAPA"!
WHRRR WHRRR KRACH!
BRRRRR
HEY! SOMEBODY'S LOOKING IN THE WINDOW!
WHAT ?!
MUST BE MY ROTTEN BROTHER ...
NOBODY'S HERE...
NO KIDDING? MUST HAVE BEEN A TRICK OF THE LIGHT.
WE'RE ON THE SECOND FLOOR, TOO.

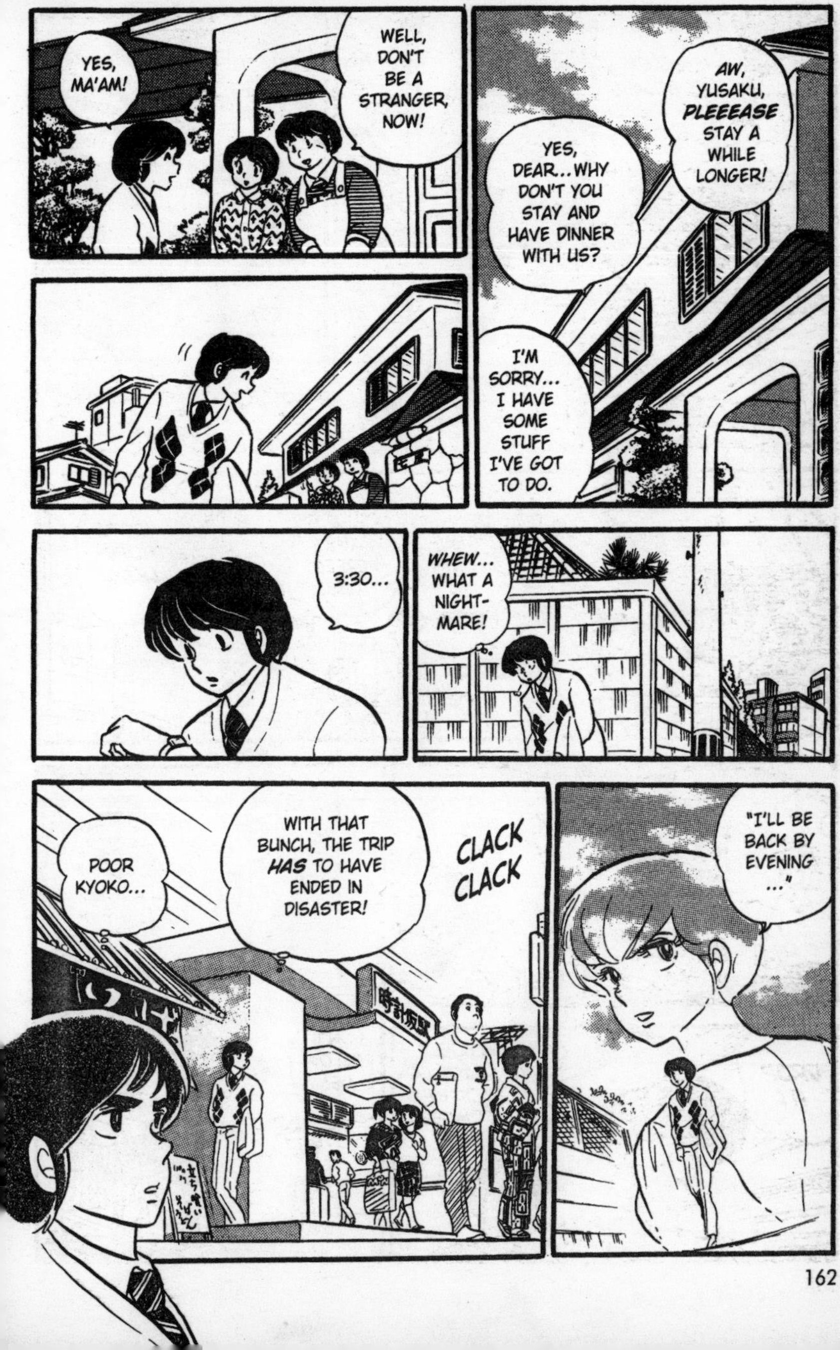

AW, YUSAKU, PLEEEASE STAY A WHILE LONGER!
YES, DEAR...WHY DON'T YOU STAY AND HAVE DINNER WITH US?
I'M SORRY... I HAVE SOME STUFF I'VE GOT TO DO.
WELL, DON'T BE A STRANGER, NOW!
YES, MA'AM!
WHEW... WHAT A NIGHT-MARE!
3:30...
"I'LL BE BACK BY EVENING ..."
CLACK CLACK
WITH THAT BUNCH, THE TRIP HAS TO HAVE ENDED IN DISASTER!
POOR KYOKO...

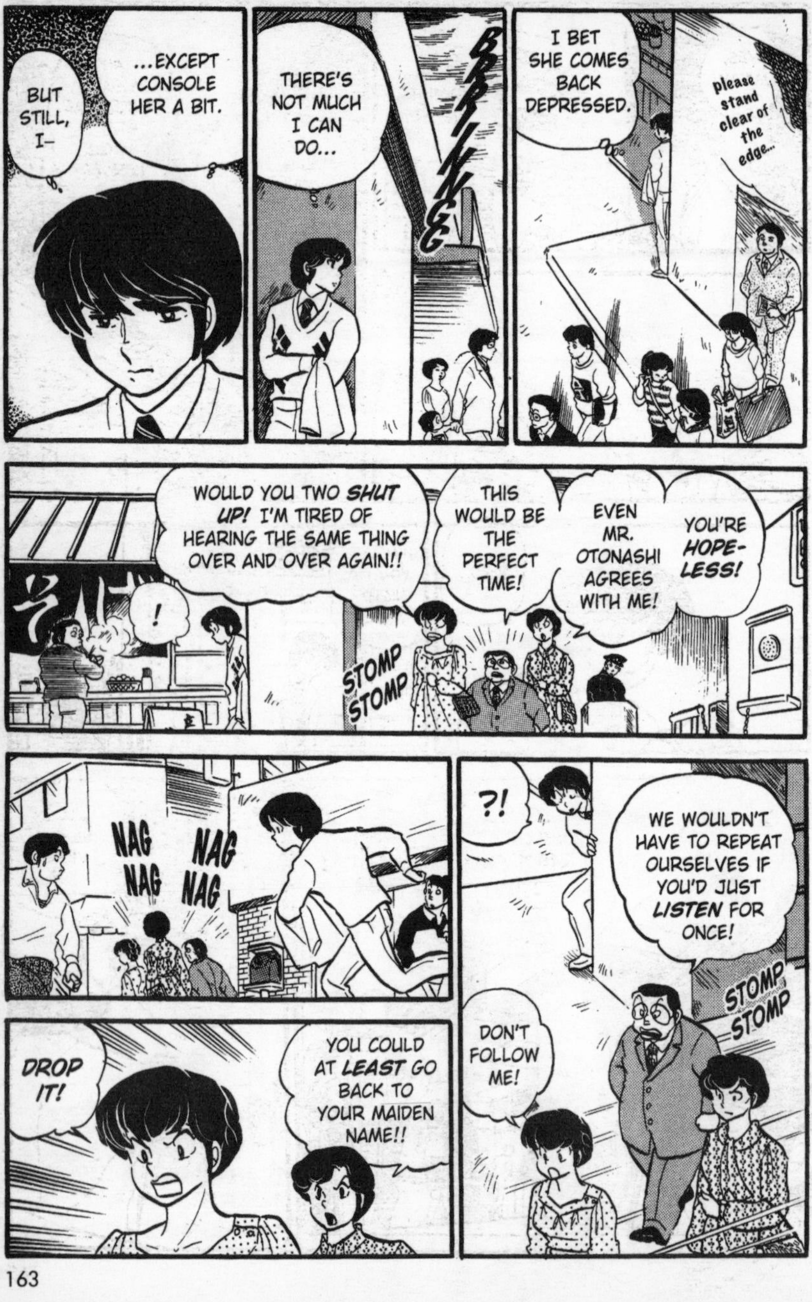
I BET SHE COMES BACK DEPRESSED.
please stand clear of the edge...
BRRINNGG
THERE'S NOT MUCH I CAN DO...
...EXCEPT CONSOLE HER A BIT.
BUT STILL, I–
YOU'RE HOPELESS!
EVEN MR. OTONASHI AGREES WITH ME!
THIS WOULD BE THE PERFECT TIME!
WOULD YOU TWO SHUT UP! I'M TIRED OF HEARING THE SAME THING OVER AND OVER AGAIN!!
STOMP STOMP
!
?!
WE WOULDN'T HAVE TO REPEAT OURSELVES IF YOU'D JUST LISTEN FOR ONCE!
STOMP STOMP
DON'T FOLLOW ME!
NAG NAG
NAG NAG
YOU COULD AT LEAST GO BACK TO YOUR MAIDEN NAME!!
DROP IT!

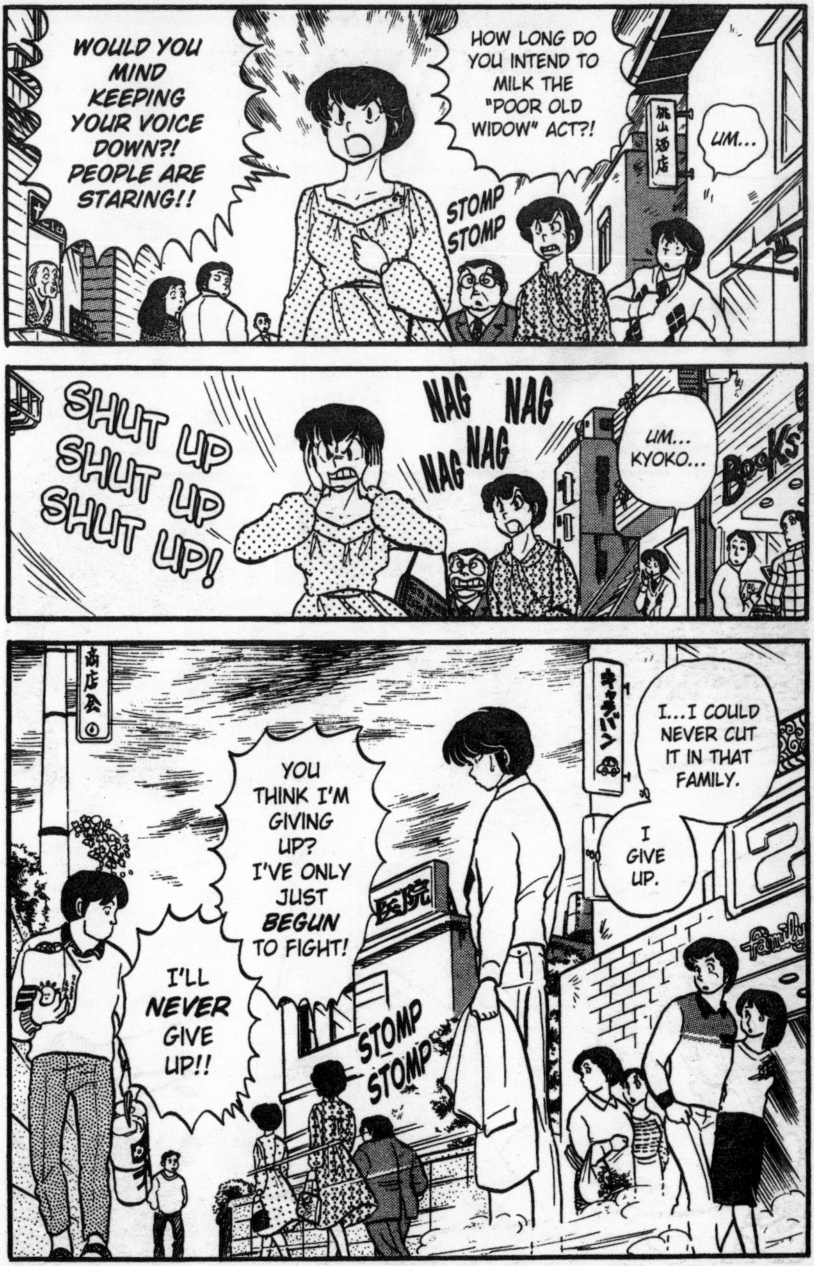
UM...
HOW LONG DO YOU INTEND TO MILK THE "POOR OLD WIDOW" ACT?!
WOULD YOU MIND KEEPING YOUR VOICE DOWN?! PEOPLE ARE STARING!!
STOMP STOMP
UM... KYOKO...
NAG NAG NAG NAG
SHUT UP SHUT UP SHUT UP SHUT UP!
I...I COULD NEVER CUT IT IN THAT FAMILY.
I GIVE UP.
YOU THINK I'M GIVING UP? I'VE ONLY JUST *BEGUN* TO FIGHT!
I'LL *NEVER* GIVE UP!!
STOMP STOMP

PART NINE

MIXED (UP) DOUBLES

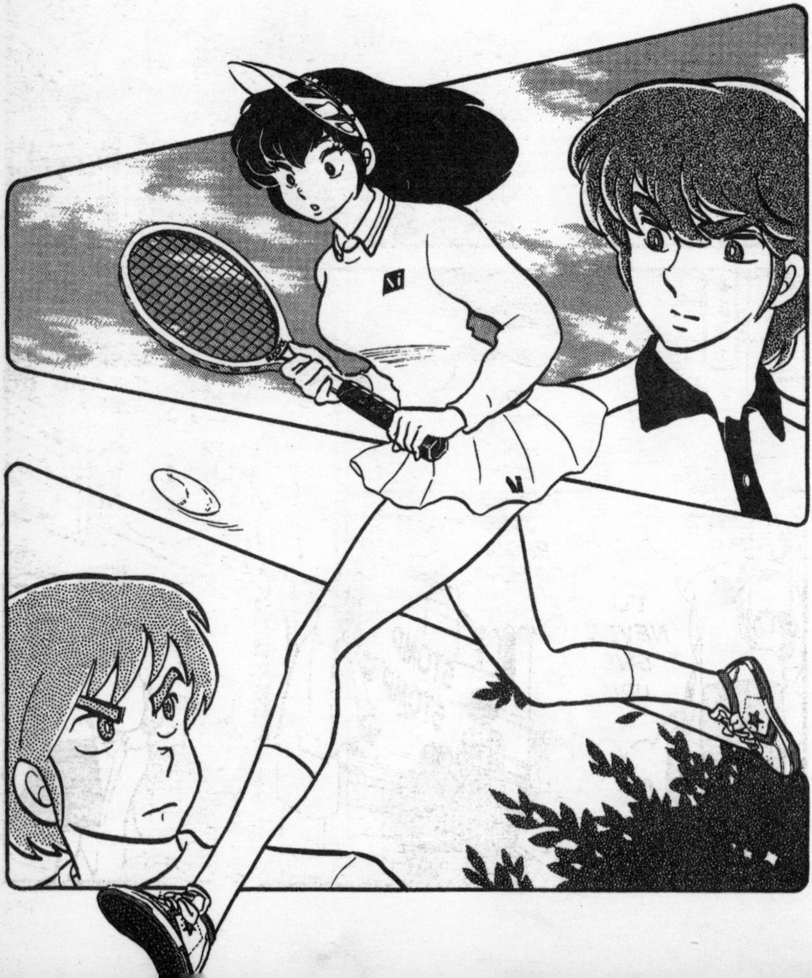

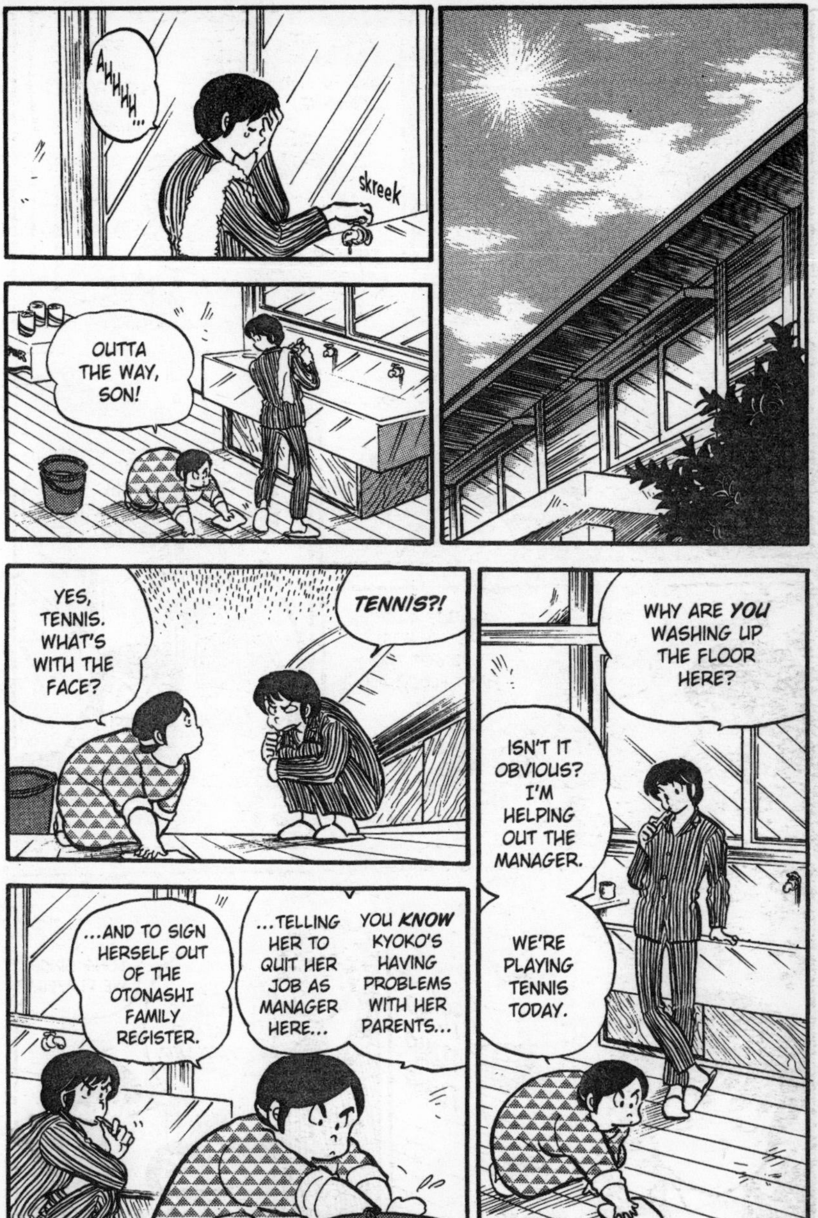
AHHHH...
skreek
OUTTA THE WAY, SON!
WHY ARE *YOU* WASHING UP THE FLOOR HERE?
ISN'T IT OBVIOUS? I'M HELPING OUT THE MANAGER.
WE'RE PLAYING TENNIS TODAY.
TENNIS?!
YES, TENNIS. WHAT'S WITH THE FACE?
YOU *KNOW* KYOKO'S HAVING PROBLEMS WITH HER PARENTS...
...TELLING HER TO QUIT HER JOB AS MANAGER HERE...
...AND TO SIGN HERSELF OUT OF THE OTONASHI FAMILY REGISTER.

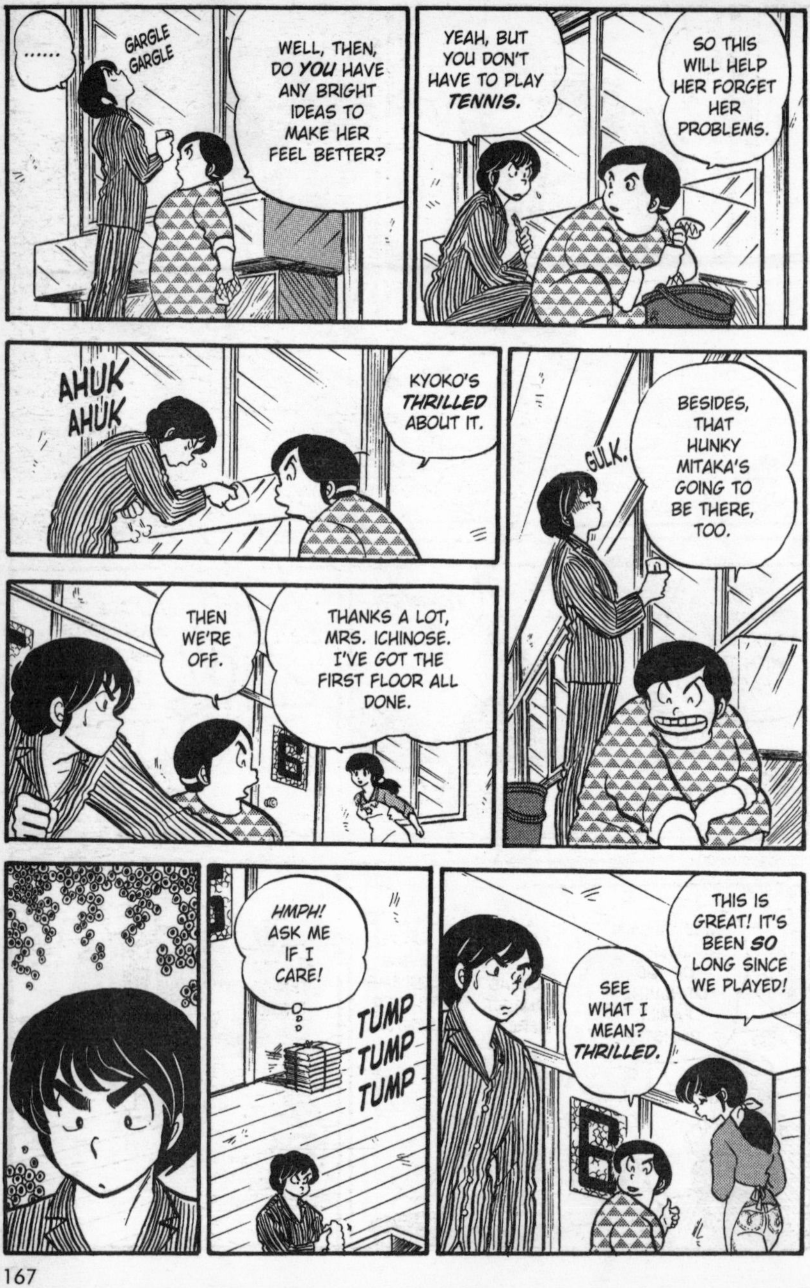
SO THIS WILL HELP HER FORGET HER PROBLEMS.
YEAH, BUT YOU DON'T HAVE TO PLAY *TENNIS.*
WELL, THEN, DO *YOU* HAVE ANY BRIGHT IDEAS TO MAKE HER FEEL BETTER?
GARGLE GARGLE
......
GULK.
BESIDES, THAT HUNKY MITAKA'S GOING TO BE THERE, TOO.
KYOKO'S *THRILLED* ABOUT IT.
AHUK AHUK
THANKS A LOT, MRS. ICHINOSE. I'VE GOT THE FIRST FLOOR ALL DONE.
THEN WE'RE OFF.
THIS IS GREAT! IT'S BEEN *SO* LONG SINCE WE PLAYED!
SEE WHAT I MEAN? *THRILLED.*
HMPH! ASK ME IF I CARE!
TUMP TUMP TUMP

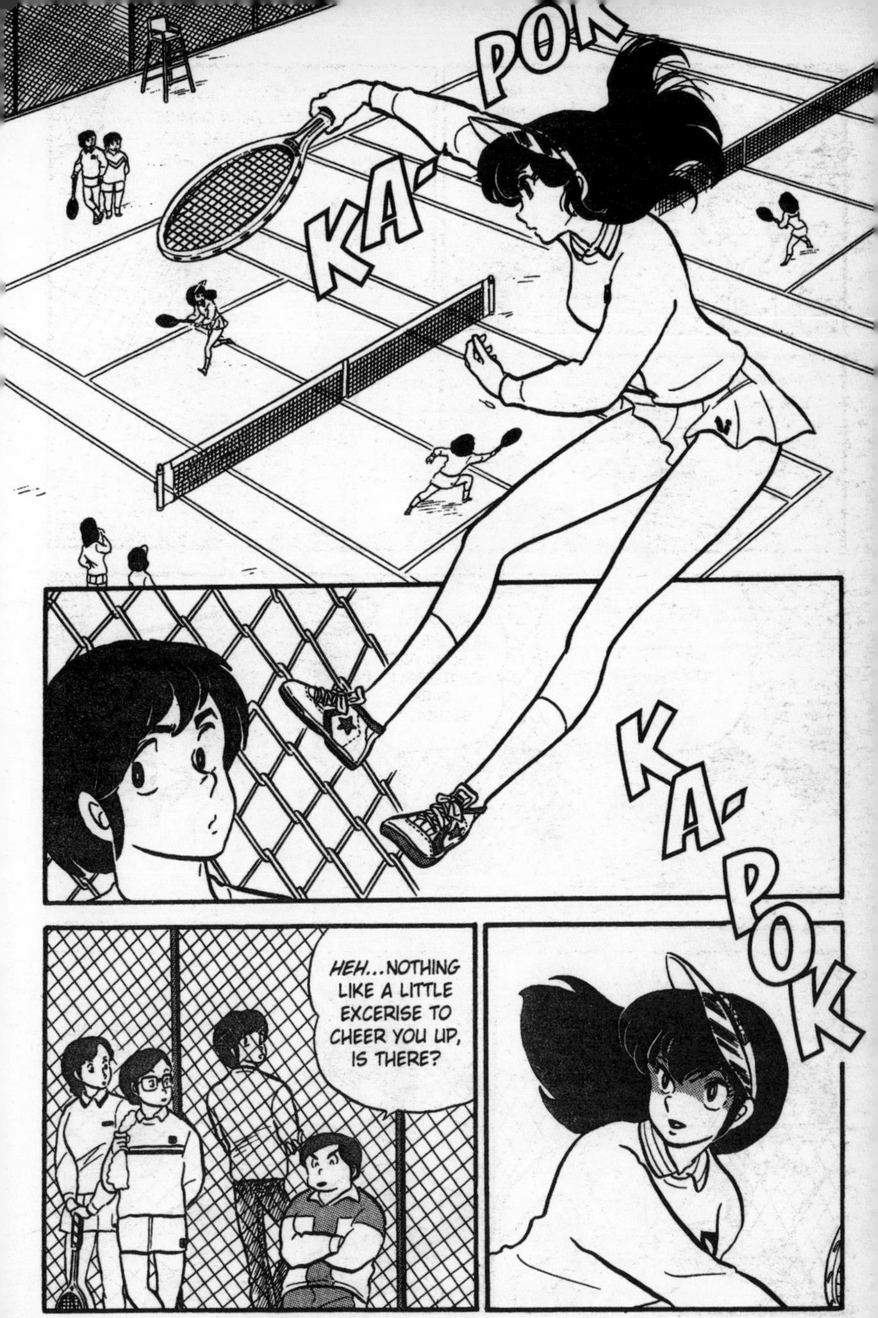
KA-PON
KA-KA-POK
HEH...NOTHING LIKE A LITTLE EXCERISE TO CHEER YOU UP, IS THERE?

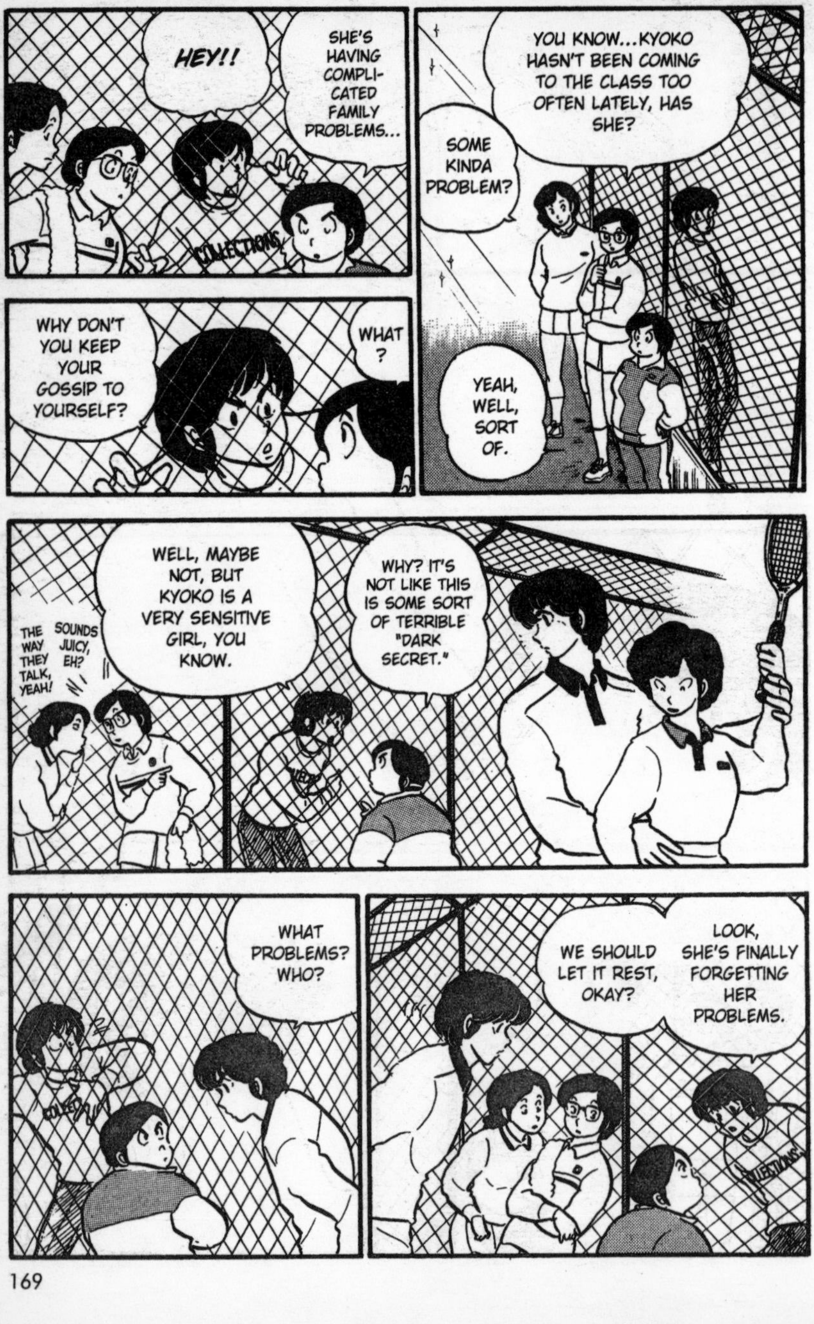
YOU KNOW...KYOKO HASN'T BEEN COMING TO THE CLASS TOO OFTEN LATELY, HAS SHE?
SOME KINDA PROBLEM?
YEAH, WELL, SORT OF.
SHE'S HAVING COMPLICATED FAMILY PROBLEMS...
HEY!!
WHAT?
WHY DON'T YOU KEEP YOUR GOSSIP TO YOURSELF?
WHY? IT'S NOT LIKE THIS IS SOME SORT OF TERRIBLE "DARK SECRET."
WELL, MAYBE NOT, BUT KYOKO IS A VERY SENSITIVE GIRL, YOU KNOW.
SOUNDS JUICY, EH?
THE WAY THEY TALK, YEAH!
LOOK, SHE'S FINALLY FORGETTING HER PROBLEMS.
WE SHOULD LET IT REST, OKAY?
WHAT PROBLEMS? WHO?

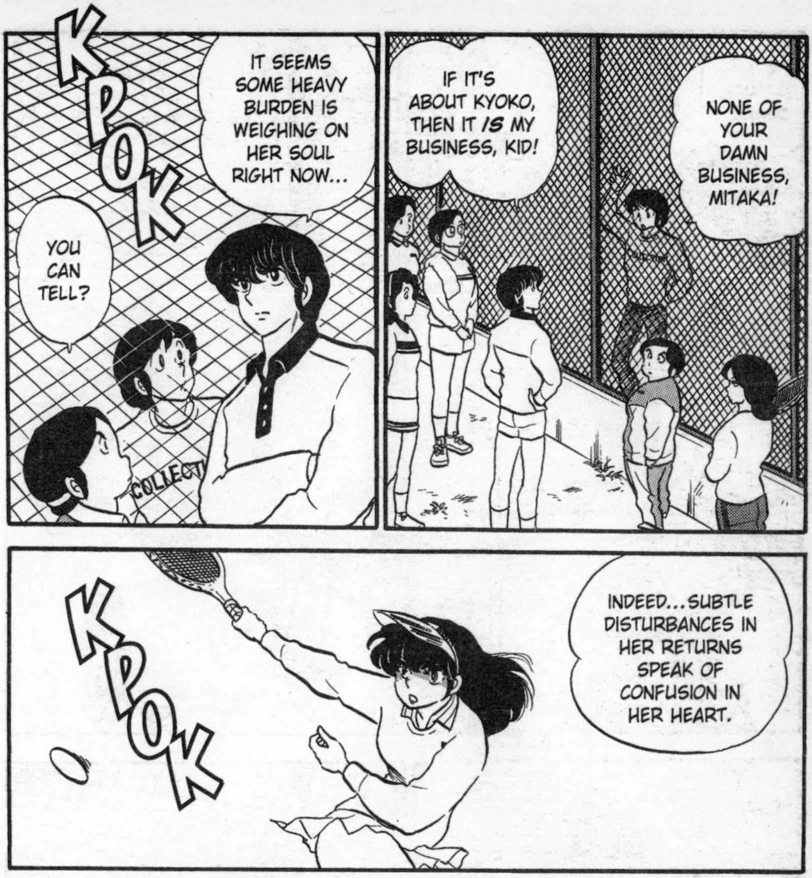
NONE OF YOUR DAMN BUSINESS, MITAKA!
IF IT'S ABOUT KYOKO, THEN IT *IS* MY BUSINESS, KID!
IT SEEMS SOME HEAVY BURDEN IS WEIGHING ON HER SOUL RIGHT NOW...
KPOK
YOU CAN TELL?
INDEED...SUBTLE DISTURBANCES IN HER RETURNS SPEAK OF CONFUSION IN HER HEART.
KPOK
WOW...
YOU REALLY **ARE** A PRO, AREN'T YOU?
WELL... *AHEM.*
YOU'RE PULLING OUR LEG, RIGHT?
YOU CAN TELL?
SHKK

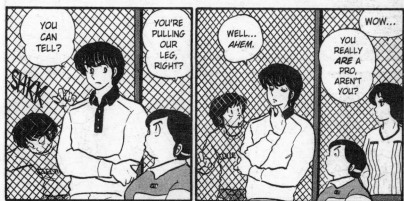

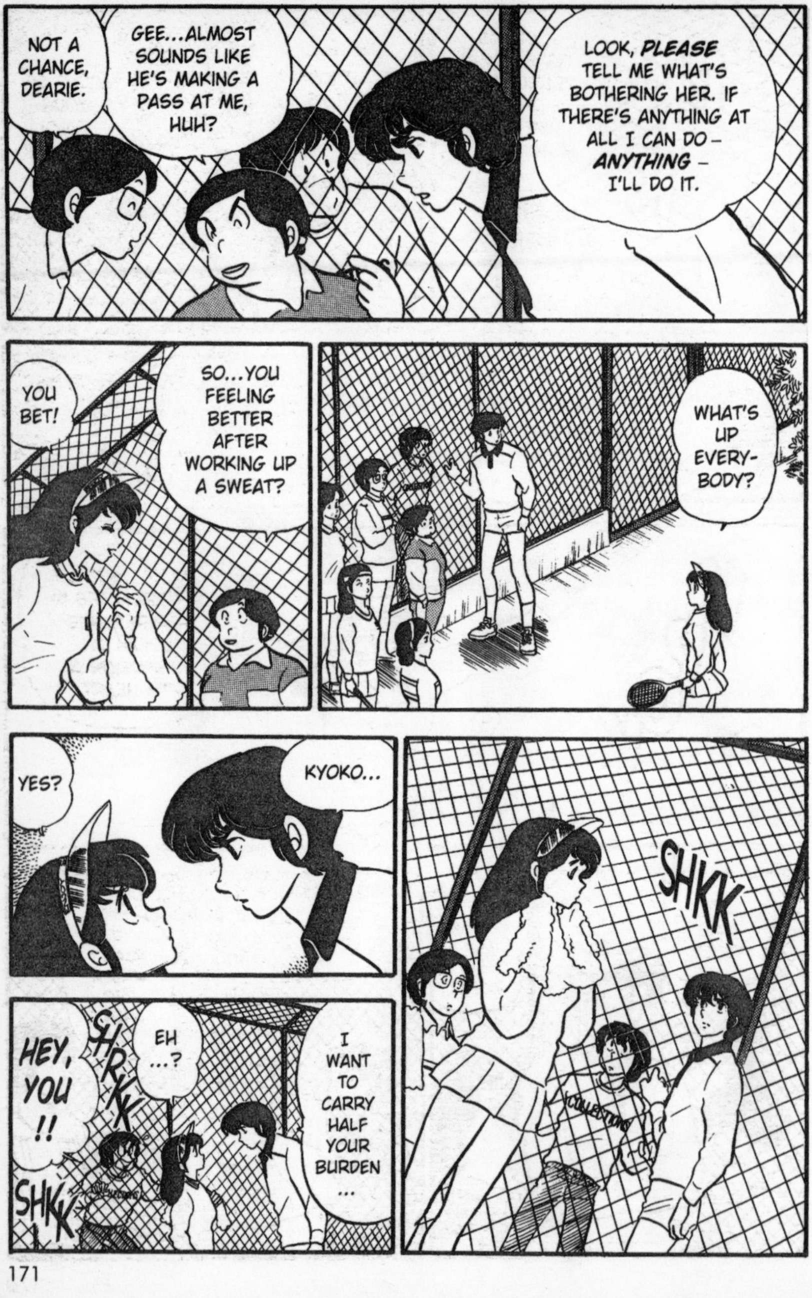
LOOK, PLEASE TELL ME WHAT'S BOTHERING HER. IF THERE'S ANYTHING AT ALL I CAN DO – ANYTHING – I'LL DO IT.
GEE...ALMOST SOUNDS LIKE HE'S MAKING A PASS AT ME, HUH?
NOT A CHANCE, DEARIE.
WHAT'S UP EVERY-BODY?
SO...YOU FEELING BETTER AFTER WORKING UP A SWEAT?
YOU BET!
SHKK
KYOKO...
YES?
I WANT TO CARRY HALF YOUR BURDEN ...
EH ...?
SHRKK
HEY, YOU !!
SHKK

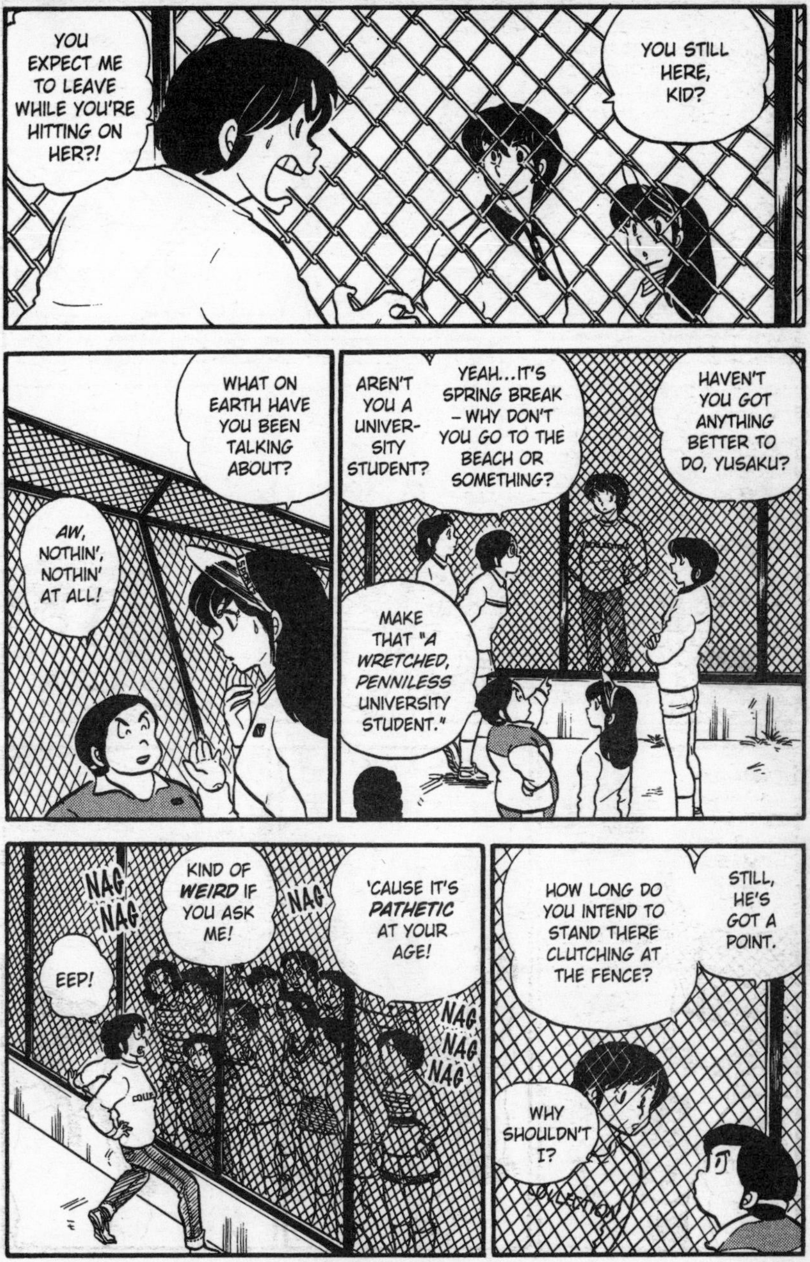
YOU STILL HERE, KID?
YOU EXPECT ME TO LEAVE WHILE YOU'RE HITTING ON HER?!
HAVEN'T YOU GOT ANYTHING BETTER TO DO, YUSAKU?
YEAH...IT'S SPRING BREAK –WHY DON'T YOU GO TO THE BEACH OR SOMETHING?
AREN'T YOU A UNIVER-SITY STUDENT?
MAKE THAT "A *WRETCHED, PENNILESS* UNIVERSITY STUDENT."
WHAT ON EARTH HAVE YOU BEEN TALKING ABOUT?
AW, NOTHIN', NOTHIN' AT ALL!
STILL, HE'S GOT A POINT.
HOW LONG DO YOU INTEND TO STAND THERE CLUTCHING AT THE FENCE?
WHY SHOULDN'T I?
'CAUSE IT'S *PATHETIC* AT YOUR AGE!
NAG
KIND OF *WEIRD* IF YOU ASK ME!
NAG NAG
EEP!
NAG NAG NAG

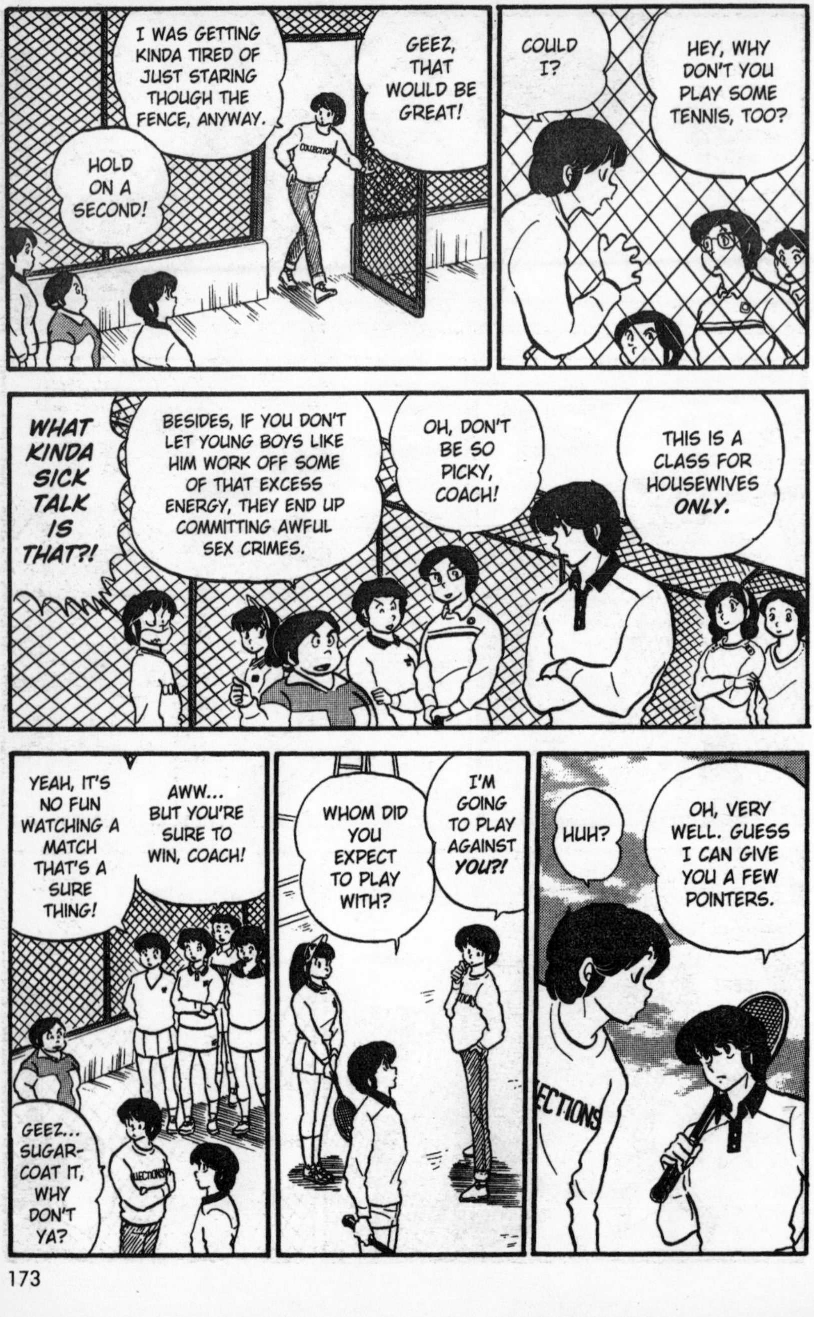
HEY, WHY DON'T YOU PLAY SOME TENNIS, TOO?
COULD I?
GEEZ, THAT WOULD BE GREAT!
I WAS GETTING KINDA TIRED OF JUST STARING THOUGH THE FENCE, ANYWAY.
HOLD ON A SECOND!
THIS IS A CLASS FOR HOUSEWIVES ONLY.
OH, DON'T BE SO PICKY, COACH!
BESIDES, IF YOU DON'T LET YOUNG BOYS LIKE HIM WORK OFF SOME OF THAT EXCESS ENERGY, THEY END UP COMMITTING AWFUL SEX CRIMES.
WHAT KINDA SICK TALK IS THAT?!
OH, VERY WELL. GUESS I CAN GIVE YOU A FEW POINTERS.
HUH?
I'M GOING TO PLAY AGAINST YOU?!
WHOM DID YOU EXPECT TO PLAY WITH?
AWW... BUT YOU'RE SURE TO WIN, COACH!
YEAH, IT'S NO FUN WATCHING A MATCH THAT'S A SURE THING!
GEEZ... SUGAR-COAT IT, WHY DON'T YA?

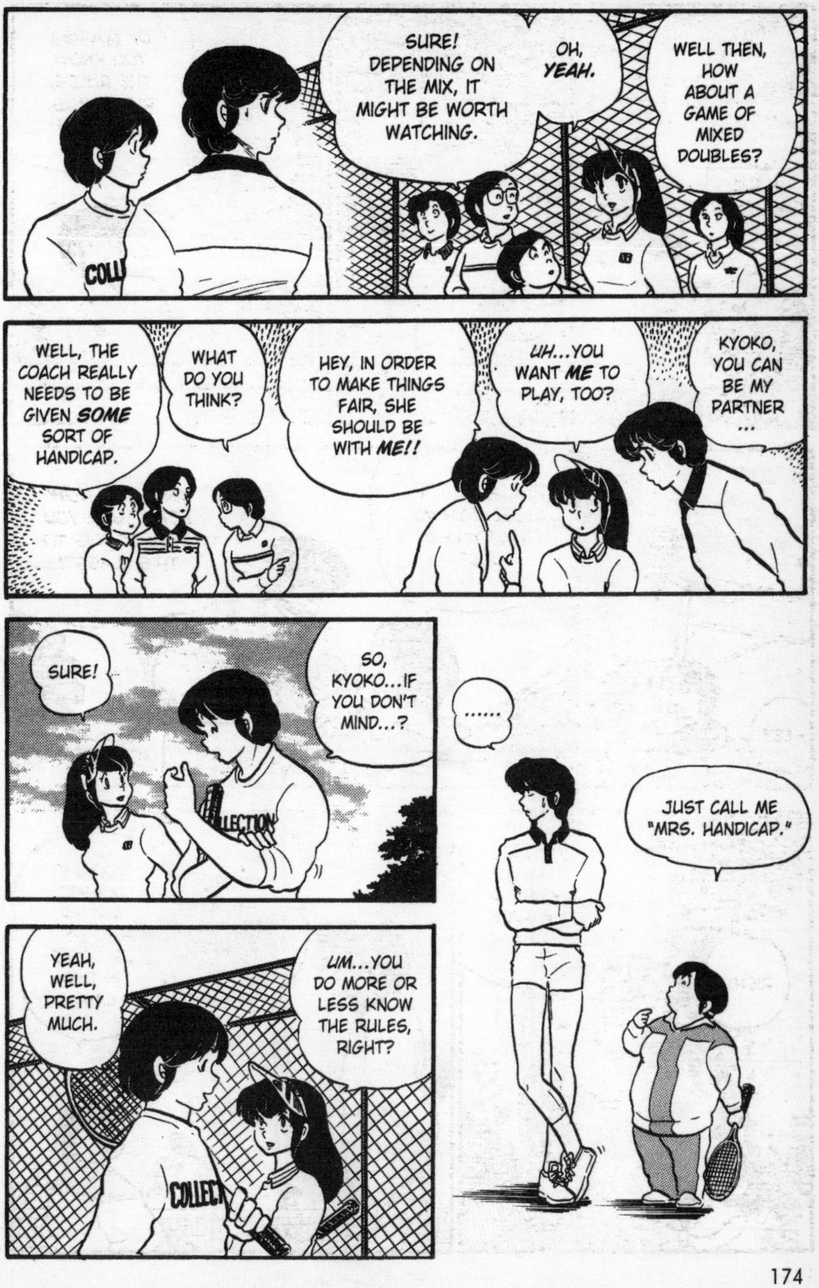
WELL THEN, HOW ABOUT A GAME OF MIXED DOUBLES?
OH, YEAH.
SURE! DEPENDING ON THE MIX, IT MIGHT BE WORTH WATCHING.
KYOKO, YOU CAN BE MY PARTNER ...
UH...YOU WANT ME TO PLAY, TOO?
HEY, IN ORDER TO MAKE THINGS FAIR, SHE SHOULD BE WITH ME!!
WHAT DO YOU THINK?
WELL, THE COACH REALLY NEEDS TO BE GIVEN SOME SORT OF HANDICAP.
......
JUST CALL ME "MRS. HANDICAP."
SO, KYOKO...IF YOU DON'T MIND...?
SURE!
UM...YOU DO MORE OR LESS KNOW THE RULES, RIGHT?
YEAH, WELL, PRETTY MUCH.

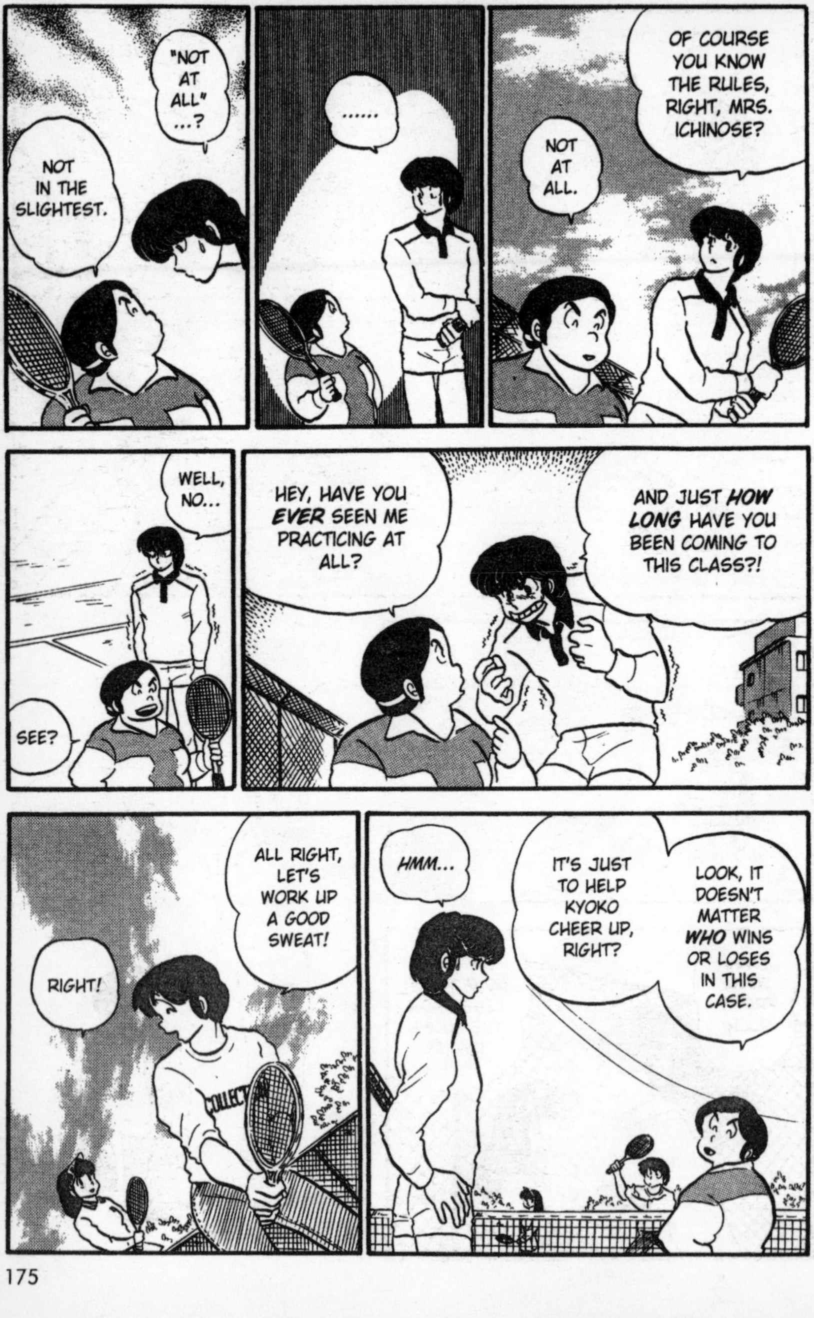
OF COURSE YOU KNOW THE RULES, RIGHT, MRS. ICHINOSE?
NOT AT ALL.
......
"NOT AT ALL" ...?
NOT IN THE SLIGHTEST.
AND JUST **HOW LONG** HAVE YOU BEEN COMING TO THIS CLASS?!
HEY, HAVE YOU **EVER** SEEN ME PRACTICING AT ALL?
WELL, NO...
SEE?
LOOK, IT DOESN'T MATTER **WHO** WINS OR LOSES IN THIS CASE.
IT'S JUST TO HELP KYOKO CHEER UP, RIGHT?
HMM...
ALL RIGHT, LET'S WORK UP A GOOD SWEAT!
RIGHT!

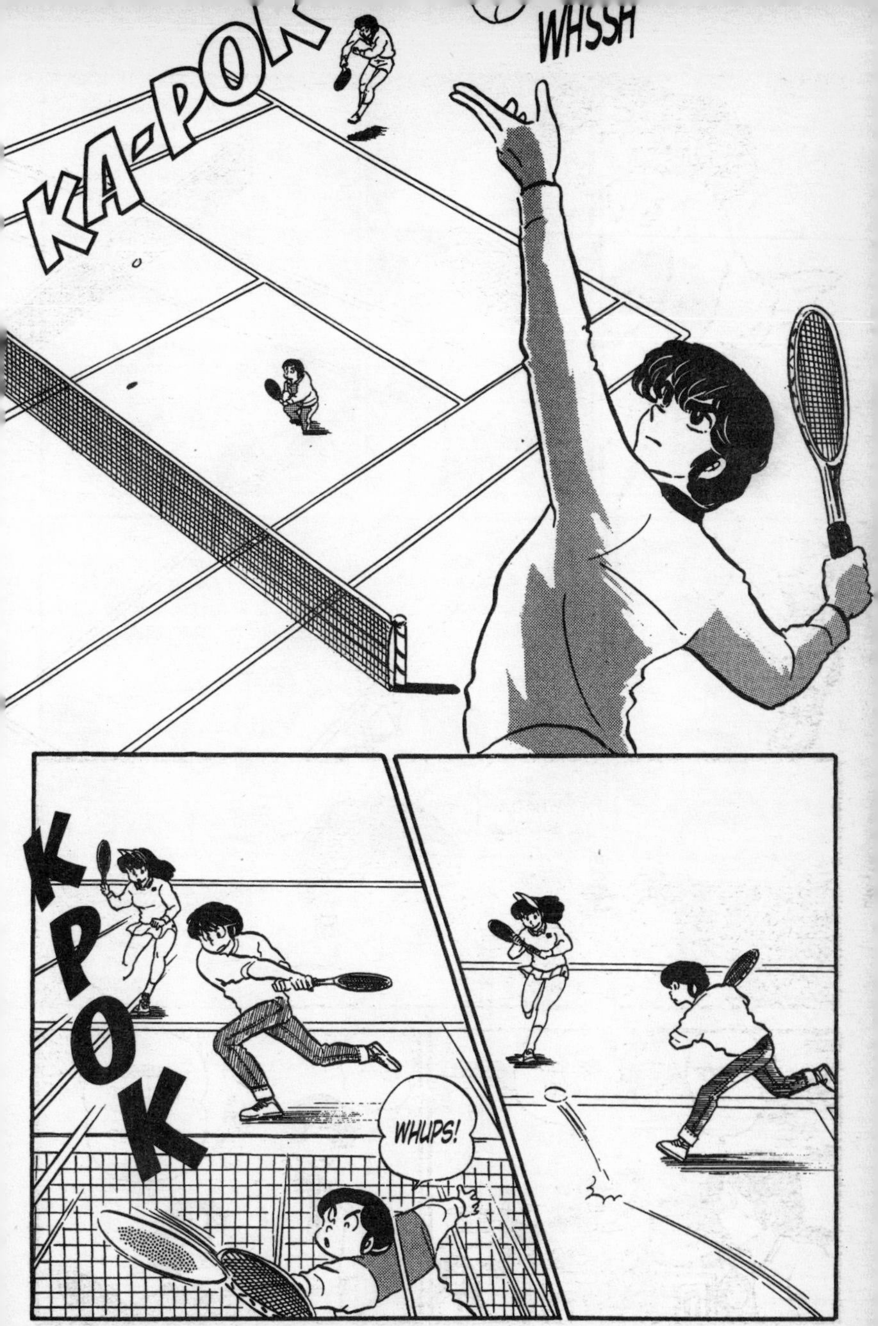
WHSSH
KA-POK
KPOK
WHUPS!

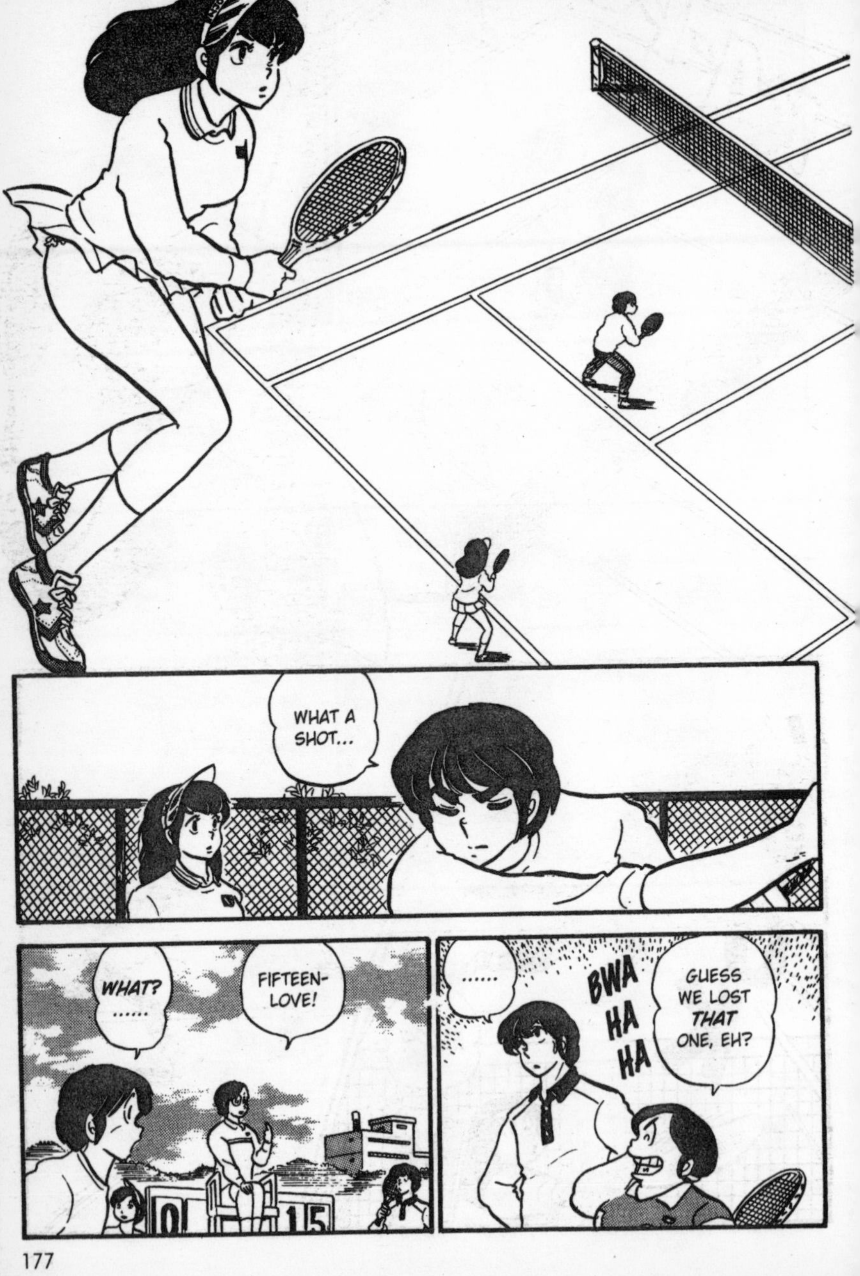
WHAT A SHOT...
GUESS WE LOST *THAT* ONE, EH?
BWA HA HA
......
FIFTEEN-LOVE!
WHAT? ......
0
15

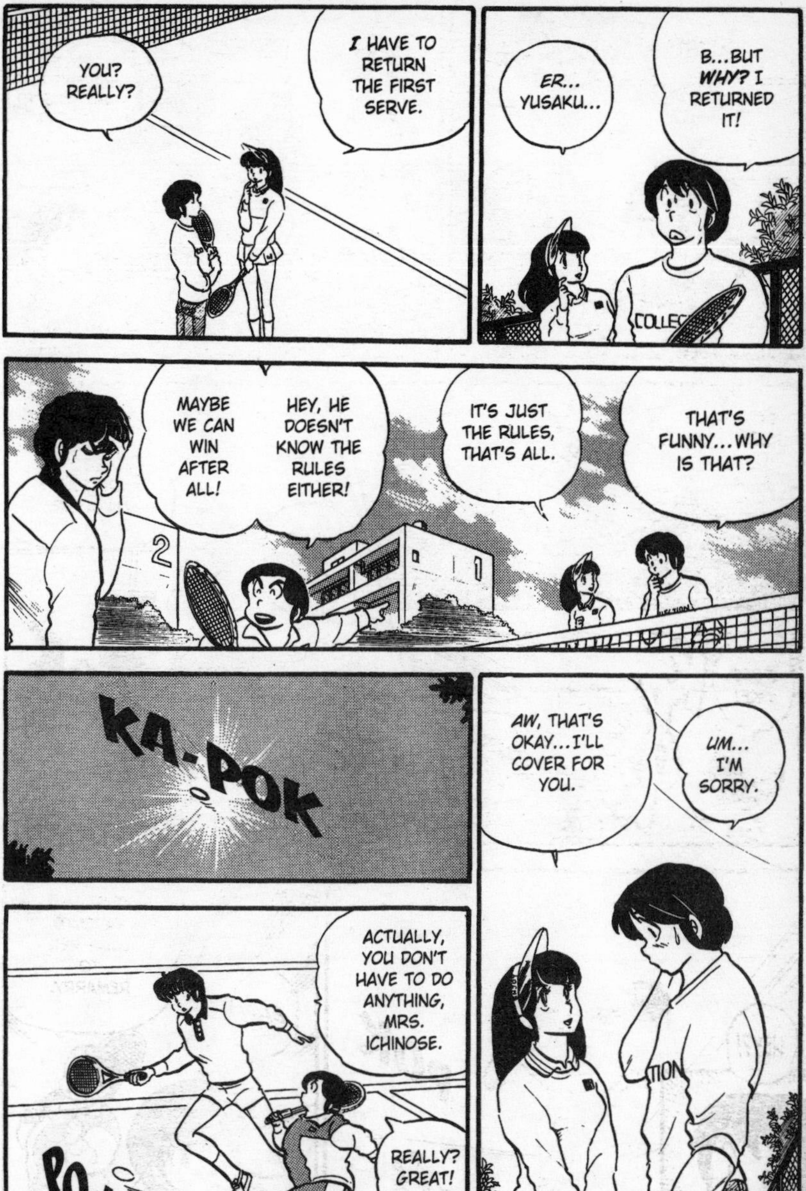
B...BUT WHY? I RETURNED IT!
ER... YUSAKU...
I HAVE TO RETURN THE FIRST SERVE.
YOU? REALLY?
THAT'S FUNNY...WHY IS THAT?
IT'S JUST THE RULES, THAT'S ALL.
HEY, HE DOESN'T KNOW THE RULES EITHER!
MAYBE WE CAN WIN AFTER ALL!
UM... I'M SORRY.
AW, THAT'S OKAY...I'LL COVER FOR YOU.
KA-POK
ACTUALLY, YOU DON'T HAVE TO DO ANYTHING, MRS. ICHINOSE.
REALLY? GREAT!
POK

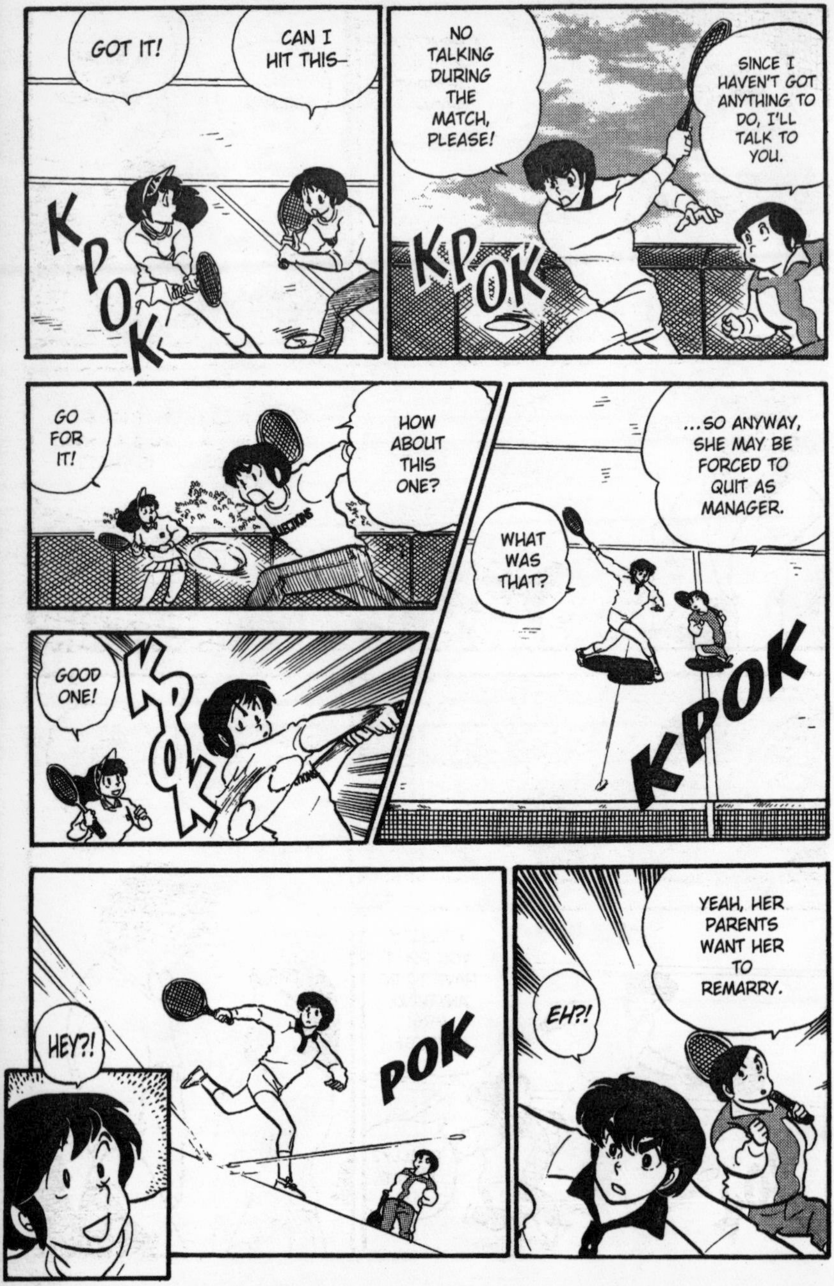
SINCE I HAVEN'T GOT ANYTHING TO DO, I'LL TALK TO YOU.
NO TALKING DURING THE MATCH, PLEASE!
KPOK
CAN I HIT THIS–
GOT IT!
KPOK
...SO ANYWAY, SHE MAY BE FORCED TO QUIT AS MANAGER.
WHAT WAS THAT?
KPOK
HOW ABOUT THIS ONE?
GO FOR IT!
KPOK
GOOD ONE!
YEAH, HER PARENTS WANT HER TO REMARRY.
EH?!
POK
HEY?!

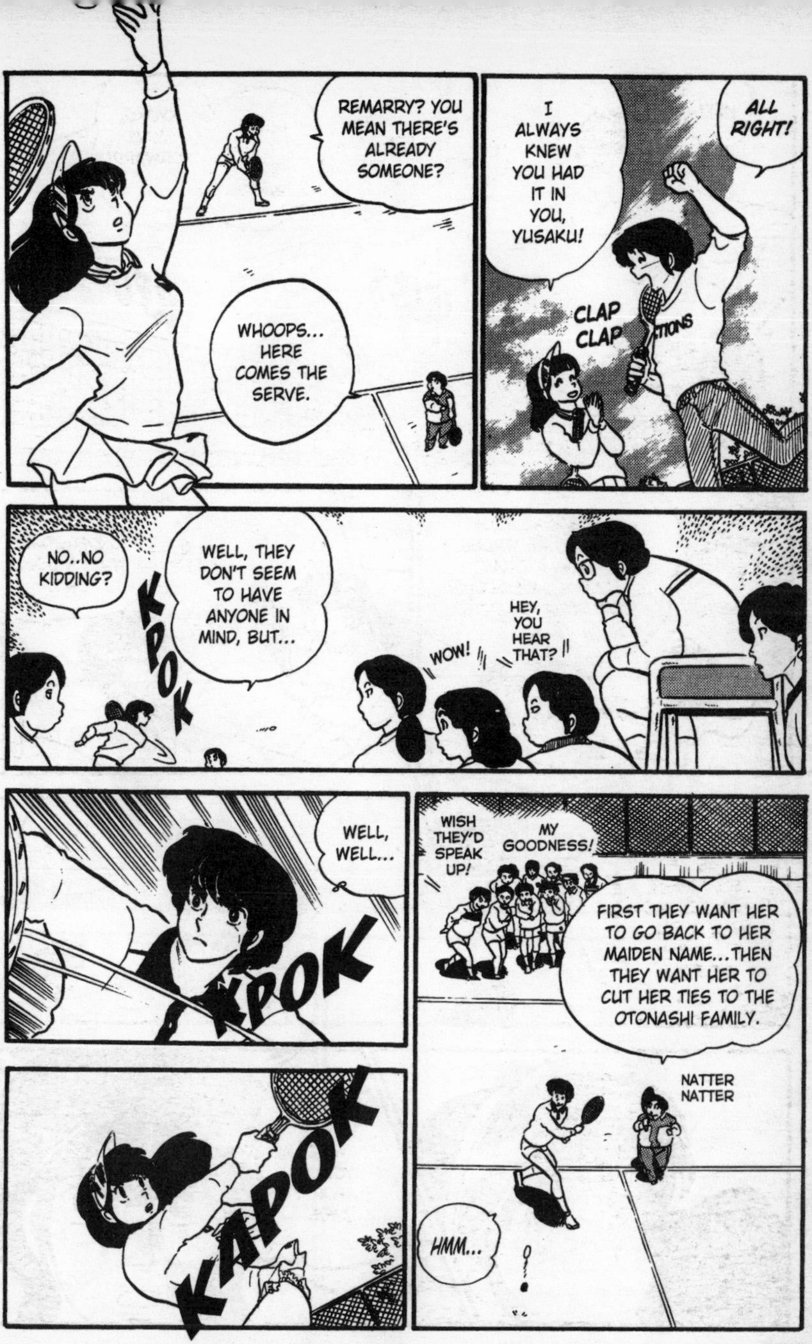
ALL RIGHT!
I ALWAYS KNEW YOU HAD IT IN YOU, YUSAKU!
CLAP CLAP
REMARRY? YOU MEAN THERE'S ALREADY SOMEONE?
WHOOPS... HERE COMES THE SERVE.
HEY, YOU HEAR THAT?
WOW!
WELL, THEY DON'T SEEM TO HAVE ANYONE IN MIND, BUT...
KPOK
NO..NO KIDDING?
MY GOODNESS!
WISH THEY'D SPEAK UP!
FIRST THEY WANT HER TO GO BACK TO HER MAIDEN NAME...THEN THEY WANT HER TO CUT HER TIES TO THE OTONASHI FAMILY.
NATTER NATTER
HMM...
WELL, WELL...
KPOK
KAPOK

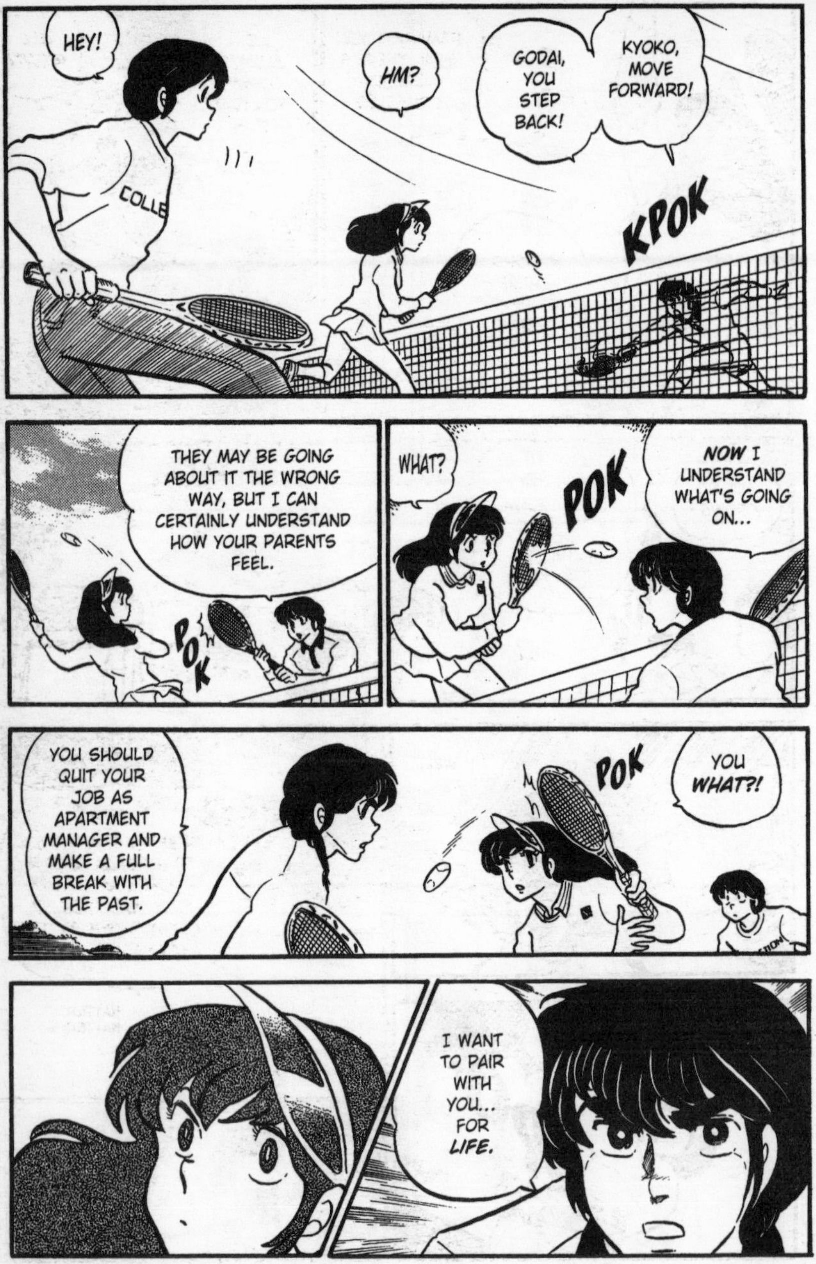
KYOKO, MOVE FORWARD!
GODAI, YOU STEP BACK!
HM?
HEY!
KPOK
NOW I UNDERSTAND WHAT'S GOING ON...
POK
WHAT?
THEY MAY BE GOING ABOUT IT THE WRONG WAY, BUT I CAN CERTAINLY UNDERSTAND HOW YOUR PARENTS FEEL.
POK
YOU WHAT?!
POK
YOU SHOULD QUIT YOUR JOB AS APARTMENT MANAGER AND MAKE A FULL BREAK WITH THE PAST.
I WANT TO PAIR WITH YOU... FOR LIFE.

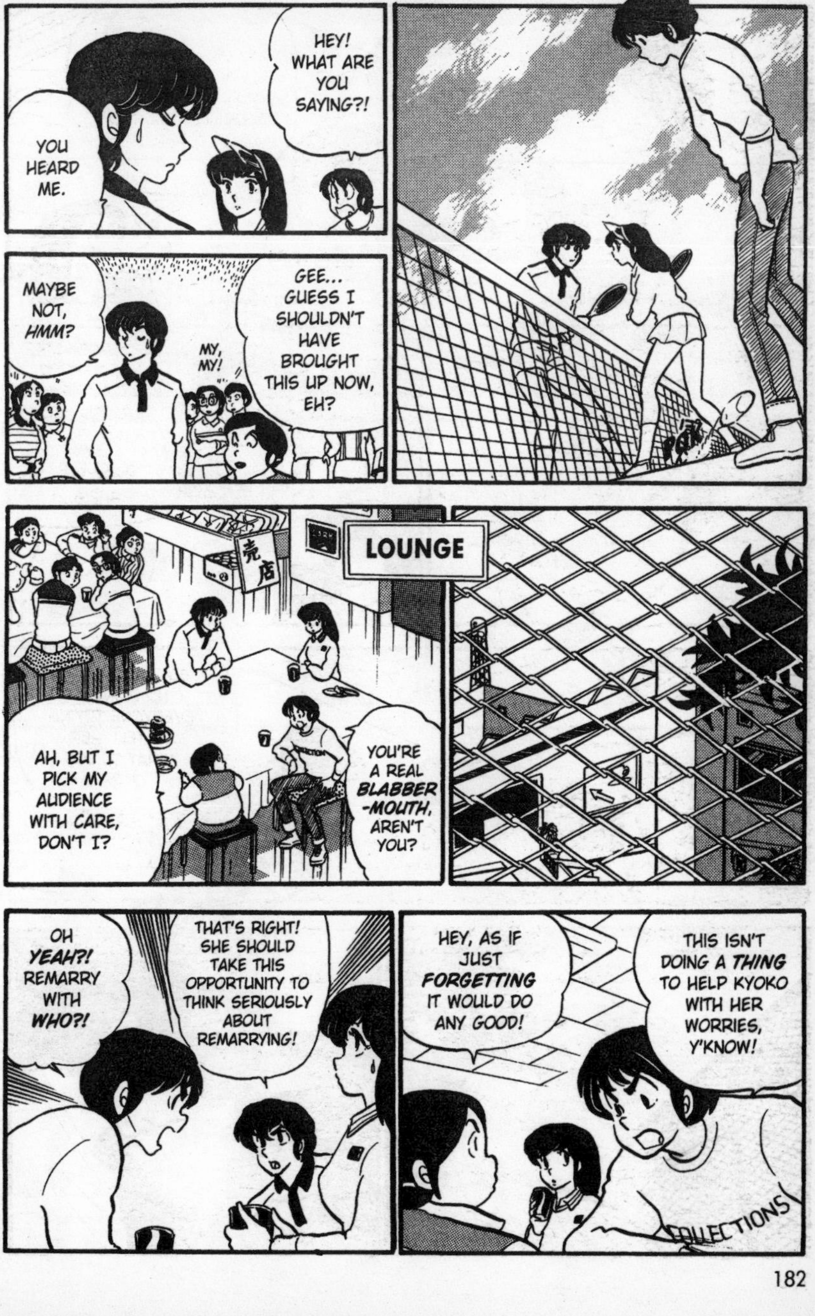
HEY! WHAT ARE YOU SAYING?!
YOU HEARD ME.
GEE... GUESS I SHOULDN'T HAVE BROUGHT THIS UP NOW, EH?
MY, MY!
MAYBE NOT, *HMM*?
LOUNGE
売店
YOU'RE A REAL *BLABBER-MOUTH*, AREN'T YOU?
AH, BUT I PICK MY AUDIENCE WITH CARE, DON'T I?
THIS ISN'T DOING A *THING* TO HELP KYOKO WITH HER WORRIES, Y'KNOW!
HEY, AS IF JUST *FORGETTING* IT WOULD DO ANY GOOD!
COLLECTIONS
THAT'S RIGHT! SHE SHOULD TAKE THIS OPPORTUNITY TO THINK SERIOUSLY ABOUT REMARRYING!
OH *YEAH?!* REMARRY WITH *WHO?!*

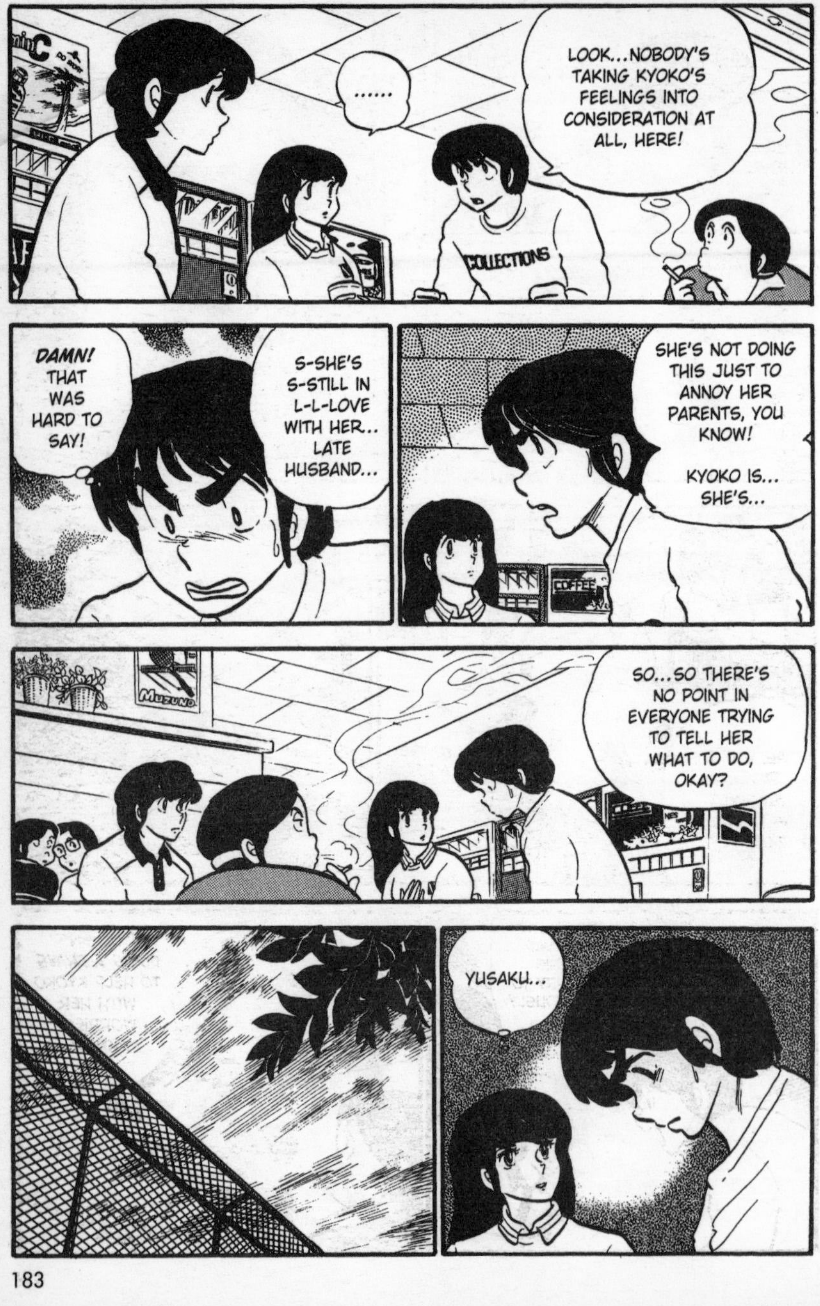
LOOK...NOBODY'S TAKING KYOKO'S FEELINGS INTO CONSIDERATION AT ALL, HERE!
......
COLLECTIONS
SHE'S NOT DOING THIS JUST TO ANNOY HER PARENTS, YOU KNOW!
KYOKO IS... SHE'S...
COFFEE
S-SHE'S S-STILL IN L-L-LOVE WITH HER... LATE HUSBAND...
DAMN! THAT WAS HARD TO SAY!
SO...SO THERE'S NO POINT IN EVERYONE TRYING TO TELL HER WHAT TO DO, OKAY?
MUZUNO
YUSAKU...

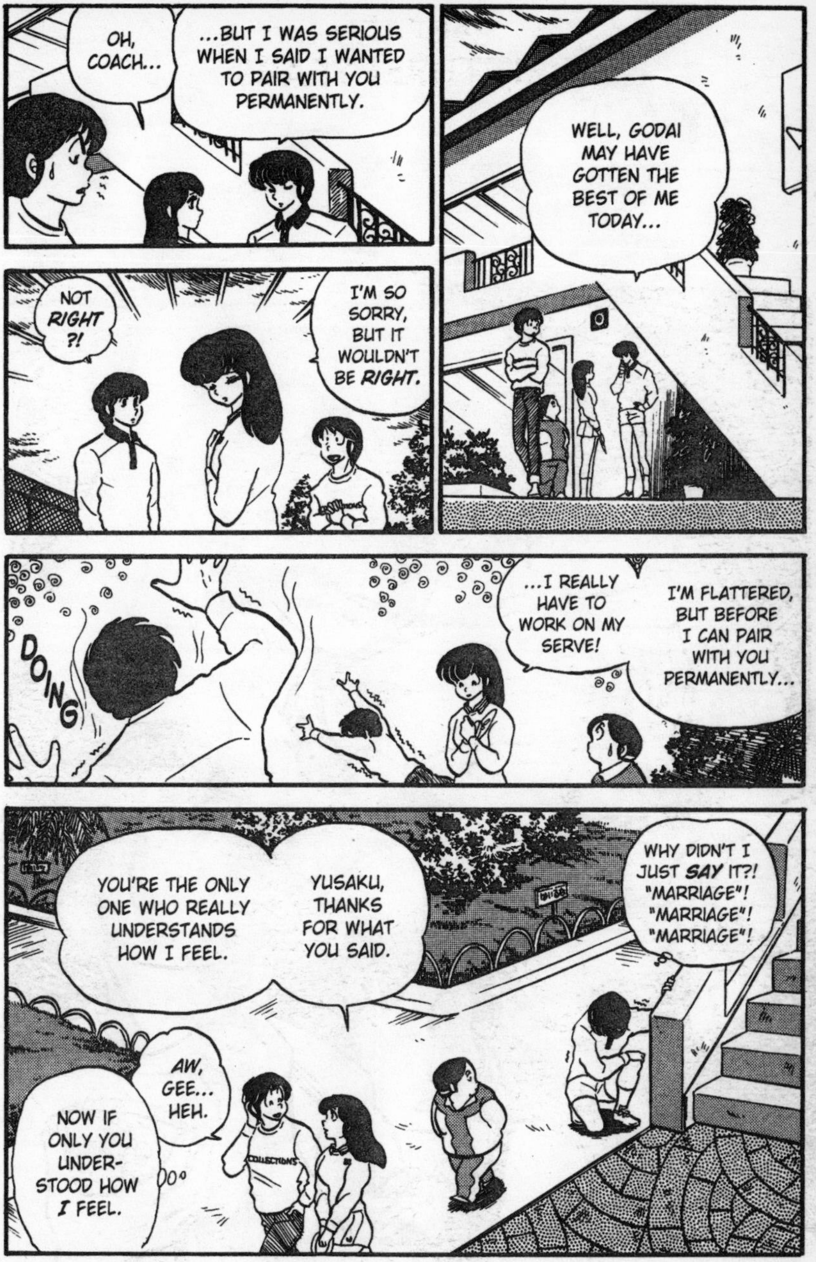
WELL, GODAI MAY HAVE GOTTEN THE BEST OF ME TODAY...
...BUT I WAS SERIOUS WHEN I SAID I WANTED TO PAIR WITH YOU PERMANENTLY.
OH, COACH...
I'M SO SORRY, BUT IT WOULDN'T BE *RIGHT*.
NOT *RIGHT* ?!
I'M FLATTERED, BUT BEFORE I CAN PAIR WITH YOU PERMANENTLY...
...I REALLY HAVE TO WORK ON MY SERVE!
DOING
WHY DIDN'T I JUST *SAY* IT?! "MARRIAGE"! "MARRIAGE"! "MARRIAGE"!
YUSAKU, THANKS FOR WHAT YOU SAID.
YOU'RE THE ONLY ONE WHO REALLY UNDERSTANDS HOW I FEEL.
AW, GEE... HEH.
NOW IF ONLY YOU UNDER-STOOD HOW *I* FEEL.

PART TEN

WAIT THREE YEARS

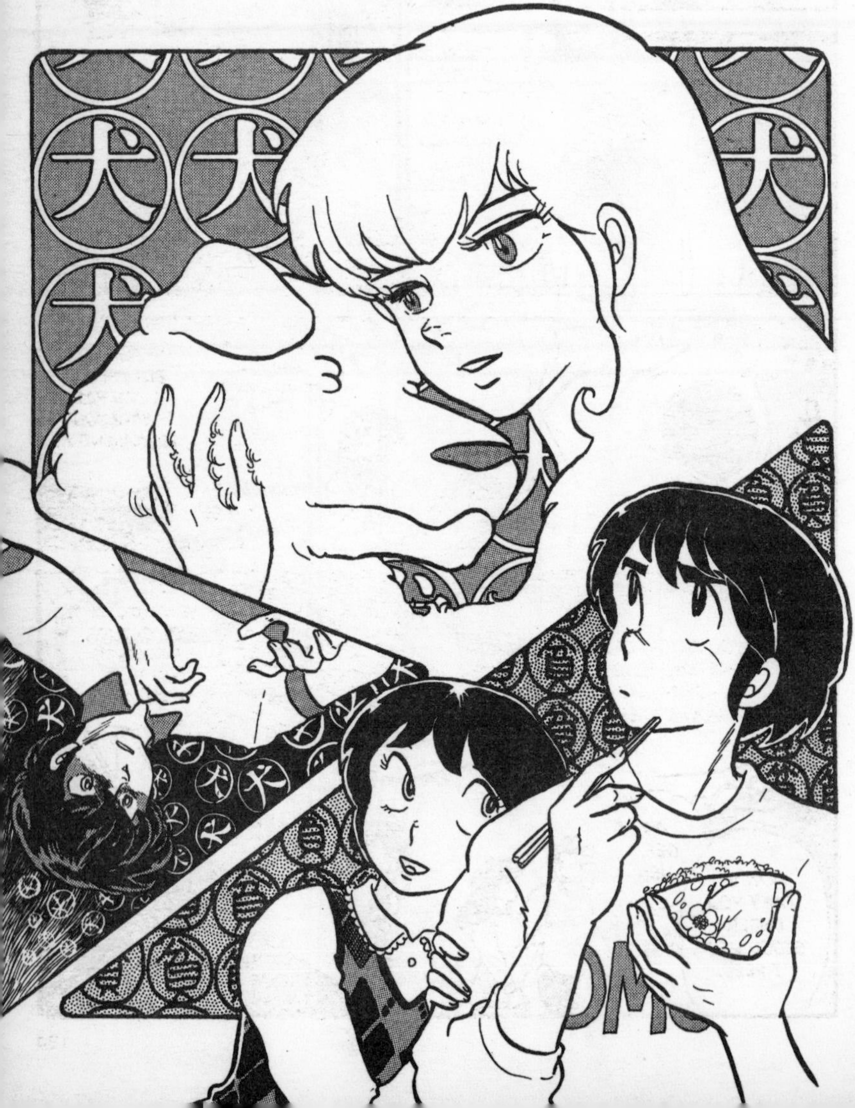

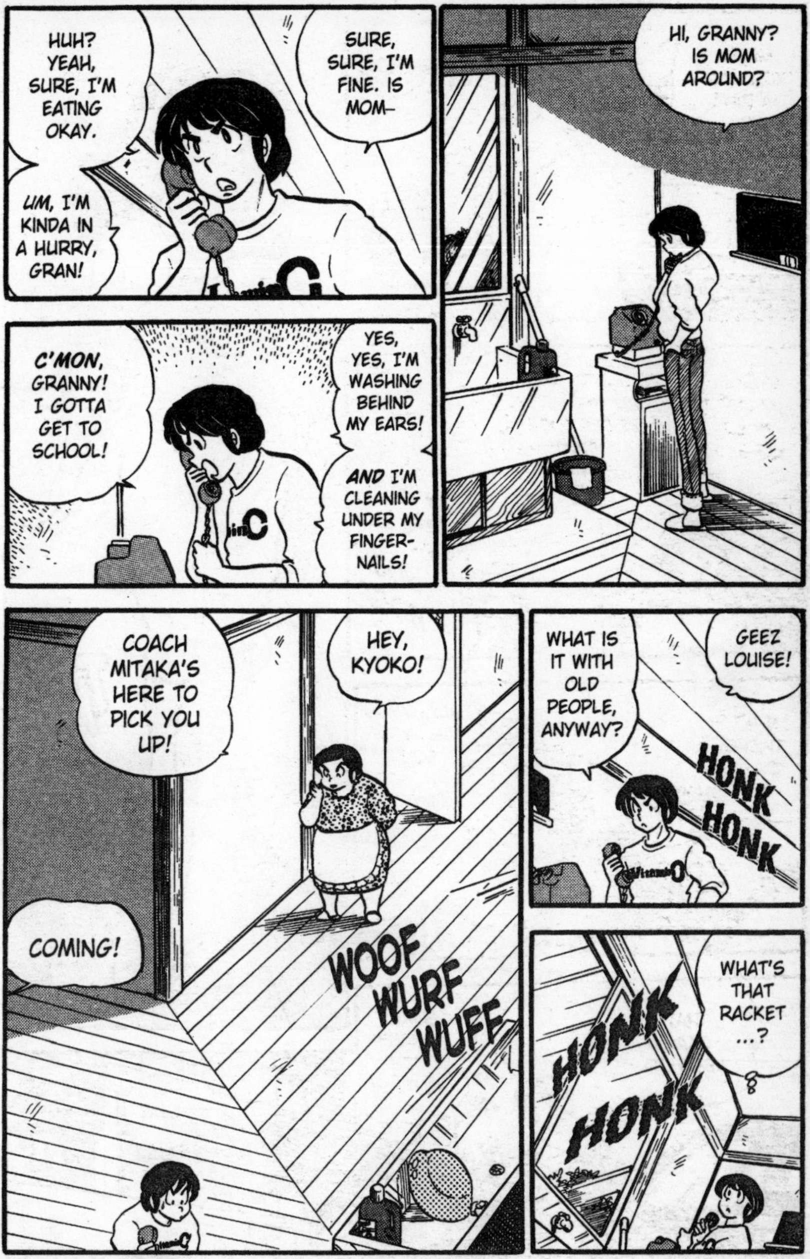
HI, GRANNY? IS MOM AROUND?
SURE, SURE, I'M FINE. IS MOM–
HUH? YEAH, SURE, I'M EATING OKAY.
UM, I'M KINDA IN A HURRY, GRAN!
YES, YES, I'M WASHING BEHIND MY EARS!
AND I'M CLEANING UNDER MY FINGER-NAILS!
C'MON, GRANNY! I GOTTA GET TO SCHOOL!
GEEZ LOUISE!
WHAT IS IT WITH OLD PEOPLE, ANYWAY?
HONK HONK
WHAT'S THAT RACKET ...?
HONK HONK
HEY, KYOKO!
COACH MITAKA'S HERE TO PICK YOU UP!
WOOF WURF WUFF
COMING!

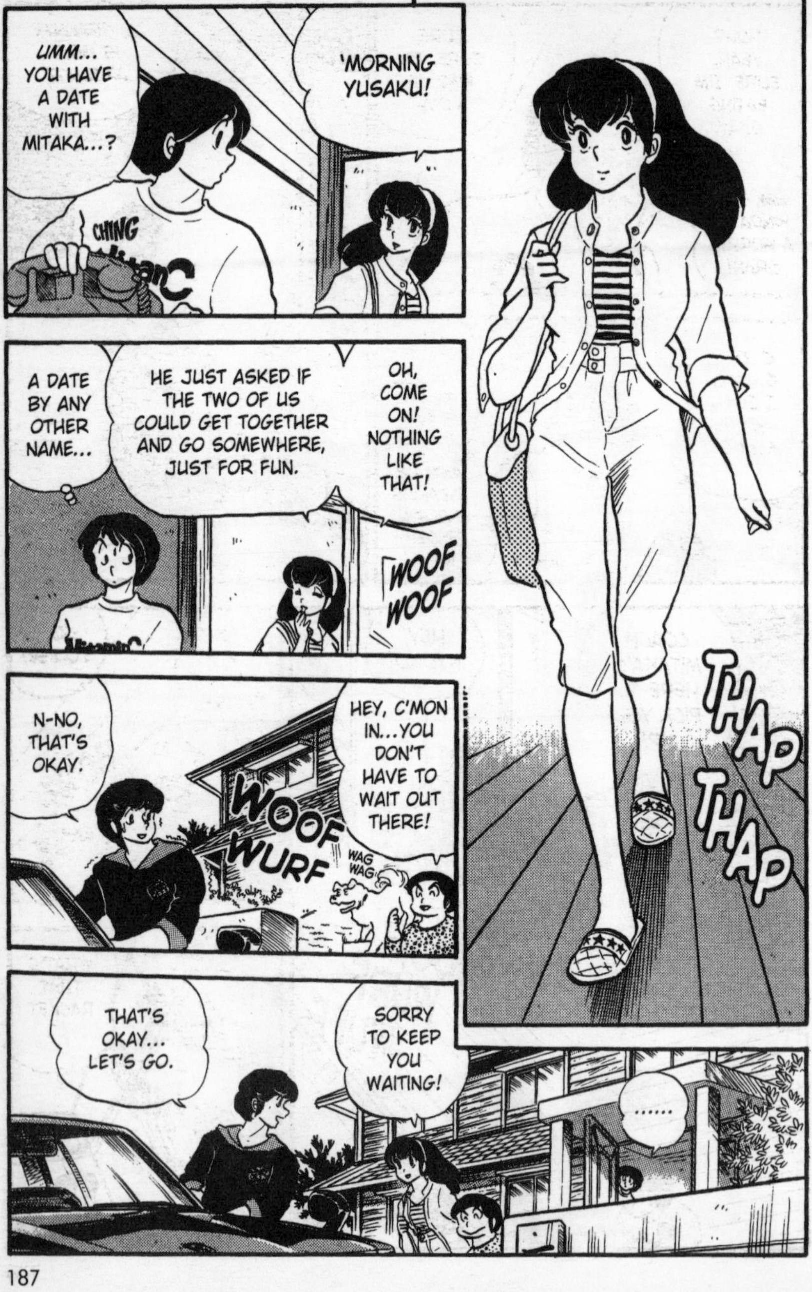
THAP THAP
'MORNING YUSAKU!
UMM... YOU HAVE A DATE WITH MITAKA...?
OH, COME ON! NOTHING LIKE THAT!
HE JUST ASKED IF THE TWO OF US COULD GET TOGETHER AND GO SOMEWHERE, JUST FOR FUN.
A DATE BY ANY OTHER NAME...
WOOF WOOF
HEY, C'MON IN...YOU DON'T HAVE TO WAIT OUT THERE!
WAG WAG
WOOF WURF
N-NO, THAT'S OKAY.
......
SORRY TO KEEP YOU WAITING!
THAT'S OKAY... LET'S GO.

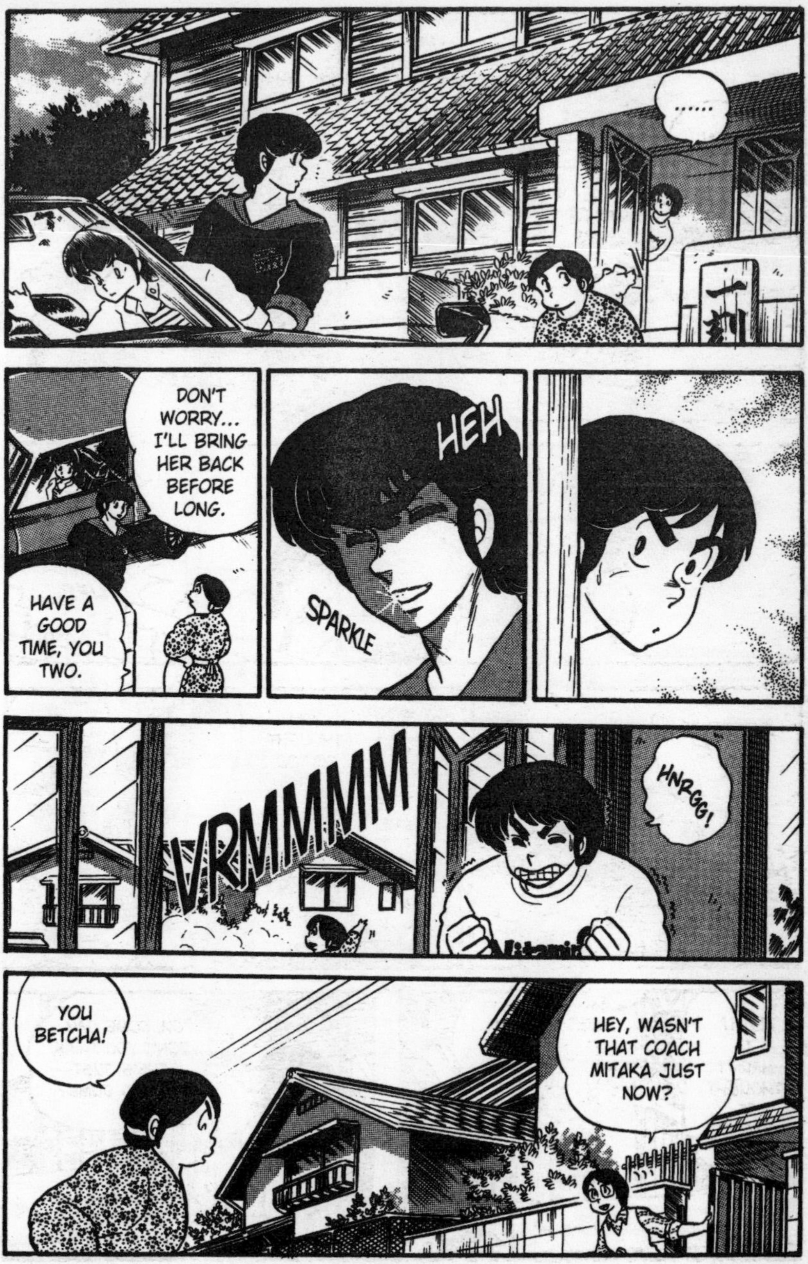
……
HEH
SPARKLE
DON'T WORRY... I'LL BRING HER BACK BEFORE LONG.
HAVE A GOOD TIME, YOU TWO.
HNRGG!
VRMMMM
HEY, WASN'T THAT COACH MITAKA JUST NOW?
YOU BETCHA!

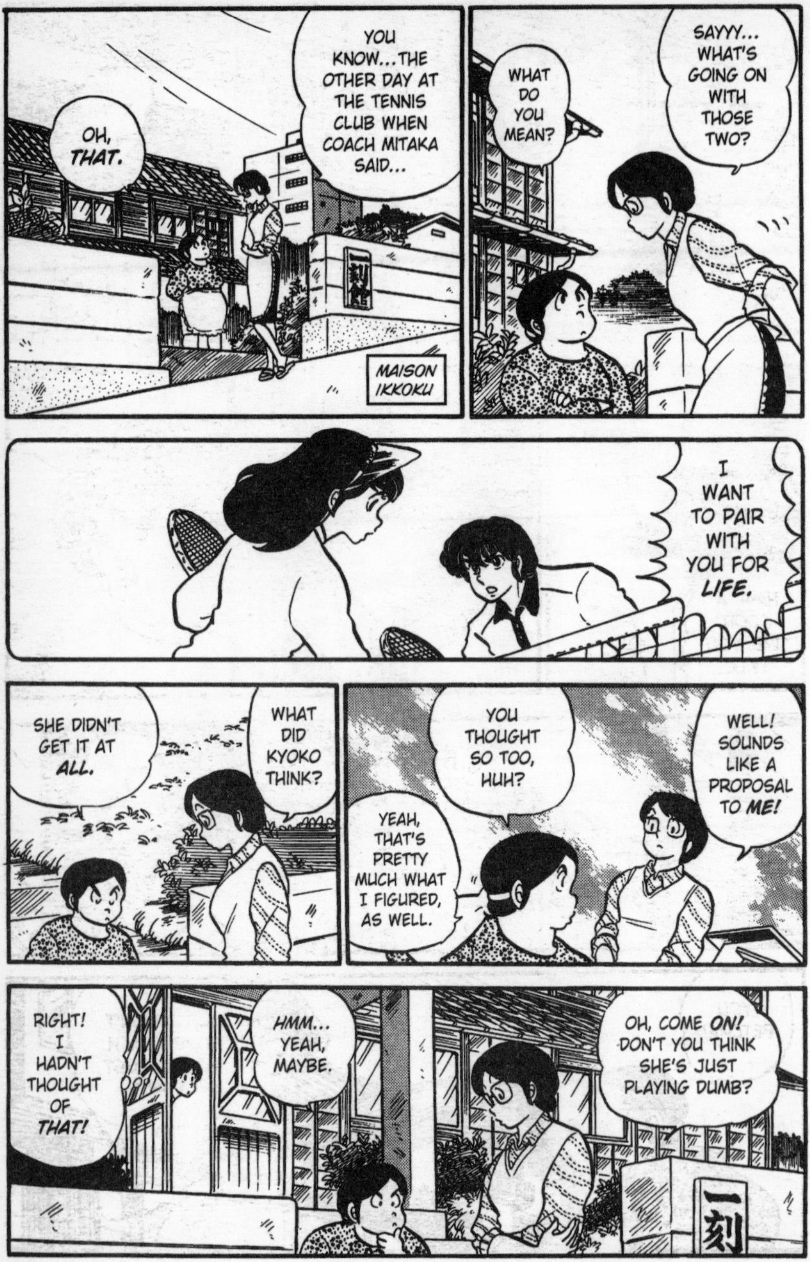
SAYYY... WHAT'S GOING ON WITH THOSE TWO?
WHAT DO YOU MEAN?
YOU KNOW...THE OTHER DAY AT THE TENNIS CLUB WHEN COACH MITAKA SAID...
OH, *THAT.*
MAISON IKKOKU
I WANT TO PAIR WITH YOU FOR *LIFE.*
WELL! SOUNDS LIKE A PROPOSAL TO *ME!*
YOU THOUGHT SO TOO, HUH?
YEAH, THAT'S PRETTY MUCH WHAT I FIGURED, AS WELL.
WHAT DID KYOKO THINK?
SHE DIDN'T GET IT AT *ALL.*
OH, COME *ON!* DON'T YOU THINK SHE'S JUST PLAYING DUMB?
HMM... YEAH, MAYBE.
RIGHT! I HADN'T THOUGHT OF *THAT!*
一刻

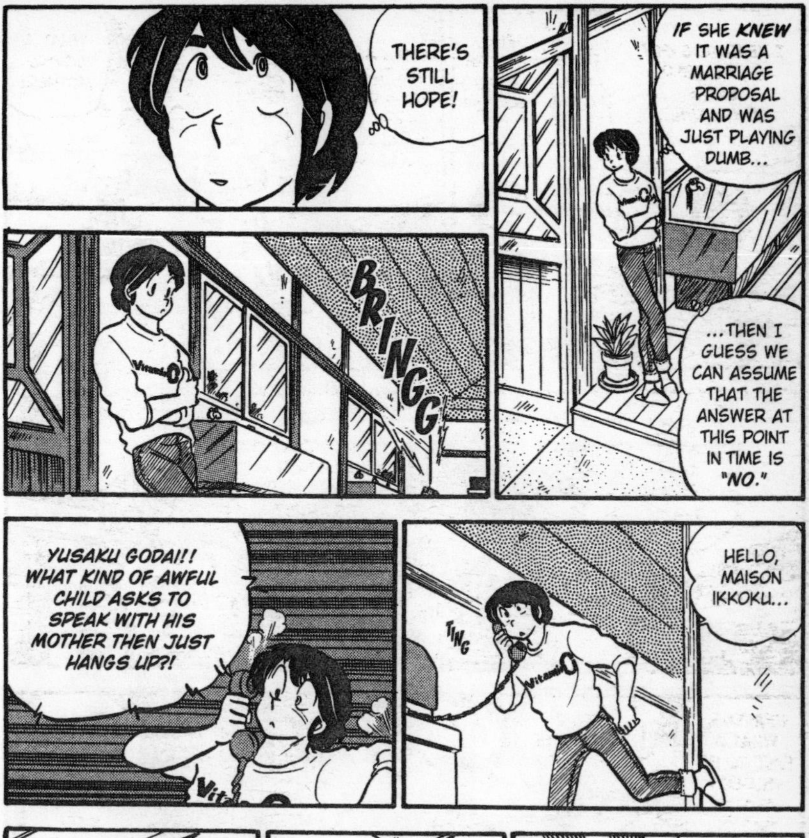
IF SHE KNEW IT WAS A MARRIAGE PROPOSAL AND WAS JUST PLAYING DUMB...
...THEN I GUESS WE CAN ASSUME THAT THE ANSWER AT THIS POINT IN TIME IS "NO."
THERE'S STILL HOPE!
BRINGG
HELLO, MAISON IKKOKU...
TING
YUSAKU GODAI!! WHAT KIND OF AWFUL CHILD ASKS TO SPEAK WITH HIS MOTHER THEN JUST HANGS UP?!
LOOK, MOM, LEMME GET STRAIGHT TO THE POINT–
MONEY !!
I HAVEN'T GOTTEN MY CHECK THIS MONTH YET!
......
MOM? HELLO?
I FORGOT.
WHA?
MOM !!

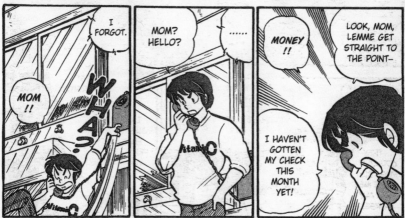

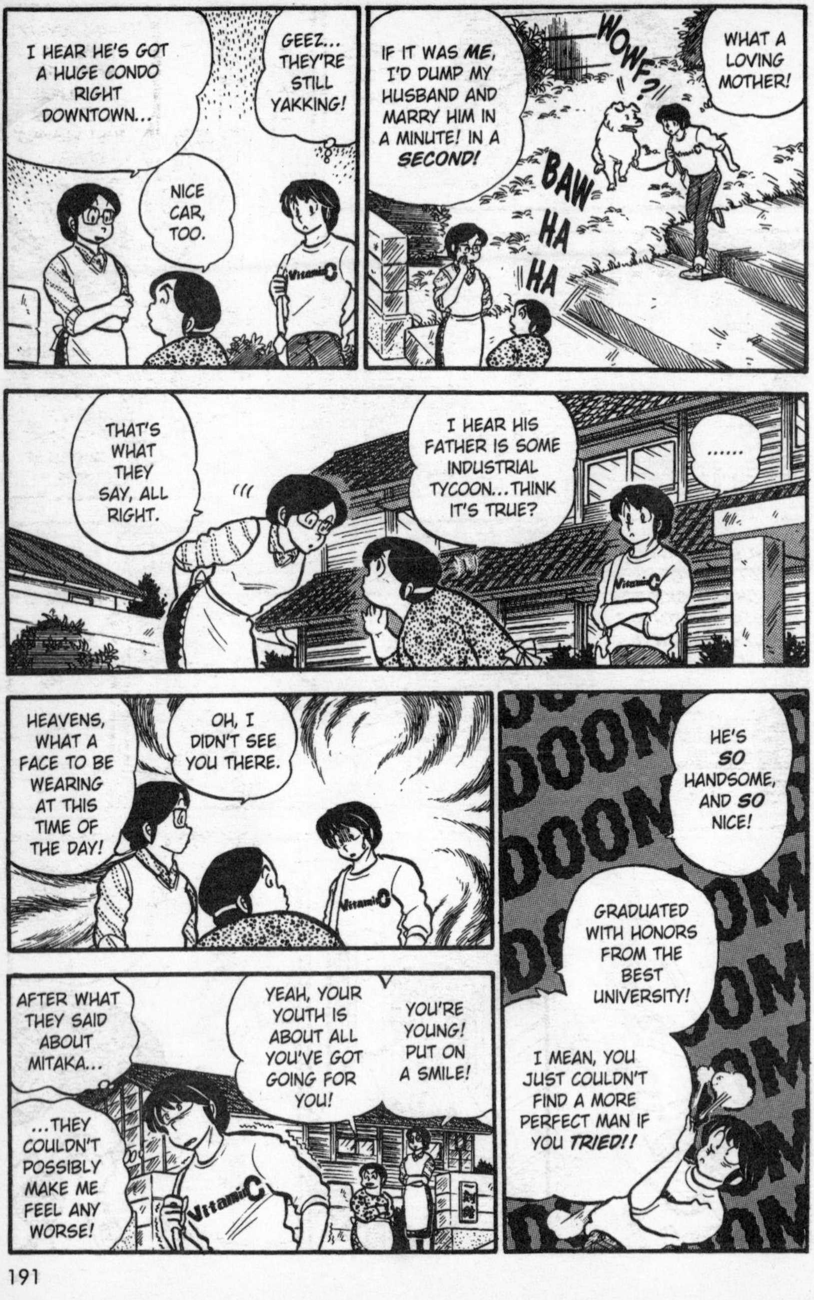
WHAT A LOVING MOTHER!
WOWF?
IF IT WAS *ME*, I'D DUMP MY HUSBAND AND MARRY HIM IN A MINUTE! IN A *SECOND!*
BAW HA HA
GEEZ... THEY'RE STILL YAKKING!
I HEAR HE'S GOT A HUGE CONDO RIGHT DOWNTOWN...
NICE CAR, TOO.
......
I HEAR HIS FATHER IS SOME INDUSTRIAL TYCOON...THINK IT'S TRUE?
THAT'S WHAT THEY SAY, ALL RIGHT.
DOOM DOOM DOOM
HE'S *SO* HANDSOME, AND *SO* NICE!
GRADUATED WITH HONORS FROM THE BEST UNIVERSITY!
I MEAN, YOU JUST COULDN'T FIND A MORE PERFECT MAN IF YOU *TRIED!!*
OH, I DIDN'T SEE YOU THERE.
HEAVENS, WHAT A FACE TO BE WEARING AT THIS TIME OF THE DAY!
YOU'RE YOUNG! PUT ON A SMILE!
YEAH, YOUR YOUTH IS ABOUT ALL YOU'VE GOT GOING FOR YOU!
AFTER WHAT THEY SAID ABOUT MITAKA...
...THEY COULDN'T POSSIBLY MAKE ME FEEL ANY WORSE!

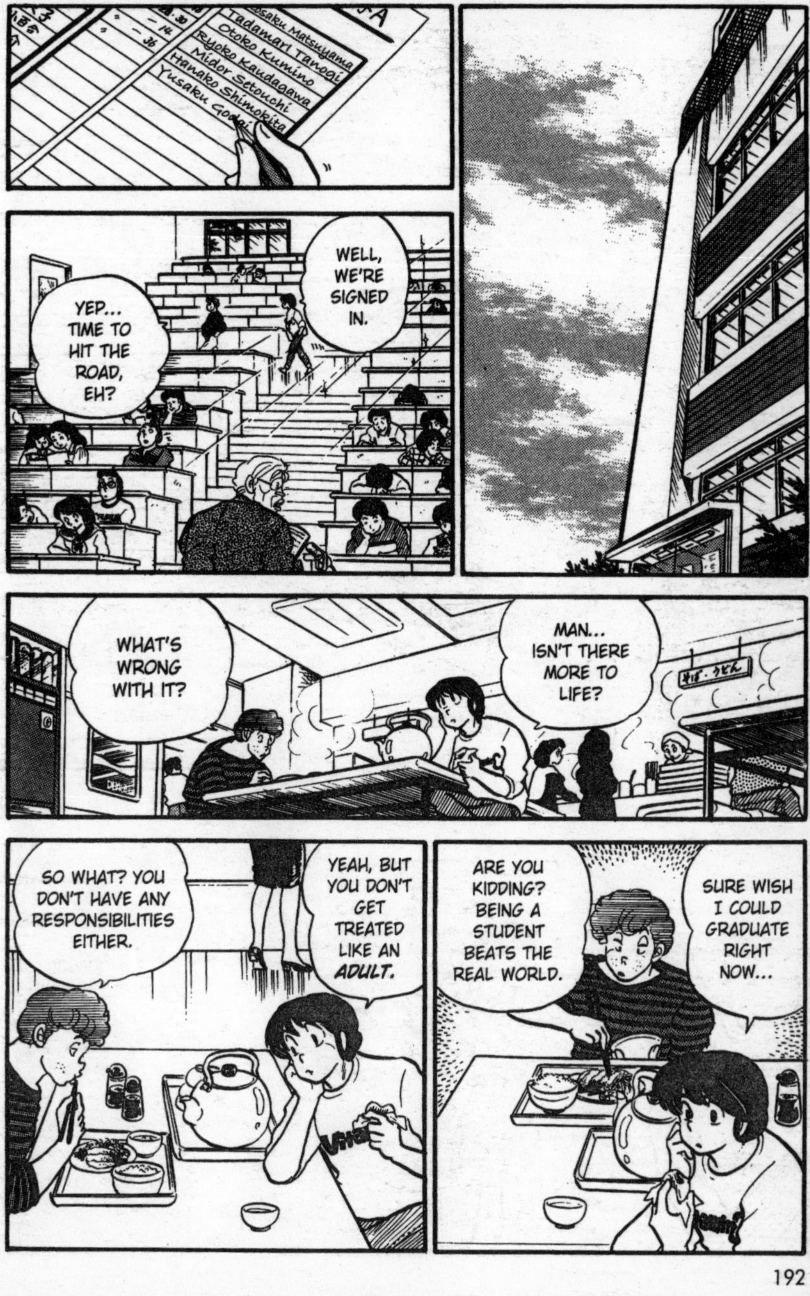
Tadamari Tanogi
Otoko Kumino
Ryoko Kaudagawa
Midor Setouchi
Hanako Shimokita
Yusaku Godai
WELL, WE'RE SIGNED IN.
YEP... TIME TO HIT THE ROAD, EH?
MAN... ISN'T THERE MORE TO LIFE?
WHAT'S WRONG WITH IT?
SURE WISH I COULD GRADUATE RIGHT NOW...
ARE YOU KIDDING? BEING A STUDENT BEATS THE REAL WORLD.
YEAH, BUT YOU DON'T GET TREATED LIKE AN ***ADULT.***
SO WHAT? YOU DON'T HAVE ANY RESPONSIBILITIES EITHER.

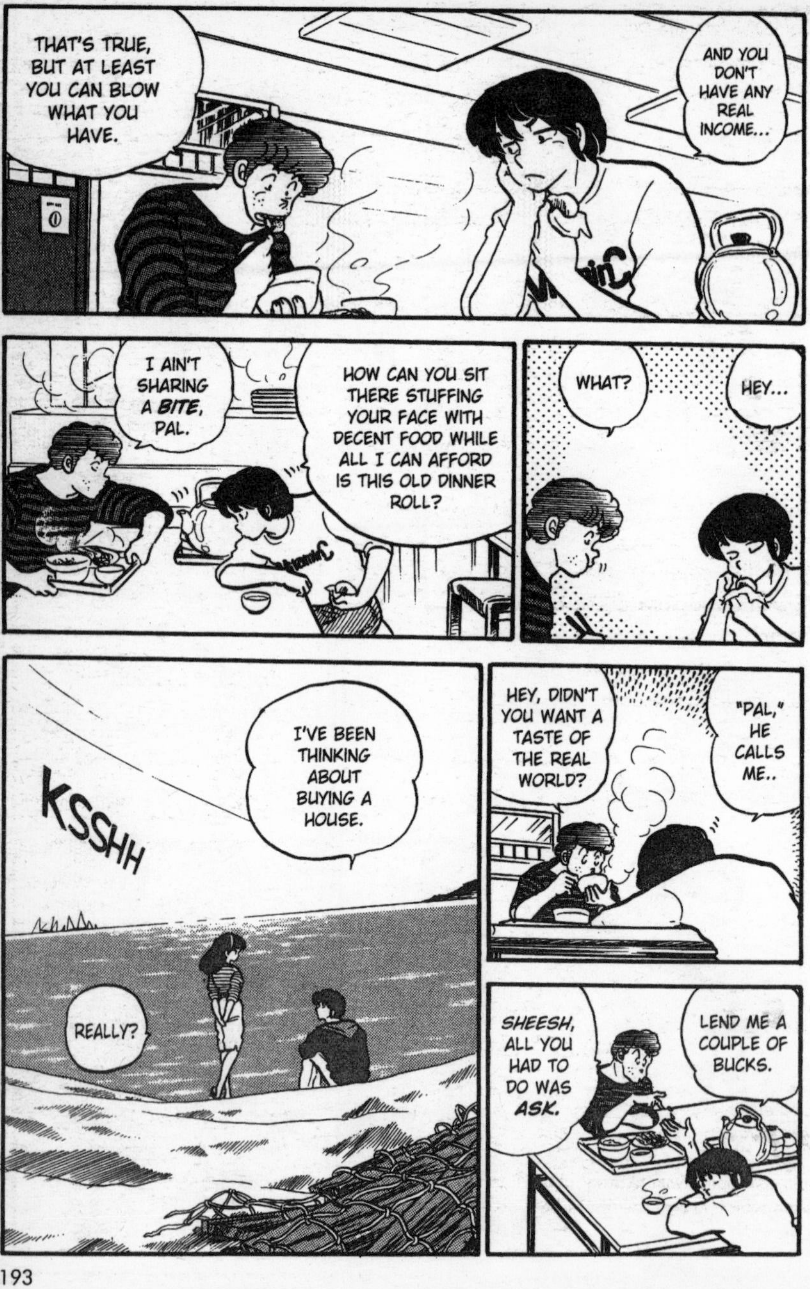
AND YOU DON'T HAVE ANY REAL INCOME...
THAT'S TRUE, BUT AT LEAST YOU CAN BLOW WHAT YOU HAVE.
HEY...
WHAT?
HOW CAN YOU SIT THERE STUFFING YOUR FACE WITH DECENT FOOD WHILE ALL I CAN AFFORD IS THIS OLD DINNER ROLL?
I AIN'T SHARING A *BITE*, PAL.
"PAL," HE CALLS ME..
HEY, DIDN'T YOU WANT A TASTE OF THE REAL WORLD?
LEND ME A COUPLE OF BUCKS.
SHEESH, ALL YOU HAD TO DO WAS *ASK*.
I'VE BEEN THINKING ABOUT BUYING A HOUSE.
KSSHH
REALLY?

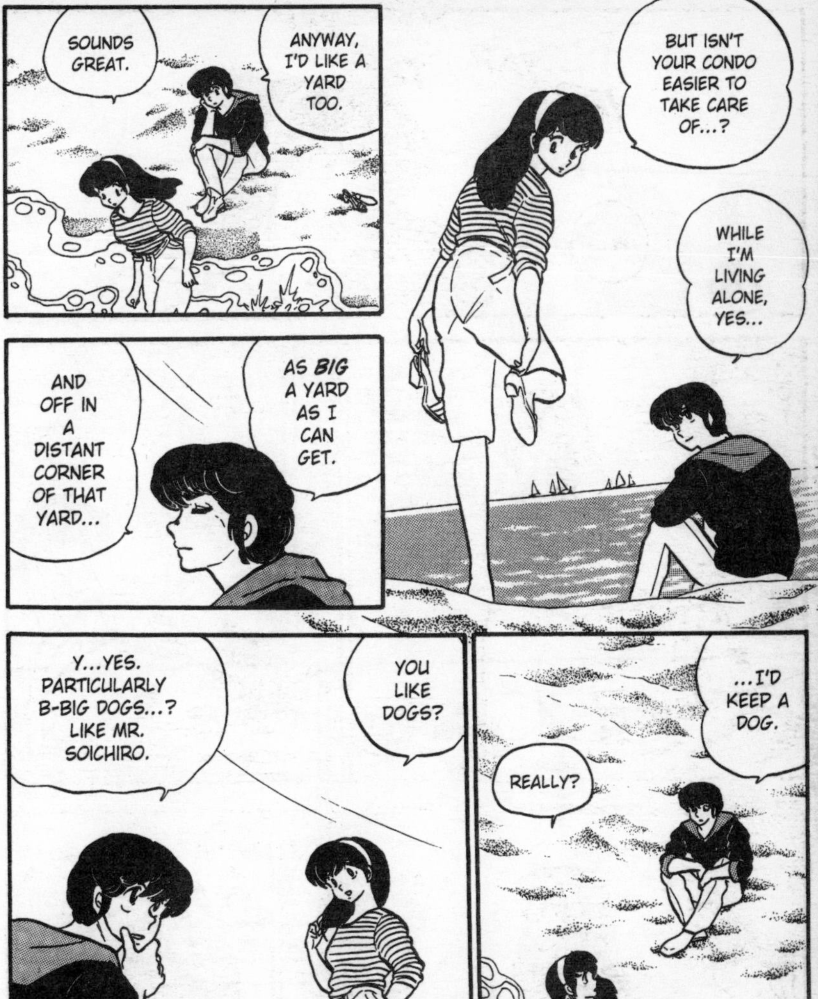
BUT ISN'T YOUR CONDO EASIER TO TAKE CARE OF...?
WHILE I'M LIVING ALONE, YES...
ANYWAY, I'D LIKE A YARD TOO.
SOUNDS GREAT.
AS *BIG* A YARD AS I CAN GET.
AND OFF IN A DISTANT CORNER OF THAT YARD...
...I'D KEEP A DOG.
REALLY?
YOU LIKE DOGS?
Y...YES. PARTICULARLY B-BIG DOGS...? LIKE MR. SOICHIRO.

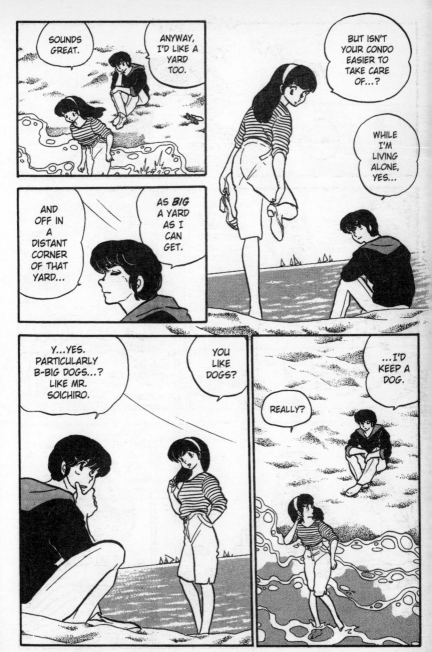

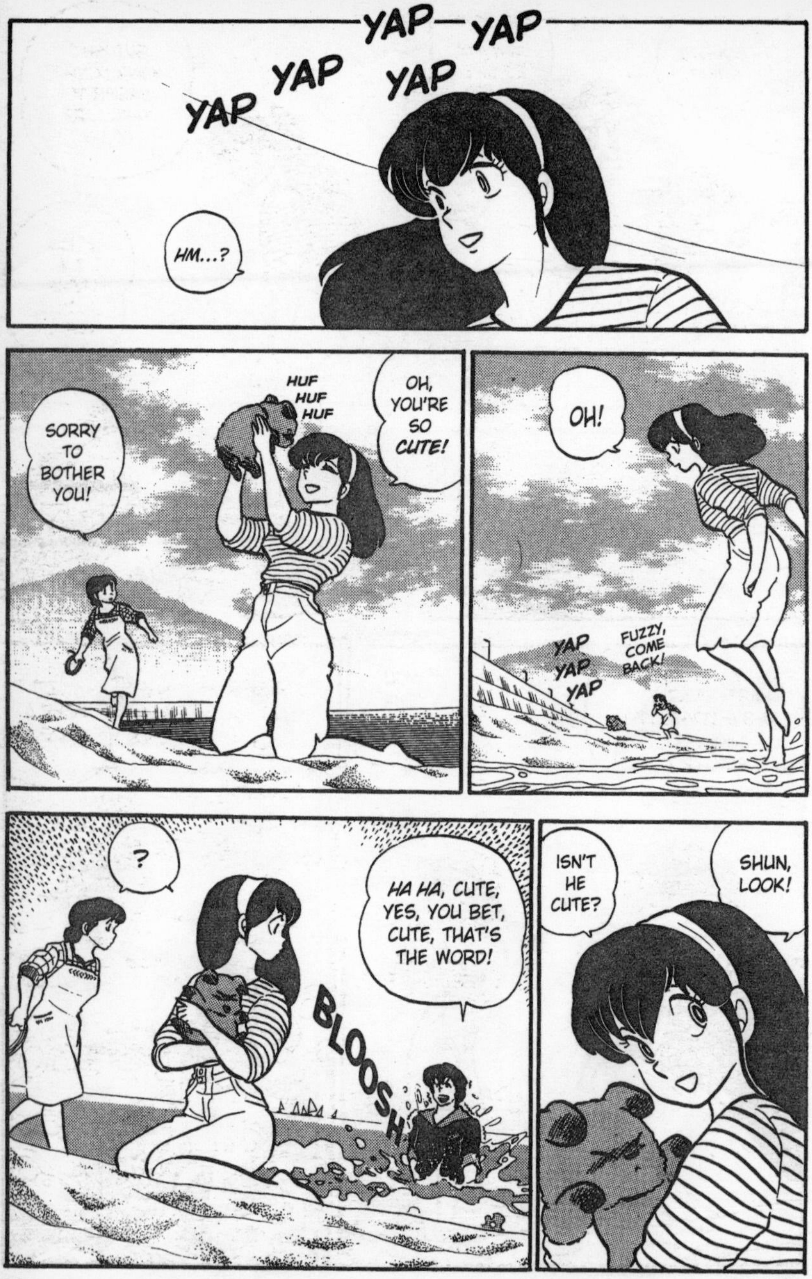
YAP YAP YAP YAP YAP
HM...?
OH!
YAP YAP YAP
FUZZY, COME BACK!
OH, YOU'RE SO CUTE!
HUF HUF HUF
SORRY TO BOTHER YOU!
SHUN, LOOK!
ISN'T HE CUTE?
HA HA, CUTE, YES, YOU BET, CUTE, THAT'S THE WORD!
BLOOSH
?

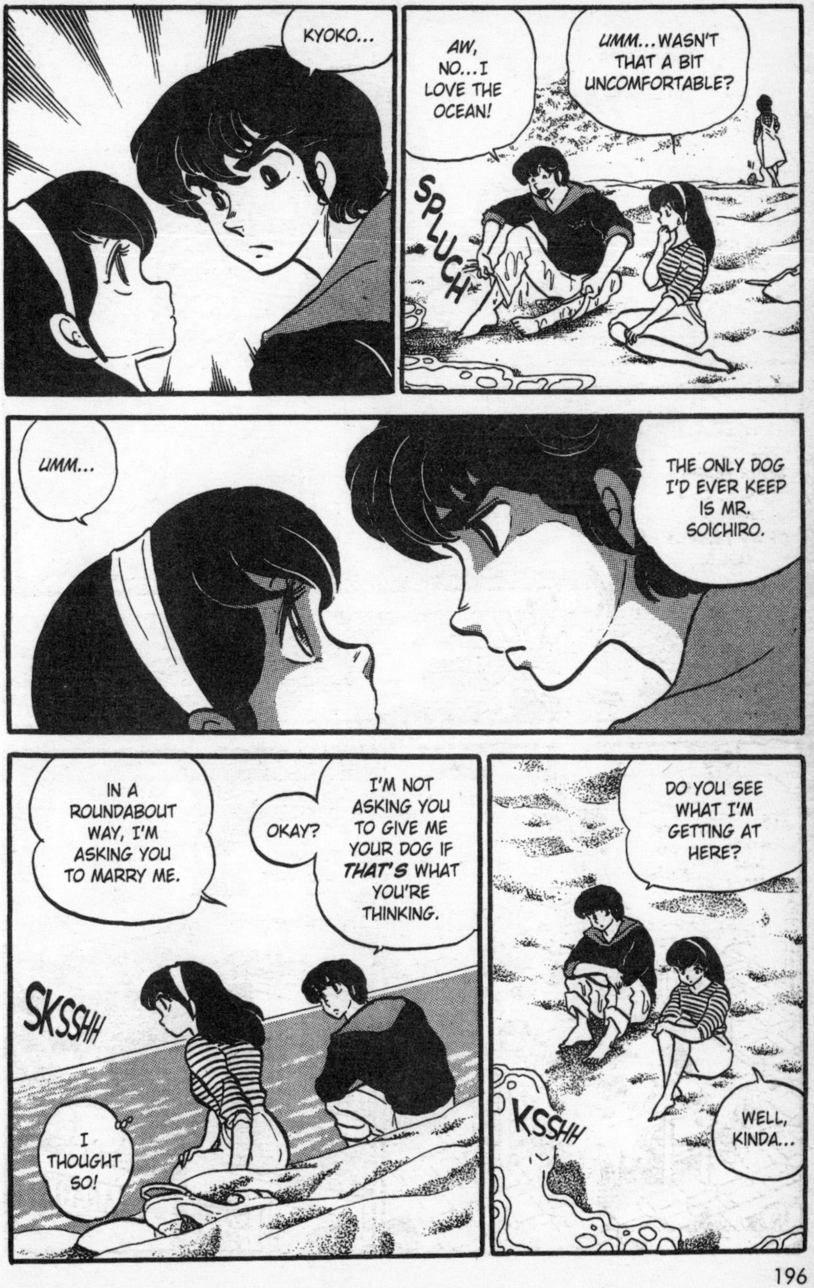
UMM...WASN'T THAT A BIT UNCOMFORTABLE?
AW, NO...I LOVE THE OCEAN!
SPLUCH
KYOKO...
THE ONLY DOG I'D EVER KEEP IS MR. SOICHIRO.
UMM...
DO YOU SEE WHAT I'M GETTING AT HERE?
WELL, KINDA...
KSSHH
I'M NOT ASKING YOU TO GIVE ME YOUR DOG IF *THAT'S* WHAT YOU'RE THINKING.
OKAY?
IN A ROUNDABOUT WAY, I'M ASKING YOU TO MARRY ME.
SKSSHH
I THOUGHT SO!

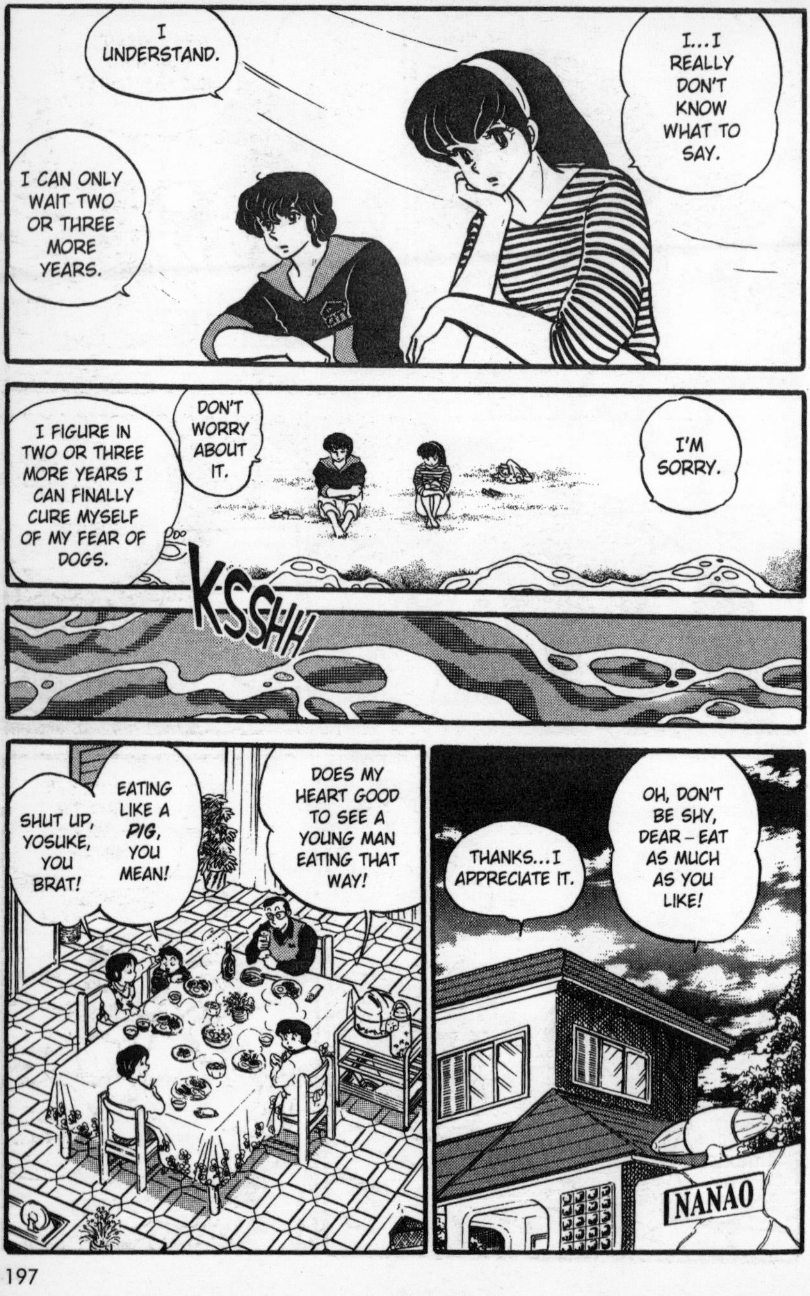
I...I REALLY DON'T KNOW WHAT TO SAY.
I UNDERSTAND.
I CAN ONLY WAIT TWO OR THREE MORE YEARS.
I'M SORRY.
DON'T WORRY ABOUT IT.
I FIGURE IN TWO OR THREE MORE YEARS I CAN FINALLY CURE MYSELF OF MY FEAR OF DOGS.
K-S-SHH
OH, DON'T BE SHY, DEAR – EAT AS MUCH AS YOU LIKE!
THANKS...I APPRECIATE IT.
NANAO
DOES MY HEART GOOD TO SEE A YOUNG MAN EATING THAT WAY!
EATING LIKE A *PIG*, YOU MEAN!
SHUT UP, YOSUKE, YOU BRAT!

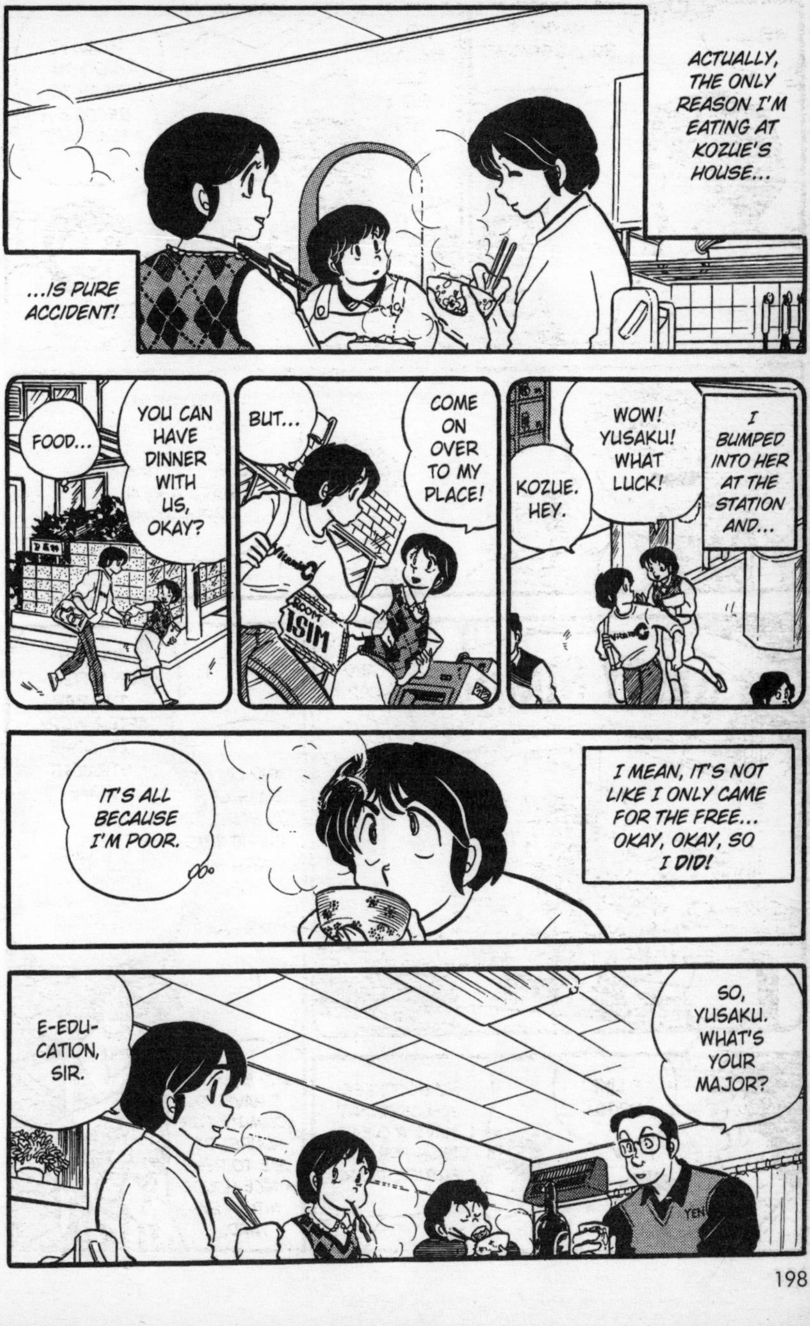
ACTUALLY, THE ONLY REASON I'M EATING AT KOZUE'S HOUSE...
...IS PURE ACCIDENT!
I BUMPED INTO HER AT THE STATION AND...
WOW! YUSAKU! WHAT LUCK!
KOZUE. HEY.
COME ON OVER TO MY PLACE!
BUT...
YOU CAN HAVE DINNER WITH US, OKAY?
FOOD...
I MEAN, IT'S NOT LIKE I ONLY CAME FOR THE FREE... OKAY, OKAY, SO I DID!
IT'S ALL BECAUSE I'M POOR.
SO, YUSAKU. WHAT'S YOUR MAJOR?
E-EDU-CATION, SIR.
YEN

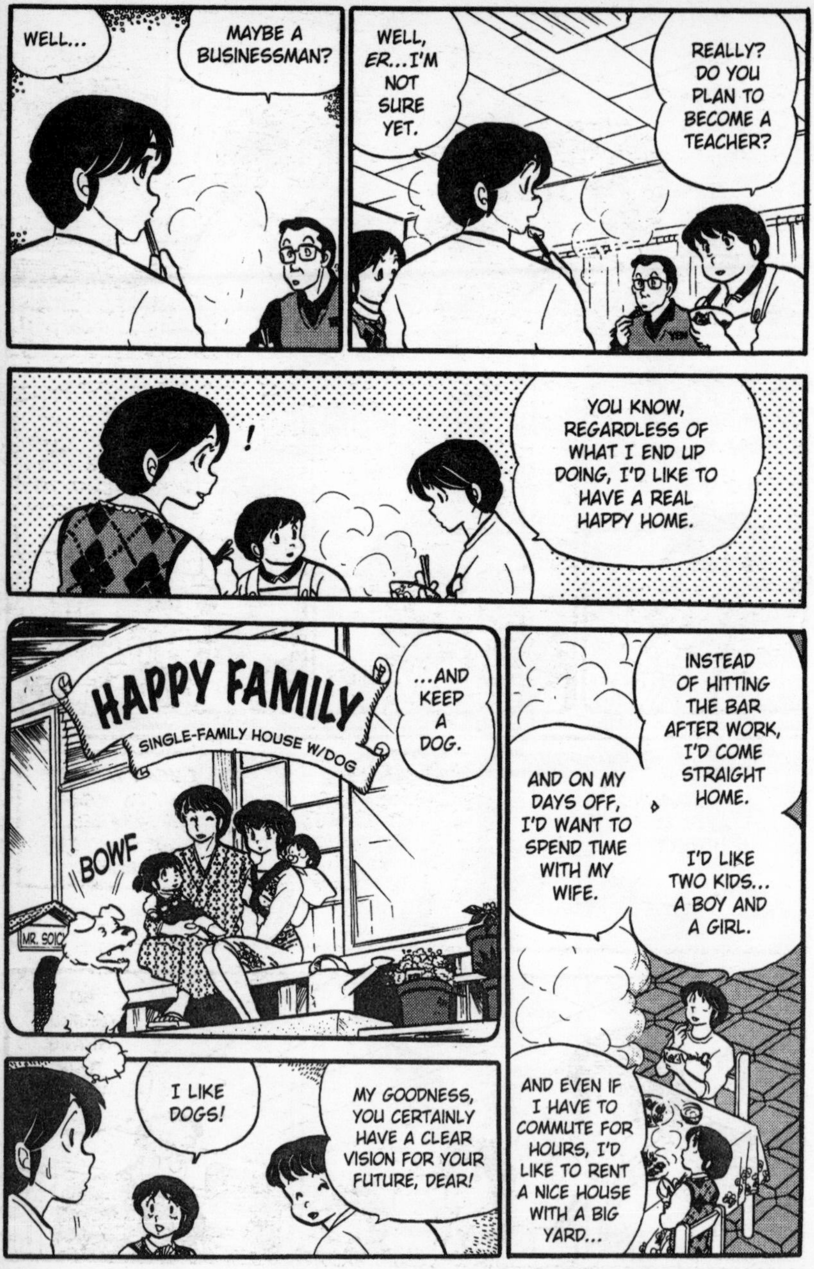
REALLY? DO YOU PLAN TO BECOME A TEACHER?
WELL, ER...I'M NOT SURE YET.
MAYBE A BUSINESSMAN?
WELL...
YOU KNOW, REGARDLESS OF WHAT I END UP DOING, I'D LIKE TO HAVE A REAL HAPPY HOME.
!
INSTEAD OF HITTING THE BAR AFTER WORK, I'D COME STRAIGHT HOME.
AND ON MY DAYS OFF, I'D WANT TO SPEND TIME WITH MY WIFE.
I'D LIKE TWO KIDS... A BOY AND A GIRL.
AND EVEN IF I HAVE TO COMMUTE FOR HOURS, I'D LIKE TO RENT A NICE HOUSE WITH A BIG YARD...
...AND KEEP A DOG.
HAPPY FAMILY
SINGLE-FAMILY HOUSE W/DOG
BOWF
MY GOODNESS, YOU CERTAINLY HAVE A CLEAR VISION FOR YOUR FUTURE, DEAR!
I LIKE DOGS!

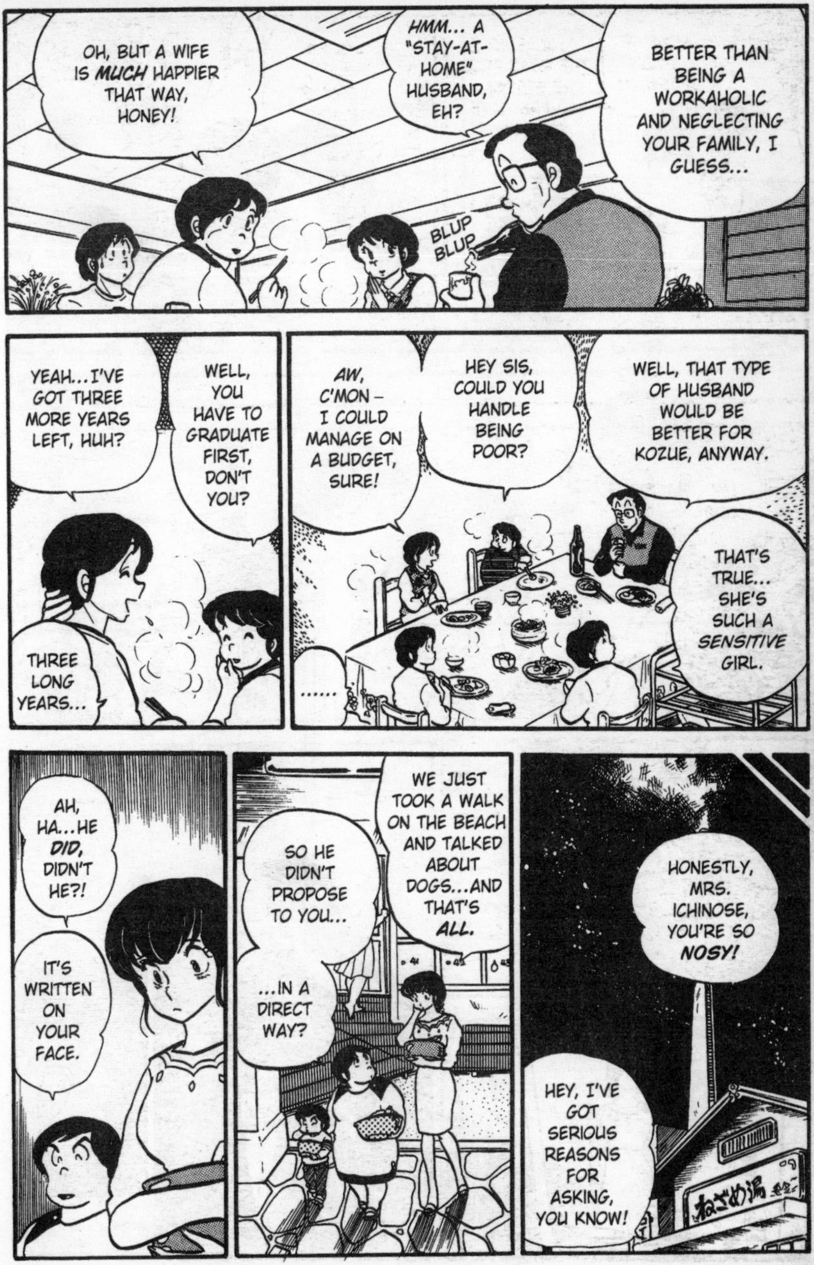
BETTER THAN BEING A WORKAHOLIC AND NEGLECTING YOUR FAMILY, I GUESS...
HMM... A "STAY-AT-HOME" HUSBAND, EH?
OH, BUT A WIFE IS ***MUCH*** HAPPIER THAT WAY, HONEY!
BLUP BLUP
WELL, THAT TYPE OF HUSBAND WOULD BE BETTER FOR KOZUE, ANYWAY.
HEY SIS, COULD YOU HANDLE BEING POOR?
AW, C'MON – I COULD MANAGE ON A BUDGET, SURE!
THAT'S TRUE... SHE'S SUCH A *SENSITIVE* GIRL.
......
WELL, YOU HAVE TO GRADUATE FIRST, DON'T YOU?
YEAH...I'VE GOT THREE MORE YEARS LEFT, HUH?
THREE LONG YEARS...
HONESTLY, MRS. ICHINOSE, YOU'RE SO ***NOSY!***
HEY, I'VE GOT SERIOUS REASONS FOR ASKING, YOU KNOW!
ねざめ湯
WE JUST TOOK A WALK ON THE BEACH AND TALKED ABOUT DOGS...AND THAT'S ***ALL.***
SO HE DIDN'T PROPOSE TO YOU...
...IN A DIRECT WAY?
AH, HA...HE ***DID,*** DIDN'T HE?!
IT'S WRITTEN ON YOUR FACE.

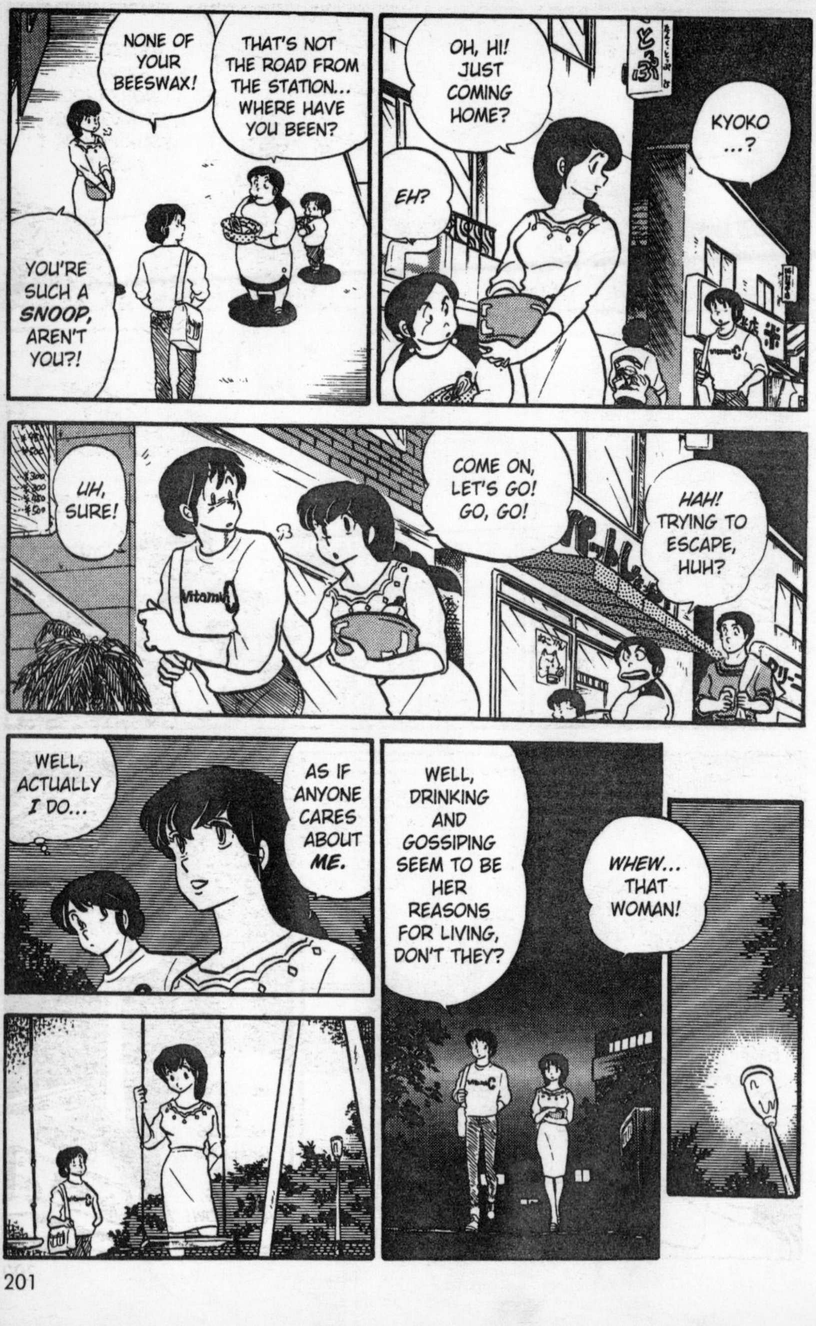
KYOKO ...?
OH, HI! JUST COMING HOME?
EH?
THAT'S NOT THE ROAD FROM THE STATION... WHERE HAVE YOU BEEN?
NONE OF YOUR BEESWAX!
YOU'RE SUCH A SNOOP, AREN'T YOU?!
HAH! TRYING TO ESCAPE, HUH?
COME ON, LET'S GO! GO, GO!
UH, SURE!
WHEW... THAT WOMAN!
WELL, DRINKING AND GOSSIPING SEEM TO BE HER REASONS FOR LIVING, DON'T THEY?
AS IF ANYONE CARES ABOUT ME.
WELL, ACTUALLY I DO...

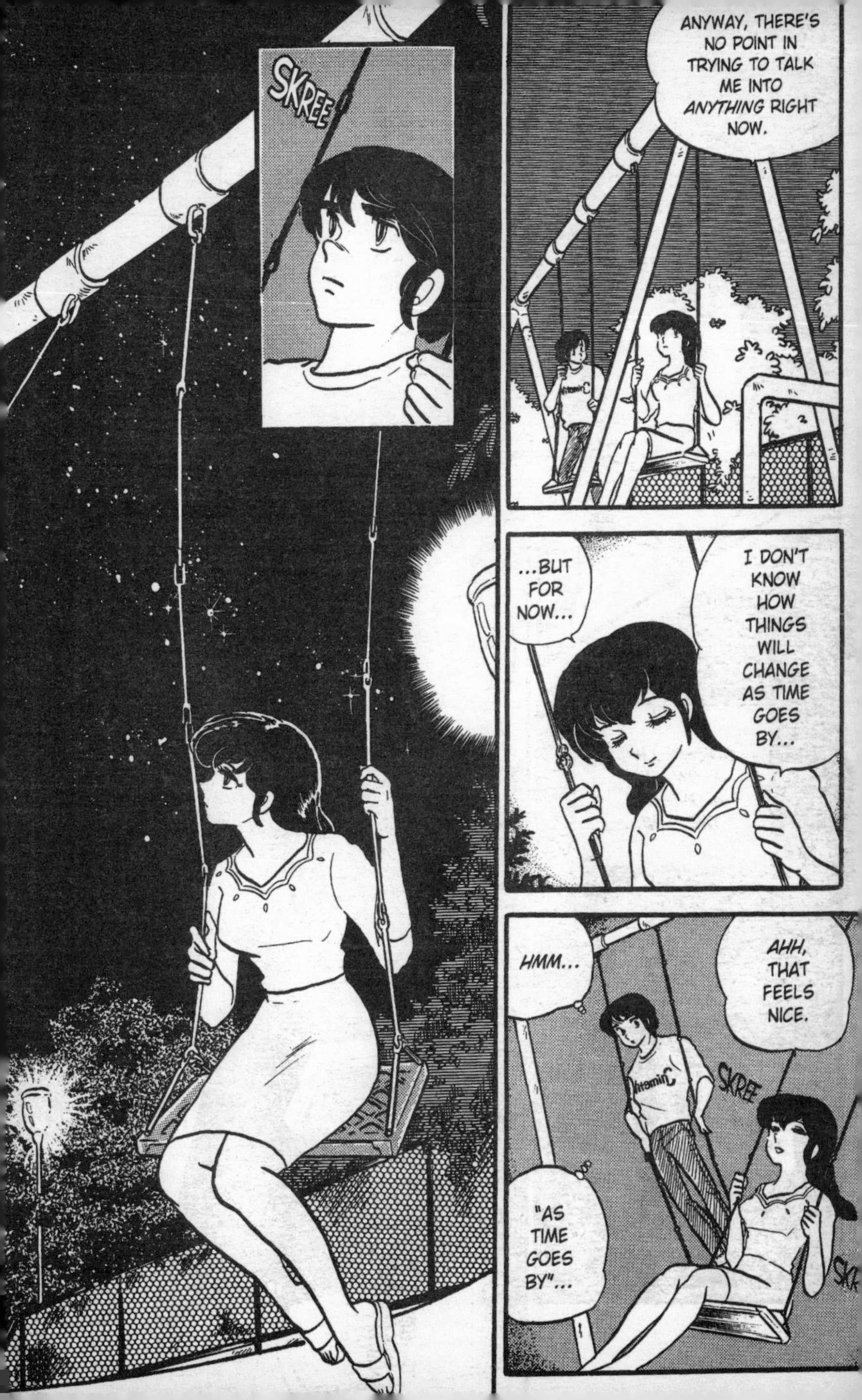
ANYWAY, THERE'S NO POINT IN TRYING TO TALK ME INTO *ANYTHING* RIGHT NOW.
I DON'T KNOW HOW THINGS WILL CHANGE AS TIME GOES BY...
...BUT FOR NOW...
AHH, THAT FEELS NICE.
SKREE
HMM...
"AS TIME GOES BY"...
SKREE

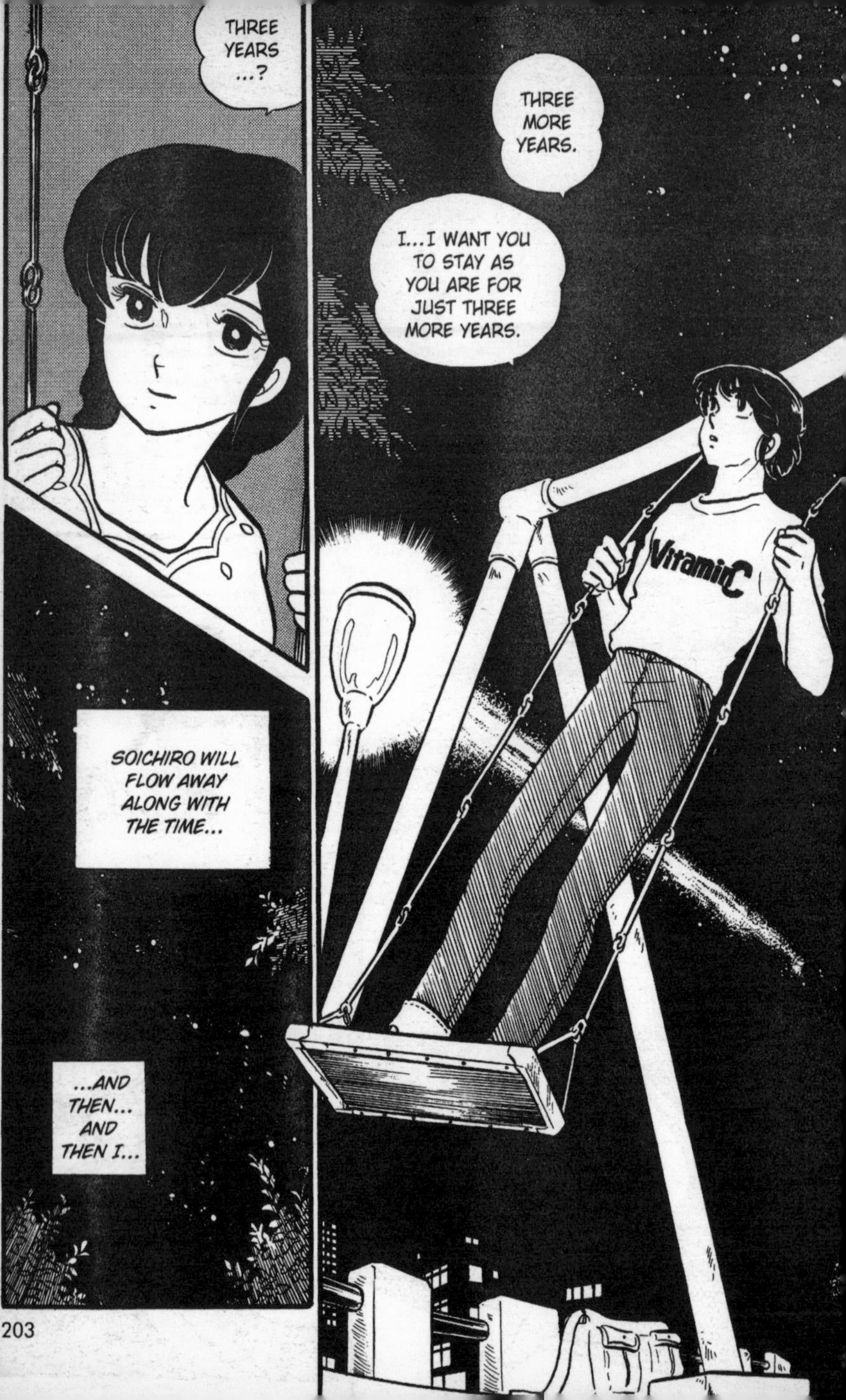
THREE MORE YEARS.
I...I WANT YOU TO STAY AS YOU ARE FOR JUST THREE MORE YEARS.
THREE YEARS ...?
SOICHIRO WILL FLOW AWAY ALONG WITH THE TIME...
...AND THEN... AND THEN I...

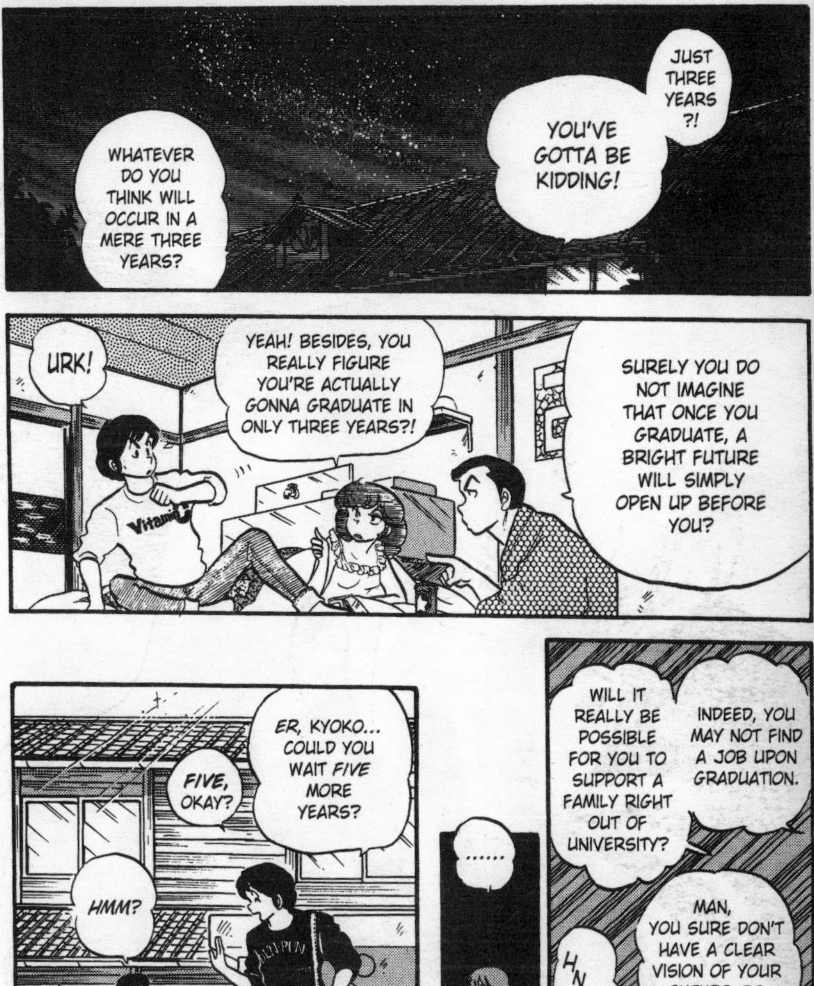

JUST THREE YEARS ?!
YOU'VE GOTTA BE KIDDING!
WHATEVER DO YOU THINK WILL OCCUR IN A MERE THREE YEARS?
SURELY YOU DO NOT IMAGINE THAT ONCE YOU GRADUATE, A BRIGHT FUTURE WILL SIMPLY OPEN UP BEFORE YOU?
YEAH! BESIDES, YOU REALLY FIGURE YOU'RE ACTUALLY GONNA GRADUATE IN ONLY THREE YEARS?!
URK!
INDEED, YOU MAY NOT FIND A JOB UPON GRADUATION.
WILL IT REALLY BE POSSIBLE FOR YOU TO SUPPORT A FAMILY RIGHT OUT OF UNIVERSITY?
MAN, YOU SURE DON'T HAVE A CLEAR VISION OF YOUR FUTURE, DO YA?!
HNNNK!
......
ER, KYOKO... COULD YOU WAIT FIVE MORE YEARS?
FIVE, OKAY?
HMM?
WUFF?

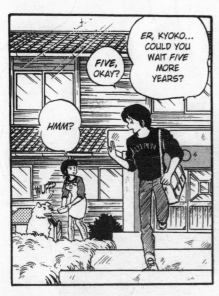

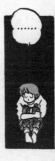

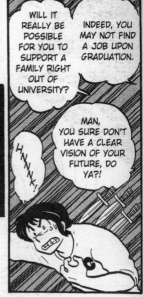

PART ELEVEN
THE BLACK WIDOW'S BITE

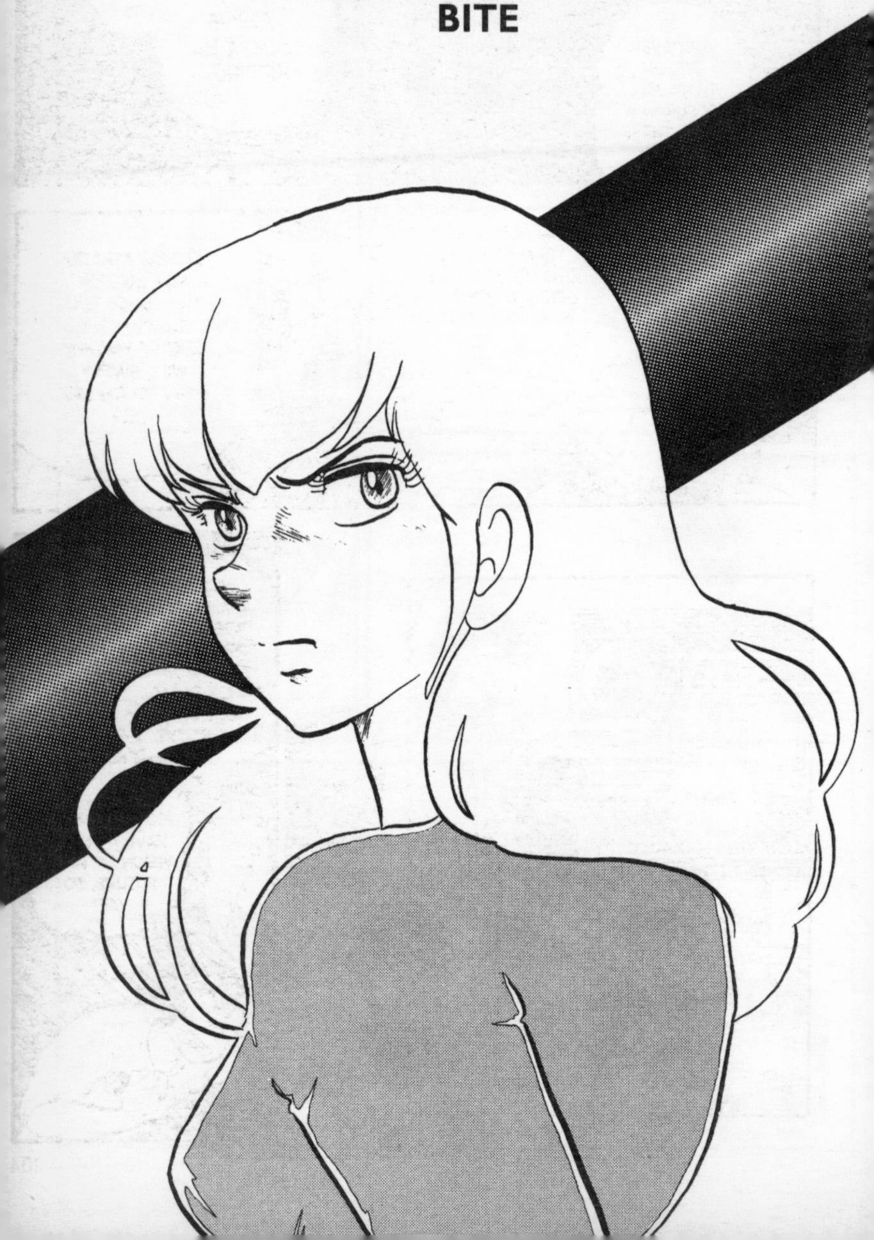

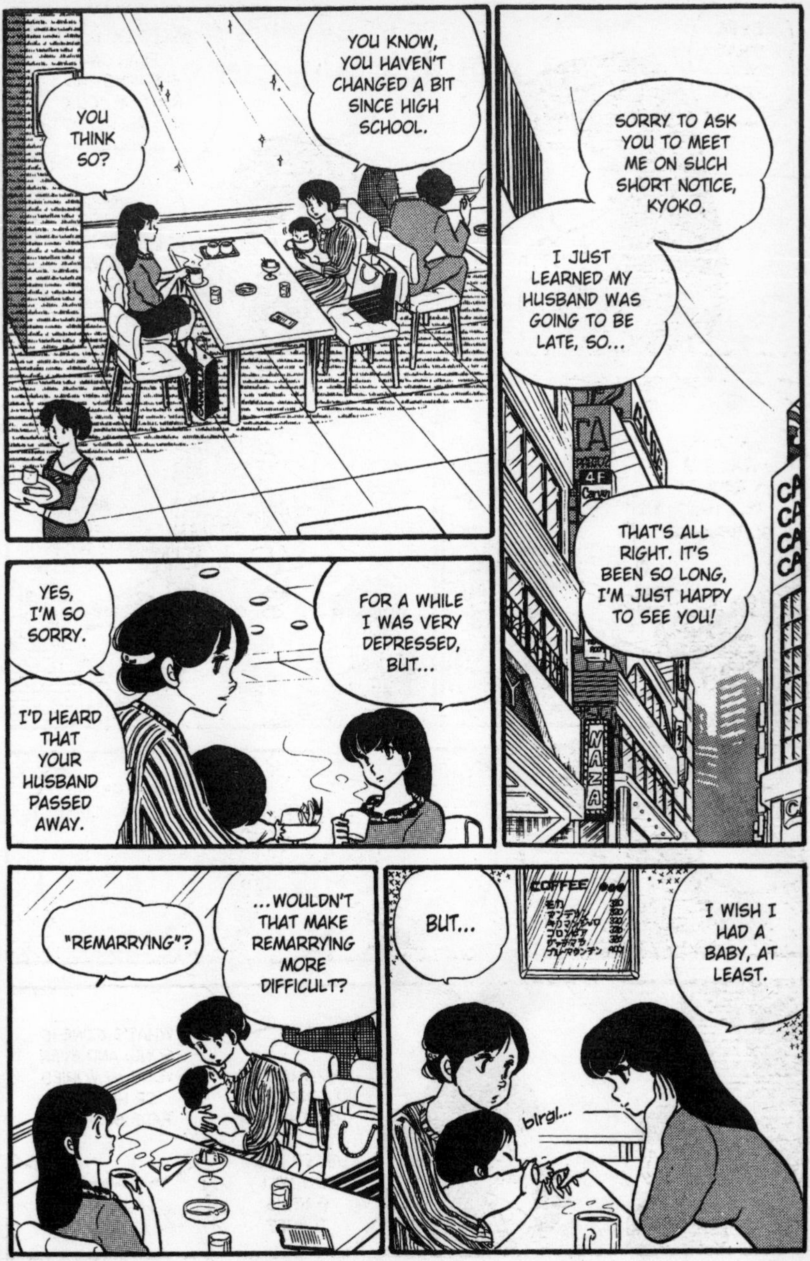
SORRY TO ASK YOU TO MEET ME ON SUCH SHORT NOTICE, KYOKO.
I JUST LEARNED MY HUSBAND WAS GOING TO BE LATE, SO...
THAT'S ALL RIGHT. IT'S BEEN SO LONG, I'M JUST HAPPY TO SEE YOU!
YOU KNOW, YOU HAVEN'T CHANGED A BIT SINCE HIGH SCHOOL.
YOU THINK SO?
YES, I'M SO SORRY.
I'D HEARD THAT YOUR HUSBAND PASSED AWAY.
FOR A WHILE I WAS VERY DEPRESSED, BUT...
COFFEE
I WISH I HAD A BABY, AT LEAST.
BUT...
blrgl...
...WOULDN'T THAT MAKE REMARRYING MORE DIFFICULT?
"REMARRYING"?

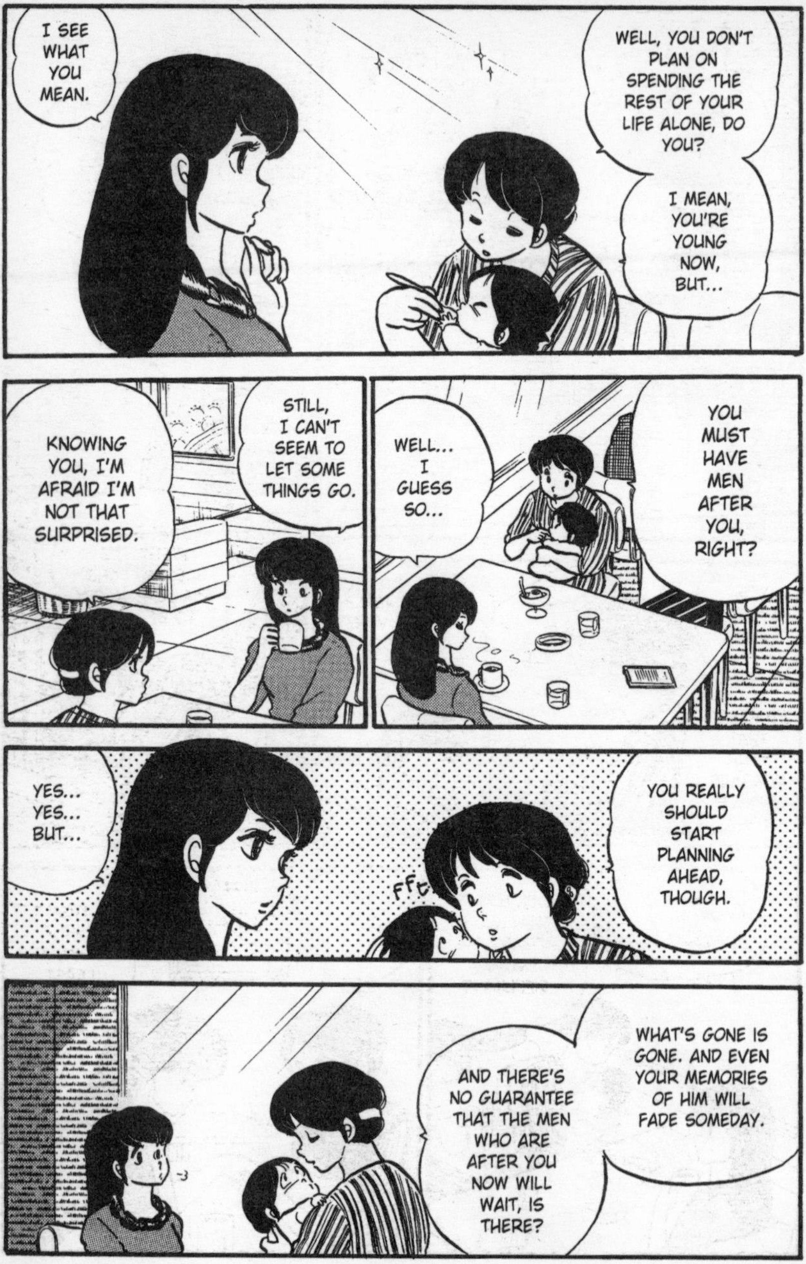
WELL, YOU DON'T PLAN ON SPENDING THE REST OF YOUR LIFE ALONE, DO YOU?
I MEAN, YOU'RE YOUNG NOW, BUT...
I SEE WHAT YOU MEAN.
YOU MUST HAVE MEN AFTER YOU, RIGHT?
WELL... I GUESS SO...
STILL, I CAN'T SEEM TO LET SOME THINGS GO.
KNOWING YOU, I'M AFRAID I'M NOT THAT SURPRISED.
YOU REALLY SHOULD START PLANNING AHEAD, THOUGH.
FFt
YES... YES... BUT...
WHAT'S GONE IS GONE. AND EVEN YOUR MEMORIES OF HIM WILL FADE SOMEDAY.
AND THERE'S NO GUARANTEE THAT THE MEN WHO ARE AFTER YOU NOW WILL WAIT, IS THERE?

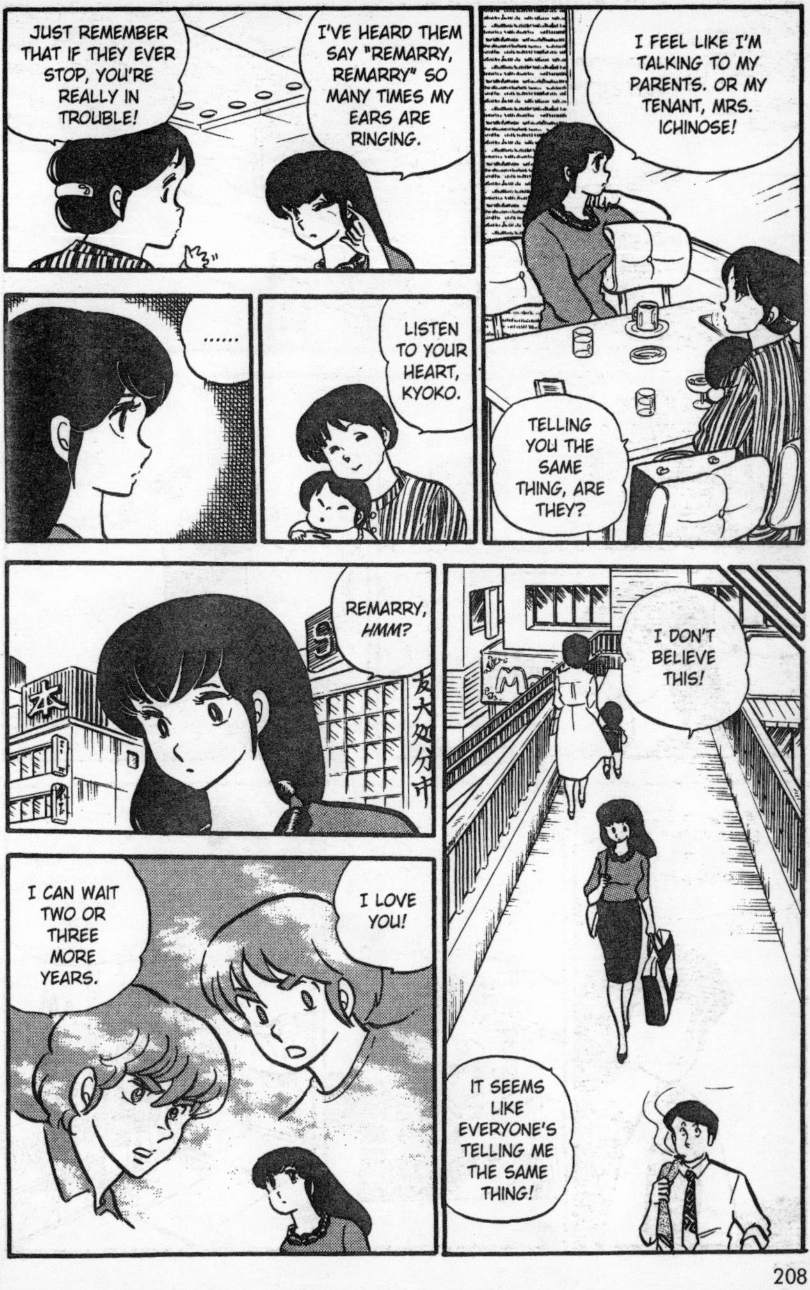
I FEEL LIKE I'M TALKING TO MY PARENTS. OR MY TENANT, MRS. ICHINOSE!
TELLING YOU THE SAME THING, ARE THEY?
I'VE HEARD THEM SAY "REMARRY, REMARRY" SO MANY TIMES MY EARS ARE RINGING.
JUST REMEMBER THAT IF THEY EVER STOP, YOU'RE REALLY IN TROUBLE!
LISTEN TO YOUR HEART, KYOKO.
......
I DON'T BELIEVE THIS!
IT SEEMS LIKE EVERYONE'S TELLING ME THE SAME THING!
REMARRY, *HMM?*
I LOVE YOU!
I CAN WAIT TWO OR THREE MORE YEARS.

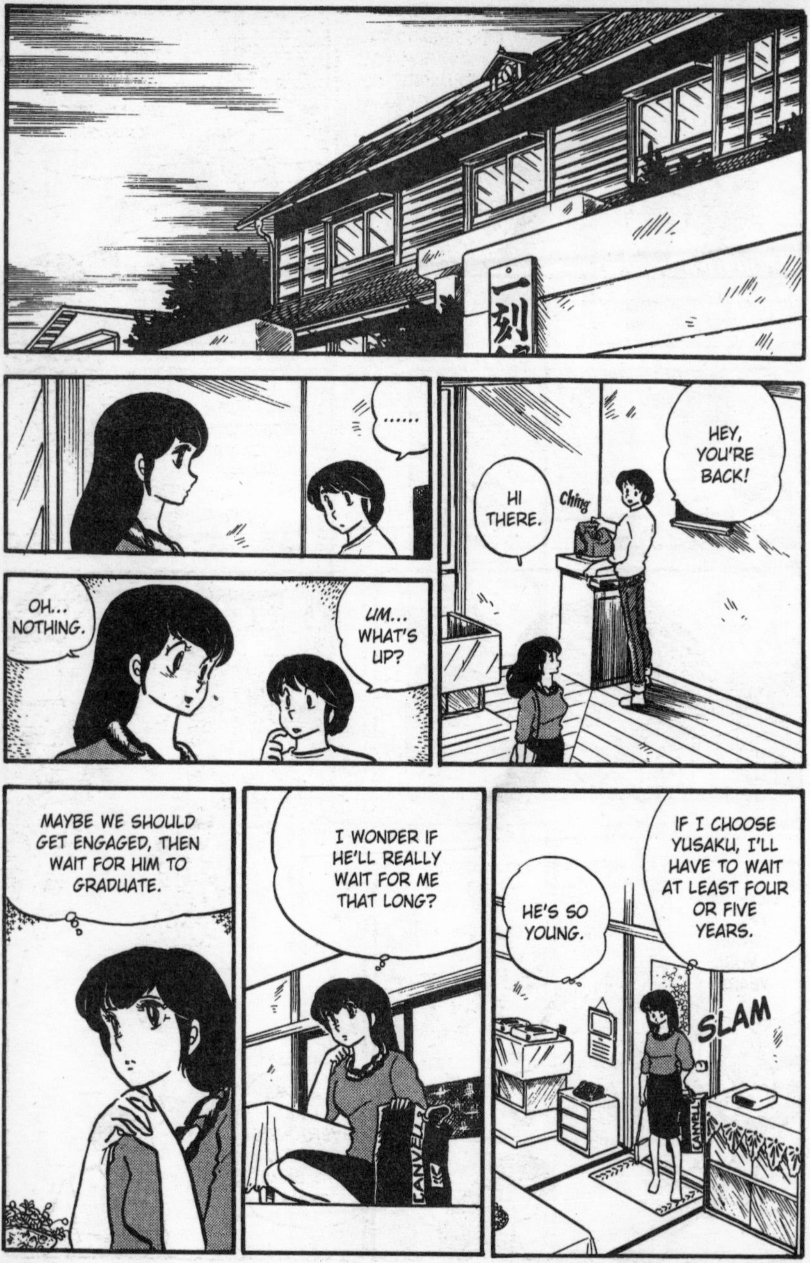
一刻
HEY, YOU'RE BACK!
Ching
HI THERE.
......
UM... WHAT'S UP?
OH... NOTHING.
IF I CHOOSE YUSAKU, I'LL HAVE TO WAIT AT LEAST FOUR OR FIVE YEARS.
HE'S SO YOUNG.
SLAM
CANVELL
I WONDER IF HE'LL REALLY WAIT FOR ME THAT LONG?
CANVELL
MAYBE WE SHOULD GET ENGAGED, THEN WAIT FOR HIM TO GRADUATE.

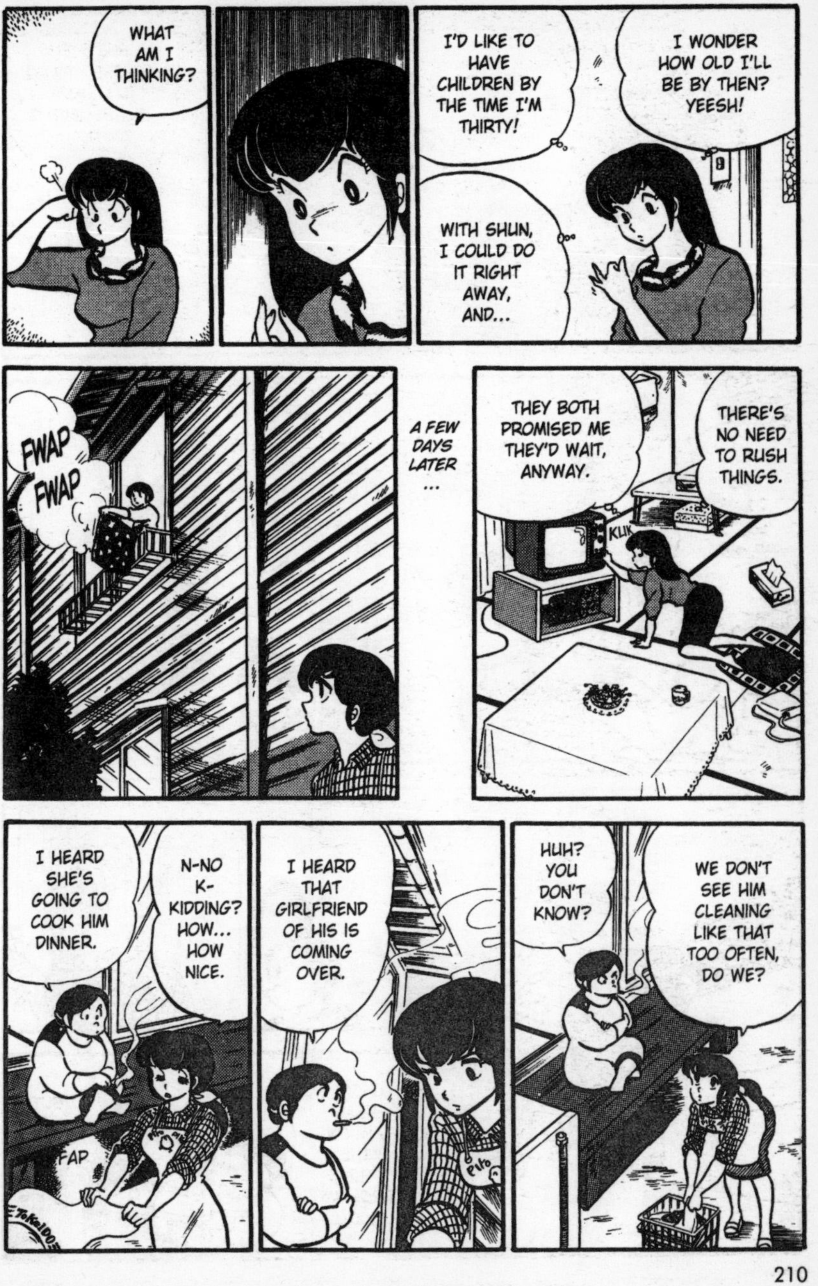
I WONDER HOW OLD I'LL BE BY THEN? YEESH!
I'D LIKE TO HAVE CHILDREN BY THE TIME I'M THIRTY!
WITH SHUN, I COULD DO IT RIGHT AWAY, AND...
WHAT AM I THINKING?
THERE'S NO NEED TO RUSH THINGS.
THEY BOTH PROMISED ME THEY'D WAIT, ANYWAY.
KLIK
A FEW DAYS LATER ...
FWAP
FWAP
WE DON'T SEE HIM CLEANING LIKE THAT TOO OFTEN, DO WE?
HUH? YOU DON'T KNOW?
I HEARD THAT GIRLFRIEND OF HIS IS COMING OVER.
N-NO K-KIDDING? HOW... HOW NICE.
I HEARD SHE'S GOING TO COOK HIM DINNER.
FAP

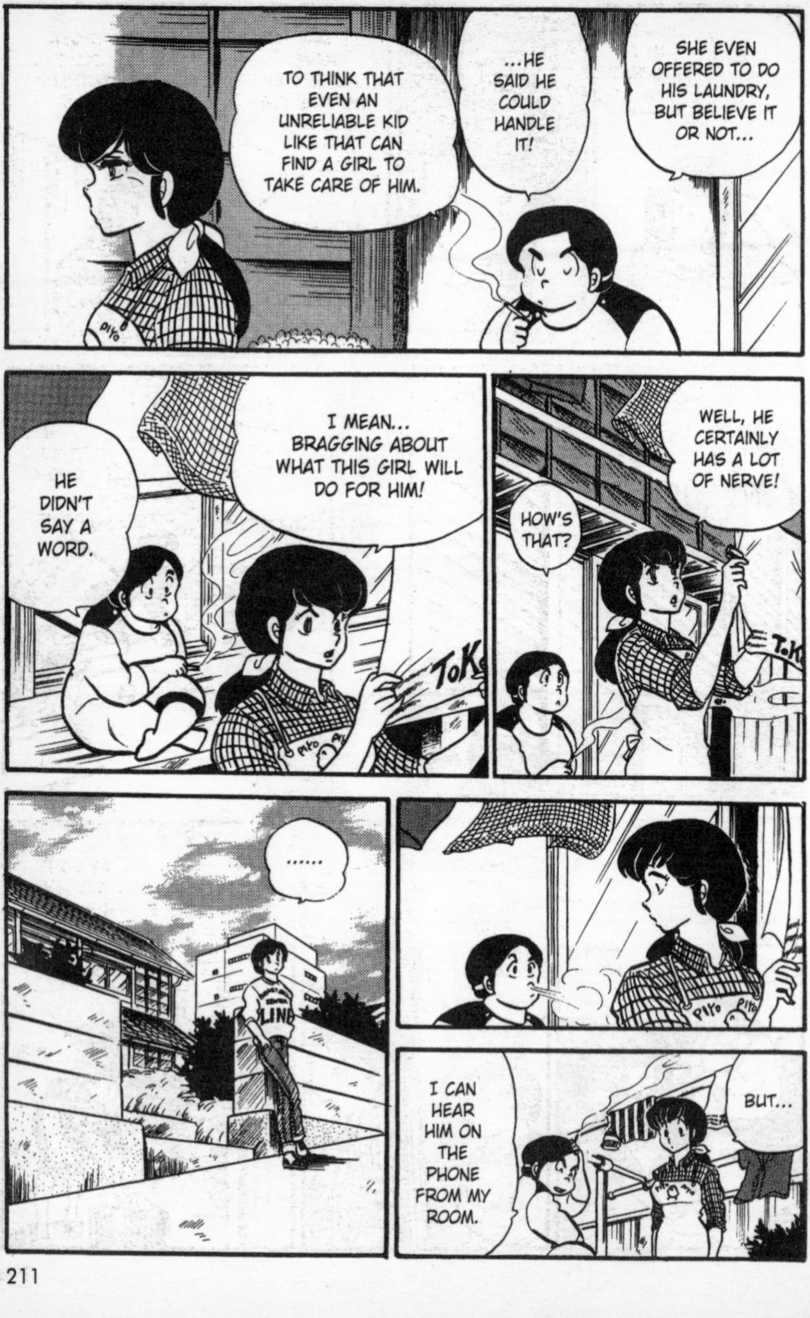
SHE EVEN OFFERED TO DO HIS LAUNDRY, BUT BELIEVE IT OR NOT...
...HE SAID HE COULD HANDLE IT!
TO THINK THAT EVEN AN UNRELIABLE KID LIKE THAT CAN FIND A GIRL TO TAKE CARE OF HIM.
WELL, HE CERTAINLY HAS A LOT OF NERVE!
HOW'S THAT?
I MEAN... BRAGGING ABOUT WHAT THIS GIRL WILL DO FOR HIM!
HE DIDN'T SAY A WORD.
BUT...
I CAN HEAR HIM ON THE PHONE FROM MY ROOM.
....

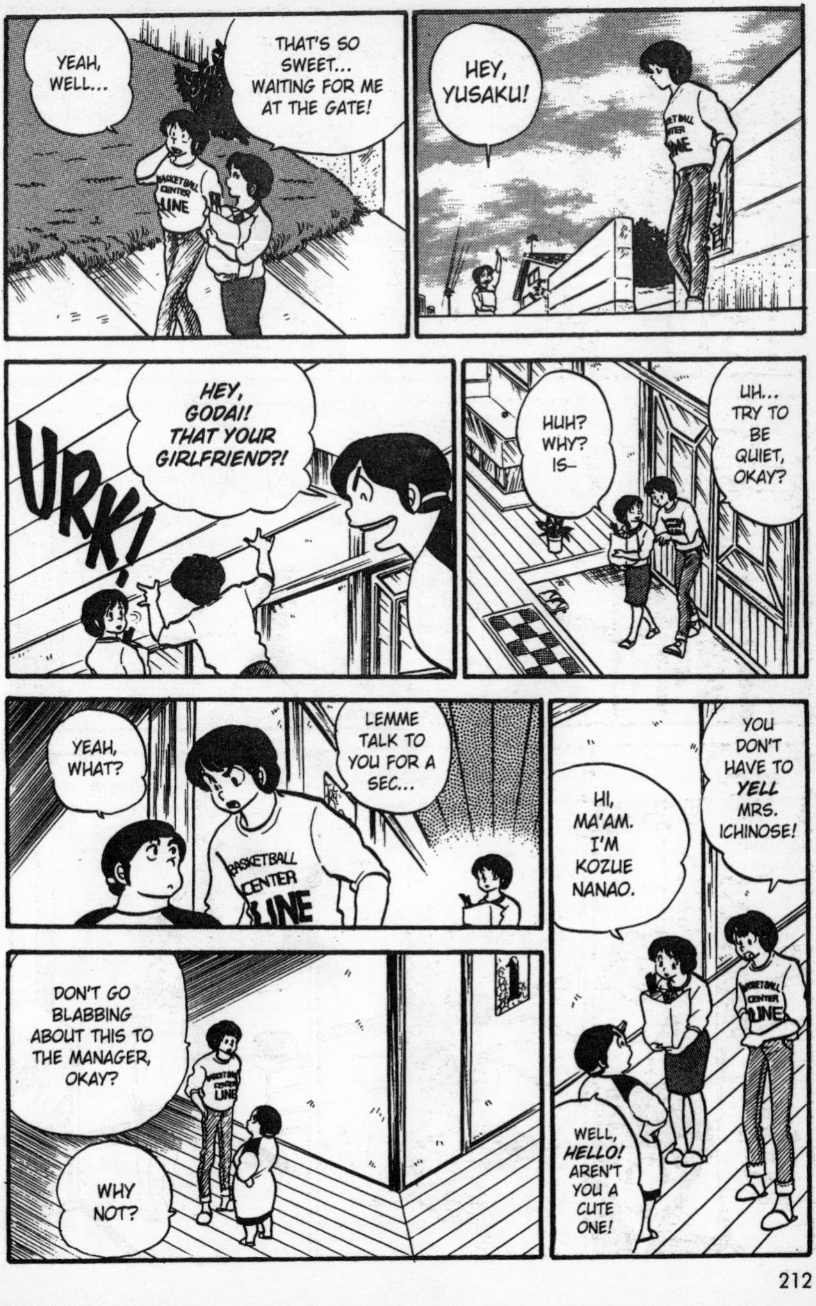
HEY, YUSAKU!
THAT'S SO SWEET... WAITING FOR ME AT THE GATE!
YEAH, WELL...
UH... TRY TO BE QUIET, OKAY?
HUH? WHY? IS—
HEY, GODAI! THAT YOUR GIRLFRIEND?!
URK!
YOU DON'T HAVE TO YELL MRS. ICHINOSE!
HI, MA'AM. I'M KOZUE NANAO.
WELL, HELLO! AREN'T YOU A CUTE ONE!
LEMME TALK TO YOU FOR A SEC...
YEAH, WHAT?
DON'T GO BLABBING ABOUT THIS TO THE MANAGER, OKAY?
WHY NOT?

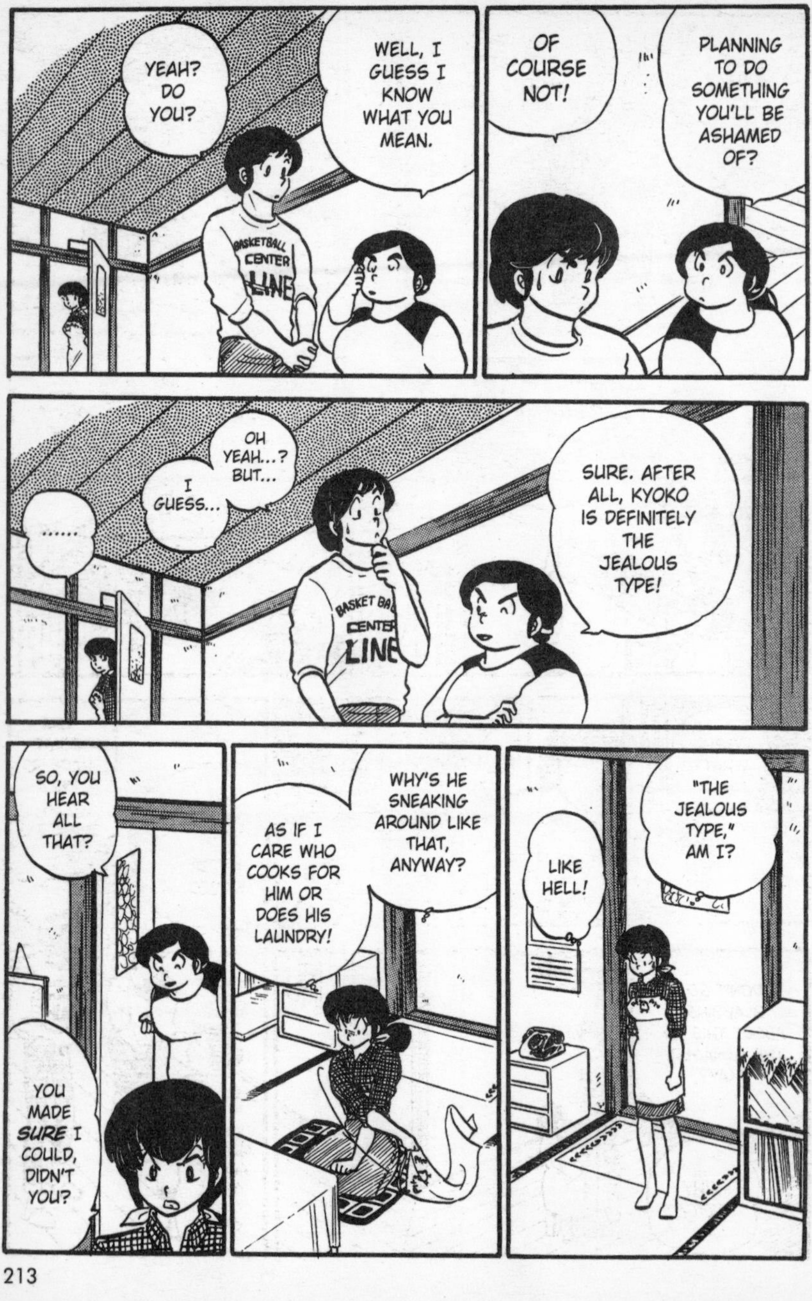
PLANNING TO DO SOMETHING YOU'LL BE ASHAMED OF?
OF COURSE NOT!
WELL, I GUESS I KNOW WHAT YOU MEAN.
YEAH? DO YOU?
BASKETBALL CENTER LINE
SURE. AFTER ALL, KYOKO IS DEFINITELY THE JEALOUS TYPE!
OH YEAH...? BUT...
I GUESS...
......
BASKET BALL CENTER LINE
"THE JEALOUS TYPE," AM I?
LIKE HELL!
WHY'S HE SNEAKING AROUND LIKE THAT, ANYWAY?
AS IF I CARE WHO COOKS FOR HIM OR DOES HIS LAUNDRY!
SO, YOU HEAR ALL THAT?
YOU MADE *SURE* I COULD, DIDN'T YOU?

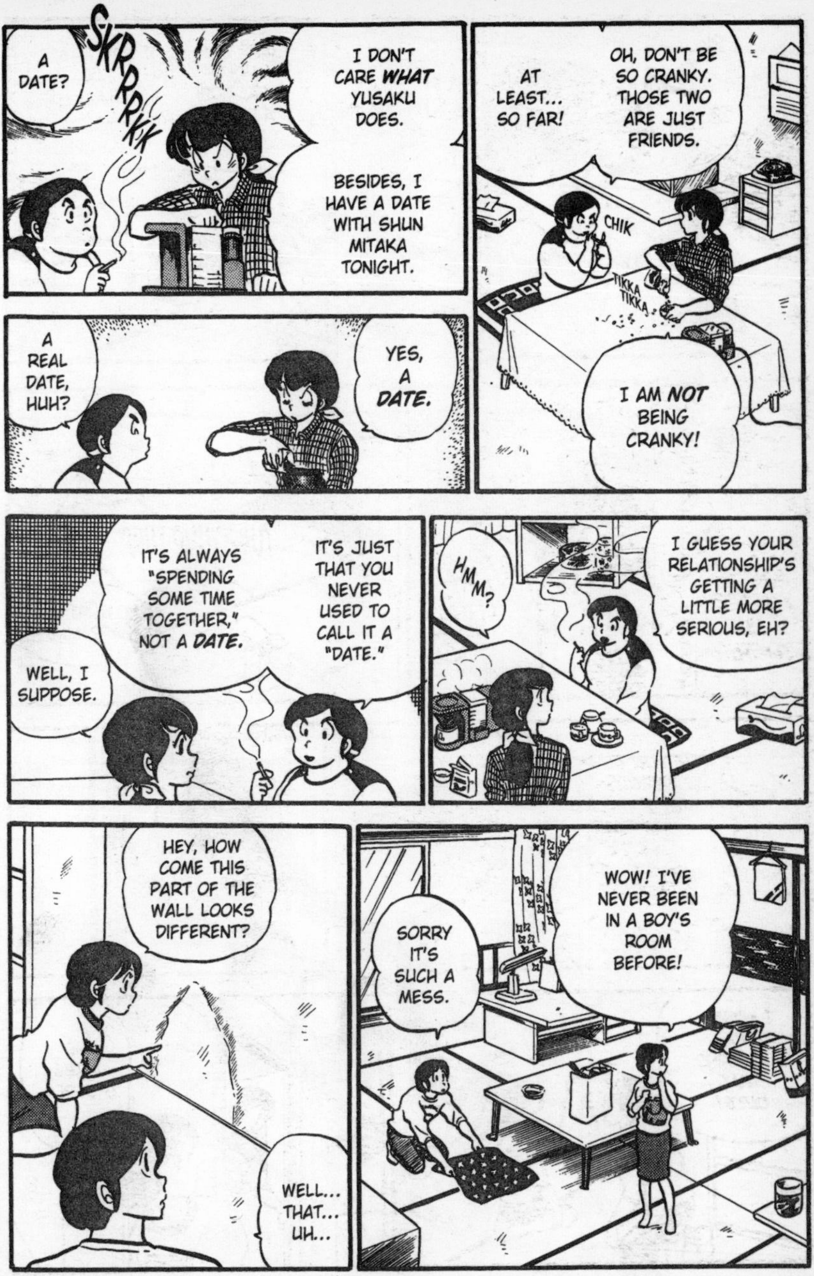
OH, DON'T BE SO CRANKY. THOSE TWO ARE JUST FRIENDS.
AT LEAST... SO FAR!
CHIK
TIKKA TIKKA
I AM **NOT** BEING CRANKY!
I DON'T CARE **WHAT** YUSAKU DOES.
BESIDES, I HAVE A DATE WITH SHUN MITAKA TONIGHT.
SKRRRKK
A DATE?
YES, A **DATE.**
A REAL DATE, HUH?
I GUESS YOUR RELATIONSHIP'S GETTING A LITTLE MORE SERIOUS, EH?
HMM?
IT'S JUST THAT YOU NEVER USED TO CALL IT A "DATE."
IT'S ALWAYS "SPENDING SOME TIME TOGETHER," NOT A **DATE.**
WELL, I SUPPOSE.
WOW! I'VE NEVER BEEN IN A BOY'S ROOM BEFORE!
SORRY IT'S SUCH A MESS.
HEY, HOW COME THIS PART OF THE WALL LOOKS DIFFERENT?
WELL... THAT... UH...

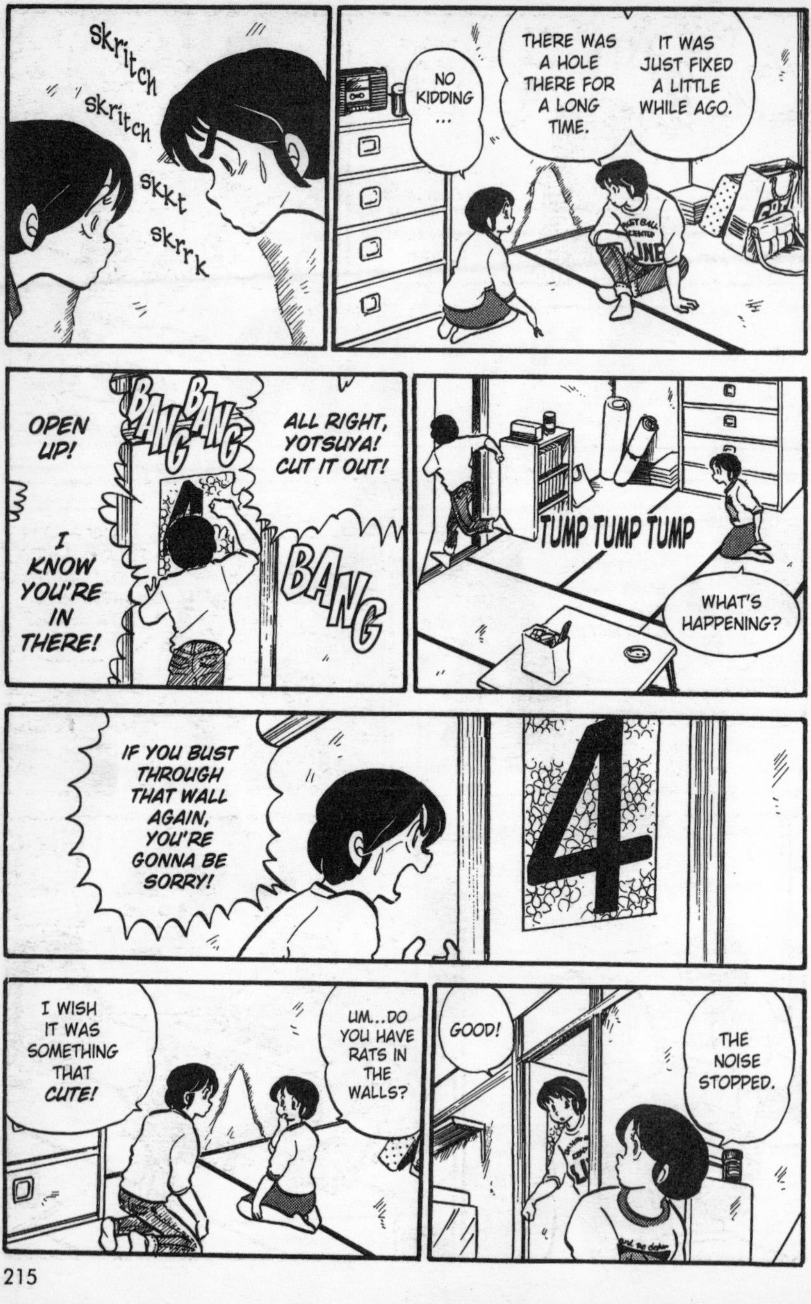
THERE WAS A HOLE THERE FOR A LONG TIME.
IT WAS JUST FIXED A LITTLE WHILE AGO.
NO KIDDING ...
skritch
skritch
skkt
skrrk
TUMP TUMP TUMP
WHAT'S HAPPENING?
ALL RIGHT, YOTSUYA! CUT IT OUT!
BANG
BANG BANG
OPEN UP!
I KNOW YOU'RE IN THERE!
IF YOU BUST THROUGH THAT WALL AGAIN, YOU'RE GONNA BE SORRY!
THE NOISE STOPPED.
GOOD!
UM...DO YOU HAVE RATS IN THE WALLS?
I WISH IT WAS SOMETHING THAT CUTE!

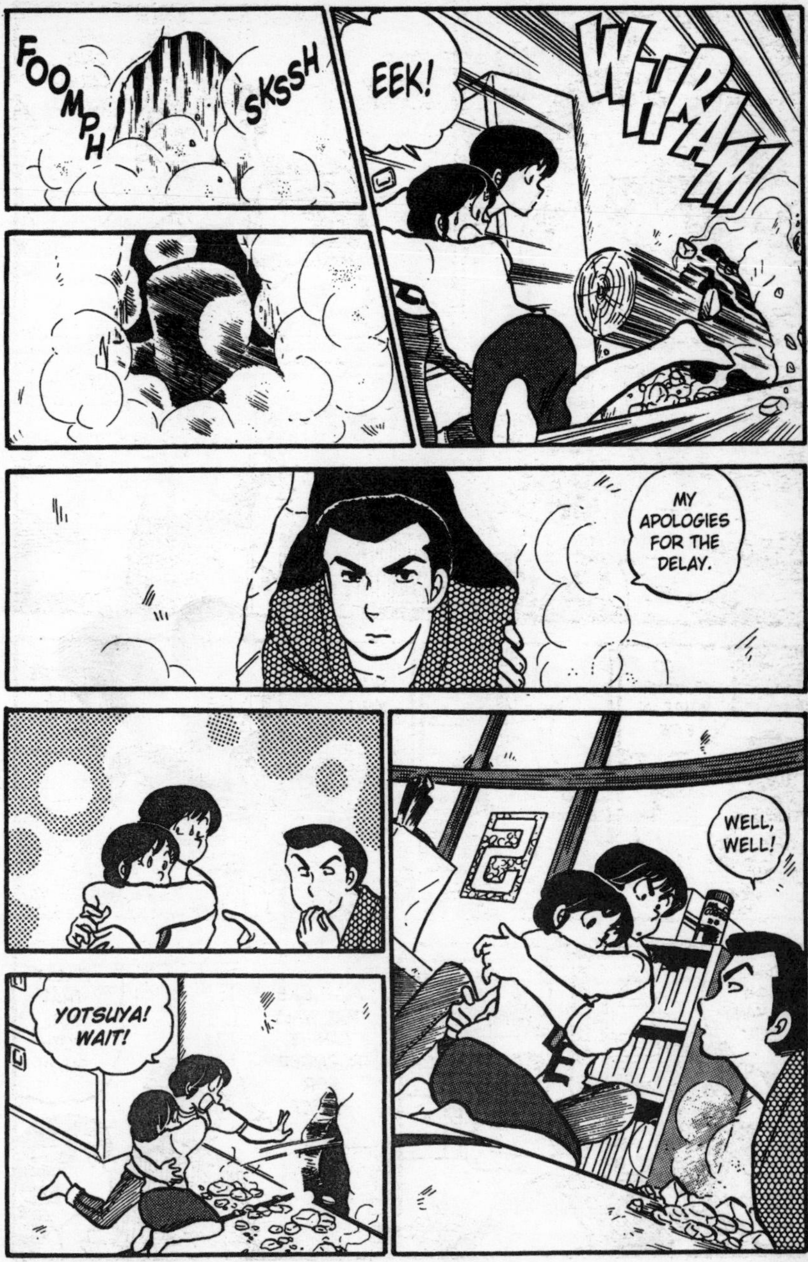
EEK!
WHRAM
SKSSH
FOOMPH
MY APOLOGIES FOR THE DELAY.
WELL, WELL!
YOTSUYA! WAIT!

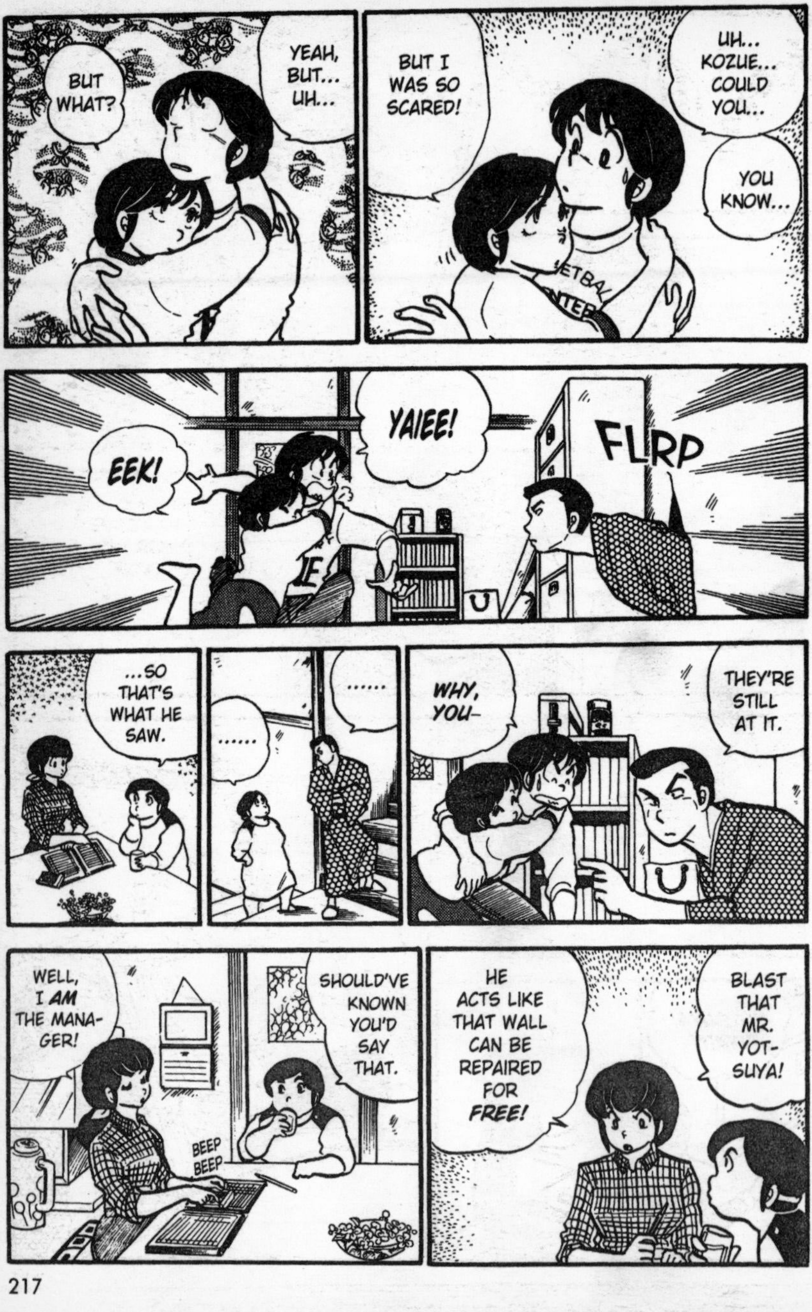
UH... KOZUE... COULD YOU...
YOU KNOW...
BUT I WAS SO SCARED!
YEAH, BUT... UH...
BUT WHAT?
FLRP
YAIEE!
EEK!
THEY'RE STILL AT IT.
WHY, YOU–
......
......
...SO THAT'S WHAT HE SAW.
BLAST THAT MR. YOT-SUYA!
HE ACTS LIKE THAT WALL CAN BE REPAIRED FOR FREE!
SHOULD'VE KNOWN YOU'D SAY THAT.
BEEP BEEP
WELL, I AM THE MANA-GER!

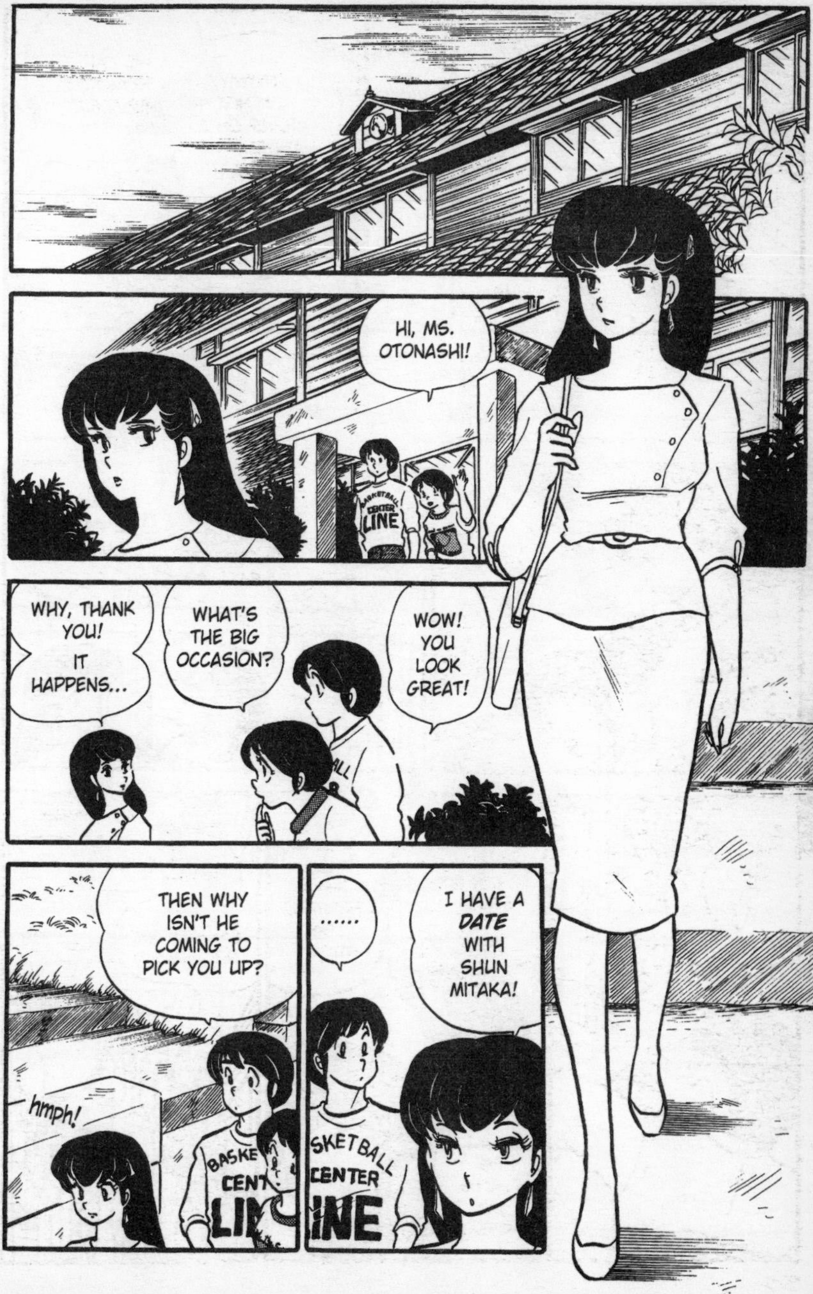
HI, MS. OTONASHI!
WOW! YOU LOOK GREAT!
WHAT'S THE BIG OCCASION?
WHY, THANK YOU! IT HAPPENS...
I HAVE A *DATE* WITH SHUN MITAKA!
......
THEN WHY ISN'T HE COMING TO PICK YOU UP?
hmph!

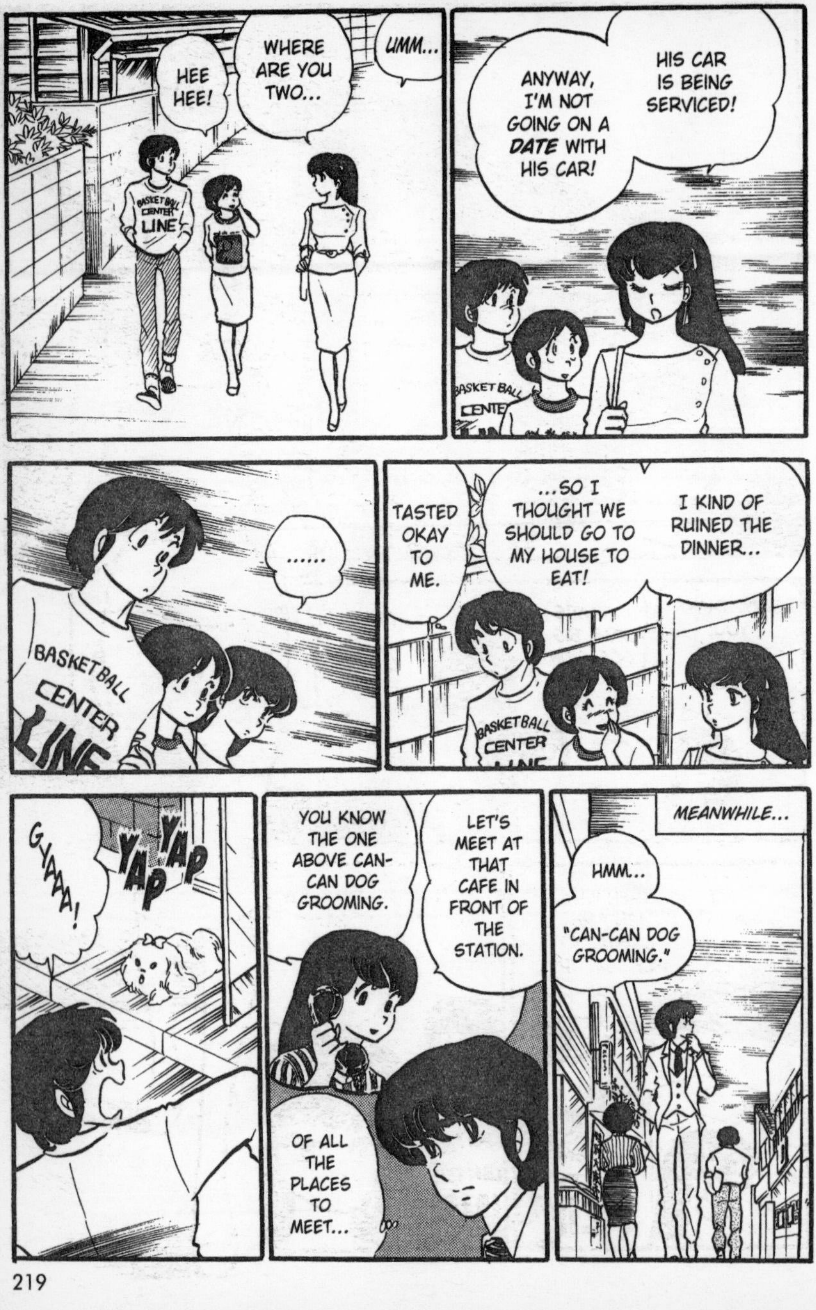
HIS CAR IS BEING SERVICED!
ANYWAY, I'M NOT GOING ON A *DATE* WITH HIS CAR!
UMM...
WHERE ARE YOU TWO...
HEE HEE!
BASKETBALL CENTER LINE
I KIND OF RUINED THE DINNER...
...SO I THOUGHT WE SHOULD GO TO MY HOUSE TO EAT!
TASTED OKAY TO ME.
BASKETBALL CENTER
......
BASKETBALL CENTER LINE
MEANWHILE...
HMM...
"CAN-CAN DOG GROOMING."
LET'S MEET AT THAT CAFE IN FRONT OF THE STATION.
YOU KNOW THE ONE ABOVE CAN-CAN DOG GROOMING.
OF ALL THE PLACES TO MEET...
YAP YAP
GYAAAA!

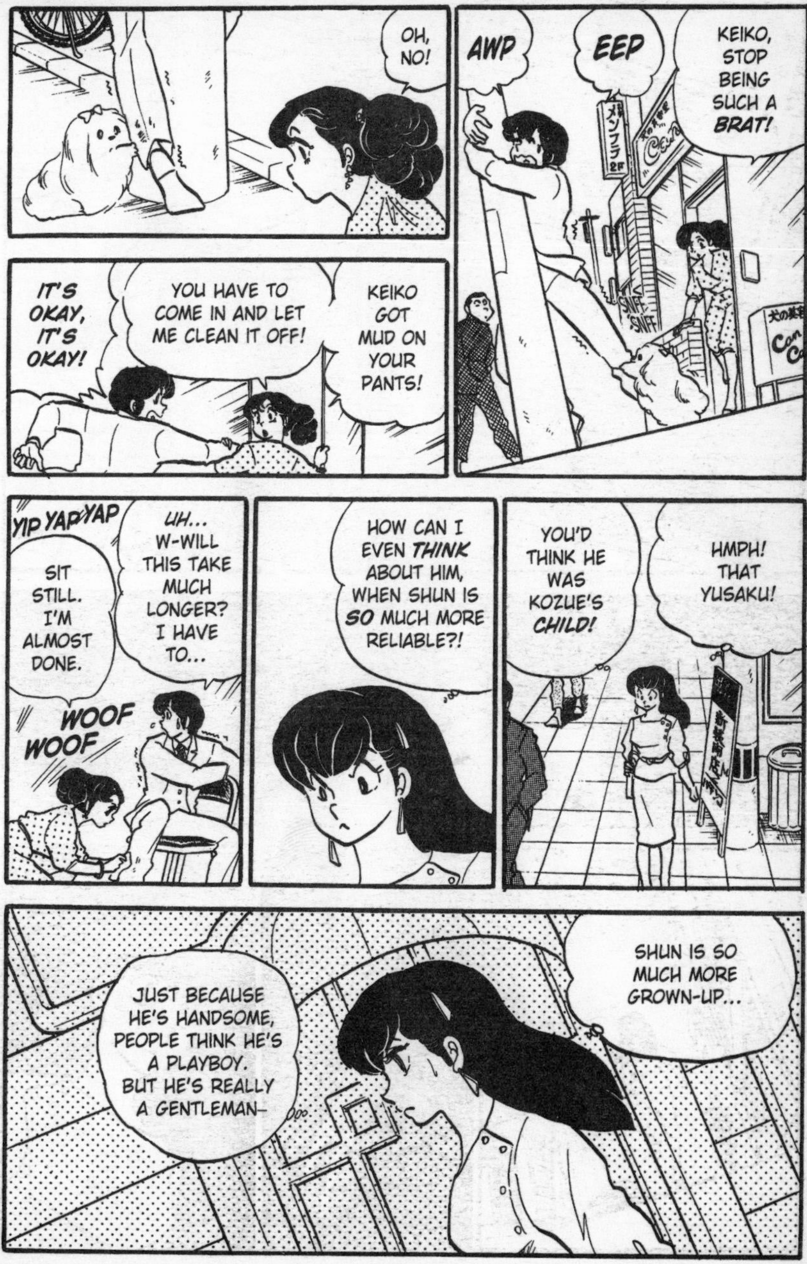
KEIKO, STOP BEING SUCH A BRAT!
EEP
AWP
SNIFF SNIFF
OH, NO!
KEIKO GOT MUD ON YOUR PANTS!
YOU HAVE TO COME IN AND LET ME CLEAN IT OFF!
IT'S OKAY, IT'S OKAY!
HMPH! THAT YUSAKU!
YOU'D THINK HE WAS KOZUE'S CHILD!
HOW CAN I EVEN THINK ABOUT HIM, WHEN SHUN IS SO MUCH MORE RELIABLE?!
UH... W-WILL THIS TAKE MUCH LONGER? I HAVE TO...
YIP YAP YAP
SIT STILL. I'M ALMOST DONE.
WOOF WOOF
SHUN IS SO MUCH MORE GROWN-UP...
JUST BECAUSE HE'S HANDSOME, PEOPLE THINK HE'S A PLAYBOY. BUT HE'S REALLY A GENTLEMAN–

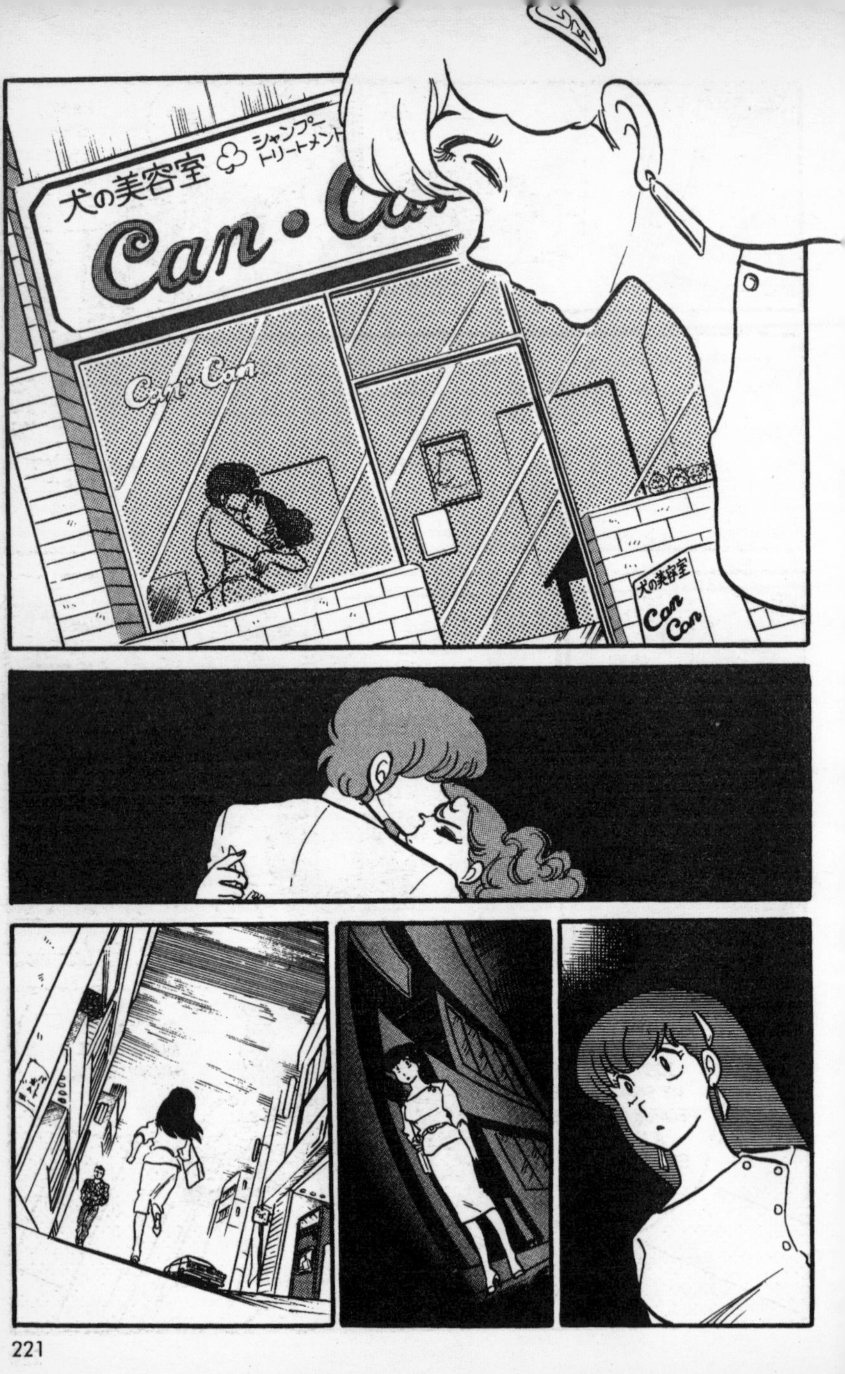
犬の美容室
シャンプー
Can・Can
犬の美容室
Can
Can

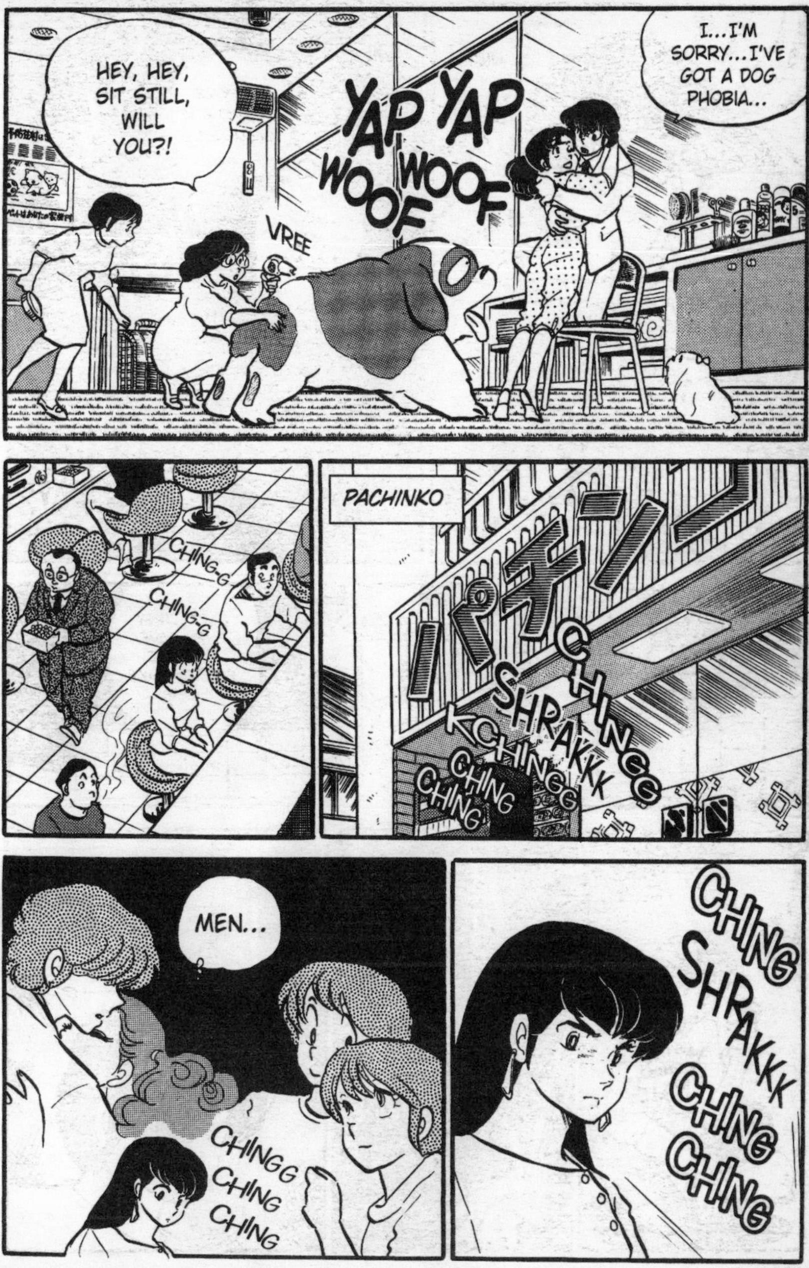
I...I'M SORRY...I'VE GOT A DOG PHOBIA...
YAP YAP WOOF WOOF
HEY, HEY, SIT STILL, WILL YOU?!
VREE
PACHINKO
CHINGG
SHRAKKK
KCHINGG
CHING CHING
CHING-G
CHING-G
CHING
SHRAKKK
CHING
CHING
CHING
MEN...
CHINGG
CHING
CHING

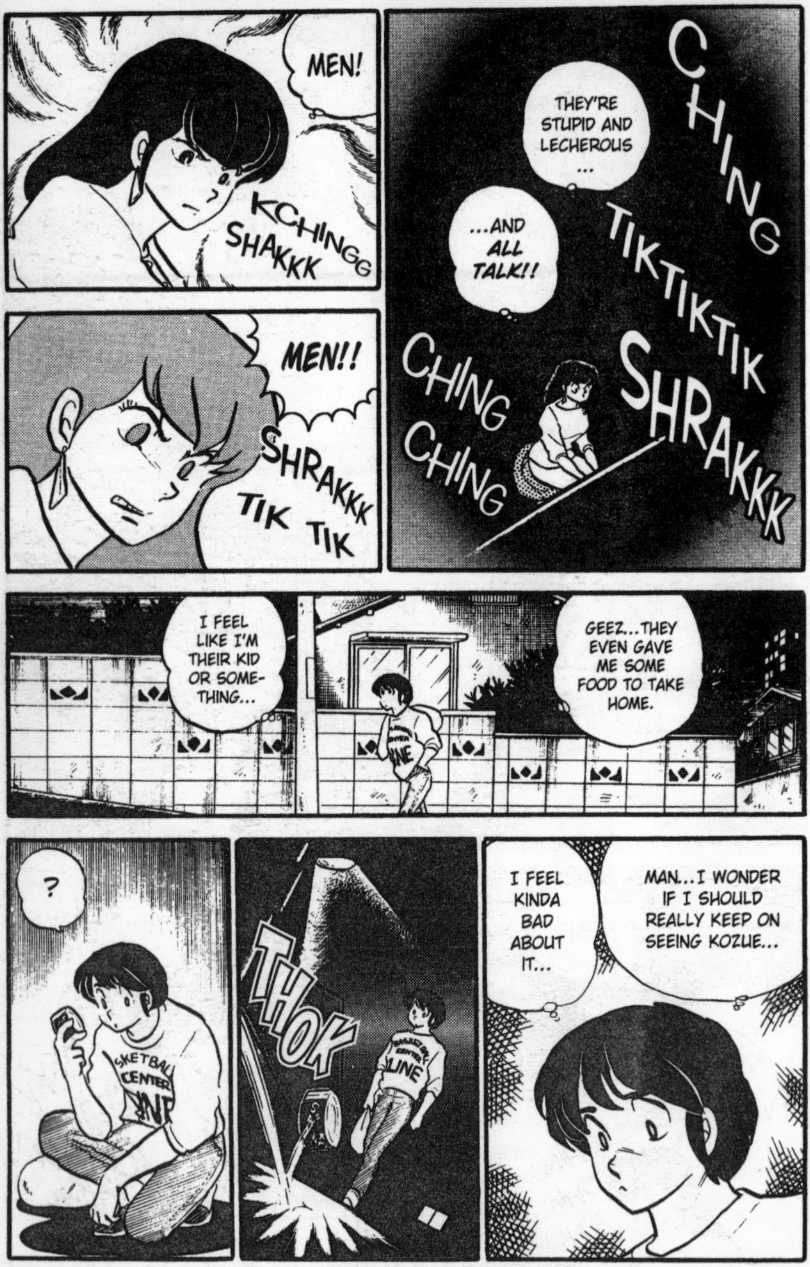
CHING
THEY'RE STUPID AND LECHEROUS ...
TIKTIKTIK
...AND ALL TALK!!
SHRAKKK
CHING CHING
MEN!
KCHINGG SHAKKK
MEN!!
SHRAKKK TIK TIK
GEEZ...THEY EVEN GAVE ME SOME FOOD TO TAKE HOME.
I FEEL LIKE I'M THEIR KID OR SOME-THING...
MAN...I WONDER IF I SHOULD REALLY KEEP ON SEEING KOZUE...
I FEEL KINDA BAD ABOUT IT...
THOK
?

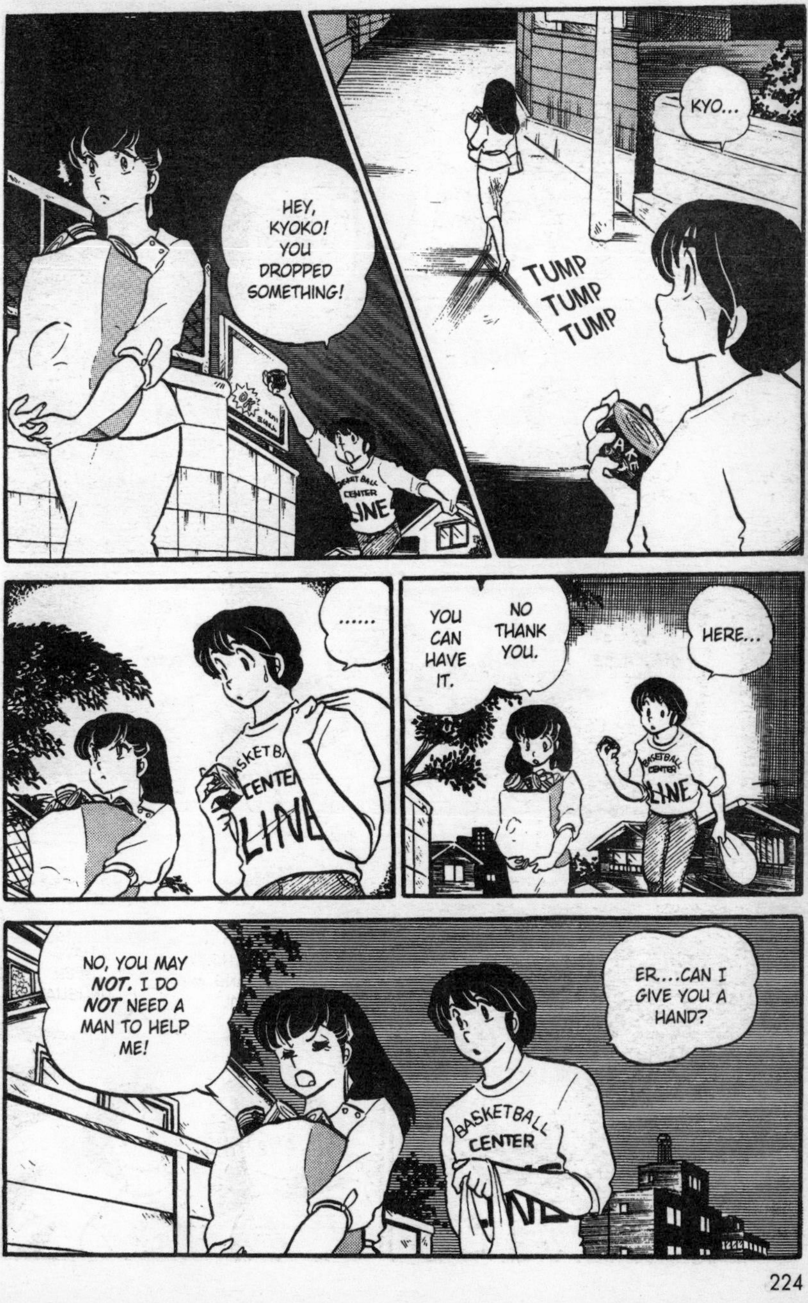
KYO...
TUMP TUMP TUMP
HEY, KYOKO! YOU DROPPED SOMETHING!
HERE...
NO THANK YOU.
YOU CAN HAVE IT.
......
ER...CAN I GIVE YOU A HAND?
NO, YOU MAY NOT. I DO NOT NEED A MAN TO HELP ME!

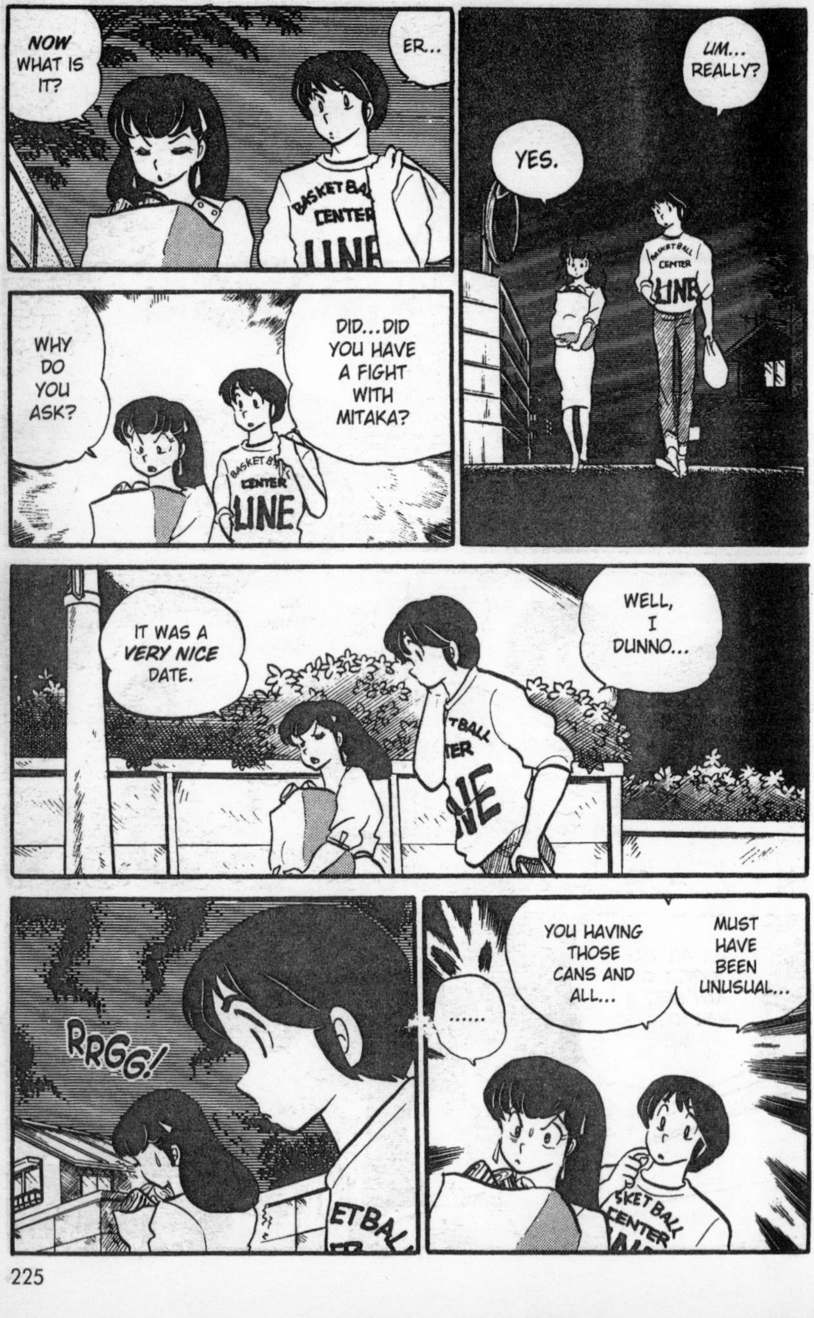
UM... REALLY?
YES.
ER...
NOW WHAT IS IT?
DID...DID YOU HAVE A FIGHT WITH MITAKA?
WHY DO YOU ASK?
WELL, I DUNNO...
IT WAS A VERY NICE DATE.
YOU HAVING THOSE CANS AND ALL...
MUST HAVE BEEN UNUSUAL...
......
RRGG!

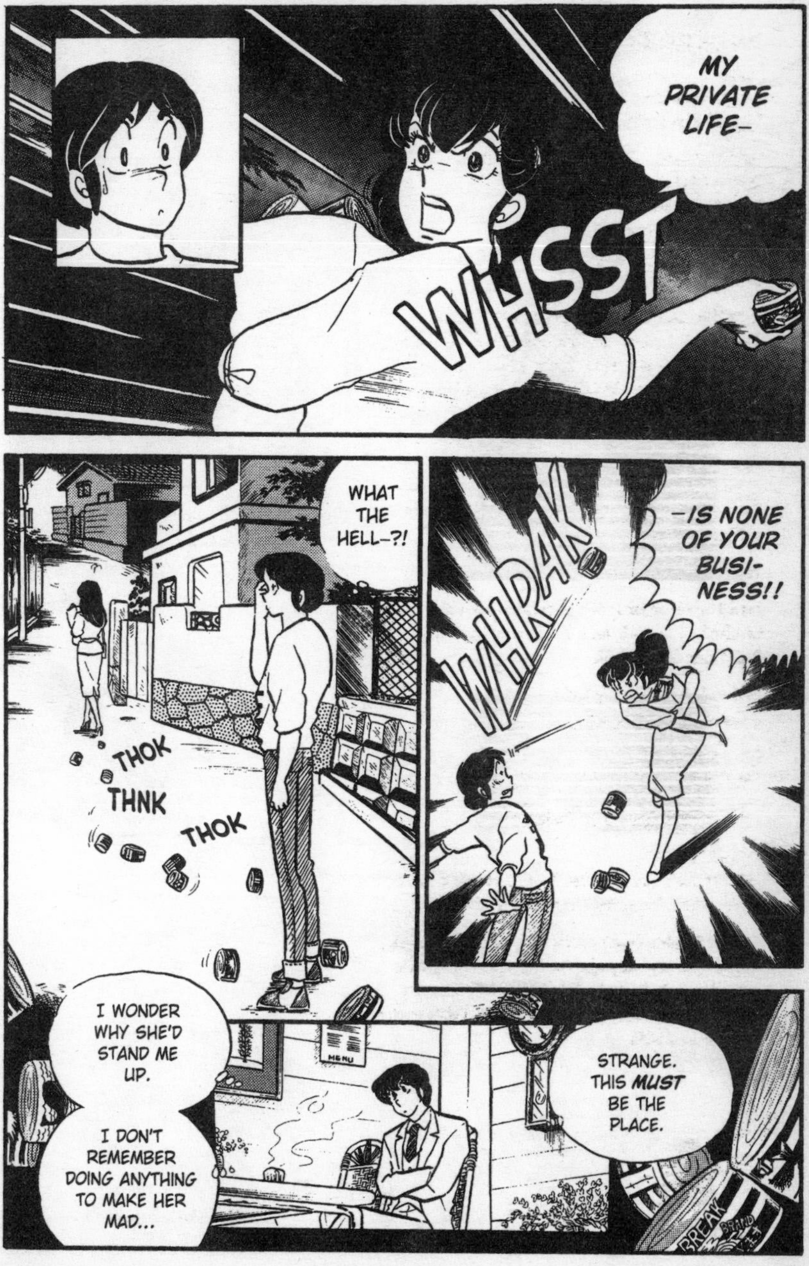
MY PRIVATE LIFE–
WHSST
–IS NONE OF YOUR BUSI- NESS!!
WHRAK
WHAT THE HELL–?!
THOK
THNK
THOK
STRANGE. THIS *MUST* BE THE PLACE.
I WONDER WHY SHE'D STAND ME UP.
I DON'T REMEMBER DOING ANYTHING TO MAKE HER MAD...

MAISON IKKOKU

VOLUME 3
Gollancz Manga Edition
Story and Art by Rumiko Takahashi

Translation/Gerard Jones, Matt Thorn & Mari Morimoto
Touch-up & Lettering/Susan Daigle-Leach
Design/Nozomi Akashi
Editors-1st Edition/Satoru Fujii & Trish Ledoux
Editors-2nd Edition/Elizabeth Kawasaki & Alvin Lu
UK Cover Adaptation/Sue Michniewicz

10 9 8 7 6 5 4 3 2 1

The right of Rumiko Takahashi to be identified as the author of this
work has been asserted by her in accordance with the Copyright,
Designs and Patents Act 1988.

A CIP catalogue record for this book is
available from the British Library

ISBN 0 57507 838 3
EAN 9 780 57507 838 3

Printed and bound at Mackays of Chatham, PLC

PARENTAL ADVISORY
Maison Ikkoku is rated T+ for Teen Plus. Contains realistic and
graphic violence. Recommended for older teens (16 and up).

The Orion Publishing Group's policy is to use papers that are natural,
renewable and recyclable products and made from wood grown in
sustainable forests. The logging and manufacturing processes are
expected to conform to the environmental regulations of the country
of the country of origin.

www.orionbooks.co.uk

ABOUT THE ARTIST

Rumiko Takahashi, born in 1957 in Niigata, Japan, is the acclaimed creator and artist of **Maison Ikkoku, InuYasha, Ranma 1/2** and **Lum * Urusei Yatsura**.

She lived in a small student's apartment in Nakano, Japan, which was the basis for the **Maison Ikkoku** series, while she attended the prestigious Nihon Joseidai (Japan Women's University). At the same time, Takahashi also began studying comics at Gekiga Sonjuku, a famous school for manga artists run by Kazuo Koike, author of **Crying Freeman** and **Lone Wolf and Cub**. In 1978, Takahashi won a prize in Shogakukan's annual New Comic Artist Contest and her boy-meets-alien comedy **Lum * Urusei Yatsura** began appearing in the weekly manga magazine **Shonen Sunday**.

Takahashi's success and critical acclaim continues to grow, with popular titles including **Ranma 1/2** and **InuYasha**. Many of her graphic novel series have also been animated, and are widely available in several languages.

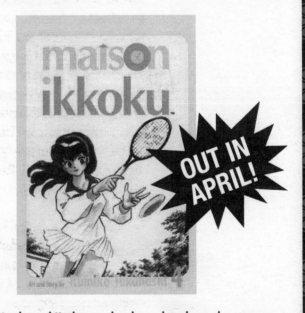

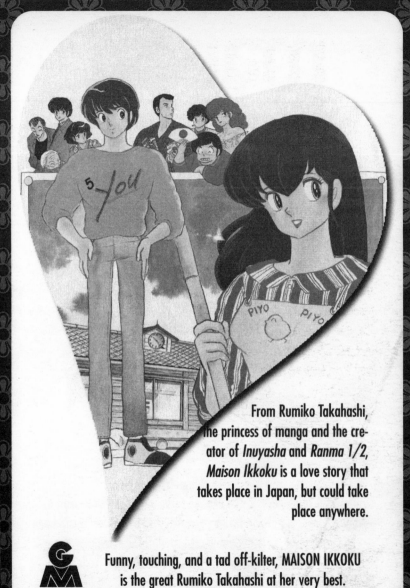

From Rumiko Takahashi, the princess of manga and the creator of *Inuyasha* and *Ranma 1/2*, *Maison Ikkoku* is a love story that takes place in Japan, but could take place anywhere.

GOLLANCZ MANGA

Funny, touching, and a tad off-kilter, MAISON IKKOKU is the great Rumiko Takahashi at her very best.

find out more at www.orionbooks.co.uk

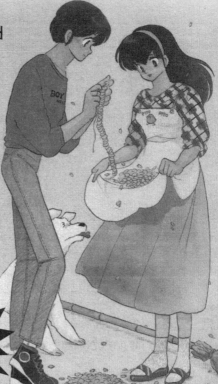

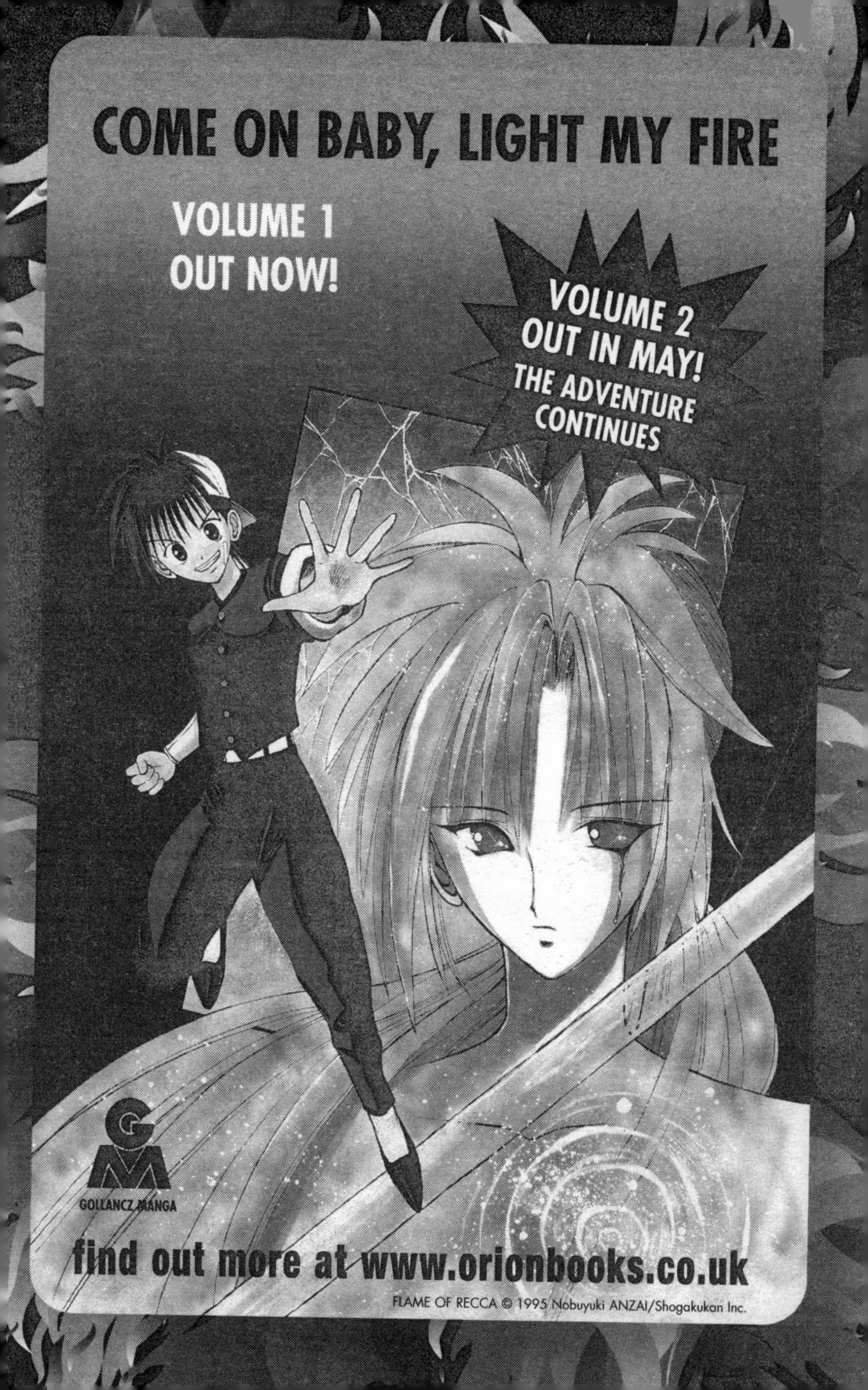

COME ON BABY, LIGHT MY FIRE
VOLUME 1
OUT NOW!
VOLUME 2
OUT IN MAY!
THE ADVENTURE
CONTINUES
GOLLANCZ MANGA
find out more at www.orionbooks.co.uk
FLAME OF RECCA © 1995 Nobuyuki ANZAI/Shogakukan Inc.

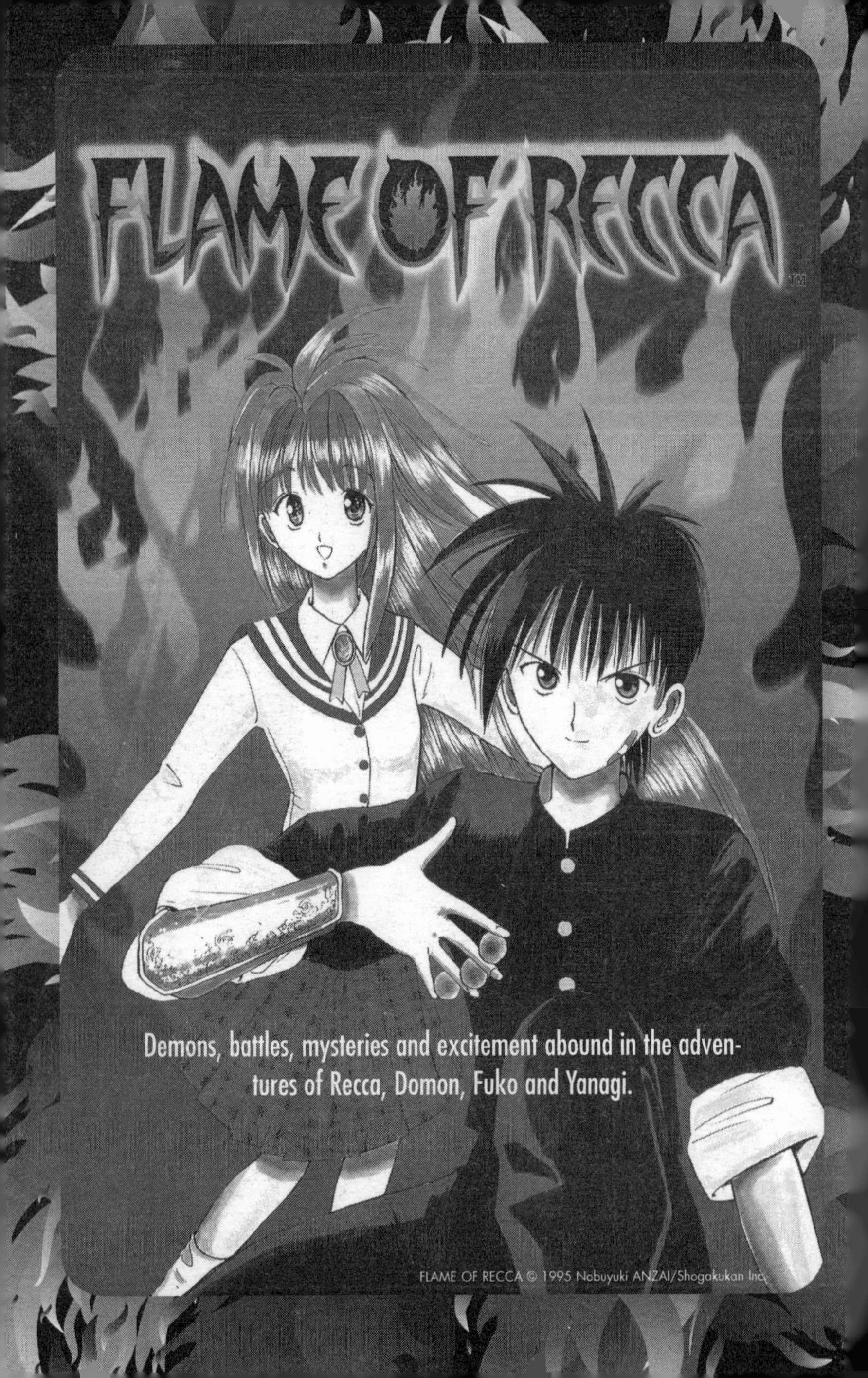
FLAME OF RECCA™
Demons, battles, mysteries and excitement abound in the adventures of Recca, Domon, Fuko and Yanagi.
FLAME OF RECCA © 1995 Nobuyuki ANZAI/Shogakukan Inc.

Spooky crimes, baffling robberies, and comic would-be detectives, no crime's too tough to crack for Jimmy! ... especially not his personal case: to find the mysterious masked men and make them change him back ... All the clues are here — can you solve the case before Jimmy does?

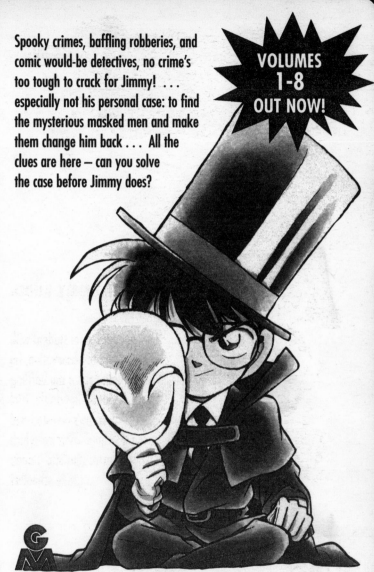

GOLLANCZ MANGA

find out more at www.orionbooks.co.uk

CASE CLOSED™

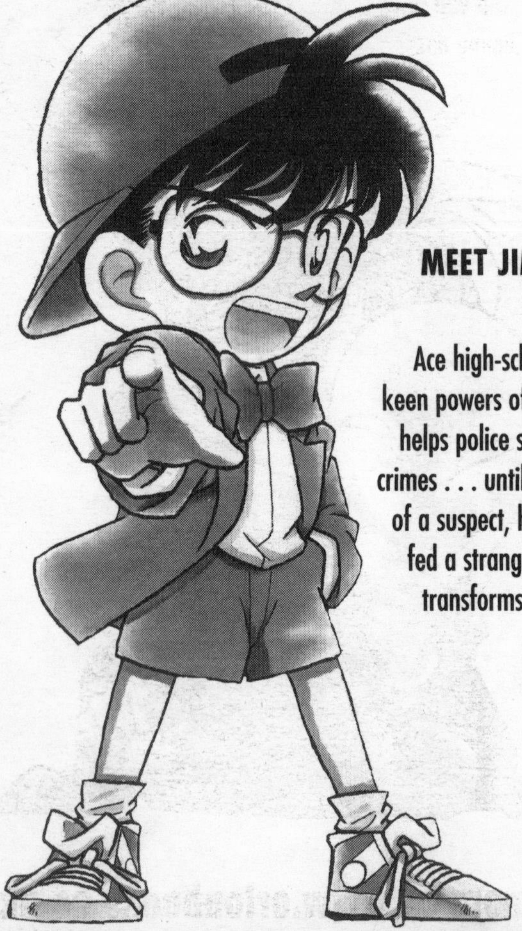

MEET JIMMY KUDO.

Ace high-school student with keen powers of observation, he helps police solve the baffling crimes . . . until, hot on the trial of a suspect, he's accosted and fed a strange chemical which transforms him into a puny grade schooler!

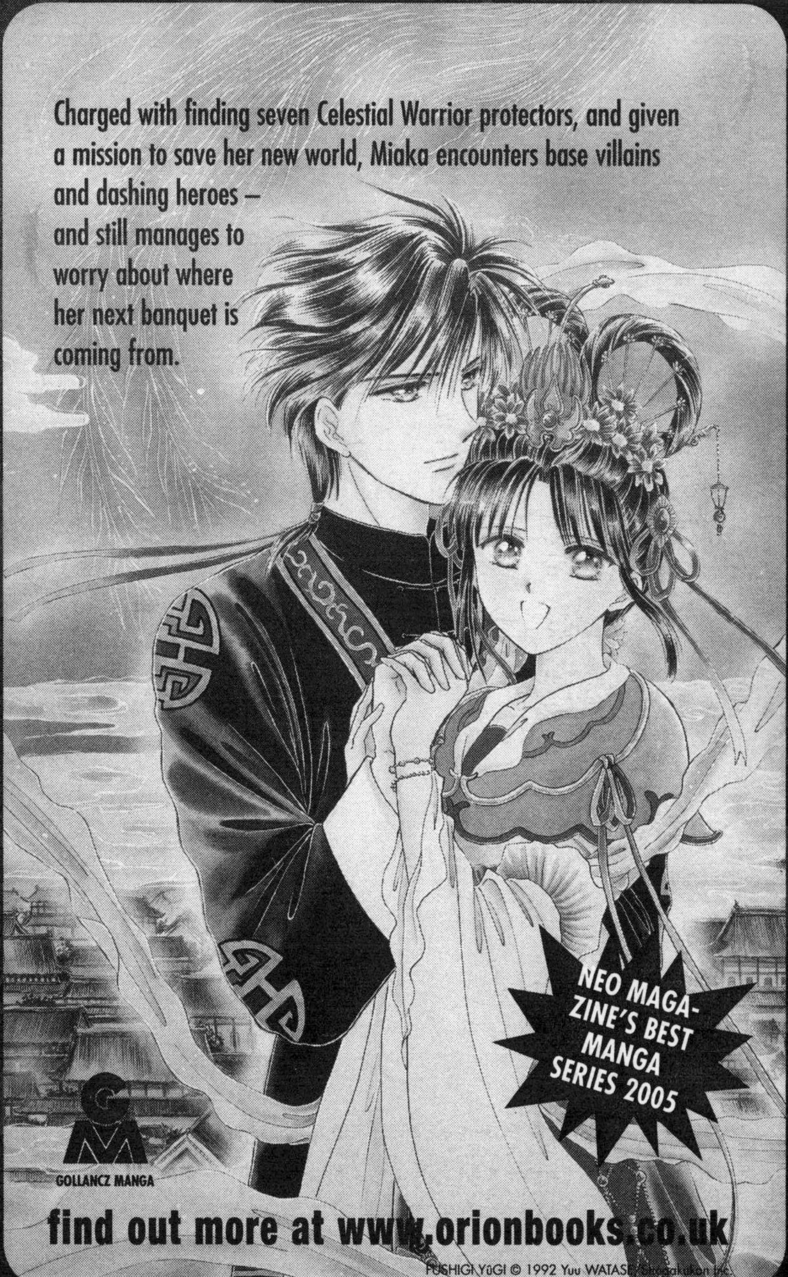
Charged with finding seven Celestial Warrior protectors, and given a mission to save her new world, Miaka encounters base villains and dashing heroes – and still manages to worry about where her next banquet is coming from.
NEO MAGAZINE'S BEST MANGA SERIES 2005
GOLLANCZ MANGA
find out more at www.orionbooks.co.uk
FUSHIGI YûGI © 1992 Yuu WATASE/Shogakukan Inc.

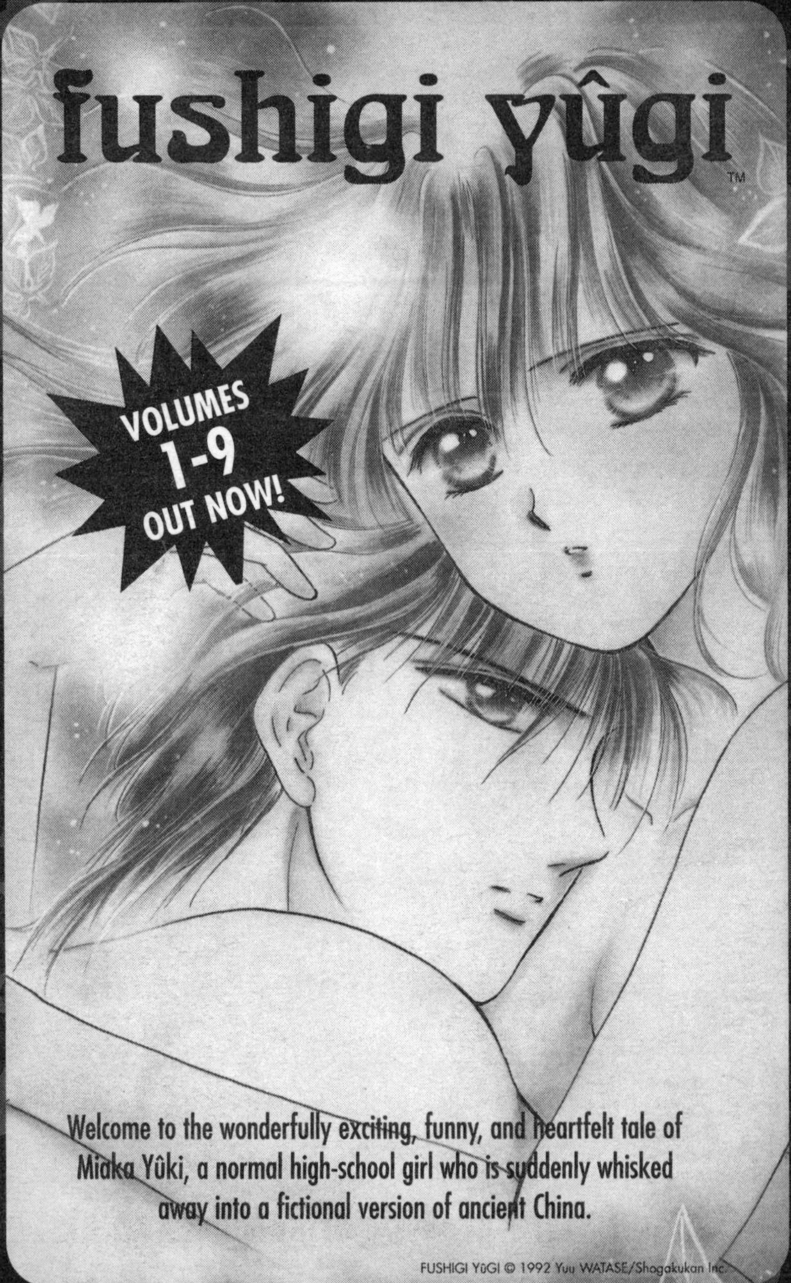

fushigi yûgi

™

VOLUMES 1-9 OUT NOW!

Welcome to the wonderfully exciting, funny, and heartfelt tale of Miaka Yûki, a normal high-school girl who is suddenly whisked away into a fictional version of ancient China.

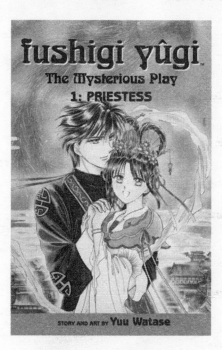

COMPLETE OUR SURVEY AND
LET US KNOW WHAT YOU THINK!

❑ Please do NOT send me information about Gollancz Manga, or other Orion titles, products, news and events, special offers or other information.

Name: _____

Address: _____

Town: _____ County: _____ Postcode: _____

❑ Male ❑ Female Date of Birth (dd/mm/yyyy): ___ / ___ / _____
(under 13? Parental consent required)

What race/ethnicity do you consider yourself? (please check one)

❑ Asian   ❑ Black   ❑ Hispanic

❑ White/Caucasian   ❑ Other: _____

Which Gollancz Manga series did you purchase?

❑ Case Closed   ❑ Dragon Ball   ❑ Flame of Recca   ❑ Fushigi Yûgi
❑ Maison Ikkoku   ❑ One Piece   ❑ Rurouni Kenshin   ❑ Yu-Gi-Oh!
❑ Yu-Gi-Oh! Duelist

What other Gollancz Manga series have you tried?

❑ Case Closed   ❑ Dragon Ball   ❑ Flame of Recca   ❑ Fushigi Yûgi
❑ Maison Ikkoku   ❑ One Piece   ❑ Rurouni Kenshin   ❑ Yu-Gi-Oh!
❑ Yu-Gi-Oh! Duelist

How many anime and/or manga titles have you purchased in the last year?
How many were Gollancz Manga titles?

Anime	Manga	GM
❑ None	❑ None	❑ None
❑ 1-4	❑ 1-4	❑ 1-4
❑ 5-10	❑ 5-10	❑ 5-10
❑ 11+	❑ 11+	❑ 11+

Reason for purchase: (check all that apply)

- ❑ Special Offer ❑ Favourite title ❑ Gift
- ❑ In store promotion If so please indicate which store: ______
- ❑ Recommendation ❑ Other ______

Where did you make your purchase?

- ❑ Bookshop ❑ Comic Shop ❑ Music Store
- ❑ Newsagent ❑ Video Game Store ❑ Supermarket
- ❑ Other: ______ ❑ Online: ______

What kind of manga would you like to read?

- ❑ Adventure ❑ Comic Strip ❑ Fantasy
- ❑ Fighting ❑ Horror ❑ Mystery
- ❑ Romance ❑ Science Fiction ❑ Sports
- ❑ Other: ______

Which do you prefer?

- ❑ Sound effects in English
- ❑ Sound effects in Japanese with English captions
- ❑ Sound effects in Japanese only with a glossary at the back

Want to find out more about Manga?

Look it up at www.orionbooks.co.uk, or www.viz.com

THANK YOU!

Please send the completed form to:

Manga Survey
Orion Books
Orion House
5 Upper St Martin's Lane
London, WC2H 9EA

All information provided will be used for internal purposes only.
We promise not to sell or otherwise divulge your details.

NO PURCHASE NECESSARY. Requests not in compliance with all terms of this form will not be acknowledged or returned. All submissions are subject to verification and become property of Gollancz Manga.